P9-DDX-252

Lincoln Christian College

YALE JUDAICA SERIES

EDITOR

LEON NEMOY

ASSOCIATE EDITORS

SAUL LIEBERMAN HARRY A. WOLFSON

Volume XVI

THE CODE OF MAIMONIDES

(*MISHNEH TORAH*)

BOOK FIVE

PUBLISHED FOR

JUDAICA RESEARCH AT YALE UNIVERSITY

through the combined assistance of the

LOUIS M. RABINOWITZ FOUNDATION

and the

JACOB ZISKIND CHARITABLE TRUST

The Code of Maimonides

BOOK FIVE

THE BOOK OF HOLINESS

TRANSLATED FROM THE HEBREW BY

LOUIS I. RABINOWITZ

AND

PHILIP GROSSMAN

NEW HAVEN AND LONDON, YALE UNIVERSITY PRESS

1965

Copyright © 1965 by Yale University.

Set in Granjon type,
and printed in the United States of America
by Vail-Ballou Press, Inc., Binghamton, N.Y.

All rights reserved. This book may not be reproduced, in whole or in part, in any form (except by reviewers for the public press), without written permission from the publishers.

Library of Congress catalog card number: 49-9495

EDITOR'S NOTE

After the first draft of the present translation was completed by Dr. Rabinowitz in 1949, the increasing pressure of his official duties as Chief Rabbi of Johannesburg and the Transvaal made it necessary for him to withdraw from the work. In 1956 it was turned over to Dr. Grossman, who proceeded to prepare, with constant reference to Dr. Rabinowitz's draft, a new translation, with a greatly expanded apparatus of notes and a completely rewritten introduction. The work as it appears in this volume is thus entirely Dr. Grossman's, and he alone bears the responsibility for it.

Illness, however, prevented Dr. Grossman from taking care of the final stages of the work.* The table of contents and the indices were therefore compiled entirely by me, while the introduction, bibliography, and glossary were put into shape by me from Dr. Grossman's drafts. The translation itself was once more collated by me with the Hebrew text in order to make the terminology more precise and uniform, in line with several valuable suggestions made, with his usual generosity, by Professor Harry A. Wolfson. A number of minor corrections and stylistic improvements were also made at the same time.

L. N.

New Haven, Connecticut
May 1964

* Dr. Grossman, a native of New Haven, received his rabbinical diploma at Yeshiva University in New York and his doctorate in Semitics at Yale University (1939). After a period of service in the ministry, he returned to New Haven in order to devote his entire time to research and teaching. He died on April 12, 1964, aged 67.

Blackwells
98.74 (Set)
7 Oct 72
46088

CONTENTS

(Sec. 14); covering up blood should be done preferably by slaughterer, but if he fails to do so, any other person noticing the blood must cover it up (Sec. 15); covering up blood should be done with reverence, not with contempt (Sec. 16).

INTRODUCTION

The fifth Book of the Code was named by Maimonides the Book of Holiness (in Hebrew *Sefer Ḳĕḏušah*), and he appropriately took for his text the Psalmist's verse *Order my footsteps by Thy word, and let not any iniquity have dominion over me* (Ps. 119:133). This Book is thus meant to set forth the rule and exercises of holy living as prescribed by divine ordinance. It comprises three Treatises:

I. Laws Concerning Illicit Intercourse
II. Laws Concerning Forbidden Foods
III. Laws Concerning *Šĕḥiṭah*.

The third Treatise is really a subdivision of the second, inasmuch as it deals with the ordinances which, if properly observed, make animal flesh fit for human consumption through a valid procedure of slaughtering and a painstaking examination of the animal's organs to assure its freedom from any disease or other disqualifying mark which would render it prohibited as food.

The Concept of Holiness

In the introduction to the Code, while discussing the title and contents of this Book, Maimonides points out the fundamental importance of these regulations and the high moral purpose that underlies them. "I will include in it," he says, "the Commandments Concerning Illicit Intercourse and the Commandments Concerning Forbidden Foods, for it is in these matters that the Omnipresent One has sanctified us and has separated us from the heathens, namely in matters of forbidden unions and forbidden foods, for in reference to both of these it is written, *And ye shall be holy unto Me, for I, the Lord, am holy, and have set you apart from the peoples, that ye should be Mine* (Lev. 20:26), *I am the Lord, your God, who have set you apart from the peoples* (*ibid.* 20:24)."

What is put here so concisely is developed in greater detail by Maimonides in his major philosophical work, the *Guide of the Perplexed:*[1] "It is . . . the object of the . . . Law to make man reject, despise, and reduce his desires, as much as is in his power. He should only give way to them when absolutely necessary. It is well known that it is intemperance in eating, drinking, and sexual intercourse that people mostly rave and indulge in, and these very things counteract the ulterior perfection of man . . . and generally disturb the social order of the country and the economy of the family. For by following entirely the guidance of lust . . . man loses his intellectual energy, injures his body, and perishes before his time." Envy, hatred, and eventually violence are the inevitable results of his subservience to his animal instincts, and it is a mark of divine wisdom that the commandments seek to forestall precisely this dire result. The purpose of the Law is to lead man to purity and holiness by training him to suppress sensuality or at least to reduce it to the minimum. Hence when at Mount Sinai Moses was commanded to *sanctify* (Exod. 19:10) the children of Israel, he properly interpreted the divine command by directing the Israelites to *come not at your wives* (*ibid.* 19:15), indicating clearly that holiness is the antithesis of sensuality; and the same thought underlies the injunction concerning the Nazirite that *he shall be holy* (Num. 6:5) by way of total abstinence from wine. Consequently, as the Sifra[2] states it, the ordinance which serves as the preamble to the Scriptural exposition of the commandments interdicting illicit intercourse, *Sanctify yourselves therefore, and be ye holy* (Lev. 20:7), signifies that sanctification and purification are effected by way of obedience to, and performance of, the divine commandments, just as defilement is incurred by way of disobedience and transgression of these commandments. Therefore, personal cleanliness and fastidiousness are likewise the aim of the Law, although in themselves they are meaningless if they are not coupled with deeds that are pure, and

1. Friedlaender's translation (New York, n.d.), *3*, 158.
2. Sif Lev. 11:44.

intellect and heart that are free from evil principles and bad habits.

Elsewhere in the same philosophical work [3] Maimonides applies this general principle to the explanation of the moral as well as practical motives behind the seemingly formal prohibitions of sexual and dietary indulgences. He repeatedly stresses the disciplinary intent of all laws relating to illicit sexual connection and interdicted food in counteracting the worldly tendency to regard pleasure as the end and purpose of man's existence. The injurious nature of most forbidden foods is obvious.[4] Pork, though seemingly wholesome, is high in moisture and waste, and moreover swine are notorious for their unclean habits and indiscriminate feeding. And as for fat, its indigestibility makes it more suitable for fuel than for food. Mixture of meat and milk [5] makes for gross food, and was in all probability also an ingredient of the ritual of heathen worship. The procedure of šĕḥiṭah,[6] while conceding the natural need of the human organism for animal as well as vegetable food, is meant to bring about the extinction of life in the quickest and least painful manner, and to abolish the primitive cruelty of haphazard killing, or, still worse, eating the flesh of a living animal or one in which life has not yet become completely extinct. The humanitarian purpose of the prohibition of slaughtering the dam and her young on the same day is self-evident, as is the prohibition of capturing a mother bird together with her chicks or eggs. Indeed, the compelling conclusion is that if even such purely mental cruelty may not be inflicted upon a bird, how much more should it not be inflicted upon the foremost of God's creatures, one's fellow man.

In this conception of the central position of chastity and temperance as the higher discipline intended by divine revelation, Maimonides follows a well-trodden path in Jewish thought. As early as the first century Philo [7] had pointed out that Scripture demands neither Spartan austerity nor Ionian sybaritism, but

3. *Guide, 3,* 159. 4. *Ibid.*, p. 251. 5. *Ibid.*, p. 253.
6. *Ibid.*, p. 253–54.
7. *Special Laws,* 4.17 (Colson's translation [London, 1954], *8,* 69 ff.).

follows a middle course; he suggested that the prohibition of certain beasts, birds, and fishes rests on the assumption that they are particularly appetizing, and that abstention from them is bound to generate firm self-control in man. From another point of view, Naḥmanides [8] (thirteenth century) placed particular emphasis upon the logical tie between the Scriptural terms of holiness and separation, for where there is holiness there is separation from excess in all things, and vice versa. It is noteworthy, says Naḥmanides, that while Scripture condemns illicit sexual and dietary indulgence, it does not expressly set limits to indulgence within the confines of lawful wedlock and permitted diet. It would thus be seemingly possible for the libertine and glutton to claim that he does not violate the divine intent so long as he satisfies his appetite, however excessively, with his wedded wife and with ritually clean comestibles. Consequently Scripture, in addition to particularizing the formally forbidden indulgences, deems it necessary to add a general injunction that man should be holy, i.e. separate, from all excess even in matters essentially permitted. Hence man should not indulge in sexual intercourse to any extent beyond that necessary for the propagation of the species, nor consume wine in quantities leading to disgrace and illness. In another context [9] Naḥmanides declares that in general it is proper for man to eat all food by which he may sustain his life. The Scriptural dietary prohibitions are meant only to safeguard the purity of man's soul, for heavy and gross food inevitably engenders heaviness and grossness of soul. But even food which is not in itself contaminating, such as ṭĕrefah, must be avoided as a matter of self-discipline and as a path to holiness, for that was the primary reason for its exclusion from the catalogue of permitted diet.

In a more pithy manner, this juxtaposition of the divine and bestial in man is expressed in the Talmud (B. Ḥag̱ 16a): "Six things are said of the children of man. In three they are like the ministering angels: they have understanding, they walk erect, and they speak the holy tongue. In the other three they are like the

8. Commentary to Lev. 19:2.

9. *Ibid.* to Exod. 22:30.

beasts: they eat and drink, they propagate, and they relieve themselves." On this the sixteenth century mystic Elijah de Vidas remarks[10] that of the latter three, evacuation of waste is one of the natural human functions inherited from Adam and therefore beyond one's control. The other two beastlike traits, however—eating and drinking, and propagation—are subject to man's discretion, and Scripture therefore enjoins him to sanctify himself therein. Consequently, "man should not eat merely to satisfy his craving, like a beast, lest his spirit should become like a beast's spirit that goes downward to the earth"—instead of soaring up ward to heaven—"and the same applies also to propagation." In short, the path to holy living, whereby man becomes worthy of God, lies through self-disciplined abstention from that which is characteristic of the bestial, and wholehearted practice of that which is characteristically divine.

The Contents of the Book of Holiness

The first Treatise, dealing with the Laws Concerning Illicit Intercourse, may be divided as follows: Chapters 1–3, degrees of forbidden union; Chapters 4–9, the menstruant woman; Chapter 10, the woman delivered of a child; Chapter 11, the woman suffering from flux; Chapter 12, intercourse between Israelite and heathen; Chapters 13–14, admissible and inadmissible proselytes; Chapter 15, bastardy; Chapter 16, male person with maimed privy organs; Chapters 17–20, proven and unproven priestly descent; Chapters 21–22, general remarks on marriage and chastity. This Treatise thus covers every aspect of the law regulating the intimate life of the individual, and Maimonides concludes it with his moral lesson, reminiscent of Plotinus'[11] admonition to "chisel away from thy soul what is superfluous, straighten that which is crooked, purify and enlighten what is dark . . . until virtue shines before thine eyes with its divine splendor."

The second Treatise, dealing with forbidden foods, is a logical

10. *Rešiṯ ḥoḵmah* (Lemberg, 1861), 94a.

11. *Enneads,* 1, 6, 9 (Inge's translation, *The Philosophy of Plotinus* [London, 1923], 2, 165).

sequel to the Treatise which deals with "forbidden fruit," inasmuch as both are concerned with the ideal of holiness. And since this Treatise confines itself to articles of food that are forbidden at all times, it does not treat of those whose interdict is limited or temporary, such as leaven, which is prohibited during Passover, the grapevine and its products, which are forbidden to the Nazirite for the duration of his period of Naziriteship, and articles of food that are prohibited because of their consecration to the altar or to the sanctuary. The rules governing these are set forth in their respective places elsewhere in the Code.

Chapters 1–5 of the second Treatise deal with permitted and forbidden domestic animals, wild beasts, birds, fishes, and locusts, and with the general prohibition of other insects and creeping things. This is followed by a discussion of the interdict of blood (Chapter 6), fat (Chapter 7), the sinew of the thigh vein (Chapter 8), and the mixture of meat with milk (Chapter 9). With this the rules concerning the prohibition of living creatures are concluded, and Maimonides then proceeds with the laws governing prohibited agricultural produce, new corn, and produce of mixed seeds (Chapter 10), which in turn is followed by the involved legislation concerning heathen wine (Chapters 11–13). Chapters 14–16 codify the regulations specifying the manner in which forbidden foods may be rectified or neutralized by admixture of permitted foods, while the last Chapter (17) sets forth a number of rules relating to various particulars, including personal hygiene and sanitation. Here again Maimonides closes his discourse with another reminder of the interpenetration of the physical and the spiritual.

The third Treatise, which is in fact an appendix to the second, is headed "Laws Concerning Šĕḥiṭah," and covers all matters that affect the rendering of the flesh of permitted animals fit for human consumption. Actually it is only the first four chapters that deal with the Jewish method of slaughtering, its proper place and time, the qualifications of slaughterers, and other details that make the slaughtering valid or invalid, as the case may be. Chapters 5–11 deal with the physical defects in an animal which render its flesh unfit even if the act of slaughtering itself has been performed in full accordance with the law. In discussing these defects, Maimonides uses his own classification, and Chapter 10 contains a tabular catalogue of seventy such defects. Chapter 12 deals with the prohibition of slaughtering a mother animal and its young on the same day, and Chapter 13 sets forth the details of the law commanding the release of a mother bird before taking her chicks or eggs from her nest. The last Chapter (14) deals with the duty to cover up the blood of beasts and birds after slaughter, and Maimonides concludes the Book with the Scriptural declaration *Thy word is a lamp unto my feet, and a light unto my path* (Ps. 119:105), thus once more stressing man's duty to approach as far as possible the divinely set exemplar of the holy life.

The Sources

The primary source of Maimonides' codification, next to Scripture, is the Mishnah and the Gemara, and the relationship between the Book of Holiness and the Talmudic text may be summarized as follows:

In the first Treatise, the rules relating to illicit intercourse correspond to Chapters 7–11 of the Mishnaic Tractate Sanhedrin, while the rules governing menstruation and flux are taken from the Tractate Niddah, which is devoted entirely to that subject. Chapters 12–14 of the Treatise cover matters dealt with in various places of the Talmud, although to be sure the regulations governing the admission of proselytes form the subject of the minor Talmudic Tractate Gerim ("Proselytes"), but this is in fact a much later compilation and not really an integral part of the Talmudic corpus. The regulations concerning bastardy, waifs, and foundlings are derived from Chapter 4 of Ḳiddušin, the laws regulating priestly marriages from Chapter 5 of Yeḇamot, and the contents of Chapter 16 of the Treatise, dealing with male persons whose sexual organs have been maimed, are based upon the second Section of Chapter 8 of the same Talmudic Tractate.

The three distinct parts of the second Treatise—forbidden living creatures, forbidden agricultural produce, and forbidden heathen wine—are derived from various parts of the Talmud, the first from Ḥullin, the second from ʿOrlah, and the third from Chapters 4–5 of ʿĂbodah Zarah.

The third Treatise stems entirely from the Tractate Ḥullin, and in conformity with the latter Maimonides includes in it the prohibition of slaughtering mother and young on the same day and the duty to release the mother bird before taking her chicks or eggs, although these matters do not, strictly speaking, come under the heading of forbidden foods and belong rather in a separate place.

In addition to the Mishnah Maimonides takes account of its interpretations and applications as made by the Palestinian and Babylonian Amoraim and contained in the two Talmuds. The Tosefta, the two Mĕḵiltas, Sifra, and Sifre, as well as other Tannaitic sources, some of which are at present either lost or known only from quotations in later compilations, were also fully utilized by him. The Midrashic literature is also often incorporated, particularly where Maimonides wishes to refer to some historical circumstance or to bring home a moral lesson. Thus in I, xiii, 16, when discussing the circumstances under which Samson and Solomon had married wives of idolatrous origin, Maimonides draws not only upon the Palestinian Talmud but also upon the Midrash Rabbah, in order to demonstrate that these women were indeed formally proselytized, even though their conversion was in fact insincere and not lasting. Again in I, xxii, 21, Maimonides utilizes the Midrash on Proverbs in proof of the view that mind and thought directed to the study of Torah and to the understanding of wisdom are the most effective preventatives of unchaste inclinations and lascivious impulses.

The Gaonic codes, compilations, commentaries, and responsa were known to Maimonides in their entirety, and he frequently quotes them in order to signify his agreement or disagreement, as the case may be, usually introducing their decisions with the formula "the Geonim have ruled." Sometimes, however, these are given without this identifying citation, as, for example, in I, iv, 3, where Maimonides silently incorporates in his ruling an almost exact quotation of a Gaonic interpretation. Again, in II, xiii, 11 Maimonides gives it as his own view that in dealing with heathen wine the term "heathen" should be understood as signifying actual idolaters, and not monotheistic Gentiles like Mohammedans. As a matter of fact, however, the same view was already expressed in a responsum by R. Naḥshon Gaon, and it would seem that by prefacing the ruling with the formula "it would appear to me" Maimonides meant to imply that other Geonim thought differently in this matter and that he accepted R. Naḥshon's view. To be sure, it is also not impossible that among the great mass of Gaonic writings this particular responsum had somehow escaped his notice.

Alfasi's compendium of the Talmud has likewise served Maimonides well, and he found himself in agreement with most of its rulings and decisions.

It is thus clear that in formulating the Book of Holiness, Maimonides took into full account the entire range of Jewish literature from the earliest times down to his own age, with which he was most thoroughly and minutely familiar, and made complete and painstaking use of it.

Maimonides' Methods as a Codifier

Maimonides wrote his Code in accordance with definite hermeneutic rules governing his construction and interpretation of law as transmitted in Scripture and Talmud. In fact, he had previously composed a work entitled *Seḏer 'olam,* which is unfortunately now lost, but was known to R. Bezaleel Ashkenazi (sixteenth century).[12] This work was devoted entirely to the exposition of Talmudic hermeneutics, and it seems certain that Maimonides applied the same rules, as he understood and interpreted them, in formulating the norms observed in the Code. Very probably many a knotty problem in the Code would have resolved itself if we had this work before us. What we might

12. Cf. his *Šiṭṭah mĕḵubbeṣeṯ* to B. Keṯ 81a, and his *Kĕlale hat-Talmuḏ,* ed. A. Marx, *Festschrift zum 70sten Geburtstage David Hoffmann's* (Berlin, 1914), Hebrew section, pp. 179–217.

attempt here is, therefore, no more than a summary of his hermeneutic method, as formulated by the chief commentators and interpreters of the Code, on the basis of their own study of the text.

Maimonides reproduces each ruling of the Talmud with great exactitude, including all the Talmudic refinements and allusions relating thereto. Since he is so meticulous in transmitting the Talmudic rulings, his own rulings likewise take on the character of the Gemara, with the result that they too can be discussed and analyzed after the manner of the latter. He usually prefers the interpretation nearest to the plain sense of the Scriptural text, even in such cases where this particular interpretation was rejected in the Gemara. Occasionally he quotes a Scriptural verse not referred to in the Gemara, because this verse seemed to him to present a better explanation, but he takes care to do so only when this explanation, while more acceptable or reasonable, does not affect the ruling itself.

In general Maimonides does not derive new rulings, but only records the laws set forth in the Talmud in their original wording and form, each one in its proper place. He sometimes designates a ruling as Scriptural, although it is actually an enactment of the Sages. At times he designates a ruling as being a Rabbinic enactment, while at other times he is not particular in this regard and merely states the law. Similarly, he sometimes states that a certain law was given to Moses on Mount Sinai, while at other times he does not do so.

Where two opposite opinions are quoted in the Talmud and the Sages decide in favor of one of them, Maimonides in the course of formulating the law explains the invalidity of the rejected view. At times he depends upon something which will be explained further on in the same chapter of the Code or elsewhere in it. In some instances where the Talmud assigns one meaning to a certain expression, Maimonides assigns to it another meaning, undoubtedly for reasons which he deemed sufficient.

When using the formula "this matter is a ruling according to tradition (*ḳabbalah*)," Maimonides includes in it also the enactments of the Prophets. When he uses the formula "as it is written," the Scriptural verse cited usually does indeed represent the source of the derived ruling, but sometimes the verse is merely a matter of indirect support. On the other hand, the formula "this rule is of Scribal origin" is used by him not only for rulings introduced by the Scribes but also for laws which are in fact Scriptural, but have been explained or elucidated by the Scribes and were formulated accordingly.

Where the Babylonian and Palestinian Gemaras differ, Maimonides usually decides according to the former, but occasionally he prefers the latter. The same is true of the Babylonian Gemara as against the Sifre—in some cases where the Gemara derives a ruling from one Scriptural verse while the Sifre derives it from another, Maimonides chooses the verse in Sifre as, in his opinion, the more appropriate to the subject at hand.

While Maimonides valued man-made science highly, he believed that it should be limited to its proper sphere; worldly wisdom, he thought, cannot outweigh the wisdom of the Torah, but should rather be subservient to it. He therefore held that the rulings of the Sages, being of Scriptural derivation, are inherently true, even if in some cases scientific knowledge, in a particular day and age, may seem to contradict them. Human knowledge is at best imperfect, and what is considered a scientific fact today may in any case be found to be not so tomorrow, whereas divine wisdom is perfect and immutable. Even in purely legal matters Maimonides thought that tradition and past practice are the chief pillars to be relied on in fixing the norm and rule.[13] This principle is particularly applicable to the Book of Holiness, dealing as it does, to a considerable extent, with human and animal anatomy, physiology, and pathology.

Throughout the Code, and in the Book of Holiness no less than elsewhere, Maimonides invariably inclines toward the more stringent interpretation of the law, since his principal aim is to incul-

13. See VII, vii, x, 6.

cate the higher and most nearly perfect conception of holiness that man can possibly achieve if he faithfully follows the letter and spirit of divine revelation.

Ample illustrations of most of these hermeneutic principles will be found in the notes to this translation; one need but compare the sources indicated there with the text of the Code.

Some Technical Terms

It may be useful here to define in somewhat greater detail some of the chief technical terms frequently used in the Book of Holiness. Of these, some can be represented with fair accuracy by the corresponding English equivalents; others, on the other hand, had to be retained in their Hebrew original because no English term could be found that would fit them properly and accurately.

Bastard (*mamzer*)

This Biblical term (Deut. 23:3) is explained in the Palestinian Talmud (Ḳid 3:12) as "blemished by reason of extraneous descent (*mum zar*)," which is a popular definition of the term's exact significance—a child born out of an incestuous union, i.e. one prohibited under the penalty of death at the hands of an earthly court or extinction at the hands of heaven. It is not necessarily the child of an unmarried mother (cf. 1, xv, 1).

Harlot (*zonah*)

In the original Biblical usage the word signified a woman engaged in fornication for material gain or for personal gratification. In later legal usage the term assumed a special significance, namely that of a woman who is statutorily forbidden to marry an Israelite of priestly lineage (Lev. 21:7), without necessarily implying any immoral conduct on her part. Maimonides himself (1, xviii, 1 and 5) carefully emphasizes the fact that harlotry in this legal sense is conferred upon a woman by the forbidden status of her mate, and not by sexual union. Indeed, some grave sexual transgressions—such as bestiality—do not make the guilty woman a harlot, even though she is liable to severe penalties, while on the other hand a heathen woman of unimpeachable character has, so far as marriage to a priestly Israelite is concerned, the legal status of a harlot. It is thus most essential to keep in mind the important point that in legal usage "harlot" is not at all equivalent to "prostitute," and by no means suggests a reflection upon the good character of all non-Jewish women, and most particularly of all non-idolatrous Gentile women who profess a monotheistic faith.

Profaned woman (ḥălalah)

This term is mentioned in the same Biblical verse (Lev. 21:7) and in the same context, and like "harlot" has nothing to do with moral, or even social, degradation. It signifies the female issue of a union between an Israelite priest and a woman prohibited to him by law; the mother likewise becomes profaned by reason of this unlawful union (cf. I, xix, 1).

Priest (ḳohen)

A priest is a descendant in the male line of Aaron the High Priest, whose privileges and obligations as a minister are set forth in Chapters 21–22 of the book of Leviticus. Jewish priesthood is thus hereditary, and not appointive. An unfit priest is one who is disqualified from the ministry by reason of impaired descent (*ḥalal*), ritual uncleanness, or physical blemish. The High Priest was originally installed by anointment with holy oil, but by the time of King Josiah this oil is said to have ceased, and subsequently high priests were inducted into office merely by investiture with the additional high priestly vestments. If the incumbent High Priest became temporarily unfit for duty because of ritual uncleanness, a substitute replaced him until such time as the former was again fit to serve. This substitute thereafter retained the designation as "past High Priest" (*ḳohen še-ʿaḇar*). A special priest was also appointed to serve as army chaplain (Deut. 20:2).

Šĕḥiṭah

This term signifies the ritual of slaughter of an animal for human consumption in strict compliance with the rules and procedure prescribed by Jewish law, any deviation from which, even in the slightest degree, renders the act invalid and the animal's flesh forbidden. The act of slaughtering itself is thus but a part of the procedure of šĕḥiṭah. Its Biblical source is Deut. 12:21, where the expression *wĕ-zaḇaḥta,* usually—and rather inaccurately—translated *thou shalt ḵill,* is taken to refer to the strictly regulated sacrificial slaughtering for the altar, whose procedure was subsequently extended also to slaughtering for human food, thus retaining the sacred element in the latter also (cf. III, i, 1).

Nĕḇelah

An animal disqualified for food by reason of some deviation or imperfection in the performance of the act of šĕḥiṭah upon it.

Ṭĕrefah

In contradistinction to nĕḇelah, ṭĕrefah signifies an animal which had undergone a valid act of šĕḥiṭah, but whose carcass thereupon revealed some evidence of organic defect or disease, making it unfit for consumption. This term, like the two that precede it, has no exact English equivalent.

Heathen wine

There are, so far as Jewish law is concerned, two varieties of heathen wine: libation wine (*yayin neseḵ*), or wine definitely known to have been poured out at a heathen altar or used in some other manner as an act of worship before a heathen deity, which is forbidden by Scriptural interdict under all circumstances; and undefined heathen wine (*sĕtam yenom*), concerning which it is not known whether it was or was not used for heathen libation, and which is forbidden only by Scribal enactment (cf. II, xi, 1 and 3). The important role played by wine in the ritual of heathen worship is probably responsible for the rigorous and minute regulations in Jewish law designed to ensure that Jewish individuals will have no contact whatsoever with it.

The Notes

In the preparation of the notes I have endeavored to go beyond what the commentators themselves have done, in order to illuminate the Maimonidean text. Maimonides' mind was so rich "both by art's purchase and by nature's dow'r," that it is well nigh impossible to trace all his sources, especially in view of the fact that some of them are no longer available to us. Moreover, the great commentators were concerned mainly with indicating the basic Talmudic or Gaonic authority for each Section as a whole, and did not therefore attempt to identify the other sources for the Section as well as for the particular rulings contained in it. The notes given here may thus possibly serve a double purpose for the specialist, first by indicating to him as many sources as I could find, and secondly by enabling him, through comparison of the sources referred to, to provide himself with a running commentary upon the Maimonidean text and its underlying reasoning. Maimonides' other works—particularly his commentary on the Mishnah, undertaken as a kind of *Vorarbeit* to the Code—were of course also drawn upon wherever advisable.

Among the authorities quoted, those anterior to Maimonides' time may, of course, be regarded as his direct sources. When, as frequently happens, authorities posterior to Maimonides are referred to, my purpose was obviously not mere multiplication of references—such multiplication could in fact be easily carried on almost *ad infinitum*—but to elucidate with greater certainty and clarity the ruling itself or the reasoning employed in arriving at it, where the compressed conciseness of Maimonides' style does not, at first glance, allow it. This seemed to me particularly necessary because the work of Maimonides, like that of Rashi, has the admirable quality of being equally readable to the layman, who finds that he can easily understand the lucid and logical exposition of the law, and to the expert, who is bound to recognize at once the Biblical or Talmudic source of each ruling and the interpretation given to it by Maimonides himself. Indeed the expert will bear in mind the important fact that Maimonides meant his Code to serve not only as a corpus of law but also as a profoundly conceived commentary on the Talmud. In other words, the Code was meant from the outset not to displace the Talmud but to make it more accessible and understandable, to both laymen and scholars.

In conclusion, I should like to acknowledge my everlasting gratitude to my late revered parents, Gershon and Feige-Hannah Grossman, who made it possible for me, by their self-sacrifice and devotion, to pursue my studies and to dedicate myself to a scholarly career.

Philip Grossman

THE BOOK OF
HOLINESS

COMPRISING THREE TREATISES IN
THE FOLLOWING ORDER

I. LAWS CONCERNING FORBIDDEN INTERCOURSE

II. LAWS CONCERNING FORBIDDEN FOODS

III. LAWS CONCERNING ŠĔḤIṬAH

Order my footsteps by Thy word, and let
not any iniquity have dominion over me.
(Psalms 119:133)

TREATISE I

LAWS CONCERNING FORBIDDEN INTERCOURSE

Involving Thirty-Seven Commandments,

One Positive and Thirty-Six Negative

To Wit

1. Not to have intercourse with one's mother;
2. Not to have intercourse with the wife of one's father;
3. Not to cohabit with one's sister;
4. Not to cohabit with the daughter of the wife of one's father;
5. Not to cohabit with the daughter of one's son;
6. Not to cohabit with one's daughter;
7. Not to cohabit with the daughter of one's daughter;
8. Not to marry a woman and her daughter;
9. Not to marry a woman and her son's daughter;
10. Not to marry a woman and her daughter's daughter;
11. Not to cohabit with the sister of one's father;
12. Not to cohabit with the sister of one's mother;
13. Not to cohabit with the wife of one's father's brother;
14. Not to cohabit with the wife of one's son;
15. Not to cohabit with the wife of one's brother;
16. Not to cohabit with the sister of one's wife;
17. Not to lie with an animal;
18. That a woman should not cause an animal to go in unto her;

19. Not to lie with a male;
20. Not to uncover the nakedness of one's father;
21. Not to uncover the nakedness of the brother of one's father;
22. Not to cohabit with a married woman;
23. Not to cohabit with a menstruant;
24. Not to intermarry with heathens;
25. That an Ammonite or Moabite shall not be permitted to enter the congregation of the Lord;
26. Not to repulse an Egyptian proselyte of the third generation from entering the congregation of the Lord;
27. Not to repulse an Edomite proselyte of the third generation from entering the congregation of the Lord;
28. That a bastard shall not be permitted to enter the congregation of the Lord;
29. That a eunuch shall not be permitted to enter the congregation of the Lord;
30. Not to castrate a male, even of animal, beast, or bird;
31. That a High Priest shall not marry a widow;
32. That a High Priest shall not cohabit with a widow, even out of wedlock;
33. That a High Priest shall marry only a virgin during her maidenhood;
34. That a priest shall not marry a divorced woman;
35. That he shall not marry a harlot;
36. That he shall not marry a profaned woman;
37. Not to approach lasciviously any of the women within the forbidden degrees of consanguinity, even if one has no intercourse with her.

An exposition of these commandments
is contained in the following chapters.

NOTE

In the list of the 613 commandments prefixed to the Code, those dealt with in the present treatise appear in the following order:

Positive commandment:

[33] 38. That a High Priest shall marry a virgin, as it is said: *And he shall take a wife in her virginity* (Lev. 21:13).

Negative commandments:

[1] 330. Not to uncover the nakedness of one's mother, as it is said: *She is thy mother; thou shalt not uncover her nakedness* (Lev. 18:7);

[2] 332. Not to uncover the nakedness of one's father's wife, as it is said: *The nakedness of thy father's wife shalt thou not uncover* (*ibid.* 18:8);

[3] 331. Not to uncover the nakedness of one's sister, as it is said: *The nakedness of thy sister . . . thou shalt not uncover* (*ibid.* 18:9);

[4] 333. Not to uncover the nakedness of one's sister on one's father's side or on one's mother's side, as it is said: *The nakedness of thy father's wife's daughter . . . thou shalt not uncover* (*ibid.* 18:11);

[5] 334. Not to uncover the nakedness of one's son's daughter, as it is said: *The nakedness of thy son's daughter . . . thou shalt not uncover* (*ibid.* 18:10);

[6] 336. Not to uncover the nakedness of one's daughter. Why is this commandment not explicitly stated in the

Torah? Inasmuch as the Torah forbids one's daughter's daughter, it remains silent with regard to the daughter herself. And the Sages have learned by tradition (B. Ker 5a) that the prohibition of the daughter is as much an essential part of the Torah as the other commandments concerning forbidden unions, as it is said: *Their nakedness thou shalt not uncover; for theirs is thine own nakedness* (*ibid.* 18:10);

[7] 335. Not to uncover the nakedness of one's daughter's daughter, as it is said: *The nakedness . . . of thy daughter's daughter, even their nakedness thou shalt not uncover* (*ibid.*);

[8] 337. Not to uncover the nakedness of a woman and her daughter, as it is said: *Thou shalt not uncover the nakedness of a woman and her daughter* (*ibid.* 18:17);

[9] 338. Not to uncover the nakedness of a woman and her son's daughter, as it is said: *Thou shalt not take her son's daughter* (*ibid.*);

[10] 339. Not to uncover the nakedness of a woman and her daughter's daughter, as it is said: *Thou shalt not take . . . her daughter's daughter* (*ibid.*);

[11] 341. Not to uncover the nakedness of one's father's sister, as it is said: *Thou shalt not uncover the nakedness of thy father's sister* (*ibid.* 18:12);

[12] 340. Not to uncover the nakedness of one's mother's sister, as it is said: *Thou shalt not uncover the nakedness of thy mother's sister* (*ibid.* 18:13);

[13] 342. Not to uncover the nakedness of the wife of one's father's brother, as it is said: *Thou shalt not uncover the nakedness of thy father's brother, thou shalt not approach to his wife* (*ibid.* 18:14);

[14] 343. Not to uncover the nakedness of one's son's wife,

as it is said: *Thou shalt not uncover the nakedness of thy daughter-in-law* (*ibid.* 18:15);

[15] 344. Not to uncover the nakedness of one's brother's wife, as it is said: *Thou shalt not uncover the nakedness of thy brother's wife* (*ibid.* 18:16);

[16] 345. Not to uncover the nakedness of one's wife's sister, as it is said: *Thou shalt not take a woman to her sister* (*ibid.* 18:18);

[17] 348. Not to lie with an animal, as it is said: *Thou shalt not lie with any beast* (*ibid.* 18:23);

[18] 349. That a woman shall not cause an animal to go in unto her, as it is said: *Neither shall any woman stand before a beast* (*ibid.*);

[19] 350. Not to lie with a male, as it is said: *Thou shalt not lie with mankind, as with womankind* (*ibid.* 18:22);

[20] 351. Not to uncover the nakedness of one's father himself, as it is said: *The nakedness of thy father . . . shalt thou not uncover* (*ibid.* 18:7);

[21] 352. Not to uncover the nakedness of one's father's brother himself, as it is said: *Thou shalt not uncover the nakedness of thy father's brother* (*ibid.* 18:14);

[22] 347. Not to uncover the nakedness of a married woman, as it is said: *Thou shalt not lie carnally with thy neighbor's wife* (*ibid.* 18:20);

[23] 346. Not to uncover the nakedness of a menstruant, as it is said: *Thou shalt not approach unto a woman . . . as long as she is impure by her uncleanness* (*ibid.* 18:19);

[24] 52. Not to intermarry with heathens, as it is said: *Neither shalt thou make marriages with them* (*Deut.* 7:3);

[25] 53. That an Ammonite or a Moabite shall never marry

a daughter of Israel, as it is said: *An Ammonite or a Moabite shall not enter into the assembly of the Lord* (*ibid.* 23:4);

[26] 55. Not to keep an Egyptian away from the assembly except up to the third generation, as it is said: *Thou shalt not abhor an Egyptian* (*ibid.* 23:8);

[27] 54. Not to keep the seed of Esau away from the assembly except up to the third generation, as it is said: *Thou shalt not abhor an Edomite* (*ibid.*);

[28] 354. That a bastard shall not marry a daughter of Israel, as it is said: *A bastard shall not enter into the assembly of the Lord* (*ibid.* 23:3);

[29] 360. That a eunuch shall not marry a daughter of Israel, as it is said: *He that is crushed or maimed in his privy parts shall not enter into the assembly of the Lord* (*ibid.* 23:2);

[30] 361. Not to castrate any male of any kind, whether of man, of cattle, of beast, or of fowl, as it is said: *That which hath its stones bruised, or crushed, or torn, or cut, ye shall not offer unto the Lord; neither shall ye do thus in your land* (Lev. 22:24);

[31] 161. That a High Priest shall not marry a widow, as it is said: *A widow, or one divorced, or a profaned woman, or a harlot, these he shall not take* (*ibid.* 21:14);

[32] 162. That a High Priest shall not cohabit with a widow, even out of wedlock, seeing that he would profane her thereby, as it is said: *He shall not profane his seed* (*ibid.* 21:15). He is thus warned not to profane a valid woman;

[34] 160. That a priest shall not marry a divorced woman,

as it is said: *Neither shall they take a woman put away from her husband* (*ibid.* 21:7);

[35] 158. That a priest shall not marry a harlot, as it is said: *They shall not take a woman that is a harlot, or profaned* (*ibid.*);

[36] 159. That a priest shall not marry a profaned woman, as it is said: *or profaned* (*ibid.*);

[37] 353. Not to approach women within the forbidden unions with behavior leading to the uncovering of their nakedness, such as embracing, kissing, winking, or gesturing, as it is said: *None of you shall approach to any that is near of kin to him, to uncover their nakedness* (*ibid.* 18:6). And the Sages have learned by tradition (Sif *ibid.*) that this signifies approach leading to the uncovering of their nakedness.

CHAPTER I

1. If one wantonly has connection with a woman within the forbidden unions enumerated in the Torah, he is liable to extinction, as it is said, *For whosoever shall do any of these abominations, even the souls that do them shall be cut off from among their people* (Lev. 18:29), i.e. both of them, the man and the woman. If, however, they have committed the transgression in error, they are subject to a fixed sin offering.

2. Some of the forbidden unions are punishable by death imposed by the court, in addition to extinction, liability to which is common to them all. In the case of those forbidden unions which are punishable by death imposed by the court, if witnesses were present and warning was given, and if the culprits did not desist from their act, the prescribed death penalty must be inflicted upon them.

3. Even if the culprit is a scholar, neither the death penalty nor the penalty of flogging may be inflicted unless warning was given, since the purpose of the warning in all instances is to distinguish between acts committed wantonly and those committed in error.

4. Of the forbidden unions punishable by death, some carry death by stoning, others by burning, and still others by strangulation. The following incur death by stoning: one who has intercourse with his mother, his father's wife, or his son's wife designated in the Torah as *his daughter-in-law* (Lev. 20:12); one who lies with a male or a beast; and a woman who causes an animal to go in unto her.

5. The following prohibited unions carry death by burning: one who has connection with his stepdaughter during his wife's lifetime, his stepdaughter's daughter, his stepson's daughter, his

mother-in-law, his mother-in-law's mother, or his father-in-law's mother; and one who has intercourse with his daughter, his daughter's daughter, or his son's daughter.

6. The only forbidden union punishable by strangulation is the one involving intercourse with another man's wife, as it is said, *The adulterer and the adulteress shall surely be put to death* (Lev. 20:10); for wherever death is prescribed in the Torah without further specification it signifies strangulation. If, however, the woman is the daughter of a priest, she is punishable by burning, while her paramour incurs death by strangulation, as it is said, *And the daughter of any priest, if she profane herself by playing the harlot, she profaneth her father, she shall be burnt with fire* (Lev. 21:9). If she is a betrothed maiden, both are punishable by stoning, as it is said, *If there be a damsel that is a virgin betrothed unto a man, and a man find her in the city, and lie with her; then ye shall bring them both out unto the gate of that city, and ye shall stone them with stones that they die* (Deut. 22:23–24). Also, wherever the Torah says "They shall surely die, their blood is on them," it means death by stoning.

7. All other kinds of forbidden unions are punishable by extinction only, and not by the death penalty imposed by the court. Consequently, if witnesses were present and warning was given, the court must order the culprits to be flogged, since all those punishable by extinction must be flogged.

8. If one has intercourse with a woman forbidden by a negative commandment, the rule is as follows: If wantonly, both he and she must be flogged; if in error, they are completely exempt. If one willfully has connection with a woman of the secondary degrees of propinquity, he must be flogged for disobedience, on the authority of the Scribes. On the other hand, if one has intercourse with a woman prohibited to him by a positive commandment, he is not liable to a flogging. The court, however, may at its discretion have him flogged for disobedience, in order to encourage him to avoid transgression.

9. The victim of duress is entirely exempt, both from flogging and from offering a sacrifice; needless to say, he is also exempt from the death penalty, as it is said, *but unto the damsel thou shalt do nothing* (Deut. 22:26). This holds true only when the victim is the woman, since duress cannot be applied to the man, for no erection is possible without his own intention. A woman who is subjected to duress at the beginning of intercourse, but finally acquiesces in it, is also entirely exempt, for once a man has begun sexual intercourse with her under duress, she cannot but acquiesce, seeing that human impulse and nature compel her to ultimate assent.

10. If the man inserts only the corona of the organ, he is designated "initiator" *(mĕ'areh),* from the verse, *he hath made naḳed (he'ĕrah) her fountain* (Lev. 20:18), while if he inserts the entire organ he is designated "consummator" *(gomer).* With respect to all illicit intercourse it matters not whether one is an initiator or a consummator. Even if he did not emit any semen or withdrew before consummation, once he has inserted the corona of the organ both participants are punishable by death imposed by the court, or extinction, or flagellation, or flogging for disobedience, as the case may be. And whether the man cohabits with the woman in a normal or abnormal manner, as soon as he has initiated with her, both become liable to the death penalty, or extinction, or flagellation, or flogging for disobedience. Whether they committed the act in a recumbent or an upright posture, culpability is incurred at the moment of the insertion of the organ's head.

11. If one has illicit intercourse without erection, his organ being flaccid like that of a corpse, as in the case of persons who are ill or congenitally impotent, such as a born eunuch, even if he introduces the organ with his hand, he is absolved from both extinction and flogging, and also, needless to say, from the death penalty, since this does not constitute intercourse. But he does debar the woman from eating of heave offering, and the court should sentence both of them to flogging for disobedience.

12. If one has illicit intercourse while believing it to be licit, he

is nevertheless liable, even though he had no intention of committing a forbidden act. The same obtains, too, for those forbidden by negative commandments or for the secondary degrees of propinquity. But if one has connection with a dead woman within the forbidden unions, he is entirely exempt; and needless to say he is exempt also if the dead woman was one of those forbidden by negative commandments. If one cohabits with a woman afflicted with a fatal disease, or if he lies with a beast so afflicted, he is liable. For they are still alive, even though they must eventually die of that disease. And even if the animal's windpipe and gullet have been cut, as long as it is twitching, if one has intercourse with it, he is liable, unless it first dies or he decapitates it.

13. Concerning any of the forbidden women referred to above, the rule is as follows: If she is three years and one day old, or older, and an adult male cohabits with her, he incurs the death penalty, or extinction, or flogging, while she is entirely exempt, so long as she has not become of age. If she is less than three years and one day old, both are exempt, since intercourse with her is not regarded as intercourse. Similarly, when a minor male has connection with an adult woman, if he is nine years and one day old, or over, she is punishable by extinction, or death, or flogging, while he is exempt. If he is nine years old, or less, both are exempt.

14. In the case of a man who lies with a male, or causes a male to have connection with him, once sexual contact has been initiated, the rule is as follows: If both are adults, they are punishable by stoning, as it is said, *Thou shalt not lie with a male* (Lev. 18:22), i.e. whether he is the active or the passive participant in the act. If he is a minor, aged nine years and one day, or older, the adult who has connection with him or causes him to have connection with him, is punishable by stoning, while the minor is exempt. If the minor is nine years old, or less, both are exempt. It behooves the court, however, to have the adult flogged for disobedience, inasmuch as he has lain with a male, even though with one less than nine years of age.

15. If one has connection with a hermaphrodite by way of the latter's male organ, he is liable; if by way of the latter's female organ, he is exempt. A *ṭumṭum,* however, is of doubtful sex, and consequently if one has intercourse with him, or with a hermaphrodite by way of the latter's female organ, he must be flogged for disobedience. A hermaphrodite is nevertheless permitted to take a wife.

16. If a man has connection with an animal, or causes an animal to have connection with him, both are punishable by stoning, as it is said, *And thou shalt not lie with any beast* (Lev. 18:23), i.e. whether he is the active or the passive participant in the act. Regardless of whether it is a domestic animal, a wild beast, or a fowl, in all these cases the penalty is death by stoning. Nor does Scripture differentiate between a fully grown animal and one not yet fully grown, seeing that it is said *any beast,* i.e. even a newly born beast. Whether he has connection in a natural manner or not, once he has initiated sexual contact with it, or has caused it to initiate contact with him, he is liable.

17. If a minor nine years and one day old has connection with an animal, or causes it to have connection with him, the animal must be stoned because of his deed, while he is exempt. If he is nine years old or less, the animal is not to be stoned. Likewise, if a female minor aged three years and one day causes a domestic animal or a wild beast to have connection with her, whether the animal is fully grown or not, once sexual contact has been initiated, whether in a natural manner or not, the animal is to be stoned, while she is exempt. If she is of age, both are to be stoned. If she is three years old or less, the animal is not to be stoned.

18. Similarly, if one lies with an animal by error, or if a woman by error causes an animal to have connection with her, the animal is not to be stoned because of their deed, even if they are both adults.

In any of the cases of forbidden unions, if one of the participants is an adult and the other a minor, the minor is exempt and the adult is liable, as we have explained. If one of them is awake and the other asleep, the latter is exempt. If one of them acted with deliberation and the other in error, the former is liable and the latter is only obligated to bring a sacrifice. If one of them commits the act under duress and the other by design, the former is exempt, as we have explained.

19. The witnesses to the deed are not bound to see the culprits initiate intercourse, like a painting stick being inserted in the paint tube. Once they see them in close embrace, in the manner of those engaged in the sexual act, the culprits are liable to be put to death on this evidence. It cannot be said that perchance the act of coition has nevertheless not been initiated, for this posture constitutes presumptive evidence to the effect that it has.

20. If a man is presumed to be related to a woman within the prohibited unions, he is judged in accordance with that presumption, even if there is no explicit evidence of this kinship, and flogging, burning, stoning, or strangulation is incurred on the basis of that presumption. Thus, if the presumption is that a certain woman is his sister, his daughter, or his mother, and he has intercourse with her, and there are witnesses to this act, he must be flogged, burned, or stoned, even though there is no clear evidence that she is in fact his sister, his mother, or his daughter, but merely a presumption to that effect. Indeed, it happened once that a certain woman came to Jerusalem with a child perched on her shoulder. Thereupon she reared him, the presumption being that he was her son. Later, he had intercourse with her, and when they brought her to court she was condemned to death by stoning. Support for this ruling is found in the enactment in the Torah that prescribes death for the son who curses or strikes his father. What clear evidence is there that he is in fact the father? None, only the presumption to that effect. Therefore the principle of presumption applies also to other relatives.

21. In the case of a man and a woman who, having arrived from overseas, mutually declare themselves to be man and wife,

if the presumption to that effect has prevailed in the city for thirty days, any other person having intercourse with her is punishable by death. Within the thirty days, however, no death penalty may be imposed in this case for intercourse with another man's wife.

22. If a woman is presumed among her women neighbors to be a menstruant, her husband must be flogged if he has intercourse with her during this period, for having cohabited with a menstruant. In the case of a man who suspects his wife, and she then secludes herself with another man, and thereupon one witness comes forth and testifies that she has been defiled, the rule is that if her husband is a priest, and he subsequently has intercourse with her, he must be flogged for intercourse with a harlot. For although it is only the mere root of the testimony that has been established by the one witness, she was already presumed to be a harlot.

23. In the case of the father who declares, "My daughter is betrothed to this man," even though he is trustworthy in this respect, and even if she subsequently marries that man, the rule is that if she commits adultery she is not to be stoned on the basis of her father's assertion alone, unless there are witnesses who say that she was betrothed in their presence. Similarly, if a woman says, "I have been betrothed," she may not be put to death on the basis of her own statement alone. There must be either witnesses or presumptive evidence.

CHAPTER II

1. The wife of a man's father, the wife of his son, the wife of his brother, and the wife of his father's brother—these four constitute unions which are forever forbidden to him, from the moment of either betrothal or marriage, whether they have been later divorced or not, whether during their husbands' lifetime

or after their demise, excepting only the wife of his brother who left no son by her. If he has intercourse with one of these women during the lifetime of her husband, he is guilty of a double offense, on account of near kin and for intercourse with a married woman, seeing that both these prohibitions have been violated simultaneously.

2. Consequently, if a man has intercourse with his mother—that is to say, the wife of his father—he is guilty of a double offense, whether it occurred during the father's lifetime, or after his death; first, because she is his mother, and secondly, because she is his father's wife. His brother's wife is of forbidden union to him, whether her husband is his brother on his father's side only or on his mother's side only, whether he was born in or out of wedlock. The wife of his father's brother on the mother's side only, however, constitutes merely a secondary degree of propinquity, as we have explained. A sister, whether on the father's or on the mother's side, whether born in or out of wedlock—for example, if his father or his mother had committed adultery with someone else and the sister was born out of this adultery—is of forbidden union to him, as it is said, *whether born at home or born abroad* (Lev. 18:9).

3. The daughter of one's father's wife, i.e. his sister on the father's side, is of forbidden union to him, as it is said, *the nakedness of thy father's wife's daughter, begotten of thy father, she is thy sister* (Lev. 18:11). If, on the other hand, his father had married a woman who already had a daughter by another man, this daughter is permitted to him, since she is not *begotten of his father*. Now, is he not already liable as regards her, inasmuch as she is designated as his *sister?* Why then does the Torah say further, *thy father's wife's daughter?* To make him liable also on this latter account.

4. Therefore, if one has intercourse with his sister, i.e. the daughter of the woman wedded to his father, he is guilty of a double offense; first, because of *the nakedness of thy sister* (Lev. 18:9), and secondly, because of *the nakedness of thy father's*

wife's daughter (*ibid.* 18:11). If, however, his father had raped or seduced a woman and begot a daughter by her, and he has intercourse with her, he is guilty only once, because of the fact that she is his sister, since a daughter born out of a raped woman cannot be considered the daughter of the father's wife.

5. The sister of one's mother, whether on the father's side or on the mother's side, whether born in or out of wedlock, is of forbidden union to him on account of *thy mother's sister* (Lev. 18:13). Similarly, the sister of his father, whether on the father's side or on the mother's side, whether born in or out of wedlock, is of prohibited union to him on account of *thy father's sister* (*ibid.* 18:12).

6. If one has had adulterous intercourse with a woman and begot a daughter by her, this daughter is of forbidden union to him, because she is his daughter, even though the Torah does not say, "Thou shalt not uncover the nakedness of thy daughter." For inasmuch as the Torah has forbidden *thy daughter's daughter* (Lev. 18:10), it is silent concerning the daughter herself. This prohibition, too, is, therefore, Scriptural, and is not based merely on the authority of the Scribes. Consequently, if one cohabits with one's daughter born in wedlock he is guilty of a double offense, because she is his daughter, and also because of *the nakedness of a woman and her daughter* (*ibid.* 18:17).

7. The moment a man has betrothed a woman unto himself, six of her female kin become prohibited to him, and each one of them is of forbidden union to him forever, whether he marries or divorces his wife, whether during the wife's lifetime or after her decease. They are: her mother, her mother's mother, her father's mother, her daughter, her daughter's daughter, and her son's daughter. If he has intercourse with any of them during the wife's lifetime, both incur death by burning.

8. If he has intercourse with any of them after the wife's death, both incur extinction, but not a sentence of death by the court, as it is said, *they shall be burnt with fire, both he and they* (Lev.

20:14); i.e. so long as both women, namely his wife and the woman with whom he had illicit intercourse, are living, he and the latter are punishable by burning, but if only one is living, death by burning is not required.

9. Similarly, one's wife's sister is of prohibited union to him up to the moment of his wife's death. Whether she is her sister on the mother's side or on the father's side, whether born in or out of wedlock, she is of forbidden union to him.

10. If a man transgresses and commits adultery with any one of the aforementioned seven women, whether deliberately or in error, even though both he and the adulterous woman are punishable by death imposed by the court or by extinction, his wife is not thereby rendered forbidden to him; with the sole exception of adultery with the sister of his betrothed wife, in which instance the wife becomes prohibited to him, as we have explained in the Laws Concerning Divorce.

11. If a man has adulterous intercourse with a woman, her relatives, i.e. the seven women mentioned above, are not thereby rendered forbidden to him. Nevertheless, the Sages have forbidden a man who has committed adultery with a woman to marry any one of these seven kinswomen of hers, as long as the harlot with whom he had committed adultery is living. The reason is that the harlot would come to visit her kinswoman and he may find himself alone with her, and since he has already been on intimate terms with her, he may succumb to sin and thus have intercourse with a woman of forbidden union. Not only this, but even if he was merely suspected of intercourse with a woman, he may not marry any one of her kin, until this suspected woman is dead. If, however, he has married any one of these relatives of the woman with whom he had committed adultery, he need not divorce her.

12. If one is suspected of adultery with a woman of prohibited union, or if an evil report to this effect is circulated about her and him, he may not dwell in the same alley with her nor be

seen in that group of dwellings. Indeed, it happened once that a man who was reported to be on intimate terms with his mother-in-law was sentenced by the Sages to a flogging for disobedience merely because he passed by the door of her house.

13. If a man has adulterous intercourse with a woman and her daughter, or with a woman and her sister, or the like, he is considered as having had intercourse with two unrelated women, since forbidden union can arise between them only through marriage, and not through harlotry. Similarly, if his father, son, brother, or father's brother has raped or seduced a woman, she is nevertheless permitted to him and he may marry her, seeing that Scripture says *the wife* (Lev. 18:14 ff.), whereas in this case there is no matrimony.

14. A man is permitted to marry the daughter or the mother of his father's or son's wife, as we have explained. He is also permitted to marry the wife of his brother's son. He may, moreover, marry a woman and her sister's daughter, or her brother's daughter, together. The Sages have accounted it a meritorious deed for a man to marry his sister's daughter, and the same applies to his brother's daughter, as it is said, *And hide not thyself from thine own flesh* (Isa. 58:7).

CHAPTER III

1. If a man has intercourse with the wife of a minor—even if she is a levirate wife whose husband was nine years and one day old when he consummated the marriage with her—he is exempt. Similarly, if a man has intercourse with the wife of a deaf-mute, an imbecile, a person of doubtful sex, or a hermaphrodite, or with a deaf-mute or imbecile woman who is the wife of a man of sound mind, or with a woman whose betrothal or divorce is in doubt—in all these instances he is exempt. If, however, they have committed the act deliberately, they must be flogged for disobedience.

2. If a man has intercourse with a female minor who is the wife of an adult, the rule is that if it was her father who had given her in marriage to her present husband, the adulterer is liable to death by strangulation, while she is entirely exempt, although she is then forbidden to her husband, as we have explained in the Laws Concerning the Unfaithful Wife. If, however, she has reached the age when she may exercise the right of refusal, the adulterer must be flogged for disobedience, while she continues to be permitted to her husband, even if he is a priest.

3. If a priest's daughter who is a married woman commits adultery, whether her husband is a priest or an Israelite, or even a bastard or a Temple bondsman, or anyone else of those with whom marriage is forbidden by a negative commandment, she is liable to death by burning, as it is said, *And the daughter of any priest, if she profane herself by playing the harlot, she profaneth her father: she shall be burnt with fire* (Lev. 21:9), while her paramour incurs the penalty of strangulation. Similarly, the daughter of an Israelite who is the wife of a priest is liable to strangulation, just like any other married woman who is guilty of adultery.

4. If a man has intercourse with a betrothed maiden, both of them are punishable by stoning, but not unless she is a virgin maiden who is betrothed and still resides in her father's house. If she has attained maturity, or if she has entered the bridal chamber—though the marriage has not yet been consummated—or even if her father has placed her in the care of her husband's agents to be escorted to his house, and she commits adultery while on the way, she incurs the penalty of strangulation.

5. However, if a man has intercourse with a betrothed female minor while she is still in her father's house, he is liable to stoning, but she is exempt. On the other hand, if a betrothed maiden who is the daughter of a priest commits adultery, she, too, is liable to stoning.

6. If ten men successively have intercourse with a virgin who is still under her father's control, the first one is punishable by

stoning, while all the others are liable to strangulation. This applies only when they have normal intercourse with her; if they have abnormal intercourse with her, so that she remains a virgin, they are all liable to stoning.

7. A betrothed maiden who has been manumitted or is a proselyte, even if manumitted or proselytized when she was less than three years and one day old, is liable to strangulation for adultery, just like any other married woman.

8. There is a novel rule concerning slanderous accusation of adultery. Wherein lies the innovation? If the charge is substantiated and witnesses come forth and testify that a maiden has committed adultery while she was betrothed, then, if she has committed the offense after leaving her father's authority, or indeed after she had entered the bridal chamber but before the consummation of the marriage by the husband, she is liable to stoning at the door of her father's house. In the case of other betrothed maidens, however, who have not yet left the father's authority and are therefore not subject to the aforementioned law of slander concerning those who commit adultery after leaving the father's authority, they are liable to strangulation, as we have explained. You thus learn that in the case of adultery by a married woman three kinds of capital punishment apply: some married women are liable to strangulation, some to burning, and some to stoning.

9. And where is the stoning of a betrothed maiden who has committed adultery to take place? If she had committed adultery while in her father's house, even if the witnesses did not testify until after she had entered her father-in-law's house, she is to be stoned at the door of her father's house. If she had committed adultery while in the house of her father-in-law, but before she was handed over by her father, then, even if the witnesses gave evidence only after she had returned to her father's house, she is to be stoned at the entrance of *the gate of that city* (Deut. 22:24).

10. If witnesses come forth and testify after she had attained maturity or after her husband had consummated the marriage, then, even if they affirm that the adultery was committed in her father's house during her maidenhood, she is to be stoned at the Place of Stoning.

11. If the betrothed maiden was conceived while her mother was yet a heathen and was born after her mother had become a proselyte, she is to be stoned at the gate of the city. In the case of any woman who is due to be stoned at the gate of the city, if the majority of the town's inhabitants are heathens, she should be stoned at the door of the court. In the case of one who is due to be stoned at the door of her father's house, if she has no father, or if she has a father but he has no house, she is to be stoned at the Place of Stoning. *At the door of her father's house* (Deut. 22:21) merely indicates that this is the prescribed place when such is in existence.

12. If a man has had intercourse repeatedly with a woman who is of the forbidden unions, he is punishable by extinction or by death imposed by the court for each individual act of intercourse; although the court can impose the death penalty only once, nevertheless each act of intercourse must be considered a separate transgression. Similarly, if he has committed a single act of intercourse punishable under several categories, the rule is that if he has done it in error he is obligated to bring a sacrifice for each category, notwithstanding that only one act of intercourse is involved, as will be explained in the Laws Concerning Sin Committed through Error; but if he has done it wantonly, then this one act of intercourse is regarded as constituting several transgressions. Likewise, by but one act of intercourse a man may become liable to more than one flogging, as will be explained.

13. The *designated bondmaid* (Lev. 19:20) referred to in the Torah signifies one who is half bondswoman and half freewoman and has been betrothed to a Hebrew slave, concerning whom it is said, *They shall not be put to death, because she was not free (ibid.)*. Hence, once she is completely manumitted, the death

penalty imposed by the court takes effect on her account, because she assumes the full status of a married woman, as we have explained in the Laws Concerning Matrimony.

14. Intercourse with a bondmaid of this category differs in respect to its penalties from all other prohibited intercourse mentioned in the Torah, seeing that she must be flogged, as it is said, *there shall be inquiry (ibid.),* while the man is liable to a guilt offering, as it is said, *And he shall bring his guilt offering* (*ibid.* 19:21). Regardless of whether the act in the case of this designated bondmaid was deliberate or in error, the man must bring a guilt offering. Even if he has intercourse with her repeatedly, either deliberately or in error, he need bring but one guilt offering. She, however, is liable to flogging for each individual act of intercourse committed wantonly, just as in other instances involving transgression of a negative commandment.

15. If a man merely initiates the act of intercourse with a designated bondmaid, but does not consummate it, he is exempt, so long as he does not complete the act. Moreover, he is liable only if she is an adult and a nonvirgin, and if she deliberately acquiesces in the act. If, on the other hand, she is a minor or a virgin, or has acted in error, or has been raped, or was asleep, he is exempt. Similarly, if he has intercourse with her unnaturally, he is exempt, since Scripture does not regard abnormal intercourse as equivalent to normal intercourse in the case of a designated bondmaid, as it is said concerning her, *a lying of seed* (*ibid.,* 19:20), whereas in other instances of intercourse Scripture makes no distinction between the one kind of intercourse and the other, as it is said *lyings of womankind* (*ibid.* 19:22). Scripture thus indicates that there are two ways of intercourse with a woman.

16. Wherever we have stated with regard to this bondmaid that the man is exempt, the meaning is that he is exempt from bringing an offering, while she is exempt from flogging. Nevertheless, a flogging for disobedience should be imposed upon him on the authority of the Scribes, if both of them are adults and have acted deliberately.

17. If a boy nine years and one day old has intercourse with a designated bondmaid, she is to be flogged while he is obligated to bring a guilt offering. This applies only if she is an adult and a nonvirgin, and has acquiesced in the act, as we have explained, since the man cannot be held liable to bring an offering unless she incurs the penalty of flagellation, as it is said, *there shall be inquiry . . . and he shall bring his . . . guilt offering* (*ibid.* 19:20–21).

CHAPTER IV

1. The menstruant is classed with all other forbidden unions. If a man initiates the act of intercourse with her, whether naturally or unnaturally, he is punishable by extinction, even if she is a minor three years and one day old, as in all other cases of forbidden union, seeing that a female is rendered unclean by menstruation from the very day of her birth onwards. Moreover, she becomes unclean because of flux from the age of ten days. The rule, based on tradition, is that in the case of uncleanness due to menstruation and flux there is no distinction between an adult and a minor.

2. Whether a man has intercourse with a menstruant at any time during the seven days of her period, even if she saw menstrual blood on the first day only; or whether he has intercourse with a woman delivered of a male child during the seven days after the birth, or one delivered of a female child during the fourteen days after the birth; or whether he has intercourse with a woman having a flux during the period of her flux and her subsequent computation of the days of cleanness; and regardless whether the woman is a bondwoman or a freedwoman—in all these cases he is punishable by extinction. Concerning a menstruant it is said, *she shall be in her impurity for seven days* (Lev. 15:19); with regard to a woman with flux it is said, *all*

the days of the issue of her uncleanness she shall be as in the days of her impurity (*ibid.* 15:25); regarding a woman who has given birth to a male child it is said, *as in the days of the impurity of her sickness shall she be unclean* (*ibid.* 12:2); and with respect to a woman who has given birth to a female child it is said, *she shall be unclean two weeks, as in her impurity* (*ibid.* 12:5).

3. How does this rule apply? Uncleanness depends upon counting a specified number of days, providing the woman subsequently immerses herself in the water of an immersion pool after the completion of the count. If, however, a menstruant, or a woman with flux, or a woman after childbirth, did not immerse herself, the rule is that a man who has intercourse with one of them, even if he does so after an interval of several years, is punishable by extinction, seeing that Scripture makes her cleanness dependent on both the counting of days and the immersion, as it is said *they shall bathe themselves in water* (Lev. 15:18). This verse establishes the general rule for every unclean person: He remains in his state of uncleanness until such time as he has immersed himself.

4. A heathen woman who is menstruating, or has a flux, or has just been delivered, imposes no liability upon the man who has intercourse with her. The Sages have decreed that all heathens, whether male or female, are to be regarded as in a permanent state of flux insofar as cleanness and uncleanness are concerned, whether they actually have a flux or not.

5. Any flow of blood a woman may have within thirty-three days after the birth of a male child, or sixty-six days after the birth of a female child, is designated as "blood of purification." It does not restrain a wife from her husband; rather, having immersed herself after seven days following the birth of a male child, or fourteen days following the birth of a female child, she may resume marital relations, even if blood continues to ooze.

6. All those who are obligated to undergo immersion must immerse themselves in daytime, excepting a menstruant and a

woman after childbirth. For regarding a menstruant Scripture says, *she shall be in her impurity seven days* (Lev. 15:19), implying that the entire seven days fall within her period of impurity, and that she is to immerse herself on the eighth night. Similarly, a woman who has given birth to a male child must immerse herself on the eighth night, and a woman who has given birth to a female child on the fifteenth night, because a woman after childbirth is regarded as analogous to a menstruant, as we have explained.

7. If a menstruant delays her immersion for many days, and then immerses herself, she should do so only at nighttime, for should she immerse herself by day, people might be misled, and another menstruant might proceed to immerse herself on the seventh day.

8. If the menstruant is ill, or if the place of immersion is so far away that the women cannot reach it in time and are afraid to return at night because of the danger of brigands, or because of the cold, or because the city gates are closed at night, she may immerse herself on the eighth day, or on a subsequent day, in the daytime.

9. Women having fixed periods are presumed to be clean for their husbands, unless a wife says to her husband, "I am unclean," or unless she is presumed by her women neighbors to be a menstruant. If her husband had gone to another locality leaving her in a state of cleanness, he need not ask her upon his return whether she is clean. Even if on his return he finds her asleep, he is allowed to have intercourse with her, so long as it is not within the time for her fixed period, and he need feel no apprehension that she might be menstruating. If, however, he had left her a menstruant, she is forbidden to him until she tells him, "I am clean."

10. If a woman says to her husband "I am unclean," and then reverses herself, saying, "I am clean—I only said the opposite at first in jest," she is not to be believed. If she offers a plausible

reason, however, she is to be believed. For example, if her husband demands her services while his mother or sister are with her in the courtyard, and she says, "I am unclean," but later reverses herself and says "I am clean—I said I was unclean only because of your mother or sister, lest they should see us," she is to be believed. And this obtains in all similar cases.

11. If a man, while having intercourse with his wife, and presuming her to be clean, is told by her, "I am become unclean," he must not withdraw immediately while still in a state of tumescence, since he derives as much gratification from his egress as he does from his ingress. If he does withdraw while in a state of tumescence, he is liable to extinction, as though he had cohabited with a menstruant, and this applies also to all forbidden unions. How then should he proceed? He should dig his toenails into the ground and pause for a while without moving, until the organ becomes limp, and thereupon withdraw from her.

12. A man is forbidden to have intercourse with his wife near the time of her period, lest she should have a flow of blood during intercourse, as it is said, *Thus shall ye separate the children of Israel from their uncleanness* (Lev. 15:21). How near? If it is her habit to have a flow of blood in the daytime, he is forbidden to have intercourse with her from the beginning of that day, and if it is her habit to have the flow at night, he is forbidden to have intercourse with her from the beginning of that night.

13. If her period has passed and she had no flow, she is permitted to have intercourse once her fixed period has expired. How so? If it is her wont to have a flow at midday, she is forbidden to have intercourse from the beginning of that day. If midday passes and no blood appears, she is still forbidden to have intercourse until the evening. Similarly, if it is her wont to have a flow at midnight, and midnight passes with no blood appearing, she is still forbidden to have intercourse until sunrise.

14. It is the usage of the sons and daughters of Israel always to examine themselves after intercourse. How so? The man wipes

himself with a rag set aside for him, while the woman does the same with a rag set aside for her, and they both examine the rags to determine whether blood had appeared during intercourse. The man may let his wife inspect his rag; for since she is trusted concerning her own rag, she is also trusted regarding his.

15. These pieces of cloth with which they wipe themselves must be of flax, rubbed soft and colored white, and are in this instance called test rags. The cloth used by the man is called his test rag, and the one used by the woman is called her test rag.

16. Pious women do not engage in intercourse unless they first examine themselves prior to it. A woman who has no fixed period is forbidden to have intercourse without prior examination. She must therefore use two test rags, one before and one after intercourse. A woman who has a fixed period need not use a test rag before intercourse, except for the sake of piety only. All, however, must use two test rags after intercourse, one for the man and one for the woman, even if she is pregnant, suckling, or aged. A minor female, too, should not have intercourse with a man without using two test rags, one for him and one for her. A virgin, however, or a woman who continues in the blood of her purification, requires no test rags, because blood is already oozing out of her.

17. If a man has intercourse with his wife repeatedly, they are not obligated to inspect their two test rags following each act; it is enough that he wipe himself with his test rag and she with hers after each act of intercourse during that entire night, and that they examine the test rags on the morrow. Should blood be found on his or her test rag, she is considered unclean. If she, having had intercourse and wiped herself, mislays her test rag, she must abstain from further intercourse until she first examines herself with another test rag, seeing that there may have been blood on the mislaid test rag.

18. If she had placed the test rag under a pillow or cushion, and blood is found on it, the rule is that if the spot is oblong,

she is deemed unclean, the presumption being that the spot was caused by the wiping. If the spot is round, she is considered clean, on the ground that it is nothing more than the blood of a bug crushed under the pillow.

19. If having wiped herself with the test rag which she had previously examined, and pressed it against her thigh, she finds on the morrow that there is blood on it, she is deemed unclean. It cannot be said, perchance she had crushed a bug when she pressed the rag against her thigh. If she had wiped herself with a test rag which she had not inspected beforehand, so that she is uncertain whether or not there was blood on it before she had wiped herself, and subsequently blood is found on it, the rule is that if the stain is the size of a bean or larger, she is deemed a menstruant; if smaller, she is considered clean, for it must have come from a bug.

20. If a woman has a flow of blood during intercourse, she may have intercourse again following her purification. If she notices blood a second time, she may have intercourse on a third occasion. Should she have a flow of blood on the third occasion also, she is forbidden to have intercourse with that husband ever again. When does this apply? When there is nothing else to which the bleeding may be attributed. If, however, the intercourse took place close to her period, the bleeding may be imputed to it. If she has a wound in her womb, the bleeding may be ascribed to the wound. If, on the other hand, the blood from the wound differs in appearance from the blood seen during intercourse, the bleeding cannot be attributed to the wound. A woman is to be believed when she declares, "I have a wound inside my womb, which is the source of the bleeding," and is therefore permitted to her husband, even though blood issues from the womb during intercourse.

21. If a woman has a flow of blood three times successively during intercourse, and there is nothing else to which the bleeding may be attributed, she must be divorced, and is then per-

mitted to marry another man. If upon remarriage she again has a flow of blood on three successive occasions during intercourse, she must again be divorced, and may marry a third time. If in her third marriage she once more has a flow of blood on three consecutive occurrences during intercourse, she must be once more divorced, and is henceforth forbidden to remarry until she is cured of that disease.

22. How should she examine herself to determine whether she has been cured or not? She should take a leaden tube with the forward edge folded over inwards, and insert it as far as it will go. She should then introduce into the tube a rod with a swab at its tip, and push it in until the swab reaches the neck of the womb; she should then extract the swab. If blood is found upon the tip of the swab, it is evident that the flow she had during intercourse came from the womb. If no blood whatsoever is found upon the swab, it is evident that the blood which was observed was caused by pressure against the sides of the passage, and she is therefore clean and permitted to remarry, as we have explained in the Laws Concerning Matrimony.

CHAPTER V

1. A woman may be rendered unclean through a mishap and become either a menstruant or a woman with a flux. How so? If, for example, she jumped from place to place, or saw domestic animals, wild beasts, or birds in the act of mating, and, becoming sexually excited, had a flow. And so in all similar cases; inasmuch as she has a flow, regardless of the cause, she becomes thereby unclean and conveys uncleanness, irrespective of the amount of blood involved. Even if she has a flow amounting to no more than a drop the size of a mustard seed, she has the same status as a woman from whom a considerable quantity of blood had issued.

2. All women become unclean by reason of blood in the antechamber. Even if the blood did not flow out, but was merely displaced from the womb, without issuing forth, inasmuch as it has come forth from "between the glands," the woman is deemed unclean, although the blood is still in her flesh, as it is said, *and her issue in her flesh be blood* (Lev. 15:19). How far in the womb is "between the glands"? As far as the male organ reaches at the conclusion of intercourse. The area itself of "between the glands" is considered as part of the interior region of the womb.

3. The Sages spoke by way of parable in referring to a woman's private parts. The womb, in which the foetus is formed, is called "the fountain." From it issues the blood of menstruation and of flux; it is also called "the chamber," since it is situated in the innermost region. The "whole neck of the womb" is the long passage whose extremity contracts during pregnancy to prevent the foetus from falling out, and opens wide at the time of birth. It is called "the antechamber," that is to say, the gateway to the womb.

4. At the completion of intercourse the male organ enters the antechamber, but does not reach the inner extremity thereof, remaining more or less distant from it, according to the length of the individual organ. Over the chamber and antechamber, and between them, is the place where the two female ovaries are situated, as well as the tubes in which the woman's sperm ripens. This place is called "the upper chamber." There is a kind of orifice opening from the upper chamber to the roof of the antechamber, and the Sages call this orifice "the passage." The male organ enters beyond the passage at the conclusion of intercourse.

5. All blood issuing from the chamber is unclean, excepting "blood of purification," which the Torah has declared clean, and "blood of travail," as will be explained. All blood from the upper chamber is clean, being considered like the blood of a wound in the bowels, liver, or kidneys, and the like. Blood found in the antechamber is unclean if found from the passage inwards,

it being presumed to have come from the chamber. A person incurred liability on account of it if he entered the Temple, and because of it heave offerings and hallowed things had to be burned. It cannot be said that it may have come from the upper chamber by way of the orifice, since most blood found in that part of the antechamber does come from the chamber. If blood is found in the antechamber from the orifice outwards, its uncleanness is in doubt, for it may have come from the chamber, or it may have flowed from the upper chamber through the passage. Consequently, heave offerings and hallowed things did not have to be burned on account of it, nor was a person liable on account of it if he entered the Temple.

6. Not every fluid issuing from the chamber conveys uncleanness, but only blood, as it is said, *and her issue be blood* (Lev. 15:19). Consequently, if a white or green fluid flows from the womb, even though it is viscous like blood, inasmuch as it does not have the appearance of blood, it is deemed clean.

7. Five varieties of woman's blood are deemed unclean, while all the others are deemed clean. These are: red, black, like bright crocus, like water mixed with earth, and like wine diluted with water.

8. What shade of red is meant? That whose appearance is like the first jet of human blood released during bloodletting. The woman's blood should be placed in a vessel, compared with the blood of bloodletting, and adjudged accordingly. Black blood is blood having the color of dried ink. What is the color of blood that is like bright crocus? A fresh crocus still embedded in its clod of earth should be brought, and the middle stalk, from the flower of the brightest hue, should be taken; the whole of it is like a reed, each flower having three stalks, and each stalk having three leaves. The color of the blood should be compared with the color of the center leaf of the middle stalk, and adjudged accordingly. What is meant by water mixed with earth? Earth from the valley of Sikhnin, or any similiar red earth, should be

brought and placed in a vessel and water should be poured over it until the water covers it to the thickness of a garlic skin; no set amount of water or soil is required. The mixture should then be stirred in the vessel, and the comparison should be made at that moment and in that place, while the mixture is turbid. Should the water become clear, the mixture should be stirred again.

9. In the case of these four shades of color, if the hue of the blood is like that of the liquid, or darker, the blood is deemed unclean. If lighter, it is deemed clean. How so? If the blood is darker than dried ink, the woman is deemed unclean; if lighter, as for example, the color of a black olive, of pitch, or of a raven, it is considered clean; and the same applies to the other three colors.

10. What color is meant by wine diluted with water? One part of Sharon wine of the Land of Israel, full bodied and of new vintage, should be mixed with two parts of water. If the shade of the blood is darker or lighter than this mixture, the blood is deemed clean, so long as the mixture is not of exactly the same color as the blood. A woman's statement, "I saw blood resembling this color, but lost it," must be given credence, and the Sage may then pronounce her clean or unclean, as the case may be.

11. How should the Sage compare and decide? He should take the bloodstained rag in his hand and inspect it as against the ink, the crocus leaf, the blood in the cupping vessel, the earth and water mixture, or the cup of mixed wine, and adjudicate her case according to the evidence as he sees it, declaring her to be clean or unclean. He may not look through the glass of the vessel from the outside, but at the liquid itself in the vessel. The utensil should be wide, weigh one *mina,* and hold two *loḡs,* in order to allow the light to penetrate and dispel the darkness.

12. Blood should not be examined except on a white rag and in sunlight. The Sage should shade the bloodspot with his hand, while he himself stands in the sunlight, in order that he might

see it as it actually is. The person who examines the blood need not necessarily resort to all these procedures whenever he makes the examination, for a Sage develops an expert eye for different species of blood, and upon seeing it is immediately able to declare the blood clean or unclean. However, should he be in doubt as to color, he should compare the blood with ink, cupping blood, or the other colors, and adjudicate accordingly.

13. If a woman loses a shapeless embryo, even one that is red in color, should blood accompany the embryo, she is deemed unclean; if not, she is deemed clean. And even if the lump, upon being torn open, is found to be full of blood, the woman is still deemed clean, because this is not menstrual but embryonic blood.

14. If a woman loses a torn embryo containing accumulated blood, she is deemed unclean. In case the abortion is something like a rind, a hair, dust, or a gnat, if the color of the aforesaid objects is red, they should be placed in lukewarm water. If they dissolve, she is deemed unclean, because in that case the abortion is congealed blood, and a woman who sees dried blood is deemed unclean. If they dissolve only after remaining in the lukewarm water for twenty-four hours, her uncleanness is in doubt. If they do not dissolve after twenty-four hours, they must have come from a wound, and the woman is therefore deemed clean.

15. In case the abortion is something like a locust, a fish, an insect, or a creeping thing, if the aforementioned objects are accompanied by blood, the woman is deemed unclean, otherwise she is deemed clean.

16. If a woman, having inserted a tube into the antechamber, notices blood within the tube, she is deemed clean, as it is said, *and her issue in her flesh be blood* (Lev. 15:19), that is, she is clean so long as she does not see the blood *in her flesh*, according to the wont of women, because it is not the way of a woman to see blood inside a tube.

17. If a woman urinates and blood issues with her urine,

whether she does so while standing or while sitting, she is deemed clean. Even if she feels a sensation in her body and trembles, she need not be apprehensive, for this sensation is due to the passing of the urine, inasmuch as urine cannot issue from the chamber, so that this blood must be attributed to a wound in the rectum or kidney.

18. Virginal blood is considered clean and not identical with either menstrual blood or blood of flux, because it does not issue from the fountain, but is regarded as blood issuing from a wound. What then is the law concerning a virgin's blood? If she was married when yet a minor, whether she had never before menstruated, or whether she did menstruate while in her father's house, the rule is that she is permitted to her husband until the wound heals, since any flow of blood she may have is deemed to be due to the wound. If, however, she has a flow after the wound has healed, she is considered a menstruant.

19. In case she was married while yet a maiden, if she had never before menstruated in her life, she is permitted to her husband for four days, both day and night, even while the blood is flowing, provided the wound has not healed. If, however, she had menstruated while in her father's house, and was thereupon married, the husband may have intercourse with her the first time only, and must then withdraw, this virginal blood being regarded as the onset of menstruation. An adult woman who had never before menstruated in her life is allowed the entire first night.

20. The four nights granted to a maiden who had never menstruated are allowed even if they are not consecutive. Her husband may have intercourse with her the first night, then wait even as long as two or three months, and then have intercourse for a second night, always provided the wound has not healed.

21. The same ruling obtains respecting a minor, who is granted time until the wound has healed, even if it takes more than a year. Her husband may have intercourse with her within the entire year, whether on irregular occasions or on successive days.

22. If a minor is married and attains maidenhood while being with her husband, and the blood is still flowing because of the wound, all the acts of intercourse which he had had with her while she was a minor are counted as the equivalent of one night, and he may thereafter complete the total of four days during the period of her maidenhood. Even if the remaining three days allowed to him are taken at irregular intervals and he has intercourse with her one night every two months, this is permitted, provided the wound has not healed.

23. How do we know whether the wound has healed or not? If she has a flow when standing but not when sitting; or if she has it when sitting on the ground but not when sitting on cushions or pillows, the wound has not yet healed. If the blood has ceased and she has no flow whatsoever, whether she is standing or sitting on a cushion, the wound has already healed. So also, if the blood does not cease at all, and she has a flow even when she is sitting on cushions or pillows, it is not the blood of a wound, but that of menstruation.

24. If she has a flow during intercourse, it is due to a wound. If during intercourse she has no flow, but subsequently has one not caused by intercourse, is it the blood of menstruation.

25. If a man has intercourse with a virgin without any blood coming forth, then has intercourse with her again and blood does issue, it is the blood of menstruation, even if she is a minor, for had it been virginal blood it would have appeared on the first occasion. If a man has intercourse with a child less than three years and a day old, and blood comes forth, it is deemed virginal blood.

CHAPTER VI

1. The blood of a menstruant, the blood of a woman with flux, the blood of travail, the blood of a woman in childbirth, and the

blood of purification of a woman after childbirth are all the same species of blood, coming from the fountain, and from the same source. The law concerning them differs only as regards the various times, so that one of them renders a woman clean, another renders her a menstruant, and still another renders her a woman with flux.

2. How so? When a woman becomes menstruant for the first time, or when she becomes menstruant during her period, that is the time which is fixed for her menstruation, she is deemed a menstruant during all of the seven days, whether she menstruates throughout the seven days, or sees only the first drop. If she has a flow on the eighth day, it is the blood of flux, since it is past the period of her menstruation.

3. Similarly, any flow of blood she may have in the days between one menstrual period and the next is considered to be the blood of flux. It is a rule given to Moses from Sinai that there are but eleven days between one period of menstruation and the next.

4. All of the seven days on the first of which a menstrual period has been fixed to begin for a woman are called the days of her menstruation, whether she becomes menstruant during those days or not. And why are they called the days of menstruation? Because she is prone to menstruate during that time, and all blood noticed during those days is to be regarded as menstrual blood.

5. All of the eleven days which follow the seven are called the days of her flux, whether she has an issue of blood during that time or not. And why are they called the days of her flux? Because she may have a flux during that time, and all blood which appears during those days is to be considered blood of flux. Care should be taken to differentiate between these two terms, "days of menstruation" and "days of flux."

6. During a woman's whole lifetime, from the day that her period is fixed until her death, or until the onset of her period is changed to another day, she must always count seven days from

the beginning of the day of her period, and following them eleven days, and then again seven days, and following them eleven days. She should be exceedingly careful in the matter of counting, in order that she should know, when she has a flow, whether the flow took place during the days of menstruation or during the days of flux, since throughout her life it is thus, seven days of menstruation and eleven days of flux, unless childbirth interrupts this sequence, as will be explained.

7. If a woman has a flow during the days of her flux for only one day or for two successive days, she is called a woman with flux of lesser degree, or "she who awaits day against day." If she has a flow for three successive days, she is to be considered a woman with full flux, and is referred to as a woman with flux of greater degree, or simply a woman with flux, as it is said, *and if a woman have an issue of her blood many days, not in the time of her impurity* (Lev. 15:25); *days* signifies at least two days; *many days,* at least three.

8. A woman with flux of greater degree differs from a woman with flux of lesser degree only in the matter of counting the seven days and the liability to bring an offering. For a woman with flux of greater degree must count seven days of cleanness, whereas a woman with flux of lesser degree need count only one day. In addition, a woman with flux of greater degree must bring an offering after she has been rendered clean, whereas a woman with flux of lesser degree need not do so. However, in respect to their uncleanness and the prohibition of intercourse with them, both are alike.

9. How so? If she has a flow during the days of her flux, whether the flow occurred at the beginning of the night or at the end of the day, that entire day is one of uncleanness; it is as though the flow had not ceased from the moment she noticed it until sunset, and she must wait all of that night. If she has no flow during the night, she must upon arising in the morning immerse herself after sunrise, and wait all day. If she has no flow

in the course of the day, it constitutes one day of cleanness as against the one day of uncleanness, and she is permitted to her husband in the evening.

10. If she has a flow on the second day also, whether by day or by night, after her immersion, the second day is likewise one of uncleanness and she must wait the entire third night. If she has no flow during that night, she must upon arising in the morning immerse herself after sunrise and wait all day. If she then has no flow whatsoever, that day is reckoned as one day of cleanness as against the two days of uncleanness, and she is permitted to her husband in the evening.

11. If she has a flow on the third day also, whether by day or by night, she is considered a woman with flux of greater degree, and must count seven days of cleanness free from blood, as it is said, *then she shall number to herself seven days, and after that she shall be clean* (Lev. 15:28). She must then immerse herself on the seventh day after sunrise, and is thereupon permitted to her husband in the evening. On the eighth day she is obligated to bring her offering of two turtledoves or two young pigeons.

12. If a woman with flux of lesser degree immerses herself on the night of the day of waiting, or if a woman with flux of greater degree has her immersion on the seventh night, it is as though she had not immersed herself at all, and she is comparable to a menstruant who had immersed herself during the seven days of her uncleanness.

13. If a man has intercourse with a woman having flux of greater degree on the seventh day of her counting after her immersion, or with a woman having flux of lesser degree on the day of waiting after her immersion, he is not liable to extinction, for inasmuch as she did immerse herself at a time proper for her immersion, she is clean. But on her part this is mischievous conduct, seeing that the question whether intercourse with her is culpable and whether her contact conveys uncleanness is left in suspense.

14. How are they left in suspense? If the day after her immersion passes without her having any flux, everything with which she had been in contact subsequent to her immersion is clean, and no liability whatsoever is incurred for the act of intercourse with her after her immersion. If, however, she does have a flow on that day, after her immersion, she is retroactively a woman with flux, and everything touched by her is retroactively rendered unclean. Both she and the man who had intercourse with her are then liable to an offering. Consequently she is forbidden to her husband until the evening, in order that she should not bring herself into a situation that is subject to doubt.

15. If a woman with flux counts six days of cleanness and then has a flow on the seventh day, even if it is near sunset of that day, the previous counting is canceled, and she must count anew seven days of cleanness from the morrow of the day of uncleanness.

16. If she discharges semen during the days of counting, she renders one day of no account, because she is considered comparable to a man with flux who had a nocturnal pollution, in which case he, too, renders one day of no account. If she has a flow on the tenth day of the days of her flux, and also on the eleventh and twelfth days, even though she had a flow on three successive days, she is not considered a woman with flux of greater degree; rather, she emerges from the state of a woman with flux of lesser degree into the state of a menstruant. The reason being that the twelfth day marks the beginning of her menstrual period, and a woman who becomes a menstruant during her period of menstruation is not considered a woman with flux, as we have explained.

17. What then is the meaning of that which is written in the Torah, *or if she have an issue upon the time of her impurity* (Lev. 15:25)? If she has a flow for three days adjacent to her menstrual period, she is deemed a woman with flux; for example, if she has a flow on the eighth day after her period, and also on the ninth and tenth days, these being the first, second, and third

days of the eleven days of her flux. If she has a flow on the eleventh day of her flux, and immerses herself in the evening, that is on the night of the twelfth day, and then has intercourse —even though both she and the man are deemed unclean and render unclean that upon which they sit or lie, they are nevertheless not liable to extinction, because the twelfth day cannot be combined with the eleventh to make her a woman with flux, and therefore her immersion that night has benefited her to the extent that it absolved her from liability to an offering.

18. If she immersed herself on the twelfth day after sunrise, she is forbidden to her husband until the evening, as is the case with every woman having flux of lesser degree. If, however, he transgresses and has intercourse with her, both are wholly exempt. Even if she has a flow of blood after the intercourse on the twelfth day, it is inconsequential, because this blood is menstrual, and this day cannot be combined with the previous day.

19. If she has a flow at the conclusion of the seven day period of her menstruation, at twilight, and then again on the ninth and tenth days, she is a woman with flux out of doubt, because it is possible that the first appearance of blood took place on the night of the eighth day, with the result that she had a flow on three successive days from the beginning of the days of her flux. Similarly, if she had a flow on the ninth and tenth days of her flux, and again at the conclusion of the eleventh day, at twilight, she is a woman with flux out of doubt, because it is possible that the last appearance of blood took place on the eleventh day, with the result that she had a flow on three successive days of her flux.

20. If a menstruant examines herself during the days of her menstruation and finds that the flow of blood has ceased—even if it has ceased on the second day—and if by either error or design she does not examine herself again for many days after her period, but then, upon examining herself again, finds that she is unclean, it cannot be said that during all those days she might have been unclean and that she is therefore a woman with flux; rather, she

is presumed to have been clean during all those days when she did not examine herself. If, however, she examines herself during her menstrual period and finds that she is unclean—even if she makes an examination on the seventh day, but does not examine herself at twilight of that day in order to separate herself from menstrual uncleanness, and waits instead some days, and then examines herself and finds that she is clean, she is a woman with flux out of doubt. If, on the other hand, she finds that she is unclean, she is definitely a woman with flux, since having found that she was unclean at the beginning as well as at the end of her period, the presumption is that the flow had not ceased. Even if she had found that she was clean on the first day of her menstrual period, she is nevertheless regarded as one who had found herself unclean, because the fountain is presumed to have been open during the whole of the first day.

21. If a woman with flux examines herself on the first of the days of her counting and finds that she is clean, and then does not reexamine herself until the seventh day, and again finds that she is clean, she is presumed to be clean, and is regarded as though she had examined herself throughout the seven days and found herself to be clean.

22. Similarly, if she examines herself on the first and eighth days of her counting, and finds that she is clean, she is presumed to be clean. If she examines herself on the third day of her flux and finds that the flow has ceased, but does not examine herself on the first day of her counting, and then examines herself again on the seventh day and finds that she is clean, she is likewise presumed to be clean. The same law applies to a man with flux in regard to all these examinations, namely that he is deemed clean, and the days of counting are credited in his favor.

23. Any woman whose status as a menstruant or as a woman with flux is in doubt must observe seven days of cleanness because of the doubt, and must then immerse herself on the night of the eighth day, after which she is permitted to her husband. She

must then bring the offering of a woman with flux, which must not be eaten, as will be explained in its proper place.

CHAPTER VII

1. If a pregnant woman begins to experience distress and is seized with birth pangs, blood commencing to flow before parturition, that blood is called the blood of travail. What is the law concerning it? If it comes during the days of her menstruation, it is blood of menstruation and she is deemed unclean as a menstruant; if it comes during the days of her flux she is deemed clean, as it is said with regard to a woman with flux, *and her issue in her flesh be blood* (Lev. 15:19). The Sages had it by tradition that *her issue* signifies blood flowing on her own account, and not on account of the child. This holds only if she bears a living child, but not if it is stillborn, because in the case of a stillborn child there is no blood of travail. Even if the flow of blood accompanies the travail and the pangs for a fortnight before birth, it is still considered blood of travail and is deemed clean, but if the blood begins to flow fifteen or more days before birth, it is regarded as the blood of flux, and she is deemed to have given birth while in a state of flux.

2. This applies only when the travail and the pangs have not ceased, the woman continuing to labor up to the moment of birth. If, however, she has a flow for three or more days during the period of her flux, in conjunction with pangs and travail, and then the pains cease and she is relieved from travail after these three days, and remains free from pain for twenty-four hours or more—even if the flow of blood does not cease, and even if the pangs and travail return after twenty-four hours—she is deemed to be with flux. For had the blood been due to the child, the pangs and travail would not have ceased. If she is subsequently delivered, she is regarded as having given birth while in a state of flux.

3. If she has a flow for one day without pain, then for two days

with travail, and then gives birth; or for two days without pain, and one day with travail, and then gives birth; or one day with travail, one day without pain, and one day with travail, and then gives birth, she is not regarded as having given birth while in a state of flux. If, however, she has a flow one day with travail, and two days without pain, and then gives birth; or two days with travail, and one day without pain, and then gives birth; or one day without pain, one day with travail, and one day without pain, and then gives birth, she is regarded as having given birth while in a state of flux. The general rule is that if hard travail immediately precedes delivery, it is not considered delivery in a state of flux; if delivery is preceded by a period of ease, the woman is regarded as having given birth while in a state of flux.

4. Should the day of delivery fall on the third day of the appearance of blood, even if during the whole of that day she is at ease, she is not regarded as having given birth while in a state of flux, since the day of delivery immediately followed travail. If she has a flow for two days and miscarries on the third, and the nature of the issue of the miscarriage is not known, it remains doubtful whether she is a woman with flux or a woman in childbirth.

5. What is the law concerning a woman who gives birth in a state of flux? She must continue seven days of cleanness, and thereupon have an immersion in the evening, after which she is permitted to her husband. She must then continue in the blood of purification, and thereupon bring the offering of a woman with flux and the offering of a woman after childbirth. Consequently, if she gives birth to a male child, even if the blood has ceased on the day of birth, she must count seven days of cleanness and thereafter immerse herself. If she gives birth to a female child, and her count of seven days of cleanness ends with the fourteenth day after birth, or later, she may immerse herself and is then permitted to her husband. If, however, the days of counting end within the fourteen days, she is forbidden to her husband until the night of the fifteenth day.

6. How so? If she has a flow for three days and then counts

seven days of cleanness, making a total of ten days, she is nevertheless still forbidden to her husband until the night of the fifteenth day, because she is considered a menstruant throughout the fourteen-day period after the birth of a female child. Why is it not required that the woman who is delivered while in a state of flux should count seven days after the seven days from the birth of a male child and fourteen days from the birth of a female child? Because the days after childbirth and the days of her menstruation during which she has no flow are credited in her favor in regard to the counting of the seven days, as will be explained.

7. If a woman gives birth while in a state of flux, and her blood continues to flow, she can have no blood of purification, and any flow of blood she may have is considered blood of flux. If, however, she counts seven days of cleanness, completes the fourteen days after the birth of a female child, and immerses herself, and then has a flow during the forty days of purification following the birth of a male child or the eighty days following the birth of a female child, it is deemed to be blood of purification.

8. If she counts seven days of cleanness, but does not immerse herself, and then has a flow of blood, she may immerse herself and is immediately permitted to her husband, since all the days of purification cannot properly be regarded as either days of menstruation or days of flux. The blood in itself, however, is unclean and renders unclean, and comes under the same law as the blood of a menstruant until she immerses herself.

9. If a woman, having given birth to a female child, becomes pregnant following her fourteen-day period, and the blood of travail begins to flow within the eighty days, it is deemed blood of purification even though there is no blood of travail in the case of a miscarriage, any flow of blood which she may have during the period of her purification being deemed clean until the moment of miscarriage. When the miscarriage does take place, she becomes subject to the uncleanness following childbirth, for a length of time prescribed for either a male or a female child. She

must then reckon the days of uncleanness and the days of fulfillment from the birth of the second child. Even if they are twins and she miscarries one of them on one day and the other many days later, she still must reckon the days of uncleanness and the days of fulfillment from the birth of the second child.

10. If the issue of a woman with flux ceases, but as she begins to count the seven days of cleanness, the blood of travail supervenes within these days, it does not cause them to be excluded from the count; rather, the days of travail are credited to the period of seven days. Similarly, if she gives birth during the seven days of cleanness, the birth has no effect upon the count; rather, the days of the birth are credited to the count of seven days, even though she is unclean during them, as it is said, *but if she be cleansed of her issue* (Lev. 15:28); inasmuch as she has been cleansed of her issue, even if she has contracted another kind of uncleanness, such as the uncleanness of childbirth, menstruation, or leprosy, she may nevertheless continue her count during these days. These and similar kinds of uncleanness do not cause any exclusion from the count.

11. If she has no flow during the days following childbirth or during the days of her menstruation, these days are included in the count of seven days of cleanness. If she has a flow during these periods, the days upon which the flow takes place are not included in the count, but they do not cause the exclusion of the other days from the count. She must then, after the cessation of the blood, complete the number of days counted, because only the appearance of flux renders the entire count void, whereas these accidents affect only the days on which they take place.

12. Once you understand all these principles that we have just explained, you will perceive the meaning of what the Sages have said, to the effect that it is possible for a woman to have a flow from the fountain for one hundred and fourteen consecutive days without becoming a woman with flux. How so? Two days before her menstruation, seven days of her menstrual period, two days

after her menstruation, fourteen days of the blood of travail, eighty days following the birth of a female child, seven days of another period of menstruation, and two days after that menstrual period. From this you learn that any flow a woman is apt to have after the days of fulfillment marks the beginning of her menstrual period, and her previous fixed periods are to be disregarded. Consequently, if she has a flow at the conclusion of her days of fulfillment, at twilight of the last day, she is a menstruant out of doubt; perchance it was night when she had her flow, in which case it would mark the beginning of her menstrual period.

13. We have already explained that if a menstruant has a flow throughout the seven days she is permitted to have intercourse after her immersion on the eighth night; that a woman with flux of lesser degree must await one day of cleanness, immerse herself, and is then allowed to have intercourse in the evening; that a woman with flux of greater degree must count seven days of cleanness, immerse herself, and is then permitted to have intercourse on the eighth night; that only eleven days intervene between one period of menstruation and the next, and that during those eleven days she may become a woman with flux of either lesser or greater degree.

14. Once you keep in mind all these principles, you will perceive the meaning of what the Sages have said, namely that a woman who is presumed to have a flow all her life on alternate days may have intercourse first on the eighth night and on the following day, which is the first day after her menstrual period, so that in eighteen days she may have intercourse on four nights only. She may not have intercourse on her days of cleanness, because each day of cleanness must be awaited against each day of uncleanness. Consequently, if she has a flow on each day of uncleanness at the beginning of the night, she may have intercourse on the eighth day only, which is the first day after her menstrual period.

15. If it is her custom to have a flow for two days, then have

none for the next two days, she may have intercourse on the eighth, the twelfth, the sixteenth, and the twentieth days.

16. If it is her custom to have a flow for three days, then have none for the next three days, she may have intercourse on two of the three days of cleanness which follow her menstrual period, because one of the three must be awaited against the two days of uncleanness adjacent to her menstrual period. After this she may never have intercourse again, because she is presumed to be a woman with flux of greater degree, but can never have seven days of cleanness.

17. If her customary schedule is four days of uncleanness followed by four days of cleanness, she may have intercourse on the day after her menstrual period, but after that she may never have intercourse again.

18. If her customary schedule is five days of uncleanness followed by five days of cleanness, she may have intercourse on three days following her menstrual period, but after that she may never have intercourse again.

19. If her customary schedule is six days of uncleanness followed by six days of cleanness, she may have intercourse only on five days after her menstrual period, but after that she may never have intercourse again.

20. If her customary schedule is seven days of uncleanness followed by seven days of cleanness, she may have intercourse during the first week of cleanness adjacent to her menstrual period. A week of uncleanness ensues, which establishes her status as a woman with flux, and the subsequent week of cleanness serves for the count, and she is therefore forbidden to have intercourse during this week. The result is that she may have intercourse for only one week out of four, so that in the course of her life she may have intercourse only on eighteen days every eighteen weeks. How so? During the fifth week she is deemed a woman with flux, and thus the sixth week, during which she is clean, serves for

the count. On the seventh week she is again a woman with flux, and the eighth week serves for the count. Of the ninth week during which she has a flow, five days are days of menstruation and two days mark the beginning of her flux. She must therefore await one day of the tenth week of cleanness, and then may have intercourse during the ensuing six days. Of the eleventh week during which she has a flow, two days mark the conclusion of her days of flux, and five days mark the beginning of her menstruation, and she may have intercourse during five days of the twelfth week of cleanness. On the thirteenth week she is a woman with flux, and the fourteenth week serves for counting. Similarly, on the fifteenth week she is a woman with flux, and the sixteenth week serves for counting; on the seventeenth week she is a woman with flux, and the eighteenth week serves for counting. In this manner she must count forever. Thus the result is that in each period of eighteen weeks she may have intercourse on eighteen days. Had this abnormality not befallen her, and had she been a normal menstruant for seven days and then clean for eleven days, she would have been permitted to have intercourse during eleven weeks out of every eighteen, which adds up to seventy-seven days.

21. When, however, she has one week of uncleanness, followed by one week of cleanness, she may have intercourse on eighteen days, which is approximately one quarter of the normal number of seventy-seven days. That is what the Sages meant when they said, "She may have intercourse for a quarter of her days."

22. If her schedule is eight days of uncleanness followed by eight days of cleanness, she may have intercourse for fifteen days out of forty eight. How so? Of the eight days of uncleanness at the beginning, seven are the days of her menstruation, and the eighth is the day of flux adjacent to her menstrual period. She must then await one day out of the ensuing eight days of cleanness, and may thereupon have intercourse on the following seven. After this follow eight days of uncleanness, of which two mark the completion of her days of flux and six are the days of her

menstrual period. Of the eight days of cleanness which follow, one completes the seven days of her menstruation, and she may then have intercourse for a second period of seven days. Thereupon eight days of uncleanness come around, of which four mark the completion of the days of her flux, and four are days of her menstrual period. Thus it comes about that she is a woman with flux of greater degree and must count seven days of cleanness. Of the next eight days of cleanness which follow seven serve for counting, and she may have intercourse on the eighth. The result is that she may have intercourse on fifteen days out of every forty-eight.

23. If her schedule is nine days of uncleanness followed by nine days of cleanness, she may have intercourse on eight days out of these eighteen forever. How so? Of the nine days of uncleanness, seven are days of her menstrual period and two are days of flux adjacent to her period of menstruation. She must therefore wait one day of the nine days of cleanness, and may then have intercourse on the subsequent eight, and so on forever after.

24. If her schedule is ten days of uncleanness followed by ten days of cleanness, or a longer period, up to a thousand days of uncleanness followed by a thousand days of cleanness, the days when she may have intercourse are the same in number as the days of her flux. How so? Of the ten days of uncleanness, seven are the days of her menstrual period and three are days of flux. Of the ten days of cleanness, she must count seven, and may then have intercourse on the remaining three. Thus there are three days of flux and three days of intercourse. The same applies if there are a hundred days of uncleanness followed by a hundred days of cleanness; of the hundred days of uncleanness, seven are the days of menstruation and ninety-three are days of flux. Of the hundred days of cleanness she must count seven, so that ninety-three are left free for intercourse. So with a thousand days, and so with any number of days, in this wise.

CHAPTER VIII

1. There are women who have a fixed period and women who have no fixed period; in the latter case a woman does not perceive it in herself until the blood comes forth, so that she has no fixed day for its appearance. The woman who has a fixed period has a set day, be it every twentieth day, or every twenty-fourth day, or more, or less.

2. A woman who has a regular period perceives it in herself prior to the appearance of blood. She may yawn and sneeze, and feel pain in the pit of the stomach and in the lower part of the abdomen; the hair upon her flesh may stand up, or her flesh may become heated, or she may show other symptoms of similar nature. These premonitory signs, or only one of them, come upon her at the time set for her on the day of her fixed period.

3. We have already explained that a woman who has no fixed period is forbidden to have intercourse until after she has examined herself, while a woman who has one is forbidden to have intercourse all through the time of the fixed period. If it occurs in daytime, she is forbidden to have intercourse during that entire day, and if it occurs at night, she is forbidden to have intercourse during that entire night. She must always count the days of her menstruation and the days of her flux from the beginning of her fixed period.

4. Consequently, a woman must take care to determine the day and the hour at which her period is fixed. If her habit is to have a flow on the twentieth day, and that day comes with no appearance of blood, but blood does appear on the twenty-third day, both the twentieth and the twenty-third are prohibited days with regard to intercourse. Similarly, if she has a flow on the next occasion on the twenty-third day and not on the twentieth, these two days are still forbidden. If, however, the blood flows for the

third time on the twenty-third day, and not on the twentieth, the twentieth day becomes a day of cleanness and her fixed period is transposed to the twenty-third day, for no woman may consider her period fixed unless it has befallen her regularly three times, nor may she account herself clean from a previous fixed period until it has thrice failed to befall her on the appointed day.

5. Any regular period which is fixed through an accidental cause, even if the flow recurs several times at regular intervals, is not considered a fixed period, because the flow of blood is due to the mishap. If a woman jumps and has a flow as a result of it, and then jumps again and has a flow, her period must nevertheless be fixed only according to the days on which she has a flow without jumping. How so? If she jumps on the first day of the week and has a flow, and after twenty days jumps again on the first day of the week and has a flow, and then after nineteen days she jumps on the Sabbath and does not have a flow, but on the next day has a flow without jumping, her period is accordingly fixed for the first day of the week after the twentieth, since it is now known that the regularity of the day, and not the jumping, is the cause of her flow, this day having already been fixed three times. And so on in all similar cases.

6. If she has a flow on the fifteenth day of one month, the sixteenth day of the following month, the seventeenth day of the next month, and the eighteenth day of the month following, her fixed period is set down as an irregular one. If the fourth month arrives and she has a flow on the seventeenth thereof, her fixed period is still not yet regular, and whatever day it is on which she has a flow she must be on the alert for the return of the same day. If when that day comes around she has no flow, that day is forthwith regarded as clean and not as the day of her fixed period, once being enough, since a threefold failure of the flow is required only if the flow has thrice previously occurred on that particular day.

7. If her habit is to have a flow on the fifteenth, and it changes to the sixteenth, both days are prohibited. If it changes to the

seventeenth, the sixteenth becomes permitted and the seventeenth forbidden, while the fifteenth remains prohibited. If it changes to the eighteenth, the eighteenth becomes prohibited, and all the other days become permitted.

8. If it is her habit to have a flow on the twentieth day, and it changes to the twenty-second, both days are prohibited. If on the twentieth of the next month she has no flow, but has it on the twenty-second, both days are still forbidden. If she has a flow on the twentieth day of the following month, the twenty-second day becomes clean, since she has now returned to her original period, so that the twenty-second day drops out, because her period was not fixed on it three times.

9. A woman may not establish her fixed period within the days of her menstruation on which she has a flow, because once she has a flow on a certain day, she may not establish her regular period throughout the ensuing seven days. Similarly, a woman may not establish her fixed period within the days of her flux, which are eleven days. She may, however, establish her fixed period on those days of her menstruation on which she has no flow. If her regular period is established during the days of her flux, she must be on the alert for the return of the same date, and any fixed period which she may establish during the days of her flux drops out if the flow fails to befall her even once. It need not necessarily fail three times, for the presumption of suspended menstruation obtains during those days.

10. How is she to be on the alert for the return of this date? If she has a flow during it, even for only one day, she must continue in her menstruation out of doubt, and is forbidden to have intercourse on that day, even if she has no flow during the remaining days of her period. Should she have a flow for three days, she is deemed a woman with flux.

11. A woman who is always diligent in examining herself, even if she has a regular period, is praiseworthy, because it is possible for blood to appear at a time other than her fixed period. Through-

out the eleven days of her flux, however, she is presumed to be clean and needs no examination; but after the days of her flux have passed, she is obligated to examine herself.

12. If she forgets and does not examine herself, whether by accident or by design, she is presumed to be clean, until she examines herself and finds that she is unclean.

13. If a woman does not examine herself on the date of her fixed period, but does so after the lapse of some time and finds herself unclean, even though she is considered unclean retroactively to the date of her fixed period—as will be explained in connection with the Laws Concerning Uncleanness and Cleanness—she does not also render retroactively unclean the man with whom she had intercourse, and need count only from the time of the onset of her flow. If, on the other hand, she finds herself clean, she is presumed to have been clean.

14. Similarly, if a woman has a flow due to a wound in her fountain, even if it happens at the time of her fixed period, she is deemed clean and the blood is considered clean, because the laws of uncleanness of fixed periods rest on the authority of the Scribes, as will be explained in the Laws Concerning Such as Render Couch and Seat Unclean.

15. A blind woman must examine herself and show the test rag to a woman neighbor. Deaf-mute and imbecile women require normal women to examine them and to establish their fixed periods for them, after which they are permitted to their husbands.

16. If a woman who, because of some error, does not know the date of her regular period has a flow, she must be on the alert as to whether she is a woman with flux. Therefore, if she has a flow for one or two days, she must continue for the remainder of the seven days; perchance this blood indicates her menstrual period. If she has a flow for three days, she must count seven days of cleanness; perchance she is in the midst of the days of her flux.

17. How should she proceed to regulate her fixed period, in

order to determine whether she is definitely or doubtfully a woman with flux, so as to ascertain the days of her flux? It all depends upon the days on which she has a flow. How so? If she has a flow for one or two days, she must complete the count of the seven days, and then begin to count the eleven days from the expiry of these seven.

18. If she has a flow for three successive days, she is a woman with flux out of doubt, since the first day may have preceded her menstruation, and the other two may constitute the beginning of it. Similarly, if she has a flow for four successive days she is a woman with flux out of doubt, since the first two of these days may have preceded her menstruation, and the other two may mark its onset. She must therefore continue for five days to complete her menstrual period, and then count eleven days of flux following these five days.

19. Similarly, if she has a flow for nine successive days, she is a woman with flux out of doubt, since the first two of them may have preceded her menstruation, and the other seven of them may be the days of menstruation, so that she must begin to count eleven days after the lapse of these nine, when the flow has ceased. Likewise, if she has a flow for eleven successive days, she is a woman with flux out of doubt, since the first two may have preceded her menstruation, the next seven may be the days of her menstruation, and the last two may have followed her menstruation, and thus nine days of her flux still remain for her to count.

20. If she has a flow for twelve successive days she is definitely a woman with flux, for even if the first two have preceded her menstruation, and the next seven constitute the days of her menstruation, there are still three days remaining after her menstruation, leaving eight more days of her flux. Similarly, if she has a flow for thirteen days, seven days remain of her flux, these being the days of counting.

21. If she continues to have a flow of blood, be it even for a thousand days, once the blood stops she must count seven days of

cleanness. After these seven days, any flow is considered as marking the days of menstruation, in the case of a woman who has erred as to her fixed period.

22. You thus learn that a woman who is in error must count, from the time the flow of blood ceases, not less than seven, nor more than eighteen days, after which any flow of blood is considered as marking the days of her menstruation. How so? If she has a flow for one day and then the blood stops, she must count seventeen days: six days to complete her menstrual period and eleven days of her flux, after which the days of her menstruation begin anew. If she has a flow for thirteen days or more, she must count seven days from the time the flow of blood stops, after which the days of her menstruation begin anew, as we have explained.

CHAPTER IX

1. According to the Torah, a woman is not rendered unclean as a result of menstruation or flux until such time as she experiences a sensation and has a flow of blood issuing in her flesh, as we have explained. She is then unclean only from the time that she has the flow and forward. If she experiences no sensation, and then examines herself and finds the blood within, i.e. in the antechamber, the presumption is that it was accompanied by a sensation, as we have explained.

2. On the authority of the Scribes, however, a woman who sees a bloodstain on her flesh or on her garments, even if she feels no sensation and even if she examines herself and finds no blood, is deemed unclean, as though she had found blood within, i.e. in her flesh. This uncleanness is subject to doubt: perchance this stain had come from the blood of the chamber.

3. Similarly, on the authority of the Scribes, a woman who has

a flow at a time other than her fixed period, or who sees a bloodstain, is unclean retroactively for twenty-four hours. If she had examined herself within this twenty-four hour period and found that she was clean, she is deemed unclean retroactively only up to the time of the examination. But even though she is by rabbinical enactment unclean retroactively, she does not render unclean retroactively the man with whom she had intercourse, as we have explained. She must begin the count of the days of her menstruation or bloodstain only from the time that she had a flow or found the stain. Moreover, a bloodstain observed by a woman upsets her normal count: perchance the bloodstain had come from the chamber, thus disarranging her fixed period.

4. A woman who has a flow during her fixed period does not render anything unclean retroactively, but only at her particular time. The same applies to a pregnant woman, a woman giving suck, a virgin, or an old woman; it is enough for them that they render unclean only from their own particular time; they do not do so retroactively. When is a woman considered pregnant? From the time that the foetus becomes discernible, that is, at three months. A woman who gives suck is so regarded for a full twenty-four months, even if during that period her child dies, or she weans it, or gives it to a nurse.

5. A virgin is one who has never had a menstrual flow, even if she has had a discharge of blood due to marital intercourse or childbirth. An old woman is one who has had no flow for ninety days at a time adjacent to her old age. When does her old age set in? When she no longer resents being called an old woman. In the case of a woman who is pregnant, suckling, or old, the same law applies to either a bloodstain or an actual flow of blood, and they do not render unclean retroactively. In the case of a virgin who has never had a flow and is still a minor, a bloodstain is considered clean until such time as she has a flow for three fixed periods.

6. What is the difference between a stain found on a woman's flesh and one found on her garment? A stain found on her flesh

has no minimum size, while one found on her garment does not render unclean unless it is the size of a Cilician bean, that is, the stain's square area must equal the area of nine lentils placed three by three. If it is smaller than this it is considered clean. If there are several drops, they cannot be combined; but elongated stains may be combined.

7. If the stain is found on an article which is not susceptible to uncleanness, it is considered clean and she need have no scruples concerning it. How so? If she sits on a vessel made of hewn stone, earth, or mixed manure and earth, or upon fishskins, or on top of an earthenware vessel, or on a piece of cloth less than three fingerlengths square, and blood is subsequently found upon them, she is deemed to be clean. Even if she examines the ground before sitting down, and subsequently, upon arising, finds a stain on it, she is still deemed to be clean. The reason is that the Sages have made no enactment concerning a stain found on an article not susceptible to uncleanness, nor concerning an article which is susceptible to uncleanness, unless the latter is white. Thus a woman need have no scruples in regard to stains found on colored articles. Consequently, the Sages have recommended that women should wear colored garments in order to free them from the regulations pertaining to bloodstains.

8. A woman does not become unclean because of a bloodstain unless the blood is found on her flesh opposite her private parts, and not on any other part of her body. How so? If the bloodstain is found on her heel she becomes unclean, since the heel may have touched her secret parts while she was sitting. Similarly, if the stain is found on the inner side of her legs or feet—that is, those parts which touch one another when she stands foot to foot and leg to leg—she is deemed unclean. If it is found on the tip of her great toe, she is unclean, since it may have dripped from the chamber onto her foot while she was walking. The same applies to any place upon which menstrual blood may have spurted while she walked; if blood is found there, she becomes unclean. Similarly, if blood is found on her hands, even on the joints of

her fingers, she is unclean, since hands touch things automatically. If, however, the blood is found on the outer part of her legs or feet, or on their sides, and needless to say, if it is found from the thighs upwards, she is deemed clean, since it can only be blood which had spurted on her from some other source.

9. Whether the bloodstain found on her flesh is elongated like a thong, or is circular, or consists of separate drops, or extends lengthwise across the breadth of the thigh, or looks as though it ran from below upwards, once it is opposite her private parts she is deemed unclean. It cannot be said that the stain would not have had this shape if it had dripped from the body, since in regard to all blood found in these places the more stringent view must prevail, even in the presence of doubt.

10. If a stain is found on her shift, from the girdle downwards, she is deemed unclean; if from the girdle upwards, she is deemed clean. In case the stain is on her sleeve, if the place where it is found reaches opposite the private parts, she is deemed unclean, otherwise she is deemed clean.

11. If it is her custom to take off her shift and cover herself with it at night, she is deemed unclean wherever the bloodstain may be located on it; the same applies to blood found on her girdle.

12. If she had been wearing a shift which remained on her person for three days or more, outside of the time of her fixed period, and if upon examination she finds on it three stains, or one large stain equal to three stains of minimum size, she is deemed a woman with flux out of doubt, since a drop of blood may have dripped from her private parts each day. Similarly, if she had been wearing three garments previously examined, which remained on her person for three days during the days of her flux, and she finds a stain on each one, she is deemed a woman with flux out of doubt, even if the stains are located opposite one another.

13. If she finds one stain smaller than three stains of minimum

size, the rule is as follows: If she examines herself throughout the twilight of the first day and finds that she is clean, but fails to examine her shift, and on the third day finds this stain which is smaller than three stains of minimum size, she need have no anxiety in regard to flux. If, on the other hand, she has not examined herself throughout the twilight, inasmuch as she did not examine her shift and it remained on her person for three days during the days of her flux, she should have anxiety in regard to flux, even if the stain is smaller than three stains of minimum size.

14. If she finds a stain on her shift one day and then has a flow for two successive days, or if she has a flow for two days and then sees a stain on the third day, she is deemed a woman with flux out of doubt.

15. If a woman sees a stain and then has a flow, the stain is considered for a period of twenty-four hours to be due to the flow, whether she had examined herself at the time she discovered the stain and found that she was clean, or whether she did not so examine herself. If, however, she sees one stain after another within twenty-four hours, the one stain cannot be connected with the other unless she had examined herself during the interval, for if a period of cleanness had intervened between the appearance of the stains, they cannot be combined towards the requisite number of stains to render her a woman with flux.

16. How so? In case she sees a stain in the first hour on Friday, even if she had not examined herself and does not know whether she is clean or unclean, and thereupon has a flow before the first hour of the Sabbath, she need not count from the time of seeing the stain, but should assign the stain to the flow. If she then has a flow again on the first and second days of the week, she becomes a woman with flux. If she has a flow in the second hour on the Sabbath, she is deemed unclean for two days, namely Friday, on which she found the stain, and the Sabbath, on which she had the flow, since both of these did not take place within twenty-four

hours. If, therefore, she then has a flow again on the first day of the week, there should be anxiety in regard to flux.

17. In case she has no flow on the Sabbath, but sees a second stain in the first hour of the Sabbath, the rule is as follows: If she had examined herself on Friday and found that she was clean, she need begin the count only from the time of the appearance of the second stain on the Sabbath, since both stains occurred within twenty-four hours. If she had not examined herself and does not know whether a period of cleanness intervened between them, she must count from Friday, and if she then has a flow on the first day of the week she should have anxiety in regard to flux.

18. If she sees the second stain in the second hour of the Sabbath, she is deemed unclean for two days, whether she had examined herself previously or not, since the stains did not appear within twenty-four hours of one another. If she then has a flow on the first day of the week after the lapse of twenty-four hours, she should have anxiety in regard to flux. In case she sees a third stain in the first hour of the first day of the week, the rule is as follows: If a period of cleanness has intervened, they cannot be combined, and she need have no anxiety in regard to flux; but if she had not examined herself, she should have anxiety.

19. In the case of any stain which, according to what we have said above, renders her unclean, if she can possibly ascribe it to some other cause and say, "This stain may have come from such-and-such a thing," the rule is as follows: If the stain is on her garment, she is deemed clean, since the intent of the Sages was to be lenient, rather than restrictive, in this matter. If the stain is found on her flesh, and the matter is in doubt, it remains unclean, and cannot be ascribed to that cause. If, however, she merely has more reason to trace it to her flesh than to her shift, even though she may trace the stain to her flesh, so long as it is in doubt, it remains clean.

20. How so? If, after she had slaughtered a domestic animal, a wild beast, or a fowl, or had busied herself with anything that

may cause bloodstaining, or had sat down by the side of those so engaged, or had walked through the butchers' market, blood is found on her garment, she is deemed clean, since she may trace the origin of the stains to these things.

21. In case the stain is found on her flesh only, if it is located from her girdle downwards, she is unclean. If she had tumbled or jumped, she is likewise unclean, even if the blood is located from her girdle upwards, for had this blood come from the slaughtering or from the market, it should have been found also on her garment; but since it was found only on her flesh and not on her garment, she is deemed unclean.

22. Should she have a wound, even one that has healed, if it is possible for her to scratch it open and draw blood, and if blood is found on her flesh, she may ascribe it to the wound, and so in all similar cases.

23. If the stain is found on both her flesh and her garments, she may ascribe it to any cause that she may have. For instance, she may ascribe it to a louse which may have been killed as she sat down, so that this blood had come from the louse. What is the maximum size of such a stain? That of a bean; if the stain is found to be larger than a bean, she may not ascribe it to the louse, even if a crushed louse is found upon the stain. So long as the stain is larger than a bean it cannot be attributed to the louse.

24. Similarly, she may attribute the stain to her son or her husband, if they had been handling anything connected with blood, or if their hands were bloodstained. Or if one of them had a wound, she may trace the stain to them and claim that they had come in contact with her without her being aware of it, and that this blood was due to them.

25. No presumption is permissible whereby blood found in one place is traced to another place. How so? If a woman has a wound on her shoulder, and blood is found on her leg, it cannot be said that her hand may have touched first the wound and then the leg.

The same applies to all similar cases, whether the blood is found on her body or on her garment.

26. If two women are busied with a bird which holds no more than a *sela'* of blood, and subsequently a stain the size of a sela' is found on each one of them, both are deemed unclean. If a woman is handling a quantity of blood which cannot produce a stain larger than a bean, and then a stain the size of two beans is found on her, she may ascribe one half of the stain to the blood with which she was busied, and the other half to a louse. If the stain is found to be larger than two beans, the woman is deemed unclean.

27. If she is handling red blood, she may not attribute a stain of black blood to that circumstance. If she is occupied with a bird which has blood of various tints, and a bloodstain similar in color to one of these is found on her, she may trace it to the bird. If she was wearing three garments, so long as she can trace the blood to something else, she may do so even if the stain is on the innermost garment; if, on the other hand, she cannot trace the stain to another cause, she may not do so even if the stain is on the outermost garment. How so? Should she pass through the butchers' market, even if the stain is found only on the innermost garment, she may ascribe it to the market. If she had not passed through the butchers' market or some similar place, she is deemed unclean, even if the stain is found only on the outermost garment. If she is in doubt as to whether she had passed through the market or not, or had handled blood or not, she may not ascribe it to another cause.

28. In any city where swine are kept or into which they are customarily brought, a woman need have no anxiety concerning bloodstains found on her garment.

29. If a woman lends her shift to a menstruant, whether the latter is a heathen or an Israelite, and then wears it again without examination and finds a stain upon it, she may trace the stain to the menstruant who had worn the shift. If she lends it to a woman

with flux of lesser degree on the day of her uncleanness, or to a woman continuing in the blood of purification, or to a virgin whose blood is clean, she may likewise trace it to them. If on the other hand she lends the shift to a woman with flux of lesser degree on the day of her waiting, or to a woman with flux of greater degree during her seven days of cleanness, and then wears it again without examination and finds a bloodstain upon it, both the borrower and the lender are adversely affected, since it may be due to either of them. If she lends the shift to a woman observing the period of uncleanness for a stain, she may not trace the stain to her, because one stain cannot be traced to another.

30. If a woman examines both the shift and herself and finds both clean, and then lends the shift to her neighbor who wears it, and if a stain is found on it upon its return, the borrower is deemed unclean. The stain may not be attributed to the owner of the shift, since she had examined it before lending it.

31. If a tall woman dons the shift of a short woman, and a stain is found upon it, she is deemed unclean if the stain is situated opposite her private parts; if not, she is deemed clean, since the stain must have been caused by the short woman.

32. If three women wear the same shift one after another, and thereupon a stain is found upon it, or if all three together sleep in the same bed, and a stain is found under one of them, all three are deemed unclean. If, however, one of them immediately examines herself and finds that she is unclean, the other two are deemed clean.

33. If they all examine themselves and find that they are clean, the one who is not capable of having a flow may ascribe the stain to the one who is so capable, in which case the former is deemed clean, while the latter is deemed unclean. How so? If one of them is pregnant and the other is not, the pregnant woman is deemed clean and the other is deemed unclean. If one is giving suck and the other is not, the former is deemed clean. If one is past the menopause and the other is not, the former is deemed clean. If one

is a virgin and the other is not, the virgin is deemed clean. If all are pregnant, past the menopause, giving suck, or virgins, all are deemed unclean.

34. If three women climb into bed by way of the foot of the bed and sleep in it, and blood is then found under the middle one, all three are deemed unclean. If the bloodstain is found under the one on the inside, she and the woman next to her are deemed unclean, while the outer one remains clean. If blood is found under the latter, she and the woman next to her are deemed unclean, while the one on the inside remains clean. If they climb into bed in a manner other than by way of the foot of the bed, and therefore not in order, and blood is then found under one of them, all are deemed unclean.

35. This applies only when they all had examined themselves and found that they were clean, and none of them can attribute the bloodstain to her companion, as we have explained. But if one of them had examined herself and found that she was clean, while her companion had not examined herself, the former may attribute the stain to the latter, and the latter is deemed unclean.

36. Any stain found on a garment which a woman cannot ascribe to any cause involving blood does not render unclean until it is ascertained that it is a bloodstain. If there is doubt as to whether it is blood or red dye, seven substances are to be applied to it in the prescribed order. If the stain disappears or grows faint, it is a bloodstain and the woman is therefore unclean; if it remains as it was, it is a dye, and she is deemed clean.

37. These are the seven substances in their prescribed order: tasteless saliva, masticated grit of peas, fermented urine, alkali, niter, Cimolian earth, and potash. The stain must be rubbed thrice with each substance, applying it to and fro each time. If they are applied out of order or all of them at once, they are ineffective. If they are applied in reverse order, the ones applied last, which are the first in the prescribed order, are regarded as valid. Next, the substances which are last in the prescribed order and which

had been wrongly applied first, should be applied again in the prescribed order, until all seven have been applied in the correct order.

38. What is tasteless saliva? It is the saliva of a person who has tasted nothing since the beginning of the night and has slept from the latter half of the night until the morrow; his saliva, before he breaks his fast, is called tasteless. That is, provided he did not engage in much speaking aloud until three hours of the day had passed. If, however, he had arisen betimes and had reviewed his daily lesson before the passing of the third hour, his saliva is not considered tasteless, because speaking aloud weakens its strength and reduces it to water. What is masticated grit of peas? It is grit which has been masticated until the peas are well mixed with saliva. What is fermented urine? Urine three days old or more.

39. Any woman who is unclean on account of a bloodstain and who had found the stain during the days of her menstruation is considered a menstruant out of doubt and must observe seven days of cleanness and immerse herself on the eighth night; thereafter she is permitted to her husband. If she finds the stain during the days of her flux, she is a woman with flux of greater or lesser degree out of doubt, as has been explained in this chapter. She must continue unclean for one day if she is a woman with flux of lesser degree, or count seven days of cleanness if she is a woman with flux of greater degree, out of doubt. All this is on the authority of the Scribes, as we have explained. Consequently, if one has intercourse with her willfully, he must be flogged for disobedience, but both are exempt from an offering.

CHAPTER X

1. Every woman in confinement is considered as unclean as a menstruant, even if she has no flow. It does not matter whether

she gives birth to a living child, a stillborn child, or even a mere foetus. If it is a male, she must continue unclean for the number of days prescribed for a male, and if it is a female, for the number of days required for a female, provided its formation is complete. An embryo, whether male or female, is not fully formed in less than forty days.

2. If a woman has a miscarriage within forty days of conception, even on the fortieth day, the laws of uncleanness of childbirth do not apply to her. If she miscarries on the forty-first day subsequent to intercourse, she is a woman after childbirth out of doubt, and she must therefore continue unclean for the number of days prescribed for a male child, a female child, and a menstruant, concurrently. If the human shape of the foetus is so indistinct as to be visually unrecognizable, she must continue unclean for the number of days prescribed for both a male and a female. Such an embryo is called an articulated foetus.

3. What is meant by an articulated foetus? At the beginning of the formation of a human being, the body resembles a lentil; the two eyes are like two eyeballs of a fly, widely spaced; the two nostrils are like two eyeballs of a fly placed close to one another; and the mouth is open like a fine hair. The foetus has no clear-cut hands or feet. After its form has become more clearly defined than this, but before its sex can be determined, it should be examined not with water but with oil, since oil renders it clear. One should take a chip of wood with a smooth tip and pass it from the top downwards over the place of the genitals. If the chip gets caught, it is certain that the embryo is male. If the place of the genitals looks like a split barley corn, the embryo is female, and no further examination is required. In respect to all these stages of the articulation of the foetus, no days of purification are appointed until the foetus has grown hair.

4. In the case of a woman who has a miscarriage of a white-colored lump, the rule is that if, upon being torn open, a bone is found in it, she is deemed unclean through childbirth. If the

abortion is a foetus filled with water, blood, worm-shaped matter, or flesh, inasmuch as it has not yet become articulated, she need have no scruples as to whether she had given birth to a child.

5. If the newborn infant emerges from its mother's side, the mother is not deemed unclean through childbirth. Nor need she on its account observe days of uncleanness and days of purification, for it is said, *If a woman conceive seed and bear a male child* (Lev. 12:2), thus implying that she gave birth from the place where she had conceived the seed. If a woman gives birth to a child from her side after hard travail, the blood of travail which issues from the womb is considered blood of flux or of menstruation, while the blood that comes from the side is deemed unclean. If, however, no blood had come forth by way of the womb, the woman is deemed clean, even though the blood which has emerged from her side is unclean, since a woman is not deemed unclean unless the discharge has issued through her private parts.

6. If the foetus is severed in her womb and emerges limb by limb, whether it comes out in the order of the limbs—for instance, first the foot, then the leg, and then the thigh—or whether it comes out of order, she is not deemed unclean through childbirth until most of the body has emerged. If, however, the whole head comes out in one piece, it is regarded as equivalent to most of the body. If the foetus is not severed at first and comes out normally, it is regarded as having been born when the major portion of the forehead has emerged, even if the foetus is severed subsequently.

7. If the foetus puts forth its hand from the womb and then withdraws it, the mother is deemed unclean through childbirth, on the authority of the Scribes, but need not continue in the blood of purification until the whole foetus or at least the larger portion of it has emerged, as we have explained.

8. If the abortion is something resembling a domestic or wild animal, or a bird, but its face is human, it is considered a human

child. If it is male, the mother must continue unclean for the number of days prescribed for a male; and if it is female, she must continue unclean for the number of days prescribed for a female. If its sex is not recognizable, she must continue unclean for the number of days prescribed for both a male and a female, even though the rest of the body resembles an animal or a bird. Should the face not be human, even if the rest of the body is that of a complete human being, the hands and feet being like human hands and feet, and the sex being clearly male or female, it is not accounted human young, and the mother is not deemed unclean through childbirth.

9. What is meant by a human face? The forehead, the eyebrows, the eyes, the jaws, and the chin must be human. Even if the mouth, the ears, and the nose resemble those of an animal, it is nevertheless accounted human young.

10. If the abortion resembles a snake, the mother is deemed unclean through childbirth, since the eyeball of a snake is round like that of a human being. If the abortion is shaped like a human being, but has wings of flesh, the mother is likewise deemed unclean through childbirth. In case the abortion is born with only one eye or one thigh, if they are on one side of the body, it is considered as one half of a human being, and the mother is deemed unclean through childbirth; if they are situated in the middle of the body, the mother is deemed clean, because such a creature is not regarded as human.

11. If the foetus is born with an obstructed gullet, or if it lacks everything from the navel downwards and is therefore shapeless, or if its skull is shapeless, or if its face is covered over so that it is unrecognizable, or if it has two backs and two spines, or if the abortion consists of a head which has no recognizable articulation, or an arm without recognizable lines—a foetus of any of these kinds is not accounted human young and the mother is not deemed unclean through childbirth. If, however, the abortion consists of an arm or a leg with recognizable lines, the presump-

tion is that it has come from a complete foetus, and it may be counted towards the major part of the limbs thereof.

12. Sometimes the residue of the blood from which the human being is formed congeals into a piece of flesh which looks like an ox tongue and is wrapped around part of the child's body. This is called a sandal, and can never be formed except together with the child, whereas a piece of flesh formed separately, without a foetus, is not called a sandal. The majority of foetuses have no sandal. At times also some object may strike the pregnant woman's belly, injure the foetus, and cause the formation of something like such a sandal. Sometimes a recognizable face remains in the foetus, while at other times the foetus withers and changes its appearance, and the blood which is upon it coagulates leaving no recognizable face. Consequently, should a woman have an abortion of a male child with a sandal, even if the sandal shows no distinct face, she must continue unclean for the number of days prescribed for both a male and a female, since this sandal may have been female. The Sages in this case have leaned toward stringency by ruling that she be deemed unclean through the sandal also on account of human young, even though it shows no actual face, since in any case she is deemed unclean through childbirth because of the accompanying human young.

13. The thick membrane, like a wine skin, in which the foetus is formed, and which encompasses both the foetus and the sandal —if there is a sandal with it—and which the foetus bursts open at the moment of birth in order to emerge, is called the caul. At the beginning of its formation it is like the thread of the woof, hollow like a trumpet, and as thick as the craw of a fowl. A caul cannot be less than a handbreadth in size.

14. If the abortion consists of the caul, the mother must continue unclean for the number of days prescribed for both a male and a female, not because the caul counts as human young, but because there can be no caul without young. If she aborts a foetus and then a caul, there is cause for concern that the caul

may belong to another young, and it cannot be maintained that it belongs to the abortion, since a caul can be attributed to a viable child only. If therefore she gives birth to a viable child and then aborts a caul, even if this takes place twenty-three days later, it is ascribed to the child. No anxiety need be felt that there may have been another child, rather it may be assumed that the newborn child had burst open the caul and had emerged from it.

15. If, however, she first aborts a caul, and subsequently gives birth to a viable child, there is reason for apprehension that this caul may belong to another young, and it cannot be ascribed to the child born after it, because it is not the way of the caul to precede the child. If part of the caul emerges on one day and part on the morrow, she must begin counting the days of uncleanness from the first day, but for the sake of stringency she is allowed to count the days of purification only from the second day.

16. If the abortion resembles an animal or a bird, and the caul is attached to it, no concern need be felt that it may belong to a child. If, however, it is not attached to it, the stringency involving a double birth must be imposed upon the mother, since it can be said that the articulated formation which was in the caul had dissolved, and that the caul of this formation which resembles a domestic or wild animal had also dissolved.

17. In all these cases where apprehension is felt that there is a child because of the caul, days for purification are not appointed to the mother. Any woman, therefore, who aborts within forty days of conception anything other than a human young or a foetus whose form is not yet complete, is deemed to be a menstruant or a woman with flux, if blood had issued with it. If it comes away dry, without blood, she is deemed clean.

18. If a woman gives birth to male and female twins, she must continue unclean for the number of days prescribed for a female. If she gives birth to a child of doubtful sex or a hermaphrodite, she must continue unclean for the number of days prescribed for both a male and a female. If she gives birth to twins, of which

one is a male and the other of doubtful sex or a hermaphrodite, she likewise must continue unclean for the number of days prescribed for both a male and a female. If one is a female and the other of doubtful sex or a hermaphrodite, she must continue unclean for the number of days prescribed for a female only, since in the case of a child of doubtful sex or a hermaphrodite there is doubt as to whether it is male or female.

19. If a woman presumed to be pregnant gives birth, and it is not known what she has given birth to—for instance, if she was crossing a river and aborted into the river, or into a pit, or if she dropped the abortion and a beast dragged it away—the presumption is that it was a human young, and she must continue unclean for the number of days prescribed for both a male and a female. If, however, she was not presumed to be pregnant and had an abortion the nature of which is not known, she is deemed to be a woman in confinement out of doubt, and she must continue unclean for the number of days prescribed for a male, a female, and a menstruant.

20. What is the procedure in cases where it was stated that she must continue unclean for the number of days prescribed for both a male and a female? She is forbidden to her husband for fourteen days after the birth, as in the case of a woman who had given birth to a female. For the first seven days she is considered definitely unclean, and for the latter seven doubtfully so. She need observe only forty days of purification, as in the case of a woman who had given birth to a male. If she has a flow after forty days and up to the eightieth day, it is not considered blood of purification but blood of a menstruant or of a woman with flux, out of doubt, if it came during the days of her flux, as we have explained. Similarly, if she has a flow on the eighty-first day alone, she is deemed a menstruant out of doubt and must continue unclean for the seven days prescribed for a menstruant. For she may have given birth to a female, in which case she has no fixed period for menstruation until after the completion of the eighty days, as we have explained.

21. What is the procedure in cases where it was stated that she

must continue unclean for the number of days prescribed for a male, a female, and a menstruant? She is forbidden to her husband for fourteen days after the birth, as though she had given birth to a female, and if she has a flow on the eighty-first day she is considered a menstruant out of doubt. Similarly, if she has a flow on the seventy-fourth and on the eighty-first days she is considered a menstruant out of doubt. Likewise, if she has a flow on the forty-first day, even if she had it on the thirty-fourth day also, she is considered a menstruant out of doubt and is forbidden to her husband until the night of the forty-eighth day, as though she had given birth to a male. She need observe no days of purification at all like a menstruant, and in this respect she is regarded as though she had not given birth. Any flow which she may have from the day of her abortion until the eightieth day, if it falls in the days of her menstruation, renders her a menstruant out of doubt from the seventh day after the abortion; if it falls during the days of her flux, it renders her a woman with flux out of doubt, since during all the days of fulfillment she has no fixed period. Similarly, if she has a flow on the eighty-first day, she is still in ill plight and is considered a menstruant out of doubt, as we have explained, even if she had a flow for but one day. Only when her period is reestablished after the eighty days is her ill plight removed and she then reverts to the state of a definite menstruant or a woman definitely with flux. Similarly, in the period from the day of her abortion up to seven days, she would be a definite menstruant if she had the abortion during the days of her menstruation, as we have explained.

CHAPTER XI

1. All that we have heretofore stated concerning a menstruant, a woman with flux, and a woman after childbirth, is the law of the Torah, and these regulations were observed when the Great Court was in existence, composed of great Sages who could

distinguish between the various species of blood. If ever a doubt arose in anyone's mind regarding the nature of the flows, or about the days of menstruation or flux, the people concerned would go up to the Great Court and inquire, according to the Scriptural assurance, to wit, *If there arise a matter too hard for thee in judgment, between blood and blood, between plea and plea,* etc. (Deut. 17:8), that is, between the blood of menstruation and the blood of flux. In those days the daughters of Israel were careful in this matter, rigidly observing their fixed periods and always counting the days of menstruation and the days of flux.

2. Now painstaking care is involved in the counting of these days, and the women were quite often in doubt, so that if a female child had a flow even on the day of her birth, from that selfsame day did they begin to count for her the days of menstruation or the days of flux, as we have explained. Consequently, a female child could not become unclean from flux before it was ten days old, for if she had a flow on the day of her birth, she would be deemed a menstruant for seven days, and counting the three days adjacent to her menstruation, this makes ten days. Thus you learn that she must begin to count the days of menstruation and the days of flux all her life from the moment she first has a flow, even if she has a flow while yet a child.

3. In the days of the Sages of the Gemara there arose many doubts concerning the flows of blood, with the result that the fixed periods were disarranged, so that all the women were unable to determine the days of menstruation and the days of flux. Consequently, the Sages leaned in the direction of stringency in this matter and enacted the rule that all the days of a woman's life should be regarded as days of flux, and that all flows of blood that she may have should be considered blood of flux out of doubt.

4. In addition to this, the daughters of Israel have imposed upon themselves a further restriction, and made it a custom that wherever Israelites may live, when any daughter of Israel

has a flow, even if it is a drop no larger than a mustard seed, she should, upon the cessation of the flow, count for herself seven days of cleanness, even if she has the flow during the period of her menstruation. It is immaterial whether she has a flow for only one day, or for two, or throughout the seven, or even longer; when the flow ceases she must count seven days of cleanness like a woman with flux of greater degree, and must then immerse herself on the eighth night, even though she is a woman with flux out of doubt, or on the eighth day in case of an emergency, as we have explained. Thereafter she is permitted to her husband.

5. Similarly, nowadays every woman in confinement is regarded as giving birth during her period of flux and must observe seven days of cleanness, as we have explained. And the custom is widespread in Iraq, Palestine, Spain, and the Maghrib that if she has a flow during the days of her fulfillment, even though she has it after the count of the seven days of uncleanness and after she had immersed herself, she must nevertheless count another seven days of cleanness after the cessation of the flow of blood, and she is accorded no days of purification whatsoever. On the contrary, any flow of blood a woman may have, whether it be the blood of travail or the blood of purification, is considered unclean, and she must count seven days of uncleanness upon the cessation of it.

6. A new enactment was instituted during the period of the Geonim, who ruled that blood of purification should no longer be observed. For the stringent procedure adopted in the days of the Sages of the Gemara applied only in such cases where the flow is of unclean blood, in which case a woman must observe seven days of cleanness, whereas for such flows of blood as she may have during the days of her purification, after counting the seven days and after immersion, there is no need for apprehension, since the days of purification are not designated for either menstruation or flux, as we have explained.

7. We have heard that in France, down to this day, it is cus-

tomary to have sexual intercourse notwithstanding the presence of blood of purification, in accordance with the law of the Gemara, after counting the days of uncleanness and after the immersion which follows the uncleanness of childbirth in a state of flux. This matter depends upon local custom.

8. Similarly, the law of virginal blood nowadays is that even if the wife is a minor who has not yet attained the age of menstruation and has never had a flow in her life, the husband may perform his marital duty for the first time and must then withdraw. Thereafter, as long as she has a flow of blood resulting from the wound, she is deemed unclean, and when the blood ceases to flow she must count seven days of cleanness.

9. Furthermore, any girl who is sought in marriage and accepts the proposal must wait for seven days of cleanness after her acceptance, and only then is she permitted to her husband, since she may, because of her desire for a man, have had a flow of a drop of blood without feeling it. Whether the woman is an adult or a minor, she must observe seven days of cleanness following her acceptance, and must then immerse herself, and thereafter she may have intercourse.

10. All these matters constitute an additional stringency which the daughters of Israel have adopted since the days of the Sages of the Gemara, and one must never depart from it. Consequently a woman who accepts a proposal when sought in marriage may not marry before she has counted these days and has immersed herself. If, however, she is marrying a scholar, she is permitted to marry at once, and may count the days of cleanness after the marriage and then immerse herself, since a scholar knows that she is forbidden to him, and will be careful not to approach her until after she has immersed herself.

11. The regulations concerning bloodstains are nowadays just as we have explained—in this matter there is neither innovation nor custom, but every bloodstain which we have stated to be clean is deemed clean, and every bloodstain that we have stated

to be unclean is unclean, and a woman must count seven days from the day that the bloodstain was found. If the stain is large enough to give rise to apprehension of flux, she must count the seven days from the day after the stain was found, since a woman who sees a stain is not subject to the same stringency as one who has a flow.

12. Likewise, in all cases where we have said that the mother is clean after childbirth, she is deemed clean at the present time also. So also is a woman who has a flow of white effusion or greenish blood, or aborts a red lump which has no blood with it, deemed clean nowadays, since the stringency applies only when there is a flow of unclean blood, and this is not considered unclean blood.

13. Similarly, if she has a wound which discharges blood, or if her urine is mixed with blood, she is deemed clean. For the only innovation here is the counting of seven days of cleanness by any woman who has a flow of unclean blood, as we have said, and the rule is that any flow of blood should be considered unclean.

14. There is a custom which prevails in some places whereby a menstruant continues through the seven days of menstruation, even if she has a flow for only one day, and thereafter continues through the seven days of cleanness; this is not a well-founded custom, but the result of an erroneous decision on the part of the authority who ruled to this effect, and no attention need be paid to it. Rather, if she has a flow for one day, she must count seven days of cleanness after that, and then immerse herself on the eighth night, which is the second night after the conclusion of her menstrual period, and thereupon she is permitted to her husband.

15. Similarly, there is a custom which prevails in some places and which is mentioned in the responsa of some of the Geonim, whereby a woman who has given birth to a male child may not have intercourse until the expiration of forty days, and in the case of a female child eighty days, even if she has had a flow

for seven days only. This, too, is not a well-founded custom, but the result of an erroneous decision in these responsa. It is a custom in the manner of the *Minim* which is prevalent in these localities, and the inhabitants thereof had learned it from the Sadducees. Indeed, it is one's duty to compel them to get it out of their minds, so that they would return to the words of the Sages, namely that a woman should count no more than seven days of cleanness, as we have explained.

16. A woman is not rid of her uncleanness, nor does she emerge from the state of forbidden union, until she immerses herself in the waters of a valid immersion pool. Nothing should interpose between her flesh and the water. The details of valid and invalid immersion pools, and of the manner of immersion, and the regulations governing interposing matter will all be explained in the Laws Concerning Immersion Pools. Should she bathe in an ordinary bath, even if all the water in the world should flow over her, she is deemed to be in the same state after the bath as she was before it, and subsequent intercourse with her involves the penalty of extinction. The only thing which raises a woman from uncleanness to cleanness is immersion in an immersion pool, or in a spring, or in waters which are like a spring, as will be explained in the Laws Concerning Immersion Pools.

17. If she has her immersion during the seven days of cleanness prescribed by present-day custom, notwithstanding that these days are subject to doubt, she is considered as though she had not immersed at all. Should she have her immersion on the seventh day, even though she is forbidden to do so in the first place, lest her husband should have intercourse with her on the seventh day after the immersion, nevertheless, inasmuch as this immersion has taken place at a proper time, the immersion avails her, even if she is definitely a woman with flux.

18. A man is forbidden to come in close contact with his wife during these seven days of cleanness, even if both she and he are

fully clothed. He should not approach her, nor touch her even with his little finger, nor eat with her out of the same dish. In general, he should conduct himself during the days of counting in the same way as he would during the days of her menstruation, since intercourse with her involves the penalty of extinction until after she immerses herself, as we have explained.

19. All tasks which a wife ordinarily performs for her husband she may also perform while she is a menstruant, except for washing his face, hands, and feet, serving him his wine, and arranging the bed in his presence; this is a precaution, lest these services should lead to forbidden intercourse. For this reason she should not eat with him out of the same dish, nor should he touch her flesh, so as not to become habituated to transgression. Similarly, she should not perform these three tasks also during the seven days of cleanness. A woman is permitted, however, to adorn herself during the days of her menstruation, in order that she should not become unattractive to her husband.

CHAPTER XII

1. If an Israelite has intercourse with a heathen woman of the other nations by way of legal marriage, or if an Israelite woman has intercourse with a heathen by way of legal marriage, they are liable to a flogging on the authority of the Torah, as it is said, *neither shalt thou have any marriage with them, thy daughter thou shalt not give unto his son, nor his daughter shalt thou take unto thy son* (Deut. 7:3). This prohibition covers both the seven Canaanitish nations and all the other nations, as is explicitly stated by Ezra, *and that we would not give our daughters unto the people of the land, nor take their daughters for our sons* (Neh. 10:31).

2. The prohibition in the Torah applies only to intercourse by way of legal marriage. If an Israelite has intercourse with a

heathen woman by way of adultery, he is, on the authority of the Scribes, liable only to the flogging prescribed for disobedience, which serves as a precaution, lest such intercourse should lead to intermarriage. If he has a continuous extramarital relationship with her, he is guilty through her for intercourse with a menstruant, a bondswoman, a heathen woman, and a harlot. If there is no continuous relationship, but merely an incidental one, he is liable only for intercourse with a heathen woman. All these prohibitions are on the authority of the Scribes.

3. This rule applies only to an Israelite. If a priest has intercourse with a heathen woman, it is on the authority of the Torah that he must be flogged, namely, for intercourse with a harlot. It is immaterial whether the harlot is heathen or Israelite, and he is liable to a flogging only for the act of intercourse, since she cannot be betrothed to him.

4. In the case of an Israelite who has intercourse with a heathen woman in public, that is, in the presence of ten or more Israelites, whether by way of legal marriage or by way of harlotry, should zealots fall upon him and slay him, they are worthy of commendation for their zeal. This is a rule given to Moses from Sinai, as evidenced by the incident of Phinehas and Zimri.

5. The zealot may fall upon them, however, only during the act of intercourse, as in the case of Zimri, as it is said, *and thrust both of them through, the man of Israel, and the woman through the belly* (Num. 25:8). Once the man has withdrawn from the woman, he may not be slain, and should the zealot slay him nevertheless, he incurs the death penalty for it. Should the zealot come to request permission from the court to slay him, he is to be given no instructions, even if the act is still in progress. And not only this, but should the zealot come forth with the intention of slaying the man, and should the man elude him and kill him in order to save himself, the man may not be put to death on that account. Should the woman be the daughter of a resident stranger, the man who has intercourse with her may not be attacked by

zealots, but should only be given the flogging prescribed for disobedience.

6. If he is neither attacked by zealots nor flogged by the court, nevertheless his punishment, as specified in post-Mosaic Scripture, is extinction, as it is said, *for Judah hath profaned the holiness of the Lord which He loveth, and hath married the daughter of a strange god; may the Lord cut off to the man that doeth this, him that calleth and him that answereth out of the tents of Jacob, and him that offereth an offering unto the Lord of hosts* (Mal. 2:11–12). If he is an Israelite, he will have none "that calleth" among the Sages, nor anyone "that answereth" among the disciples, and if he is a priest he will have none "that offereth an offering unto the Lord of hosts." Hence you learn that whosoever has intercourse with a heathen woman is considered as though he had intermarried with an idol, as it is said *hath married the daughter of a strange god,* and he is called "one who has profaned the holiness of the Lord."

7. Although this transgression does not carry the death penalty imposed by the court, let it not be considered lightly in your eyes, for it involves a detriment carried by no other kind of prohibited union. A child born out of forbidden union is regarded as one's own son in all respects and is considered a member of the Israelite community, even though he is a bastard, whereas a child by a heathen woman is not recognized as a son, as it is said, *for he will turn away thy son from following Me* (Deut. 7:4), that is, the father will turn him away from being "after the Lord."

8. Moreover, such conduct causes one to cleave to idolaters from whom the Holy One, blessed be He, had separated us, to turn away from God, and to break faith with Him.

9. In the case of a heathen who has intercourse with a daughter of Israel, if she is a married woman, he is liable to be put to death; if she is unmarried, he is not liable to be put to death.

10. If, however, an Israelite has intercourse with a heathen

woman, whether she is a minor three years and one day old or an adult, whether she is married or unmarried, even if the Israelite is only nine years and a day old, once he willfully has intercourse with her, she is liable to be put to death, because an offense has been committed by an Israelite through her, just as in the case of an animal. This law is explicitly stated in the Torah, *Behold, these caused the children of Israel, through the counsel of Balaam, to revolt, so as to break faith with the Lord . . . therefore kill every woman that has known man by lying with him* (Num. 31:16–17).

11. Slaves who have undergone immersion for the purpose of acquiring the status of slaves, and have accepted the commandments which are incumbent upon slaves, have thereby left the community of idolaters, but without entering the community of Israel. Consequently a bondswoman is forbidden to a freeman, whether she is his own bondswoman or his neighbor's, and if he has intercourse with her nevertheless he is liable to the flogging prescribed for disobedience, on the authority of the Scribes. For the Torah states explicitly that a master may give his Canaanite bondswoman to his Hebrew slave, and she is permitted to the latter, as it is said, *If his master give him a wife* (Exod. 21:4).

12. The Sages have issued no prohibition, however, against intercourse with a bondswoman, nor does the Torah hold a man liable to a flogging on account of it, unless she is designated to another man, as we have explained.

13. Nevertheless let not this transgression be esteemed lightly in your eyes, just because the Torah does not prescribe a flogging, for this also causes a man's son to depart from following after the Lord, since that bondswoman's son is likewise a slave, and is not of Israel; the man thus causes the holy seed to become profaned and to be reduced to slavery. Indeed, Onkelos, the translator of the Pentateuch into Aramaic, interpreted the verse, *There shall be no harlot of the daughters of Israel, neither shall there be a*

sodomite of the sons of Israel (Deut. 23:18), to mean intercourse with a male or female slave.

14. If a man has intercourse with a bondswoman, even if he does it publicly and even if the act is still in progress, he may not be attacked by zealots. Similarly, if he takes a bondswoman by way of legal marriage, he is, according to the Torah, not liable to a flogging, because from the moment that she had immersed herself and had accepted the commandments, she has left the status of an idolatress.

15. If the child of an Israelite woman is confused with the child of a bondswoman, both children are considered doubtful cases, and each of them is deemed a doubtful slave. The owner of the bondswoman must therefore be compelled to manumit both of them. If the Israelite child is the owner of the slave child, they must, when they reach majority, manumit each other, and they are then permitted to enter the congregation of the Lord.

16. If the confused children are females, both are considered doubtful bondswomen, and if a man has intercourse with them the resulting child is deemed a doubtful slave. Similarly, if the child of a heathen mother is confused with the child of an Israelite mother, both must be immersed for the purpose of proselytization, and each of them is regarded as a doubtful proselyte.

17. All heathens, without exception, once they become proselytes and accept all the commandments enjoined in the Torah, and all slaves, once they are manumitted, are regarded as Israelites in every respect, as it is said, *As for the congregation, there shall be one statute both for you and for the stranger* (Num. 15:15), and they may enter the congregation of the Lord immediately. That is, provided the proselyte or manumitted slave marries the daughter of an Israelite, or an Israelite marries the female proselyte or manumitted bondswoman. Excepting the four nations, Ammon, Moab, Egypt, and Edom, for if a member of one of these nations becomes a proselyte, he is considered an Israelite in all respects save the right to marry an Israelite woman.

18. What is the rule concerning them? The males of Ammon and Moab, but not the females, are forever forbidden to enter the congregation, as it is said, *An Ammonite or a Moabite shall not enter into the congregation of the Lord, even to the tenth generation* (Deut. 23:4). It is a rule given to Moses from Sinai that while a male Ammonite or Moabite is forever forbidden to marry a daughter of Israel, even their posterity for all time, an Ammonite or Moabite woman is permitted to marry an Israelite immediately, like a woman from any other nation.

19. In the case of an Egyptian or an Edomite, both males and females of the first and second generation are forbidden to enter into Israel, but the third generation is permitted to do so, as it is said, *the children of the third generation that are born unto them may enter into the assembly of the Lord* (Deut. 23:9).

20. If a pregnant Egyptian woman becomes a proselyte, the child is considered to be of the second generation. If an Egyptian proselyte of the second generation marries an Egyptian woman-proselyte of the first generation, or if an Egyptian proselyte of the first generation marries an Egyptian woman-proselyte of the second generation, the child is regarded as of the second generation, since it is said, *the children that are born unto them,* that is, Scripture makes the status of the child dependent on birth.

21. If an Ammonite proselyte marries an Egyptian woman, the child is an Ammonite. If an Egyptian proselyte marries an Ammonite woman, the child is an Egyptian. The rule with regard to these nations is that the child has the status of the father. If, however, they become proselytes, the child has the status of the lesser parent.

22. A man of the seven Canaanitish nations who became a proselyte was not forbidden by the Torah to enter the congregation. It is, however, a known fact that of these nations only the Gibeonites became proselytes, and Joshua decreed that they, both males and females, should be forbidden to enter the congregation. But this prohibition was made to apply only as long as the Temple was in existence, as it is said, *hewers of wood and*

drawers of water for the house of my God (Josh. 9:23). Their exclusion by Joshua was thus made dependent on the existence of the sanctuary.

23. They are the ones who were designated *Nethinim* ("the given ones"), because Joshua had "given" them to the service of the sanctuary. But subsequently David decreed that they should not ever enter the congregation, even when the sanctuary no longer existed, and so it is explicitly stated in Ezra, *and of the Nethinim whom David and the princes had given for the service of the Levites* (Ezra 8:20). Hence you learn that David made their exclusion independent of the sanctuary.

24. Why did he and his court issue this decree against them? Because he saw the insolence and cruelty displayed by them when they demanded the seven sons of Saul, the chosen one of the Lord, in order to hang them, and mercilessly slew them.

25. When Sennacherib, king of Assyria, arose, he mixed up all the nations, intermingling them one with the other, and exiled them from their homelands; the result was that the people who now dwell in Egypt are not the original Egyptians, nor are the Edomites now in the plains of Edom the original ones. Therefore, once these four forbidden nations have become commingled with all the other permitted nations, they all became permitted. For whosoever separates himself from them in order to become a proselyte is presumed to have issued from the majority; consequently, when nowadays a person becomes a proselyte anywhere, whether he is an Edomite, an Egyptian, an Ammonite, a Moabite, an Ethiopian, or of any other nation, and whether male or female, he is permitted to enter the congregation at once.

CHAPTER XIII

1. Israel entered into the covenant by way of three rites: circumcision, immersion, and sacrifice.

2. Circumcision was performed in Egypt, as it is said, *but no*

uncircumcised person shall eat thereof (Exod. 12:48). Our master Moses circumcised the people, for with the exception of the tribe of Levi they all had abandoned the covenant of circumcision in Egypt, and it is to the Levites that Scripture refers in saying, *for they kept Thy covenant* (Deut. 33:9).

3. Immersion took place in the wilderness before the revelation of the Torah, as it is said, *and sanctify them today and tomorrow, and let them wash their garments* (Exod. 19:10). The same is true of sacrifice, as it is said, *And he sent the young men of the children of Israel, who offered up burnt sacrifices* (*ibid.* 24:5), that is, they offered up the sacrifices on behalf of all Israel.

4. Accordingly, the rule for future generations is that when a heathen wishes to enter into the covenant, to take shelter under the wings of the Shekinah, and to assume the yoke of the Torah, he requires circumcision, immersion, and the offering of an acceptable sacrifice, while in the case of a female there must be immersion and sacrifice only, as it is said, *as ye are, so shall be the convert* (Num. 15:15), i.e. just as ye have entered the covenant by way of circumcision, immersion, and the offering of an acceptable sacrifice, so shall the proselyte in future generations enter by way of circumcision, immersion, and the offering of an acceptable sacrifice.

5. What constitutes the sacrifice of a proselyte? A burnt offering of an animal, or two turtledoves, or two pigeons, both of them as burnt offerings. At the present time, when sacrifices cannot be offered, he requires only circumcision and immersion, but when the Temple is rebuilt he will be required to offer up a sacrifice as well.

6. If a prospective proselyte is circumcised but not immersed, or vice versa, he is not considered a proselyte, until he is both circumcised and immersed. The immersion requires the presence of three witnesses, and since it must take place before a court it cannot be performed on a Sabbath, on a festival, or at night. If, however, it has already taken place, he is deemed a proselyte.

7. A proselyte who is a minor may be immersed by sanction

of the court, since this involves the bestowal of a privilege upon him. If a pregnant woman becomes a proselyte, her child needs no immersion. If the proselyte immerses himself privately, or becomes a proselyte privately, even in the presence of two witnesses, he is not regarded as a proselyte. If he comes forth and declares, "I was made a proselyte by such-and-such a court, in whose presence I was immersed," he may not enter the congregation on the strength of his own declaration, but must bring witnesses to support it.

8. If the proselyte is married to an Israelite woman or to a woman-proselyte and has children, and then declares, "I became a proselyte privately," he may be believed to the extent of invalidating his own status as a proselyte, but not to the extent of invalidating his children's status, and he must be immersed again by the court.

9. A woman-proselyte who openly and consistently conducts herself in the ways of Israel, such as having an immersion after her menstruation, separating the heave offering from her dough, and the like, or a male proselyte who conducts himself in the ways of Israel by having an immersion after his nocturnal pollution and observing all the commandments, is presumed to be a righteous proselyte, even if there are no witnesses to testify as to the court in which the rite was performed. Nevertheless, should they desire to intermarry with Israel, they should not be allowed to do so until they either bring witnesses or immerse themselves in our presence, since there is also a presumption that they are heathens.

10. If a person comes forth, however, and declares that he had been a heathen but was made a proselyte by a court, he is to be believed, since the mouth that forbids is the mouth that permits. This applies only to the Land of Israel and to times when all the inhabitants thereof are under the presumption of being Israelites. Outside of the Land he must produce proof before he may be allowed to marry an Israelite woman. As for me, I say that this represents a higher standard to ensure purity of descent.

11. Just as proselytes must be circumcised and immersed, so must slaves acquired from heathens for the purpose of slavery be circumcised and immersed. If a man acquires a slave from a heathen, and the slave anticipates him and immerses himself first in order to obtain his freedom, he thereby acquires his liberty, providing that he declares at the time of the immersion, "Behold, I immerse myself in your presence for the purpose of becoming a proselyte." If he immerses himself in the presence of his master, he need not make such a declaration, but once he immerses himself he becomes free. Consequently his master must keep hold of him in the water until he rises, whereby he remains in his possession, and the master must also inform him before the judges that he is immersing him for the purpose of bondage. The slave must immerse himself in the presence of three witnesses, and in the daytime, like a proselyte, since the immersion constitutes partial proselytism.

12. After the slave is manumitted, he must have another immersion in the presence of three witnesses and in the daytime, whereby he becomes a full proselyte and attains the status of an Israelite. He need not, however, declare that he assumes the commandments, and it is unnecessary at that time to acquaint him with the principles of the faith, since they had already been made known to him at the time of his immersion for the purpose of bondage.

13. Proselytes, slaves, and freedmen must be immersed in an immersion pool which is valid for menstruants, and anything which constitutes an interposition in the case of a menstruant does so also in the case of a proselyte, a slave, or a freedman.

14. It should not be imagined that Samson, the deliverer of Israel, or Solomon, king of Israel, who was called "the beloved of the Lord," married foreign women while these were still heathens. Rather, the essence of the matter is as follows: The proper procedure, when a man or a woman comes forth with the intention of becoming a proselyte, is to examine them; per-

chance they come to embrace the faith in order to gain money, or to qualify for a position of authority, or out of apprehension. In the case of a man, perchance he has cast his eye upon an Israelite woman. In the case of a woman, it may be that she has cast her eye upon one of the youths of Israel. If no such ulterior motive is found in them, they should be informed of the heavy weight of the yoke of the Torah, and how burdensome it is for Gentiles to observe its precepts, in order to induce them to withdraw. If they accept the yoke nevertheless and refuse to withdraw, and it is evident that they have forsaken heathenism out of love for the Torah, they should be accepted, as it is said, *And when she saw that she was steadfastly minded to go with her, she left off speaking unto her* (Ruth 1:18).

15. Consequently the court did not receive any proselytes throughout the days of David and Solomon; in the days of David, lest they should become proselytes out of apprehension, and in Solomon's time, lest they should become proselytes on account of the might, the prosperity, and the greatness which Israel then enjoyed. For whosoever forsakes heathenism for the sake of some worldly vanity is not considered a righteous proselyte. Nevertheless, many became proselytes in the presence of laymen during the days of David and Solomon, and the Great Court was apprehensive on that account. While the court did not repulse them, at any rate after they had immersed themselves, neither did it welcome them, until such time as their subsequent conduct could be observed.

16. Now since Solomon caused the women to become proselytes first, before marrying them—and so did Samson—and it is a known fact that these women had become proselytes for ulterior motives; and since Samson and Solomon made them proselytes without the sanction of the court, therefore Scripture regarded them as heathens remaining in their state of prohibition. Moreover, their later actions showed the true reason for their former ones, for they continued to worship their idols and built high places for them, which is why Scripture holds Solomon respon-

sible as though he had built them himself, as it is said, *then did Solomon build a high place* (1 Kings 11:7).

17. A proselyte who has not undergone an examination, or was not made acquainted with the commandments and the punishment for transgressing them, but was circumcised and immersed in the presence of three laymen, is deemed a proselyte. Even if it becomes known that he had become a proselyte because of some ulterior motive, once he is circumcised and immersed, he has left the status of a heathen, but apprehension should be felt concerning him until his righteousness shall have become apparent. Even if he reverts to his previous state and worships idols, he is considered merely a renegade Israelite; his act of betrothal remains valid, and it remains the finder's duty to return to him his lost property, for once a person immerses himself, he attains the status of an Israelite. That is why Samson and Solomon kept their wives, even though their secret motives were revealed.

18. It is for this reason that the Sages have declared, "Proselytes are as hard to bear for Israel as a scab upon the skin," since the majority of them become proselytes for ulterior motives and subsequently lead Israel astray, and once they become proselytes, it is a difficult matter to separate from them. An instructive example is what happened in the wilderness in the matter of the golden calf, and at Kibroth-Hattaavah, as well as in most of the trials with which the children of Israel wearied God. All of these were initiated by the mixed multitude.

CHAPTER XIV

1. In what manner are righteous proselytes to be received? When a heathen comes forth for the purpose of becoming a proselyte, and upon investigation no ulterior motive is found, the court should say to him, "Why do you come forth to become a proselyte? Do you not know that Israel is at present sorely af-

flicted, oppressed, despised, confounded, and beset by suffering?" If he answers, "I know, and I am indeed unworthy," he should be accepted immediately.

2. He should then be made acquainted with the principles of the faith, which are the oneness of God and the prohibition of idolatry. These matters should be discussed in great detail; he should then be told, though not at great length, about some of the less weighty and some of the more weighty commandments. Thereupon he should be informed of the transgressions involved in the laws of gleanings, forgotten sheaves, the corner of the field, and the poor man's tithe. Then he should be told of the punishment for violation of the commandments. How so? The court should say to him, "Be it known unto you that before entering into this faith, if you ate forbidden fat, you did not incur the penalty of extinction; if you desecrated the Sabbath, you did not incur the penalty of death by stoning. But now, having become a proselyte, should you eat forbidden fat you will incur the penalty of extinction, and if you should profane the Sabbath, you will incur the penalty of death by stoning." This, however, should not be carried to excess nor to too great detail, lest it should make him weary and cause him to stray from the good way unto the evil way. A person should be attracted at first only with pleasing and gentle words, as it is said first, *I will draw them with cords of a man,* and only then *with bonds of love* (Hos. 11:4).

3. Just as the court should inform him of the punishment for transgression, so should they tell him of the reward for the observance of the commandments. He should be assured that by performing these commandments he will be vouchsafed the life of the world to come, and that there is no perfectly righteous man but the learned man who performs these commandments properly and understands them.

4. They should say to him further, "Be it known unto you that the world to come is treasured up solely for the righteous, who are Israel. As for what you see that Israel is in distress in this world, it is in reality a boon which is laid up for them, be-

cause it is not granted them to receive the abundance of good things in this world like other peoples, lest their hearts should wax haughty and they should go astray and squander the reward of the world to come, as it is said, *But Jeshurun waxed fat and kicked* (Deut. 32:15)."

5. "Nevertheless, the Holy One, blessed be He, does not bring upon them too many calamities, lest they should altogether perish. Rather, all the heathen shall cease to exist, while they shall endure." The court should expatiate on this point, by token of their affection for him. If he then changes his mind and does not wish to accept, he should be left to go on his way. But should he again accept, there should be no further delay, and he should be at once circumcised. If he is already circumcised, a drop of blood of the covenant should be drawn from him, and the court should wait until he is completely healed, after which he should be immersed.

6. Three men must stand over him during the immersion, and inform him for the second time of some of the less weighty precepts and some of the more weighty ones, while he stands in the water. In the case of a woman, she should be attended by women who should place her in the water up to her neck, and the members of the court, who are to remain outside, should inform her of some of the less and some of the more weighty precepts, while she is in the water. She must then immerse herself in the presence of the court, the while they turn their backs and depart, so as not to see her as she emerges from the water.

7. What is meant by "a resident stranger"? A former heathen who has undertaken to forsake the worship of idols and to observe the other commandments made obligatory upon the descendants of Noah, but has been neither circumcised nor immersed. He should be accepted and regarded as one of "the pious individuals of the nations of the world." Why is he called "resident"? Because we are allowed to permit him to reside in our midst in the Land of Israel, as we have explained in the Laws Concerning Idolaters.

8. A resident stranger may be accepted only during such times as the law of the Jubilee is in force. Nowadays, however, even if he accepts the entire Torah, but with the exception of one particular, he may not be received.

9. One should not say to a slave acquired from a heathen, "Why do you come?" etc., but rather, "Is it your desire to enter into the full status of a slave of Israel, so that you might become one of the worthy slaves, or is it not?" If he answers affirmatively, he should be made acquainted with the principles of the faith and some of the less and the more weighty commandments, with their reward and punishment, as in the case of a proselyte, and he should be immersed in the same way as a proselyte. He should be informed of all this again while he is in the water. If he is unwilling to accept this, the master may bear with him for up to twelve months, and should then sell him to a heathen, it being forbidden to retain him longer than that. If, however, the slave had made a prior condition that he should not be circumcised or immersed, but should become a resident stranger, he may be kept in service as a resident stranger. A slave such as this may be kept, however, only at such time as the law of the Jubilee is in force.

10. The only unions prohibited to a heathen are his mother, his father's wife, and his sister by his mother; the prohibition extends also to a married woman, a male, and an animal, as will be explained in the Laws Concerning Kings and Wars. All other forbidden unions are permitted to him.

11. A heathen who becomes a proselyte, or a slave who has been manumitted, is regarded as if he were a newborn child. All kin prohibited to him while he was a heathen or a slave are therefore no longer considered forbidden. If both he and they become proselytes, he may not be held liable on account of forbidden unions for intercourse with any one of them at all.

12. According to the Torah, a proselyte is permitted to marry his mother or his sister by his mother if they, too, become prose-

lytes, but the Sages have forbidden it, in order that they should not say, "We have gone from a stringent sanctity to a lenient one," for heretofore she was forbidden to him, whereas now she is permitted. Similarly, if a proselyte has intercourse with his mother or sister who have remained heathens, it is regarded as no more than intercourse with a heathen woman.

13. What is the law concerning proselytes with regard to forbidden unions with kinsfolk? If, while still a heathen, the proselyte was married to his mother or his sister, and they then became proselytes, they must be separated from one another, as we have explained. But if he was married to a woman of the other forbidden unions and both he and his wife become proselytes, they need not be separated from one another. A proselyte is forbidden to his mother's kin after he becomes a proselyte, on the authority of the Scribes, but he is permitted to his father's kin, even though he knows for certain that they are his kin on his father's side. For instance, if both are twins, it is certain that they had the same father; nevertheless, the Sages did not prohibit his father's kin. Consequently, a proselyte may marry the wife of his brother on his father's side, or the wife of his father's brother, or the wife of his father, or the wife of his son, even though they had contracted the marriage with his brother, his father, his father's brother, or his son, after they also had become proselytes. Similarly, the sister of his mother by her father, or his sister by his father, or his proselyte daughter are permitted to him. He is forbidden, however, to marry his sister by his mother, his mother's sister by her mother, or the wife of his brother by his mother, if this brother by his mother married her after he had become a proselyte. If, however, his brother married her while he was a heathen, she is permitted to him.

14. If twin brothers were conceived while their mother was a non-Israelite, but were born after their mother had become a proselyte, they are liable if one marries the wife of the other.

15. If a man marries a woman-proselyte and her proselyte

daughter, or two sisters by one mother, he may dwell with one of them, but must divorce the other. If he marries a proselyte woman and she dies, he may then marry her mother or her daughter, since the prohibition is in force only during the wife's lifetime. A man is also permitted to marry two proselyte sisters by one father, since the prohibitive decree does not extend to the father's kin, as we have explained.

16. All secondary degrees of propinquity do not apply to proselytes. Consequently, a proselyte may marry his maternal grandmother, and a man may marry a woman-proselyte and her maternal grandmother, or her daughter's granddaughter; and so with all other secondary degrees of propinquity.

17. A slave may marry his mother while he is a slave; needless to say, he may also marry his daughter, his sister, or the like. Since he has already left the status of a heathen, the unions which are forbidden to the heathen are no longer forbidden to him, and since he has not yet acquired the status of an Israelite, neither are the unions forbidden to a proselyte forbidden to him.

18. It would appear to me that if a slave has intercourse with a male or with an animal, both must be put to death, since the prohibition of these unions applies equally to all mankind.

19. Manumitted slaves are equivalent to proselytes. Whatever is forbidden to proselytes is forbidden to them, and whatever is permitted to proselytes is permitted to them. A man may give his bondswoman to his slave or to his neighbor's slave. He may even deliberately hand over one bondswoman to two slaves without any further ado, since they are regarded as cattle. It is immaterial whether the bondswoman is or is not designated for a specific slave, for the laws of marriage apply only to Israelites, or to heathens marrying heathens, but not to slaves marrying slaves, or to slaves marrying Israelites.

CHAPTER XV

1. Who is accounted a bastard, as designated in the Torah? The offspring by any of the forbidden unions, except by a menstruant, whose child is considered impaired, but not a bastard. If, however, a man has intercourse with a woman of any of the other forbidden unions, whether by force or by consent, whether willfully or by error, the child born of that union is regarded as a bastard, and both male and female are eternally forbidden to marry into Israel, as it is said, *even to the tenth generation* (Deut. 23:3), that is, forever.

2. Whether a male bastard marries an Israelite woman, or an Israelite marries a female bastard, they are liable to a flogging if intercourse follows the betrothal. If he betrothes her but does not have intercourse with her, he does not incur a flogging. If he has intercourse without betrothal, he is not liable to a flogging on account of bastardy. The only case in which a man is liable to a flogging for intercourse without betrothal within one of the unions forbidden by a negative commandment, is that of a High Priest who has intercourse with a widow, as will be explained. If a man remarries his divorced wife after she had been married to someone else and been divorced, the child born of that union is considered legitimate, since she is not considered a forbidden union.

3. If a heathen or slave has intercourse with a daughter of Israel, the child is considered legitimate, whether she is unmarried or married, whether the intercourse took place by force or by consent. If a heathen or slave has intercourse with a female bastard, the child is deemed a bastard; if a male bastard has intercourse with a heathen woman, the child is considered a heathen. If this child then becomes a proselyte, it is legitimate like any other proselyte. If a male bastard has intercourse with

a bondswoman, the child is regarded as a slave. If this child is then manumitted, it is legitimate like any other manumitted slave, and is permitted to a daughter of Israel.

4. The general rule is that the child of a male slave, a male heathen, a bondswoman, or a heathen woman has the status of his mother, the father not being considered. In accordance with this rule, the Sages have permitted a male bastard to marry a bondswoman in order to rectify his offspring, since he can manumit them and make them freemen. That is indeed why the Sages did not forbid the marriage of a bondswoman to a bastard, namely, in the interests of the legitimization of the children.

5. If a man half-slave and half-free has intercourse with a married woman, the child of that union has no prospect of legitimization, since the legitimate part of him is inextricably mixed with the illegitimate one. He is therefore forbidden to marry a bondswoman, and his descendants will have his status for ever.

6. If a heathen has intercourse with a bondswoman who had immersed herself, the child is deemed a slave; if a slave who had immersed himself has intercourse with a heathen woman, the child is considered a heathen; in both cases the child assumes the status of the mother. If, however, a heathen has intercourse with a heathen bondswoman, or a heathen slave with a heathen freewoman, the child retains the status of the father.

7. A male bastard may marry a female proselyte, and a female bastard may marry a male proselyte. But the children of both these unions are deemed bastards, since the child retains the status of the impaired parent, as it is said, *into the congregation of the Lord* (Deut. 23:3), and a congregation of proselytes is not called "a congregation of the Lord."

8. If a proselyte woman marries a proselyte and gives birth to a son, even though both conception and birth have taken place after they had become proselytes, the son is nevertheless permitted to marry a female bastard. And so down to his great-grandson,

until his proselyte descent sinks into oblivion, and the fact that he is a descendant of proselytes is no longer known. After that he is forbidden to marry a bastard. This regulation applies equally to proselytes and to manumitted slaves.

9. If a proselyte marries a daughter of Israel, or if an Israelite marries a woman proselyte, their child is regarded as an Israelite in every respect and is forbidden to marry a bastard.

10. There are three classes of bastards: an assured bastard, a doubtful bastard, and a bastard on the authority of the Scribes. Who is deemed an assured bastard? The offspring of an undoubtedly forbidden union, as we have explained. A doubtful bastard is the offspring of a doubtfully forbidden union, for instance, if a man has intercourse with a woman whose betrothal to another man or whose divorce is doubtful. Similar considerations apply to a bastard on the authority of the Scribes. For instance, if a woman, having heard that her husband had died, remarries, and thereupon it comes to light that her first husband is still living, and if he then has intercourse with her while she is still wed to the second man, the resulting child is deemed a bastard on the authority of the Scribes.

11. If an unmarried woman becomes pregnant by way of adultery, she should be asked, "What is this expected child," or "this newborn child?" If she says, "It is a legitimate child, for I had intercourse with an Israelite," she is to be believed, and the child is to be considered legitimate, even if the majority of the inhabitants of the city in which she had committed adultery are such as she could not lawfully marry.

12. If the mother dies prior to this inquiry, or if she is deaf, mute, or an imbecile, or if she says, "I had intercourse with So-and-so who is a bastard," or "with So-and-so who is a *Nathin*," the child is deemed a bastard out of doubt, even if that person admits the parentage. For just as she had committed adultery with the man who admits the fact, so may she have committed adultery also with some other man. Such a child is called *šĕtuḳi*,

i.e. one who knows his mother, but does not know for certain his father.

13. The same applies to a foundling, who is called *'ăsufi,* and is considered a bastard out of doubt, since we do not know his parentage.

14. Should an unmarried woman commit adultery, and then say, "This child is the son of So-and-so," if that person is of legitimate descent the child also is deemed legitimate, but she may not be believed to the extent of establishing that the child was begotten by that particular person. It would appear to me, however, that we should take her assertion into consideration to the extent of forbidding the child to marry the relatives of that person, out of doubt. If that person is a bastard, her statement alone is insufficient to make the child an undoubted bastard, as we have explained, and he is only deemed a bastard out of doubt.

15. If, however, the man who is presumed to be the father of the child says, "This son of mine is a bastard," he is to be believed. But should the son also have sons of his own, the father is not to be believed, since Scripture gives him credence only as regards his son, as it is said, *he shall acknowledge the first-born, the son of the hated* (Deut. 21:17), i.e. acknowledge him to others.

16. Just as a man is to be believed when he says, "This my son is my first-born," so is he to be believed when he says, "This my son is a bastard," or "the son of a divorcée," or "of a woman released from levirate marriage." Similarly, if his wife is pregnant, he is to be believed if he says, "This expected child is not mine, but a bastard," and the child then becomes an assured bastard. If a man declares himself to be a bastard, he is also to be believed, to the extent of rendering himself forbidden to a daughter of Israel, but he is then equally forbidden to marry a female bastard until it has become certain that he is indeed a bastard. The same applies also to his son, but if the latter, too, has children, the father is not to be believed to the extent of invalidating his grandchildren; his testimony is effective only in regard to himself.

46088

17. If a betrothed maiden becomes pregnant while still in her father's house, the child is presumed to be a bastard, and is forbidden both to a daughter of Israel and to a female bastard. If his mother, when questioned, says, "I became pregnant by my fiancé," she is to be believed, and the child is then deemed lawful. If the fiancé contradicts her and says, "I have never had intercourse with her," the child is deemed a bastard, since even if the child had been presumed to be his son, and he had said, "This my son is a bastard," he would have been believed. The woman, however, should not be presumed to be a harlot, but her assertion, "I had intercourse with my fiancé," is to be believed, so that she is not to be considered a harlot. If she is then married to a priest, her marriage with him need not be annulled, and any child which she may have by him is deemed legitimate.

18. Should there be common gossip about a betrothed maiden involving her fiancé as well as other men, even if the fiancé has intercourse with her in the house of his father-in-law, the resulting child is deemed a bastard out of doubt. For just as she had abandoned herself to her fiancé, so may she have abandoned herself to others. If, however, she says when questioned, "This expected child is by my fiancé," the child is deemed legitimate, as we have explained.

19. If a married woman who has become pregnant says, "This expected child is not by my husband," she is not to be believed to the extent of invalidating the child, and the child is presumed to be legitimate, for the Torah accepts only the word of the father in this respect. If, however, the husband says, "It is not my child," or if he is away beyond the sea, the child is presumed to be a bastard. If she declares that she had become pregnant by a heathen or a slave, the child is nevertheless deemed legitimate, since the husband cannot contradict her in this matter. A foetus cannot remain in the womb for more than twelve months.

20. If there is a rumor abroad concerning a married woman that she had committed adultery while being under her husband,

Lincoln Christian College

and everyone gossips about her, no apprehension need be felt that her children may be bastards, since most of her intercourse is with her husband. One may, at the outset, marry her daughter, but the mother herself is under suspicion of being a harlot. If she is excessively dissolute, apprehension should be felt even concerning her children.

21. According to the Torah, a doubtful bastard is permitted to enter the congregation, as it is said, *A bastard shall not enter into the assembly of the Lord* (Deut. 23:3). An assured bastard is thus forbidden to enter the congregation, but not a bastard out of doubt. The Sages, however, have adopted a higher standard of purity of descent, and have forbidden even doubtful bastards to enter the congregation. Consequently, an assured bastard may marry an assured female bastard, but a doubtful bastard, a *šĕṯuḳi,* or a foundling is forbidden to marry a daughter of Israel.

22. A doubtful bastard is likewise forbidden to marry a bastard, or even a doubtful bastard, since one of them may not be a bastard at all, while the other may be an assured bastard. But a person who is a bastard on the authority of the Scribes may marry a woman who is likewise a bastard on the authority of the Scribes. Similarly, all other doubtful cases are forbidden to intermarry with one another.

23. How so? *Šĕṯuḳim,* foundlings, and doubtful bastards are forbidden to intermarry with one another; if they do contract a marriage, they must not continue in it, but must be divorced, and the child remains in the same doubtful state as its parents. There is no recourse for these doubtful cases, except to marry proselytes, in which case the offspring retains the status of the impaired parent.

24. How so? If a šĕṯuḳi or a foundling marries a female proselyte or a manumitted bondswoman, or if a proselyte or a manumitted slave marries a female šĕṯuḳi or foundling, the child is considered a šĕṯuḳi or a foundling.

25. If a foundling is found in a city containing heathens,

whether the majority of the inhabitants are Israelites or heathens, the child is considered a doubtful heathen as regards descent, and if he betroths an Israelite woman she must be given a divorce on account of the doubt. Whosoever slew him was not executed for it.

26. If the court immerses the child for the purpose of making him a proselyte, or if he immerses himself after he grows up, he is regarded like all other foundlings found in the cities of Israel. If the majority of the inhabitants of that city are heathens, it is permitted to give him forbidden food to eat. If the majority are Israelites, his lost articles must be restored to him, as in the case of an Israelite. If the population is equally divided, it is obligatory to support him, as in the case of an Israelite, and to clear away a pile of debris on the Sabbath in order to rescue him. With respect to civil damages, he is subject to the rule which governs every other case of doubt in financial matters, that is, the claimant against him must produce evidence.

27. It would appear to me that in any country in which there is a bondswoman or a heathen woman capable of childbearing, if a foundling found there should marry a proselyte woman, as we have explained, she is to be considered a doubtfully married woman, since such a foundling must be considered a doubtful slave or heathen. If another man has intercourse with this woman, he is exempt, since the death penalty may not be inflicted in case of doubt. And similarly, it would appear to me that if a šĕṯuḳi marries a woman who may be within the unions forbidden to him, she becomes a doubtfully married woman, since betrothal cannot take effect in the case of forbidden unions.

28. What women are they who are possibly within the unions forbidden to him? Any woman whose father or brother was living when his mother became pregnant with him, or who was divorced or widowed at that time, since she may have been the wife of his father or of his father's brother.

29. On what evidence do I base my opinion that a šĕṯuḳi or a foundling is not prohibited to every woman who may be within the unions forbidden to him? Because a legitimate child whose

mother had been questioned is not prohibited to any woman who may possibly be within the unions forbidden to him, although it is said in Scripture, *Profane not thy daughter to make her a harlot* (Lev. 19:29), and our Sages have said that if a man were to do this, the result would be that a father might marry his own daughter or a brother his own sister. If the law had been that a man who is not certain of the identity of his father may not marry a woman who might possibly be within the unions forbidden to him, the world would never have come to this pass, and it would not have happened that *the land [has] become full of lewdness* (*ibid.*). Hence you learn that forbidden unions cannot be prohibited or presumed to constitute near of kin out of doubt, until it is known for a certainty that the woman is indeed of a forbidden union. For should you maintain the contrary, all fatherless persons in the world who do not know their fathers would not be permitted to marry anyone anywhere, lest they chance upon a woman who is within the forbidden unions.

30. If a child is found abandoned in the roadway, and a man comes forth and declares, "This is my son, and I have abandoned him," he is to be believed; the same applies to the mother. If after the child is gathered up from the street, his father and mother come forth and say, "This is our child," they are not to be believed, since he is already known as a foundling. In years of famine, however, they are to be believed, since they may have abandoned him because of hunger and out of a desire that others should sustain him, and it may be for that reason that they remained silent until he was gathered up.

31. If the child is found circumcised, or swaddled, or salted, or with his eyes painted with kohl, or with an amulet hanging from his neck, or if he is found under a tree surrounded by a thicket, so that a wild beast could not reach him, and the place is near the city; or if he is found in a synagogue adjacent to the public domain, or by the side of the public domain, he is not to be considered a foundling, for once precautions had been taken that he should not die, he is presumed to be legitimate. If, however, he is

found cast away in the middle of the road, or far from the city, be it even under a tree or in a synagogue, or suspended from a tree in such a position that a wild beast could reach him, he is deemed a foundling.

32. A midwife is to be believed if she declares, "This child is a priest," or "a Levite," or "a *Nathin,*" or "a bastard," since in such a case there is no presumption of descent, and we do not know his genealogy. When does this apply? When the midwife is known to be a truthful person and no one has ever challenged her veracity. If, however, her veracity has been questioned, even by a single individual who claimed that her testimony was false, she may no longer be believed, and the child is presumed to be legitimate, but of unattested descent.

33. It is self-evident that a male *šĕṯuḳi* may not marry a female šĕṯuḳi, nor may a male foundling marry a female foundling, since their status is doubtful. Assured bastards and *Nethinim,* however, are permitted to intermarry with one another, and the offspring of the marriage is considered a bastard. A šĕṯuḳi and a foundling are permitted to intermarry with Nethinim and other proselytes, and the offspring of the marriage has a doubtful status.

CHAPTER XVI

1. If a man who is crushed or maimed in his privy parts marries a daughter of Israel and has intercourse with her, he is liable to a flogging, as it is said, *He that is crushed or maimed in his privy parts shall not enter into the assembly of the Lord* (Deut. 23:2). He may, however, marry a proselyte or a manumitted bondswoman, and even a priest whose privy parts are crushed may marry a proselyte or a manumitted bondswoman, since he does not retain his sanctity. Indeed, even a female *Nathin* or any other woman of doubtful descent is permitted to him.

2. Since a man with crushed or maimed privy parts is forbid-

den to enter the congregation, the Sages did not prohibit his marriage to a Nathin or to any other doubtful case. He is, however, forbidden to marry an assured bastard, since she is prohibited on the authority of the Torah.

3. Who is deemed "crushed in his privy parts"? A man whose testicles have been crushed. "Maimed" means a man whose genital organ has been amputated. There are three organs which may cause a male to be invalidated to enter the congregation: the genital organ, the testicles, and the tubes in which the semen is generated and which are called the testicular cords. If one of these three organs is crushed or bruised, the man is invalidated.

4. How so? If the genital organ is crushed or bruised, or if it has been amputated, cutting away the corona or higher, the man is invalidated. If, however, the head of the corona has been cut away, but there remains so much as a hair-thread of it encircling the whole organ, he is considered valid. If the organ is amputated above the corona, but in the shape of an obliquely trimmed reed pen or of a spout, he is also considered valid.

5. If the organ is perforated below the corona, it is valid. If the corona itself is perforated, and if at the time of a nocturnal pollution the semen oozes out of the perforation, it is invalid. Should the perforation subsequently close itself, the organ reverts to its validity. If it is perforated below the corona, but the other end of the perforation is higher up and in the corona, it is invalid, since a defect anywhere in the corona prevents validation.

6. If the seminal tube becomes obstructed, and the semen is seen issuing from the urinary duct, the organ is invalid.

7. If both testicles are severed, or only one, or if one of them is crushed or bruised, or is missing or perforated, it is invalid. If both testicular cords, or one of them, are severed, bruised, or crushed, they are likewise invalid.

8. If one of the testicular cords has an opening into the urinary duct, so that urine is passed from two places, from the urinary duct and from the seminal tube, it is valid.

9. All these invalidities which we have mentioned in this connection apply only to defects which are not due to an act of heaven, as when the organ has been severed by a man or a dog, or has been pierced by a thorn, and the like. If, however, the man was born with crushed or maimed privy parts or without testicles, or if he contracted a disease which caused these organs to cease functioning, or if the organs developed sores which caused them to become atrophied or to be severed, he is valid to enter the congregation, since all these are due to an act of heaven.

10. It is forbidden to mutilate the procreative organs, whether in man or in animal, beast, or bird, whether these be clean or unclean, whether in the Land of Israel or outside the Land. Even though it is said, *Neither shall ye do thus in your land* (Lev. 22:24), the Sages have learned by way of tradition that this prohibition applies everywhere, the purport of Scripture here being, "This shall not be done in Israel, whether upon their own bodies or upon the bodies of others." And whosoever practices castration is punishable by a flogging on the authority of the Torah, wherever he may be, and even if a person merely continues the process of castration begun by another person, he must be flogged.

11. How so? If one man amputates the genital organ, and then another amputates the testicles or dislocates them, and another cuts the testicular cords; or if one man crushes the genital organ, and then another dislocates it, and another amputates it, all of them must be flogged, even though the last person actually castrates a man, animal, beast, or bird which is already castrated. If a person castrates a female, whether of the human or of any other species, he is not liable to punishment.

12. If a person gives a potion of roots to a human being, or to a creature of the other species, in order to render it barren, he is not to be flogged on account of it, although it is forbidden. A woman is permitted to drink a potion of roots in order to render herself sterile, so that she would remain barren. If someone binds a man and sets a dog or another animal on him, so that it maims his privy parts, or if he holds him in water or snow until his sexual

organs become useless, he is not to be flogged, unless he performs the act of castration with his own hand. Nevertheless, it is fitting that he should be given the flogging prescribed for disobedience.

13. An Israelite is forbidden to tell a heathen to castrate his animal. If, however, the heathen takes the animal of his own accord and castrates it, it is permitted. If the Israelite uses an artifice to achieve this purpose, he is to be fined, and the animal is to be sold to another Israelite. He may sell it, however, to his own adult son, but may not sell or present it to his minor son.

CHAPTER XVII

1. Three classes of women are forbidden to all Israelites of priestly descent: a divorcée, a harlot, and a profaned woman; four are forbidden to a High Priest: the same three, and a widow. Whether he is a High Priest installed with the ceremony of anointing, or a High Priest installed by mere investiture with the additional vestments; whether he is an officiating High Priest, or a substitute High Priest; whether he is the priest anointed as the chaplain of the army—all these are enjoined to marry a virgin and are forbidden to marry a widow.

2. If a priest, whether a High Priest or a common priest, marries a woman of one of these three classes and has intercourse with her, he is liable to a flogging; but if he has intercourse with her adulterously, he is not so liable, insofar as she is a harlot, or a divorcée, or a profaned woman, for it is said, *they shall not take* (Lev. 21:7), "taking" implying both marriage and intercourse.

3. On the other hand, if a High Priest has intercourse with a widow, he must be flogged once, even if he did not betroth her, as it is said, *and he shall not profane* (Lev. 21:15). By having intercourse with her, he has profaned her and thus disqualified her for the priestly privileges. In the case of the harlot, the di-

vorcée, and the profaned woman, they have already been profaned before his intercourse. Consequently a High Priest must be flogged for intercourse with a widow only, even if there was no marriage, for he has thereby profaned her, and yet he is enjoined not to profane valid people, that is both the woman and his own progeny.

4. If a High Priest marries a widow and has intercourse with her, he must be flogged twice, once on account of *he shall not take a widow* (Lev. 21:14), and once on account of *he shall not profane*. But whether he is a High Priest or a common priest, if he marries a woman of the four aforementioned classes, but has no intercourse with her, he is not liable to a flogging.

5. Whenever he is to be flogged, she also is to be flogged, and whenever he is not to be flogged she also is not, since there is no distinction between man and woman as regards punishment, with the sole exception of the designated bondmaid, as we have explained.

6. Any priest who has intercourse with a heathen woman, whether he is a High Priest or a common priest, must be flogged for intercourse with a harlot. The reason is that she is not subject to betrothal, and he is forbidden to have intercourse with a harlot, whether Israelite or heathen.

7. A woman released from levirate marriage is forbidden to a priest on the authority of the Scribes, since she is deemed analogous to a divorcée, and if he marries her he must be flogged for disobedience on the same authority. If her status as a woman released from levirate marriage is doubtful, he is not obligated to divorce her, and both she and her child are considered legitimate. The reason is that the Sages' decree applies only to a woman whose aforementioned status is certain, not to one whose status is in doubt. Similarly, if a woman's status as a divorcée, a widow, a harlot, or a profaned woman is in doubt, he must be given the flogging prescribed for disobedience, and must dismiss her with a writ of divorcement.

8. It is a major principle with regard to all prohibitions in the Torah that one prohibition cannot take legal hold where another prohibition already exists, unless both are coincidental, or the second prohibition introduces factors additional to the first, or is more comprehensive in its application than the first.

9/10. Consequently, if a widow becomes in succession a divorcée, a profaned woman, and a harlot, and thereafter a High Priest has intercourse with her, he becomes liable to a fourfold flogging for the one act of intercourse. The reason is that a widow is forbidden to a High Priest, but permitted to a common priest; when she subsequently becomes a divorcée, an additional prohibition takes effect, in that she thereby becomes forbidden also to a common priest. Consequently, an additional prohibition has been added to the original prohibition of a widow; but she is still permitted to partake of the heave offering. When thereupon she becomes a profaned woman, again an additional prohibition is added, since she is now also forbidden to eat of the heave offering, although she is still permitted to an Israelite. When finally she becomes a harlot, thus introducing here harlotry, whereby an Israelite's wife becomes forbidden to him if she willingly commits adultery, an additional prohibition takes effect once more. The same law applies to a common priest if he has intercourse with a divorcée who has consecutively become a profaned woman and a harlot—a triple flogging must be inflicted upon him for the one act of intercourse. If, however, the sequence of her disabilities is different, he must be flogged only once.

11. If a woman is widowed or divorced from more than one husband, and then marries a priest, only one flogging must be administered for each act of intercourse. A widow is forbidden regardless of whether she is widowed from betrothal or from marriage.

12. If a High Priest's brother dies and leaves a widow, even from the betrothal, the High Priest may not enter into levirate marriage with her, but must give her her release. If she becomes

subject to levirate marriage while he is a common priest, and he is subsequently elevated to the high priesthood, he may not enter into levirate marriage with her after his elevation, even if he had betrothed her to himself by a verbal declaration while he was a common priest. If, however, he had betrothed any other widow while he was a common priest, and was subsequently elevated to the high priesthood, he may marry her after his elevation. If she is doubtfully betrothed and her fiancé dies, she is deemed a doubtful widow.

13. It is a positive commandment incumbent upon a High Priest that he may marry only a virgin maiden. Once she becomes mature, she becomes forbidden to him, as it is said, *And he shall take a wife in her virginity* (Lev. 21:13); *a wife* excludes a minor; *in her virginity* excludes a mature woman. How can she leave the status of a minor while not yet attaining the status of a mature woman? While she is a maiden. He may never marry two wives at the same time, since Scripture says, *a wife,* i.e. one, and not two.

14. A High Priest may not marry a woman who has been deflowered accidentally, even if she has never had intercourse with a man. If she had intercourse with a man unnaturally, she is considered as though she had had natural intercourse; if she had intercourse with an animal, she is permitted to a High Priest.

15. If a High Priest marries a nonvirgin, he is not liable to a flogging, but must divorce her. If he marries a mature woman or a woman who was deflowered accidentally, he may retain her. If he becomes betrothed to a nonvirgin and is subsequently elevated to the high priesthood, he may marry her after his elevation.

16. If he violates or seduces a virgin maiden, even if the violation or seduction took place while he was a common priest, and he is subsequently elevated to the high priesthood before he marries her, he may not marry her; if he does so nevertheless, he must divorce her.

17. If he betrothes a minor and she reaches maturity while she

is under him, but before the marriage, he may not marry her, since she has undergone a physical change; but if he has married her, he need not divorce her.

18. There is no difference between a woman divorced after betrothal and one divorced after marriage, but a woman who may exercise the right of refusal is permitted to a priest, even if her husband had given her a divorce and had then taken her back, and she subsequently exercised the right of refusal against him, as we have explained in the Laws Concerning Divorce. If a woman who is not liable to release from levirate marriage is so released, she is not thereby invalidated for the priesthood.

19. If a rumor is spread abroad that a certain priest had written or given a writ of divorcement to his wife, but she still lives with him and has intercourse with him, she may not be compelled to leave her husband. If she then marries another priest, she must leave the latter.

20. If a rumor is spread about her in the town that she had been betrothed and then divorced, it should be heeded, as we have explained in the Laws Concerning Divorce. If, however, rumor has it that she had been released from levirate marriage, no account need be taken of it.

21. If a rumor is current about a virgin that she had lost her virginity, no attention should be paid to it, and she may marry a High Priest. If the rumor is to the effect that she is a bondswoman, again no attention should be paid to it, and she may marry even a priest. If the town rumor has it that she had committed adultery, it too should be disregarded. Even if her husband had divorced her on the ground of transgression against Israelite custom, or because of evidence of indecent conduct, but died before he could give her the writ of divorcement, she is nevertheless permitted to a priest, since a woman cannot be rendered forbidden for these reasons, except on explicit testimony or by her own admission.

CHAPTER XVIII

1. We have learned by tradition that the term "harlot" as designated in the Torah means any woman who is not a daughter of Israel, or a daughter of Israel who has had intercourse with a man whom she is forbidden to marry—the prohibition applying equally to everyone in this category—or one who has had intercourse with an unfit priest, even though she is permitted to marry him. Consequently if a woman has intercourse with an animal, she is, although liable to death by stoning, not thereby rendered a harlot, nor is she invalidated from marrying into the priesthood, seeing that she has not had intercourse with a man. Also, if a man has intercourse with a menstruant, even though this is punishable by extinction, she is not thereby rendered a harlot, nor is she invalidated for the priesthood, since she is not forbidden to marry him.

2. Similarly, if a man has intercourse with an unmarried woman, even if she is a prostitute who has abandoned herself to everyone, and even though she is liable to a flogging, she is not thereby rendered a harlot, nor is she invalidated for the priesthood, since she is not forbidden to marry her paramour. If, however, she has intercourse with a man prohibited by a negative commandment equally applicable to all and not restricted to priests; or if she has intercourse with a man prohibited by a positive commandment—and needless to say, with a man within the forbidden unions, or with a heathen or slave—she is deemed a harlot, since she is forbidden to marry such a man.

3. Similarly, a proselyte woman or a manumitted bondswoman, even if she became a proselyte or was manumitted when less than three years old, is considered a harlot, since she is not a daughter of Israel and is forbidden to the priesthood. Hence the Sages have said that if a heathen, a slave, a *Nathin,* a bastard, an Am-

monite or Moabite proselyte, an Egyptian or Edomite proselyte of the first and second generations, a man with crushed or maimed privy parts, or an unfit priest has intercourse with an Israelite woman, he renders her a harlot and she is thereby forbidden to the priesthood. If she herself is of priestly descent, she is invalidated from eating of the heave offering. Similarly, if a nonpriest has intercourse with a woman subject to levirate marriage, he thereby renders her a harlot. A woman who is barren, however, is permitted to a priest and is not considered a harlot.

4. If a man has intercourse with a woman within the secondary degrees of propinquity, and the like—for example, if he has intercourse with a near relative of his sister-in-law whom he has released from levirate marriage, or with that sister-in-law herself—he does not thereby render her a harlot, since according to the Torah she is not forbidden to marry him, as we have explained in the Laws Concerning Levirate Marriage.

5. Hence you learn that the status of a harlot is not dependent upon forbidden intercourse, seeing that if a man has intercourse with a menstruant, a prostitute, or a woman who has previously had intercourse with an animal, the act of intercourse is a forbidden one, yet she is not thereby rendered a harlot, while on the other hand, in the case of a woman married to an unfit priest, the intercourse is permitted, as will be explained, yet she is thereby rendered a harlot. The matter is thus dependent solely upon impairment, the Sages having learned by tradition that she becomes impaired only by intercourse with a man forbidden to her, or with an unfit priest, as we have said.

6. Any woman who has intercourse with a man who renders her a harlot, whether by rape or by consent, whether willfully or by error, whether naturally or unnaturally—once he has initiated with her, she is invalidated for the priesthood, because she has become a harlot. The only condition is that she be at least three years and one day old, and that he be at least nine years and one day old. Consequently if a married woman has intercourse with

another man, whether by rape or by consent, she is invalidated for the priesthood.

7. Should the wife of a priest be raped, her husband must be flogged if he subsequently has intercourse with her, on account of the defilement involved, as it is said, *her former husband, who sent her away, may not take her again to be his wife, after that she is defiled* (Deut. 24:4), indicating the general rule that all married women who have had intercourse with other men are forbidden to their husbands. Scripture then proceeds to except the wife of an Israelite who has been raped and nevertheless remains permitted to her husband, as it is said, *neither she be taken in the act* (Num. 5:13). A priest's wife, however, remains subject to the general prohibition, seeing that she has become a harlot.

8. The raped wife of an Israelite, while permitted to her husband, is forbidden to the priesthood. If the wife of a priest says to her husband, "I have been raped," or "I have been the victim of an error, whereby some man had intercourse with me," or if a single witness comes forth and testifies against her that she had committed adultery, whether by rape or of her own will, she is not thereby forbidden to her husband, since it may be that she had set her eyes upon another man. If, however, he believes her or the witness, and gives credence to their words, he should divorce her in order to free himself from doubt.

9. If a priest's wife says to her husband, "I have been raped," even though she is permitted to her husband, as we have explained, she is nevertheless forbidden to any other priest in the world after her husband's death, seeing that she has admitted being a harlot and has thereby rendered herself prohibited, in the same manner as a person who declares a certain portion of meat forbidden to himself.

10. If a priest betrothes a minor or an adult woman and after some time has intercourse with her, and then alleges that he found her already deflowered by another man, she is rendered forbidden to him out of doubt, since it is uncertain whether the illicit act

had taken place before or after betrothal. If, however, an Israelite makes such an allegation, she does not become forbidden to him, since in this case there is a double doubt: first, whether it happened before or after betrothal, and secondly, if it happened after betrothal, whether it was against her will or with her consent, since a raped woman is permitted to an Israelite, as we have explained.

11. Consequently if a girl's father betrothes her to an Israelite when she is less than three years and one day old, and after some time the latter alleges that he found her already deflowered by another man, she becomes forbidden to him out of doubt, since in this case there is only one doubt, whether it happened against her will or with her consent, and in a doubt involving a Scriptural prohibition the more stringent alternative must prevail.

12. If a man suspects his wife of having secluded herself with another man, and she fails to drink the curse-causing water, she is forbidden to a priest, since she is a harlot out of doubt. It is immaterial whether she herself refuses to drink or whether the husband refuses to administer the potion, whether testimony is offered which prevents her from drinking, whether the court also suspects her, or whether she belongs to a category of women who are not designated to drink the curse-causing water—once she does not drink it for any reason whatsoever, she is forbidden to the priesthood out of doubt.

13. If an unmarried woman is seen to have intercourse with a man who then goes on his way, and when people thereupon say to her, "Who is this man who had intercourse with you?" replies that he is a man of legitimate status, she is to be believed. And not only this, but even if people, observing that she is pregnant, say, "By whom have you become pregnant?" and she answers that it was by a man of legitimate status, she is to be believed, and she is permitted to a priest.

14. This rule applies, however, only where the intercourse has taken place at a crossroads, or in the corners of the fields where

passers-by are frequent; moreover, the majority of the passers-by must be persons of legitimate status, and the majority of the inhabitants of the city whence these passers-by had come must also be legitimate, since in this case the Sages have established a higher standard with regard to descent by requiring a twofold majority. If, however, the majority of the passers-by are of invalid descent, such as heathens, bastards, or the like, they render her invalid, even if the majority of the inhabitants of the city whence they had come are legitimate; or if the majority of the inhabitants of the city are of invalid descent, even though the majority of the passers-by are legitimate, apprehension should be felt concerning her, since she may have had intercourse with one who invalidated her, and she is not permitted to marry a priest in the first instance. But if she does marry him, she need not be divorced.

15. If she was seen to have intercourse or became pregnant in a city, even if but one of its inhabitants is a heathen, an unfit priest, a slave, or the like, she is forbidden to be married to a priest in the first instance, since in the case of a fixed object the possibility of what is permitted and what is forbidden is assumed to be equal. If, however, she has been married, she need not be divorced, since her contention is that she had had intercourse with a valid man.

16. If she is mute, or deaf, or if she says, "I do not know with whom I have had intercourse," or if she is a minor who cannot distinguish between a valid and an invalid man, she is deemed a harlot out of doubt. If she has been married to a priest she must be divorced, unless the two majorities of those with whom she could have come in contact consist of valid men.

17. If a captive woman is ransomed when three years and one day old or more, she is forbidden to a priest, since she is a harlot out of doubt, seeing that a heathen may have had intercourse with her. If she can produce one witness to testify that she was never alone with a heathen, she is permitted to the priesthood. The evidence of even a slave, a bondswoman, or a relative is acceptable

for such testimony. If two captive women give evidence concerning each other, they are also to be believed. Since the prohibition of all doubtful cases rests only on the authority of the Scribes, they have ruled leniently with regard to a captive woman.

18. Similarly, a minor speaking in his innocence is to be believed. It happened once that a minor had been taken captive together with his mother, and talking in his innocence said, "We were taken captive among heathens; when I went out to draw water my attention remained fixed upon her, and likewise when I went out to gather firewood my attention remained fixed upon her," whereupon the Sages permitted her on the strength of this statement to marry a priest.

19. The testimony of a husband to the effect that his wife who had been taken captive had not been defiled is not acceptable, since no man may testify in his own behalf. Similarly, the wife's own bondswoman may not testify in her favor, although the bondswoman of her husband may do so. But if her bondswoman spoke in all innocence, she is to be believed.

20. If a priest gives evidence on behalf of a captive woman that she had not been defiled, he himself may not marry her, since he may have set his eyes upon her. If, however, he ransoms her and then testifies in her behalf, he may marry her, for had he not known that she had not been defiled, he would not have expended his money on her.

21. If a woman says, "I was taken captive, but have not been defiled," she is to be believed, since the mouth that forbids is the mouth that permits. This is so even if there is also one witness who testifies that she had been taken captive; but should there be two witnesses to testify that she had been taken captive, her statement that she has not been defiled is not acceptable, unless there is also one witness to the same effect. If there are two witnesses that she had been taken captive, and one of them testifies that she has been defiled, while the other contradicts him and testifies that she has not been defiled and no heathen has been alone with her until she was ransomed, she is deemed permitted to the priesthood,

even if the witness who testifies that she has not been defiled is a woman or a bondswoman.

22. If a woman says, "I was taken captive, but have not been defiled," and the court thereupon allows her to marry a priest, and subsequently two witnesses testify that she had been taken captive, she may marry a priest in the first instance, and the permission given to her may not be withdrawn. Even if the captor enters after her and we actually behold her a captive in the hands of her master, nevertheless the permission granted her previously may not be withdrawn, but she must be guarded from now on until such time as she is ransomed.

23. If two witnesses subsequently come forth and testify that she has been defiled, she must be divorced, even if she is already married and has children. If there is only one witness, his testimony is of no effect. If she says, "I was taken captive, but have not been defiled, and I have witnesses to testify that I have not been defiled," the court should not say, "Let us wait until witnesses come forth," but she should be given permission to marry at once. And not only this, but even if there is a rumor about her that there are witnesses to her defilement, permission should be granted to her until such time as these witnesses shall come forth, seeing that the Sages have ruled leniently in the case of a captive woman.

24. If a father says, "I gave my daughter in marriage and then had her divorced, she being a minor," he is to be believed. If he says, "I gave her in marriage and then had her divorced while she was a minor, but now she has attained her majority," he is not to be believed insofar as the presumption of her being a divorcée is concerned. If he says, "She was taken captive and I ransomed her," whether she is a minor or an adult, he is not to be believed, since the Torah gives credence to a father's testimony only in respect to rendering her forbidden as a married woman, as it is said, *I gave my daughter unto this man to wife* (Deut. 22:16), but not in respect to invalidating her as a harlot.

25. If a priest's wife is declared forbidden to him because she

had been taken captive, she is permitted to reside in the same courtyard with him, since this is a case of doubt, but his children and the members of his household must be with him continually to keep watch over him.

26. If a city is besieged and captured after being entirely surrounded by heathen soldiers, so that no woman could have escaped without being seen and falling into their hands, all the women in that city become invalid for the priesthood as though they had been taken captive, since heathens may have had intercourse with them. The only exceptions are those less than three years old, as we have explained.

27. If it is possible for even one woman to have escaped without the heathens' knowledge, or if there is even one hiding place in the city, even though it could hold only one woman, that woman frees them all.

28. How does that woman free them all, so that every one of the women in the city who says, "I have not been defiled," is to be believed even though she has no witnesses? The answer is that every one of the women could say, "I escaped when the city was captured," or "I was in this hiding place and was saved," and would have to be believed. Or she could even say, "I neither escaped nor hid myself, yet I have not been defiled."

29. When does this apply? When the attacking army belongs to the same kingdom and settles down in that city, without fear of pursuit; therefore apprehension need be felt that they may have had intercourse with the women. If, however, an army from another kingdom raids the territory, overruns it, and passes on, the women are not rendered forbidden, since such invaders have no leisure for intercourse, for they forthwith busy themselves with pillage and then flee. If, however, they have taken women captive so that they came under their control, these women become forbidden, even if the Israelites pursue the raiders and rescue the women from their hands.

30. If a woman is imprisoned by heathens for an offense concerning property, she is still permitted to the priesthood; but if it is for a capital offense, she is forbidden to the priesthood. Consequently if her husband is a priest, she is forbidden to him. When does this apply? When the power of the Israelites is paramount over the heathens and they fear them. When the power of the heathens is paramount over the Israelites, even if she is imprisoned for an offense concerning property, once she comes under the control of heathens she is forbidden to the priesthood, unless a witness testifies in her favor just as in the case of a captive woman, as we have explained.

CHAPTER XIX

1. Who is deemed a profaned woman? One born of a priest and a woman forbidden to him. In addition, any woman forbidden to a priest who has intercourse with him becomes thereby profaned. The priest himself, however, does not become unfit as a result of that transgression.

2. Whether the intercourse takes place against her will or with her consent, whether it is natural or unnatural, once he initiates with her she becomes profaned. This applies only when the priest is at least nine years and one day old, and the woman forbidden to him is at least three years and one day old.

3. How so? If a priest nine years and one day old and over has intercourse with a divorcée or a harlot, or if a High Priest has intercourse with one of these or with a widow, or if he marries a nonvirgin and has intercourse with her, these women are deemed profaned forever. If the woman has a child, either by him or by another priest, that child too is considered profaned. If, however, a priest betrothes a woman forbidden to the priesthood and she is widowed or divorced from the betrothal, she is not thereby rendered profaned. But if the marriage takes place, even without

intercourse, she becomes profaned, since every married woman is presumed to be a nonvirgin, even if she is found in fact to be still a virgin.

4. If a High Priest marries a mature woman, or a woman who had been accidentally deflowered, he does not thereby render her profaned. Similarly, if he has intercourse out of wedlock with a nonvirgin, he does not thereby render her profaned.

5. If a priest has intercourse with a woman within the forbidden unions—with the exception of a menstruant—or with a woman forbidden to him by a negative commandment which applies equally to all, he thereby renders her a harlot, as we have explained. If he or another priest has intercourse with her again, she becomes thereby a profaned woman, and his children by her are also considered profaned. Consequently if a priest has intercourse with a woman who is under obligation to marry her levir and she becomes pregnant from the first act of intercourse, the child is deemed valid for the priesthood, since she does not belong to one of the categories of women forbidden to the priesthood, but she herself is thereby rendered a harlot. If, therefore, he has intercourse with her a second time and she becomes pregnant again and gives birth, both she and the child are considered profaned, since it is the offspring of a union forbidden to a priest.

6. Similarly, if a priest has intercourse with a proselyte woman or a manumitted bondswoman, he renders her profaned, and his children by her are also deemed profaned. If a priest has intercourse with a menstruant, the child is considered valid and not profaned, since the prohibition of a menstruant is not peculiar to priests, but applies equally to all.

7. If a priest marries a divorcée who is pregnant, either by him or by another man, and a child is born while she is profaned, the child is considered valid, since it did not come from seed of transgression.

8. We have already explained that a woman released from levirate marriage is forbidden to a priest on the authority of the

Scribes. Consequently, if a priest has intercourse with such a woman, he renders her profaned, and her children by any other priest are also considered profaned, but all this is on the authority of the Scribes. If, however, a priest has intercourse with a woman of the secondary degrees of propinquity, she and her children by him are valid for the priesthood, since the prohibition of the secondary degrees is equally applicable to all and is not peculiar to priests.

9. If a priest has intercourse with a harlot out of doubt, such as a doubtful proselyte or manumitted bondswoman, or with a doubtful divorcée, or if a High Priest has intercourse with a doubtful widow, she is deemed doubtfully profaned, and her child is doubtfully profaned for the priesthood.

10. There are thus three classes of profaned persons: one who is profaned on the authority of the Torah, one who is profaned on the authority of the Scribes, and one who is doubtfully profaned. In the case of one doubtfully profaned, the more stringent rulings touching priests and Israelites are applicable to him. He may not eat of the heave offering nor defile himself through contact with the dead, and he must marry only a woman permitted to a priest. If he does eat of the heave offering, or defiles himself through contact with the dead, or marries a woman forbidden to a priest, he is liable to the flogging prescribed for disobedience. The same law applies to a person who is profaned on the authority of the Scribes. A person who is assuredly profaned on the authority of the Torah is considered the same as a nonpriest. He may marry a divorcée and defile himself through contact with the dead, as it is said, *Speak unto the priests, the sons of Aaron* (Lev. 21:1); even though they are sons of Aaron, they are not forbidden to defile themselves through contact with the dead unless they also perform their priestly ministrations.

11. A male of priestly descent who is forbidden to marry a harlot or a profaned woman is also forbidden to marry a proselyte or a manumitted bondswoman, who are regarded as harlots, as

we have explained. A female of priestly descent, however, may be married to an unfit priest, to a proselyte, or to a manumitted slave, since there is no interdict against valid women marrying invalid men, as it is said, *the sons of Aaron* (Lev. 21:1), not "the daughters of Aaron." It follows, therefore, that a proselyte may marry not only a bastard, but also a woman of priestly descent!

12. If proselytes or manumitted slaves intermarry, and a female child is born to them, even after a number of generations, as long as no Israelite seed has been commingled with them, that female is forbidden to a priest. Nevertheless, if the marriage has taken place, she need not be divorced, since both her conception and her birth took place while her mother was an Israelite. If, however, a proselyte or a manumitted slave marries a daughter of Israel, or if an Israelite marries a proselyte or a manumitted bondswoman, the daughter of that marriage is permitted to the priesthood in the first instance.

13. If an Ammonite proselyte, or an Egyptian proselyte of the second generation, marries a daughter of Israel, even though their intercourse is in sin and their wives are thereby rendered harlots, as we have explained, their daughters are nevertheless permitted to the priesthood in the first instance.

14. If an unfit priest marries a valid woman, his children by her are regarded as profaned, and so are his subsequent male descendants even after a thousand generations, since the son of an unfit priest is himself unfit forever. In the case of a female child, she is forbidden to the priesthood, since she is deemed profaned. If, however, an Israelite marries a profaned woman, the child is valid. If, therefore, the child is a girl, she is permitted to the priesthood.

15. Priests, Levites, and Israelites are permitted to intermarry with one another, and the child retains the status of the father. Levites, Israelites, and profaned persons are also permitted to intermarry with one another, with the child again retaining the status of the father, as it is said, *and they declared their pedigrees*

after their families, by their fathers' houses (Num. 1:18): his father's house is considered his family, and not his mother's house.

16. Levites, Israelites, unfit priests, proselytes, and manumitted slaves are permitted to intermarry with one another. If a proselyte or a manumitted slave marries a Levite or Israelite woman, or a profaned woman, the son born of that union is deemed an Israelite. If an Israelite, a Levite, or an unfit priest marries a proselyte woman or a manumitted bondswoman, the child retains the status of the father.

17. All families are presumed to be of valid descent, and it is permitted to intermarry with them in the first instance. Nevertheless, should you see two families continually striving with one another, or a family which is constantly engaged in quarrels and altercations, or an individual who is exceedingly contentious with everyone, or is excessively impudent, apprehension should be felt concerning them, and it is advisable to keep one's distance from them, for these traits are indicative of invalid descent. Similarly, if a man always casts aspersions upon other people's descent—for instance, if he alleges that certain families and individuals are of blemished descent and refers to them as being bastards—suspicion is justified that he himself may be a bastard. And if he says that they are slaves, one may suspect that he himself is a slave, since whosoever blemishes others projects upon them his own blemish. Similarly, if a person exhibits impudence, cruelty, or misanthropy, and never performs an act of kindness, one should strongly suspect that he is of Gibeonite descent, since the distinctive traits of Israel, the holy nation, are modesty, mercy, and loving-kindness, while of the Gibeonites it is said, *Now the Gibeonites were not of the children of Israel* (2 Sam. 21:2), because they hardened their faces and refused to relent, showing no mercy to the sons of Saul, nor would they do a kindness unto the children of Israel by forgiving the sons of their king, nothwithstanding that Israel showed them grace at the beginning and spared their lives.

18. If the legitimacy of a family is contested, that is, if two

witnesses testify that a bastard or an unfit priest had become blended with it, or that there is slave blood in it, it is deemed a doubtful case, and if it is a priestly family, one should not marry a woman of that family until an investigation is made of the four maternal ancestresses, i.e. eight on both sides: her mother, her maternal grandmother, the mother of her maternal grandfather, the grandmother of her maternal grandfather, and on the father's side her paternal grandmother, the mother of her paternal grandmother, the mother of her paternal grandfather, and the maternal grandmother of her paternal grandfather.

19. If the family whose legitimacy is contested is a Levitical or an Israelite one, the investigation should be extended over one more pair, making ten maternal ancestresses in all. The reason is that intermingling is more prevalent among Levites and Israelites than among priestly families.

20. Why should the investigation be limited to the female line alone? Because when men quarrel with one another they customarily taunt each other with the blemish in his descent, so that if such a blemish exists it would have been heard of before, while women, even when quarreling, do not voice such allegations of blemished descent.

21. And why must the man who wishes to marry into a family with a weakened presumption of unblemished descent undertake such an investigation, while the woman who wishes to marry into it need not do so? Because women of valid descent are not enjoined against marrying men of invalid descent.

22. If a man is called a bastard, a *Nathin,* an unfit priest, or a slave, and he remains silent, apprehension should be felt concerning him and his family, and a person should not intermarry with them unless they are investigated, as we have explained.

23. If a doubtfully unfit priest had married into a family, a widow of that family is forbidden to a priest in the first instance. If, however, the marriage has taken place, she need not be di-

vorced, because of a double doubt: first, whether the widow is or is not the relict of that unfit priest; and secondly, even if it is assumed that she is the relict of that man, it is still not certain whether he is an unfit priest or not. If, however, an assured unfit priest had married into the family, every woman of that family is forbidden to a priest until an investigation is made, and should the marriage have taken place, she must be divorced. A similar ruling obtains if a doubtful bastard or an assured bastard is commingled with the family, since the same prohibition applies to both the wife of a bastard and the wife of an unfit priest as to marrying into the priesthood, as we have explained.

CHAPTER XX

1. All priests at the present time are priests by presumption only, and may eat only the sacred gifts set apart and consumed outside of the Temple and Jerusalem, meaning the heave offering eaten on the authority of the Scribes. Heave offering and dough offering enjoined in the Torah, on the other hand, may be eaten only by a priest of proven genealogy.

2. Who is deemed a priest of proven genealogy? Whosoever has two witnesses to testify that he is a priest, the son of So-and-so who was a priest, who himself was the son of So-and-so a priest, and so on, directly to a priest who does not require investigation, that is a priest who had ministered at the altar in the Temple. For had not the Great Court investigated his genealogy, they would not have permitted him to minister. For that reason one need not pursue the investigation beyond the evidence that he had ministered at the altar, nor beyond the fact that a person was a member of the Sanhedrin, since only priests, Levites, and Israelites of proven genealogy were appointed to the Sanhedrin.

3. Dough offering at the present time, even in the Land of Israel, is not of Scriptural sanction, since Scripture says, *When ye*

come into the land whither I bring you (Num. 15:18), implying the coming of all Israel, not of only a part of it, and when they went up into the Land in the days of Ezra, not all Israel did go up. Similarly, heave offering nowadays is eaten on the authority of the Scribes, and consequently priests of the present day, who are priests by presumption only, may eat of it.

4. If witnesses testify that they saw a priest eating of the heave offering of Scriptural sanction, he is to be regarded as a priest of proven genealogy. On the other hand, a priest may not be elevated to the status of proven genealogy on the sole basis of his having pronounced the priestly benediction, or of having been called first to the reading of the Torah, or of having been present at the distribution of the heave offering from the granaries, or on the evidence of a single witness.

5. If a priest of proven genealogy declares, "This my son is a priest," the son may not be elevated to the status of proven genealogy on his father's declaration, until the father brings witnesses that he is his son.

6. If a priest of proven genealogy had gone with his wife, who is known to be of valid descent, to another country, and they both returned closely accompanied by children, and if he says, "This is the wife who had gone away with me, and these are her children," he is not required to bring witnesses concerning either the wife or the children. If, however, he says, "She died, and these are her children," he must produce witnesses that they are his children, although he is not required to bring witnesses that their mother was of valid descent, since the presumption already exists that when she had left she was a woman of valid descent.

7. If a priest of proven genealogy had gone to another country and then returned with a wife and children, and if he says, "This is the woman whom I married and these are her children," he must adduce evidence that the woman is of valid descent, although he is not required to bring witnesses that these are her children. This applies only when the children cling to her. If he

returns with two wives and presents evidence that one of them is of valid descent, even though the children are young and cling to her, he must adduce evidence in their case also, since they may be the children of the other wife, notwithstanding that they cling to the one of valid descent.

8. If he returns with children and says, "I married a woman, and she died, and these are her children," he must bring witnesses to prove both that the woman was of valid descent and that these are her children. The same rule applies respecting an Israelite or a Levite of proven descent. Only after this can we take it as attested that this son of his is indeed of valid descent, so that he is qualified for the Sanhedrin.

9. A man may not be elevated to the priesthood on the sole basis of documents. How so? If it is found written in a certain document, "So-and-so, a priest, borrowed from So-and-so, and the latter lent him, such-and-such an amount," and at the foot of the document are the signatures of the witnesses, he may not be presumed on this ground to be a priest of proven genealogy, since the witnesses have vouched only for the debt. This applies only to the question of proven genealogy, but as far as to presume him to be a priest like the present-day priests, so that he might partake of the heave offering and the dough offering eaten on the authority of the Scribes, and of other sacred gifts set apart and consumed outside of the Temple and Jerusalem, he may be elevated to the status of a priest on the sole basis of documents, as well as on the evidence of a single witness, or of the fact that he pronounced the priestly benediction, or was called first to the reading of the Torah.

10. Similarly, any priest who says, "This my son is a priest," is to be believed to the extent of enabling the son to eat of the heave offering and to be presumed a priest, and he is not required to adduce evidence concerning either his wife or his son.

11. If two men come to a country, and each one of them says, "I and my companion are priests," even though it appears as if

they were repaying a favor to each other, they are to be believed, and both should be presumed to be priests. Similarly, if one witness says, "I saw this man pronounce the priestly benediction," or "eat of the heave offering," or "present at the distribution at the granaries," or "called up first to the reading of the Torah, and a Levite was called up after him," he is presumed to be a priest on the strength of this evidence. Likewise, if the witness testifies that a certain person read the second portion of the Torah lesson after a priest, that person is presumed to be a Levite.

12. If a witness testifies that he saw a man, together with his brother, receive his allocation of heave offering which their father, a priest, had left them, before the court, that man may not be elevated to the status of a priest on the basis of this testimony, since he may have been an unfit priest who took his share of the inheritance of heave offering for the purpose of selling it.

13. Nowadays, whosoever comes forth and declares that he is a priest is not to be believed, and may not be elevated to the status of a priest on the strength of his own statement. He may not read first in the Torah lesson, nor pronounce the priestly benediction, nor eat of the sacred gifts set apart and consumed outside of the Temple and Jerusalem, until he produces one witness. Nevertheless, he thereby renders himself forbidden to a divorcée, a harlot, or a profaned woman, and may not defile himself through contact with the dead. If he does pronounce the benediction or defile himself, he is liable to a flogging. The woman who has intercourse with him becomes profaned out of doubt.

14. If, however, he speaks in all innocence, he is to be believed. How so? It happened that a man said in all innocence, "I remember, when I was a child and was borne on my father's shoulder, that they took me out of school and removed my shirt and immersed me, so that I could eat of the heave offering that evening; and my companions kept their distance from me and called me 'Johanan, the eater of dough offering'." Thereupon the saintly Rabbi Judah han-Naśi' elevated him to the status of a priest on the sole basis of his own statement.

15. An adult is to be believed if he says, "I remember that when I was a child I saw So-and-so immersing himself and then eating of the heave offering in the evening," and the presumption then is that that man is a priest, on the basis of this testimony. If someone comes forth nowadays and says, "I am a priest," and one witness testifies in his behalf that he knows that his father was a priest, he is not to be elevated to the status of a priest on the basis of this testimony, since he may be an unfit priest. He may not be elevated until there is testimony that he himself is a priest. If, however, his father was presumed to be a priest, or if two witnesses come forth and testify that his father was known to be a priest, he may be presumed to have the same status as his father.

16. If the presumption is that his father was a priest, but a rumor has gone forth about him that his mother was a divorcée or a woman released from levirate marriage, apprehension should be felt concerning him and he should be demoted. If subsequently one witness comes forth and testifies that he is of valid descent, he is to be restored to the status of priest on the strength of this testimony. If thereupon two other witnesses come forth and testify that he is an unfit priest, he should again be demoted from the status of priest. If finally one more witness comes forth and testifies that he is of valid descent, he is again to be restored to the status of priest, since this last testimony is combined with the testimony of the first witness, so that there are now two witnesses to testify that he is valid and two that he is invalid. They therefore vitiate one another, and the rumor is also rendered void, seeing that two witnesses are as good as a hundred, and he remains a priest on the presumption of his father's status.

17. If a woman does not wait three months after the death of her husband before remarrying, and then gives birth to a child, so that it is uncertain whether this is a nine-months-old child by the first husband or a seven-months-old child by the second, and one of the husbands is a priest and the other an Israelite, the child is to be considered a doubtful priest. Similarly, if the child of a priest is confused with the child of an Israelite and the two chil-

dren grow up together, each of them is to be regarded as a doubtful priest. The more stringent rulings touching both priests and Israelites apply to them: they may marry only women permitted to the priesthood and may not defile themselves through contact with the dead, but they may not eat of the heave offering, and if they marry a divorcée they must divorce her, although they are not liable to a flogging.

18. If the children of two priests are confused with one another, or if the wife of a priest, without waiting three months after the death of her husband, marries another priest, and it is unknown whether the newborn child is a nine-months-old child by the first husband or a seven-months-old child by the second, the more stringent rulings touching both fathers apply to the child: he must go into mourning for either one of them, and either one of them must go into mourning for him; he may not defile himself by contact with the corpse of either one of them, nor may either one of them defile himself by contact with his corpse; he may attend the watches to which both of them were assigned; and he may take no portion of the heave offering. If both fathers belong to the same watch and to the same subdivision, he may take one portion.

19. This rule applies only if the children were born in wedlock. If they were born out of wedlock, the Sages have ruled that the child is to be excluded from the privileges of the priesthood entirely, since he does not know his father with certainty, as it is said, *and it shall be to him and to his seed after him, the covenant of an everlasting priesthood* (Num. 25:13): so long as his seed traces its proven genealogy from him with assurance.

20. How so? If out of a group of ten priests one withdraws and commits adultery, the child is certainly a priest; nevertheless, since the child does not know for certain the father to whom he may trace his proven genealogy, he must be excluded from the privileges of the priesthood. He may neither minister in the Temple, nor eat of the heave offering, nor obtain his allocation,

but if he defiles himself through contact with the dead or marries a divorcée, he is liable to a flogging, since there exists in this case no doubt which might render these acts permissible.

CHAPTER XXI

1. Whosoever has intercourse with a woman within the forbidden unions, whether by way of the sexual organs, or by way of lustful embracing or kissing, thus deriving pleasure from carnal proximity, is liable to a flogging on the authority of the Torah, as it is said, *that ye do not any of these abominable customs* (Lev. 18:30), and it is also said, *none of you shall approach to any that is near of kin to him to uncover their nakedness* (*ibid.* 18:6); that is to say, you shall not even approach things which lead to forbidden union.

2. Whosoever indulges in these practices lays himself open to the suspicion of forbidden unions. A man is forbidden to make suggestive gestures with his hands or legs or to wink at a woman within the forbidden unions, or to jest or act frivolously with her. It is forbidden even to inhale her perfume or gaze at her beauty. Whosoever directs his mind towards these things is liable to the flogging prescribed for disobedience. He who stares even at a woman's little finger with the intention of deriving pleasure from it, is considered as though he had looked at her secret parts. It is forbidden even to listen to the singing of a woman within the forbidden unions, or to look at her hair.

3. These things are forbidden with regard to a woman prohibited to a man by a negative commandment; on the other hand, he is permitted to look at an unmarried woman, whether she is a virgin or not, and to inspect her, so that if she is pleasing in his sight he may marry her. Not only is there no suggestion of prohibition about this, but it is indeed proper to do so. He should not, however, look at her adulterously, for Scripture says, *I made*

a covenant with mine eyes, how then should I look upon a maiden? (Job 31:1).

4. A man is permitted to look at his wife while she is a menstruant, even though she is forbidden to him at that time. For while his heart will be pleased by the sight of her, nevertheless, seeing that she will become permitted to him after her menstruation, he will not be led now to temptation thereby. But he should not jest or act frivolously with her, lest he should become addicted to transgression.

5. The services of a woman are utterly forbidden to a man, whether she is an adult or a minor, a bondswoman or a manumitted woman, lest he should come thereby to sinful thoughts. What services are here referred to? Washing his face, hands, or feet, arranging his bed in his presence, and pouring his wine, since only his own wife should perform these duties for him. A man may not inquire after the well-being of a woman at all, not even through a messenger.

6. If a man innocently embraces or kisses a woman within the forbidden unions—for instance, his elder sister, maternal aunt, or the like—even though neither lust nor pleasure is involved in the act at all, it is nevertheless most disgraceful, and is forbidden, being the act of a fool. For a man should not come nigh to a woman forbidden to him under any circumstances, whether she is an adult or a minor; the sole exceptions are a mother with her son, and a father with his daughter.

7. How so? A father is permitted to embrace and kiss his daughter, and she may sleep with him with their bodies touching, and similarly a mother with her son, while the children are minors. When they come of age, the son reaching his majority, and the daughter developing firm breasts and a growth of hair, he must then sleep in his clothes, and she in hers. If the daughter feels ashamed to stand naked before her father, or if she is married, or, similarly, if the mother is ashamed to stand naked in the presence of her son, even though they are minors, once they have

reached the stage of feeling shame, they must sleep together only in their clothes.

8. Women are forbidden to engage in Lesbian practices with one another, these being *the doings of the land of Egypt* (Lev. 18:3), against which we have been warned, as it is said, *After the doings of the land of Egypt . . . ye shall not do* (*ibid.*). Our Sages have said, "What did they do? A man would marry a man, or a woman a woman, or a woman would marry two men." Although such an act is forbidden, the perpetrators are not liable to a flogging, since there is no specific negative commandment prohibiting it, nor is actual intercourse of any kind involved here. Consequently, such women are not forbidden for the priesthood on account of harlotry, nor is a woman prohibited to her husband because of it, since this does not constitute harlotry. It behooves the court, however, to administer the flogging prescribed for disobedience, since they have performed a forbidden act. A man should be particularly strict with his wife in this matter, and should prevent women known to indulge in such practices from visiting her, and her from going to visit them.

9. Since a man's wife is permitted to him, he may act with her in any manner whatsoever. He may have intercourse with her whenever he so desires, and kiss any organ of her body he wishes, and he may have intercourse with her naturally or unnaturally, provided that he does not expend semen to no purpose. Nevertheless, it is an attribute of piety that a man should not act in this matter with levity and that he should sanctify himself at the time of intercourse, as we have explained in the Laws Concerning Knowledge. A man should not turn aside from the normal way of the world and its proper procedure, since the true design of intercourse is fruitfulness and multiplication of progeny.

10. A man is forbidden to have intercourse by the light of a lamp. If it is Sabbath, and he has no other room than the one in which a light is burning, he should abstain from intercourse entirely. Similarly, an Israelite is forbidden to have intercourse during daylight, since this constitutes shameless behavior. If he is a

scholar, who would not be likely to make it a habit, he may envelop himself in darkness by spreading his cloak over himself and then have intercourse. But he should not have recourse to this expedient except in case of great need, and the way of sanctity is to have intercourse in the middle of the night only.

11. The Sages have found no pleasure in the man who indulges in sexual intercourse to excess and is as frequently with his wife as a cock is with his hen. Such conduct is a serious blemish, and brands him as a boor. The more continent a man is, the more is he praiseworthy, provided he does not neglect his marital duty without his wife's consent. Indeed, the original reason why the rule was enacted that a man who had a nocturnal pollution should not read in the Torah before immersing himself, was in order to reduce sexual intercourse.

12. Similarly, the Sages have forbidden a man to have intercourse with his wife while thinking in his heart of another woman. Nor should he have intercourse while intoxicated or in the midst of strife or hatred. Nor should he have intercourse with her against her will while she is in dread of him, nor when one of them is under a ban, nor after he has made up his mind to divorce her. If he does one of these things, the resulting children will be degenerate; some will be shameless, others will become renegades and sinners.

13. Similarly, the Sages have said that in the case of a woman who is so barefaced as to brazenly demand intercourse, or seduces a man in order to make him marry her, or persuades her husband to have intercourse with her when his intention is to visit his other wife, or does not wait three months after the death of her husband before remarrying, with the result that the parentage of the resulting child is in doubt—all children born of such women become renegades and sinners who become separated in the sufferings of exile.

14. A man is forbidden to have intercourse with his wife in public places and streets, or in gardens and orchards; he may

have it only in their dwelling, so that it should not seem like harlotry and thus cause them to accustom themselves to harlotry. If a man has intercourse with his wife in such places, he should be given the flogging prescribed for disobedience. Similarly, he who betrothes his wife by an act of intercourse, or in the market place, or without proper negotiation, is also liable to the flogging prescribed for disobedience.

15. A guest staying at an inn is forbidden to have intercourse with his wife until he returns home. Similarly, the Sages have forbidden a man to reside in the house of his father-in-law, since this constitutes shamelessness; nor should be enter a bathhouse with him.

16. Nor should a man enter a bathhouse with his father or with his sister's husband, or with his disciple. If, however, he has need of his disciple's services in the bath, it is permitted. There are localities where custom forbids two brothers to enter a bathhouse together.

17. Daughters of Israel should not walk in the market place bareheaded, regardless of whether they are unmarried or married, nor should a woman walk in the market place with her son following behind her, lest he should be seized and she should then pursue in order to retrieve him, and the rogues who had originally seized the boy for mere sport, would thereupon ravish her.

18. It is forbidden to expend semen to no purpose. Consequently, a man should not thresh within and ejaculate without, nor should a man marry a minor who cannot yet bear children. As for masturbators, not only do they commit a strictly forbidden act, but they also expose themselves to a ban. It is to them that Scripture refers in saying, *Your hands are full of blood* (Isa. 1:15), and a masturbator's act is regarded as equivalent to killing a human being.

19. Similarly, a man is forbidden to bring about an erection or unchaste thoughts deliberately. If such thoughts do enter his mind, he should direct it away from thoughts of vanity leading to wast-

age of semen, and back to words of Torah, which is *a hind of love and a doe of grace* (Prov. 5:19). A man is therefore forbidden to sleep on his back, face upwards, unless he inclines a little to one side, in order not bring about an erection.

20. Nor should he look at domestic animals, wild beasts, or birds when male and female are mating. Animal breeders, however, are permitted to insert the male organ into the female, for inasmuch as they are absorbed in their work they are not likely to think of lustful matters.

21. Similarly, a man is forbidden to gaze upon women while they are bending over their washing, and he is even forbidden to look at the brightly colored clothes belonging to a woman whom he knows, lest indecent thoughts should enter his mind.

22. If a man meets a woman in the street, he is forbidden to walk behind her, and should hasten on so as to have her walk by his side or behind him. Whosoever walks in the street behind a woman is considered a most worthless boor. A man is forbidden to pass by a harlot's door unless he keeps a distance of four cubits from it, as it is said, *and come not nigh the door of her house* (Prov. 5:8).

23. An unmarried man is forbidden to take hold of his privy parts, lest this should cause unchaste thoughts. He should not even insert his hand below the navel, for the same reason. When he urinates, he should not hold his organ, but if he is married, he may do so. Whether he is married or not, he should never put his hand to his organ, except when relieving himself.

24. One of the early pietists and most distinguished Sages prided himself on the fact that he had never in his life looked upon his circumcision, while another stated with pride that he had never looked upon his wife's figure, for his thoughts were always turned away from matters of vanity toward those of truth which take hold of the hearts of saintly men.

25. It is an injunction of the Sages that a man should marry

off his sons and daughters as near to puberty as possible, for if he leaves them unmarried they will be led to adultery or to indecent thoughts, and concerning this it is said, *and thou shalt think of thy habitation, and not sin* (Job 5:24). It is also forbidden to marry an adult woman to a minor, since this is considered the same as harlotry.

26. A man is not permitted to live without a wife, nor should he marry a barren woman or a woman too old for childbearing; a woman, on the other hand, has the right to remain unmarried or to marry a eunuch. A young man should not marry an old woman, nor an old man a young girl, since this leads to harlotry.

27. Similarly, a man who has divorced his wife after marriage should not reside with her in the same courtyard, lest they should come to adultery; if he is a priest, she should not reside even in the same alley with him. A small village is regarded in this respect as equivalent to an alley. If he owes her money, she should appoint an agent to demand repayment. If a divorced woman comes to court for a lawsuit with her divorced husband, they both should be put under a ban or be given the flogging prescribed for disobedience. If she had been divorced after betrothal, she is permitted to summon him to a lawsuit and dwell in the same courtyard, but if he is on terms of familiarity with her, she is forbidden to do so even if the divorce followed betrothal. Which one must give way? She must give way to him, but if the courtyard is her own property, he must give way to her.

28. A man is forbidden to marry a woman with the intention of subsequently divorcing her, as it is said, *Devise not evil against thy neighbor while he dwelleth securely by thee* (Prov. 3:29). If, however, he informs her at the outset that he is marrying her only for a specified period, it is permitted.

29. A man should not marry one wife in one country and another in another country, lest with the passage of time it should happen that his son would marry his own sister, or his mother's or father's sister, or the like, without being aware of it. If, how-

ever, the father is a distinguished man whose name is well known and whose children would therefore also be widely and well known, it is permitted.

30. A man should not marry a woman belonging to a family of lepers or epileptics, provided that there is a presumption based on three cases that the disease is hereditary with them.

31. If a woman had been successively married to two husbands and both died, she should not marry for a third time, but if she does so, she need not be divorced. Even if only the betrothal has taken place, the third husband may consummate the marriage. An unlettered Israelite should not marry a woman of priestly descent, since this constitutes in a way a profanation of the seed of Aaron. Should he marry her nevertheless, the Sages have said that the marriage will not prove successful, and he will die childless, or else he or she will come to an early death, or there will be strife between them. On the other hand, it is laudable and praiseworthy for a scholar to marry a woman of priestly descent, since in this instance learning and priesthood are united.

32. A man should not marry the daughter of an unlettered person, for if he should die or be sent into exile, his children would grow up in ignorance, since their mother knows not of the crown of the Torah. Nor should a man marry his daughter to an unlettered person, for one who gives his daughter in marriage to such a husband is as though he had bound her and placed her in front of a lion, seeing that the beast's habit is to smite his mate and have intercourse with her, since he has no shame. A man should go so far as to sell all his possessions in order to marry a scholar's daughter, for should he die or go into exile, his children would grow up to be scholars. Similarly, he should marry his daughter to a scholar, since there is no reprehensible thing or strife in the house of a scholar.

CHAPTER XXII

1. A man is not permitted to seclude himself with a woman within the forbidden unions, whether she is old or young, since this may lead to violation of this interdict. The only exceptions are a mother with her son, a father with his daughter, and a husband with his wife during her menstrual period. If a bride becomes menstruous before the bridegroom can have intercourse with her, he may not be secluded with her, and she should sleep with the women and he with the men. If, however, the first act of intercourse has already taken place and she then becomes unclean, he may be secluded with her.

2. Israelites are not under suspicion of sodomy with males or animals. It is therefore not forbidden to be secluded with them. Nevertheless, a man who avoids seclusion with males and animals is praiseworthy, and the greatest among the Sages used to keep their distance from animals in order not to be secluded with them. The prohibition of being secluded with women within the forbidden unions is based on the authority of tradition.

3. After the incident of Amnon and Tamar, David and his court issued a prohibition against seclusion with an unmarried woman, and as a result, although she does not come under this classification, she is nevertheless included in the prohibition of seclusion with women within the forbidden unions. Shammai and Hillel also enacted a decree forbidding seclusion with a heathen woman. Consequently, if a man secludes himself with a woman with whom he is forbidden to be secluded, whether she is Israelite or heathen, both the man and the woman should be given the flogging prescribed for disobedience, and proclamation should be made of the fact. The only exception is a married woman; although it is forbidden to be secluded with her, nevertheless, if a man has secluded himself with her, they should not

be flogged, in order to avoid the imputation that she has committed adultery, which is tantamount to the insinuation that her children are bastards.

4. If a man's wife is with him, he is permitted to be with a woman with whom seclusion is otherwise forbidden, since his wife would watch over him. On the other hand, an Israelite woman should not be secluded with a heathen, even if his wife is with him, since a heathen's wife would not watch over her husband in this regard, seeing that they have no shame.

5. Similarly, a person should not entrust an Israelite child to a heathen to be taught reading or a trade, since all heathens are suspected of sodomy. Nor should a man stable an animal in a heathen inn, even male animals with male innkeepers or females with female innkeepers.

6. Nor should a person deliver domestic animals, wild beasts, or birds to heathen herdsmen, even male animals to male heathens, or females to female heathens, because they are all suspected of copulating with animals, and we have already explained that sodomy and lying with animals are forbidden also to heathens, and it is said, *Thou shalt not put a stumbling block before the blind* (Lev. 19:14).

7. And why is it forbidden to deliver a female animal to a heathen woman? Because all heathen women are suspected of whoredom, and when her paramour comes to lie with her, it is possible that he will not find her at home and will lie with the animal instead. Indeed, even if he does find her, he may still lie with the animal.

8. One woman should not be alone even with a number of men, unless the wife of one of them is also there. Similarly, one man should not be alone with several women. If a number of men are with a number of women, no apprehension need be felt of improper seclusion. If the men are outside and the women inside, or vice versa, and a woman leaves her group and mingles with

the men, or a man mingles with the women, this is forbidden, because of improper seclusion. Even a man whose business or occupation requires him to deal with women should not be alone with them. What then should he do? He should either have his wife with him while transacting his business, or else turn to another occupation.

9. It is permitted to be alone with two women subject to the same levirate marriage, two wives of one man, a woman and her mother-in-law, a woman and her husband's daughter, or a woman and her mother-in-law's daughter, since all these usually dislike one another and would not cover up for each other. Similarly, it is permitted to be alone with a woman in the presence of her young daughter who is aware of the nature of sexual intercourse but has as yet no desire to indulge in it, because the mother would not commit adultery in her presence, for fear that she will reveal her secret.

10. It is permitted to be alone with a female child three years old or less, or with a male child nine years old or less, since the Sages have forbidden seclusion only with males and females old enough for sexual intercourse.

11. A hermaphrodite should not be alone with women, but if he does seclude himself with them he is not to be flogged, since his sex is doubtful. A man, however, may be alone with a hermaphrodite or with a person of doubtful sex.

12. If a married woman's husband is in town, there is no need for apprehension with regard to her being alone with another man, since the fear of her husband remains upon her. If, however, this other man is on terms of familiarity with her, as for instance, they having grown up together or being related to each other, she may not be alone with him even if her husband is in town. Similarly, if a man is alone with a woman in a room with the door open to a public domain, no apprehension need be felt about improper seclusion.

13. An unmarried man should not teach children, since their

mothers would come to school after their children, with the result that he may become enamored of them. Similarly, a woman should not teach little children, because of their fathers who would come to the school after their children, with the result that they may find themselves alone with her. It is not necessary, however, for the teacher to have his wife staying with him in the school, rather she may remain at home while he teaches at his place of instruction.

14. The Sages have enacted the rule that women should engage in audible conversation with one another while in the privy, so that a man should not enter there unawares and thus find himself in improper seclusion with them.

15. Even a trustworthy and virtuous man should not be appointed watchman over a courtyard where there are women, notwithstanding that his post is outside, since there is no guardian against forbidden unions. Similarly, a man is forbidden to appoint an administrator over his house, so as not to lead his wife into transgression.

16. A scholar is forbidden to dwell in the same courtyard with a widow, even if he does not seclude himself with her, in order to avoid suspicion, unless his wife is with him. Similarly, a widow is forbidden to rear a dog, because of possible suspicion. Nor should a woman acquire male slaves, even minors, for the same reason.

17. A master should not expound to three disciples at once such laws concerning forbidden unions as are not explicitly stated, since while one of them would be preoccupied with the questions put to him by his master, the other two would engage in discussion with one another and their minds would not be free to pay attention; and seeing that a man's mind is predisposed to illicit intercourse, if he is in doubt about something he had heard from his master, he would be prone to render a lenient decision. For this reason a master should expound such laws to only two

disciples at one time, so that the student who listens should have his mind free and thus understand what he hears from his master.

18. There is no prohibition in the whole of Scripture which the generality of the people experience greater difficulty in observing than the interdict of forbidden unions and illicit intercourse. The Sages have declared that when Israel was given the commandments concerning forbidden unions, they wept and accepted this injunction with grumbling and wailing, as it is said, *weeping in their families* (Num. 11:10), i.e. weeping on account of the matter of family relations.

19. The Sages have declared further that the soul of man lusts after larceny and forbidden unions and covets them. At no time can one find a community which does not contain libertines indulging in forbidden unions and illicit intercourse. And the Sages have declared also, "The majority of men are guilty of larceny, the minority of forbidden unions, and all of them together of the tendency to evil tongue."

20. Consequently, it behooves a man to subdue his inclination towards these vices and to inure himself to unbounded sanctity, pure thought, and disciplined moral disposition, so as to be saved from such transgressions. Above all, he should be on guard against improper seclusion, since this is the chief contributory factor to unchastity. The greatest of our Sages used to say to their disciples, "Warn me to beware of my daughter, warn me to beware of my daughter-in-law," in order to teach their disciples not to feel embarrassed in such matters and to keep away from improper seclusion.

21. In like manner, man should keep away from levity, drunkenness, and lewd discourse, since these are great contributory factors and degrees leading to forbidden unions. Nor should a man live without a wife, since married estate is conducive to great purity. But above all this, as the Sages have declared, a man should direct his mind and thoughts to the words of Torah and enlarge

his understanding with wisdom, for unchaste thoughts prevail only in a heart devoid of wisdom, and of wisdom it is said, *a hind of love and a doe of grace, let her breasts satisfy thee at all times, with her love be thou ravished always* (Prov. 5:19).

TREATISE II

LAWS CONCERNING FORBIDDEN FOODS

Involving Twenty-Eight Precepts,
Four Positive and Twenty-Four Negative
To Wit

1. To examine the tokens of domestic animals and wild beasts, in order to distinguish between unclean and clean;
2. To examine the tokens of birds, in order to distinguish between unclean and clean;
3. To examine the tokens of locusts, in order to distinguish between unclean and clean;
4. To examine the tokens of fishes, in order to distinguish between unclean and clean;
5. Not to eat unclean domestic animals or wild beasts;
6. Not to eat unclean birds;
7. Not to eat unclean fish;
8. Not to eat winged insects;
9. Not to eat reptiles of the earth;
10. Not to eat creeping things of the earth;
11. Not to eat fruit worms once they come out into the open;
12. Not to eat animals that move in the water;
13. Not to eat carrion;
14. To derive no benefit from an ox condemned to stoning;
15. Not to eat a diseased animal;

16. Not to eat the limb of a living thing;
17. Not to eat blood;
18. Not to eat the forbidden fat of a clean domestic animal;
19. Not to eat the sinew of the thigh vein;
20. Not to eat meat and milk together;
21. Not to cook meat and milk together;
22. Not to eat bread baked from the new harvest;
23. Not to eat parched corn of the new harvest;
24. Not to eat early barley of the new harvest;
25. Not to eat the fruit of the first three years;
26. Not to eat the mixed produce of a vineyard;
27. Not to eat untithed produce;
28. Not to drink wine of heathen libation.

An exposition of these commandments is contained in the following chapters.

NOTE

In the list of the 613 commandments prefixed to the Code, those dealt with in the present treatise appear in the following order:

Positive commandments:

[1] 149. To examine the tokens of domestic animals and wild beasts, as it is said: *These are the living things which ye may eat* (Lev. 11:2);

[2] 150. To examine the tokens of birds, in order to distinguish between unclean and clean, as it is said: *Of all clean birds ye may eat* (Deut. 14:11);

[3] 151. To examine the tokens of locusts, in order to know the clean from the unclean, as it is said: *These may ye eat of all winged swarming things* (Lev. 11:21);

[4] 152. To examine the tokens of fishes, as it is said: *These may ye eat of all that are in the waters* (*ibid.* 11:9).

Negative commandments:

[5] 172. Not to eat unclean domestic animals or wild beasts, as it is said: *These shall ye not eat of them that only chew the cud* (Lev. 11:4);

[6] 174. Not to eat unclean birds, as it is said: *And these ye shall have in detestation among the fowls* (*ibid.* 11:13);

[7] 173. Not to eat unclean fish, as it is said: *And they shall be a detestable thing unto you; ye shall not eat of their flesh* (*ibid.* 11:11);

[8] 175. Not to eat winged insects, as it is said: *And all winged swarming things are unclean unto you* (Deut. 14:19);

[9] 176. Not to eat reptiles of the earth, as it is said: *And every swarming thing that swarmeth upon the earth is a detestable thing* (Lev. 11:41);

[10] 177. Not to eat creeping things of the earth, as it is said: *Neither shall ye defile yourselves with any manner of swarming thing* (*ibid.* 11:44);

[11] 178. Not to eat fruit worms once they come out into the open, as it is said: *Even all swarming things that swarm upon the earth* (*ibid.* 11:42);

[12] 179. Not to eat animals that move in the water, as it is said: *Ye shall not make yourselves detestable with any swarming thing* (*ibid.* 11:43);

[13] 180. Not to eat carrion, as it is said: *Ye shall not eat any thing that dieth of itself* (Deut. 14:21);

[14] 188. Not to eat the flesh of an ox condemned to stoning, as it is said: *Its flesh shall not be eaten* (Exod. 21:28);

[15] 181. Not to eat a diseased animal, as it is said: *Ye shall not eat any flesh that is torn of beasts in the field* (*ibid.* 22:30);

[16] 182. Not to eat the limb of a living thing, as it is said: *Thou shalt not eat the life with the flesh* (Deut. 12:23);

[17] 184. Not to eat blood, as it is said: *Ye shall eat neither fat nor blood* (Lev. 3:17);

[18] 185. Not to eat forbidden fat, as it is said: *Ye shall eat no fat, of ox, or sheep, or goat* (*ibid.* 7:23);

[19] 183. Not to eat the sinew of the thigh vein, as it is said: *Therefore the children of Israel eat not the sinew of the thigh vein* (Gen. 32:33);

[20] 187. Not to eat meat and milk together, as it is said, the second time: *Thou shalt not seethe a kid in its mother's milk* (Exod. 34:26). And the Sages have learned by tradition (B. Ḥul 115b) that this commandment in its first occurrence (*ibid.* 23:19) forbids the seething, and in the second occurrence forbids the eating.

[21] 186. Not to cook meat and milk together, as it is said: *Thou shalt not seethe a kid in its mother's milk* (*ibid.* 23:19);

[22] 189. Not to eat bread baked from the new harvest before Passover, as it is said: *And ye shall eat neither bread, nor parched corn, nor fresh ears, until this selfsame day* (Lev. 23:14);

[23] 190. Not to eat parched corn of the new harvest, as it is said: *nor parched corn* (*ibid.*);

[24] 191. Not to eat early barley of the new harvest, as it is said: *nor fresh ears* (*ibid.*);

[25] 192. Not to eat the fruit of the first three years, as it is said: *Three years shall it be as forbidden unto you; it shall not be eaten* (*ibid.* 19:23);

[26] 193. Not to eat the mixed produce of a vineyard, as it is said: *Thou shalt not sow thy vineyard with two kinds of seed; lest the fullness of the seed which thou hast sown be forfeited together with the increase of the vineyard* (Deut. 22:9), signifying that the eating thereof is forbidden;

[27] 153. Not to eat untithed produce, signifying produce growing out of the earth and subject to heave offering and tithe, from which the heave offering has not yet been separated, as it is said: *And they shall not profane the holy things of the children of Israel, which they set*

apart unto the Lord (Lev. 22:15); that is to say, things from which heave offering is to be separated unto the Lord shall not be made profane by being eaten while not yet tithed;

[28] 194. Not to drink wine of heathen libation, as it is said: *Who did eat the fat of their sacrifices, and drank the wine of their drink offering?* (Deut. 32:38).

CHAPTER I

1. It is a positive commandment that one must know the tokens which distinguish such animals, beasts, fowl, fish, and locusts as are permitted to be eaten, from those which are not permitted, as it is said, *Ye shall therefore separate between the clean beast and the unclean, and between the unclean fowl and the clean* (Lev. 20:25); and it is also said, *to make a difference between the unclean and the clean, and between the living thing that may be eaten and the living thing that may not be eaten* (*ibid.* 11:47).

2. The tokens in animals and beasts are specified in the Torah. They are two, the cloven hoof and the chewing of the cud, and both must be present. An animal or beast which chews the cud has no front teeth in its upper jaw. Every animal which chews the cud has cloven hoofs, with the sole exception of the camel. And every animal which has cloven hoofs chews the cud, with the exception of the pig.

3. Consequently, if a person finds an animal in the wilderness whose species he cannot identify, but whose hoofs are split, he should examine its mouth; if it has no front teeth in its upper jaw, he may be certain that it is a clean animal, provided that he can recognize a camel. If he finds an animal whose muzzle had been cut away, he should examine its hoofs. If they are cloven, the animal is clean, provided that he can recognize a pig. If he finds an animal with both muzzle and hoofs cut away, he should, after slaughtering, examine the end of the tail. If he finds that the flesh runs crosswise, it is a clean animal, provided he can recognize the wild ass, since its flesh also runs crosswise.

4. If a clean animal gives birth to a young which resembles an unclean animal, even if it has no cloven hoofs and does not chew the cud, but is entirely like a horse or an ass, it is nevertheless deemed permissible for consumption. This, however, applies only

when the birth takes place in a person's presence; if he leaves a cow in calf among his herd, and returns to find a young resembling a pig following it, even though it suckles from the cow, it is deemed a doubtful case and therefore forbidden, since it is possible that it was born of an unclean animal and became attached to the clean.

5. If an unclean animal gives birth to a young resembling a clean animal, even if it has cloven hoofs and does chew the cud, and completely resembles an ox or a sheep, it is forbidden for consumption. The rule is thus that the offspring of an unclean animal is unclean, and the offspring of a clean animal is clean. An unclean fish found in the belly of a clean fish is forbidden, and a clean fish found inside an unclean fish is permitted, since it did not grow from it but was swallowed.

6. If a clean animal gives birth to a creature with two backs and two spines, or if such a creature is found in the mother's womb, that creature is forbidden to be eaten. This is the "cloven" which was forbidden by the Torah, as it is said, *Nevertheless, these shall ye not eat of them that chew the cud or of them that have the cloven hoof, the 'cloven'* (Deut. 14:7), that is, a creature which is born "cloven" into two animals.

7. The same applies to an animal in whose womb is found a young resembling a bird; even if the shape is that of a clean bird, it is forbidden. Of that which is found inside an animal, only that which has cloven hoofs is permitted.

8. Of all the animals and beasts in the world, only the ten species enumerated in the Torah are permitted. Three of them are species of animals, namely the ox, the sheep, and the goat, while the remaining seven are species of beasts, namely the hart, the gazelle, the roebuck, the wild goat, the pygarg, the antelope, and the mountain sheep. They and their subspecies, such as the wild ox and the buffalo, which are species of the ox, are permitted. All these ten species, together with their subspecies, both chew the cud and have cloven hoofs. Therefore, if one recognizes them, he has no need to examine either their muzzles or their feet.

9. Although all the aforementioned kinds are permitted to be eaten, one must nevertheless differentiate between clean animals and clean beasts, since the fat of beasts is permitted and their blood must be covered, whereas partaking of the fat of an animal carries the penalty of extinction, but its blood need not be covered.

10. The tokens of a beast are known by tradition. Every species which has cloven hoofs, chews the cud, and has branching horns, such as the hart, is certainly a clean beast. Of those whose horns do not branch out, if the horns are ringed like those of an ox, notched like those of a goat, with the notches dovetailing one with the other, and rounded like the horns of a gazelle, they are deemed clean beasts. But the horns must have all these three tokens, rings, notches, and roundness.

11. This rule refers only to unfamiliar species; as for the seven species enumerated in the Torah, once a person recognizes them, he may eat their fat and must cover their blood, even if he finds no horns at all.

12. The wild ox is a species of animal, and the oryx, though having only one horn, is deemed a beast. Whenever one is in doubt whether a creature is a species of animal or a species of beast, its fat is forbidden, but no flogging is incurred for eating it, and its blood must be covered.

13. A hybrid creature which is the offspring of a clean animal and a clean beast is the one called *koy*. Its fat is forbidden, but no flogging is incurred for eating it, and its blood must be covered. An animal of an unclean species can never become pregnant by an animal of a clean species.

14. The tokens of a clean bird are not specified in the Torah, which enumerates only the unclean species, all others being permitted. There are twenty-four forbidden species, as follows: the great vulture; the bearded vulture; the osprey; the *da'ah* (kite), which is the same as the *ra'ah* enumerated in Deuteronomy (14:13); the *'ayyah* (falcon), which is the same as the *dayyah* mentioned in Deuteronomy; another species of *'ayyah,* since

Scripture says *the 'ayyah after its kind* (Lev. 11:14), proving that there are two species of it; the raven; the starling, since with regard to the raven Scripture says, *after its kind* (Lev. 11:15), which includes the starling; the ostrich; the nighthawk; the seamew; the hawk; the *surinka,* which is a species of hawk, since with regard to the hawk Scripture says, *after its kind* (Lev. 11:16); the little owl; the cormorant; the great owl; the horned owl; the pelican; the carrion vulture; the stork; the heron; another species of heron, since Scripture says, *after its kind* (Lev. 11:19); the hoopoe; and the bat.

15. Whosoever is expert in these species and in their names may eat any bird which does not belong to them, nor is examination necessary. Clean birds are permitted to be eaten by tradition, that is, if it is commonly accepted in a particular place that a particular species is a clean bird. A hunter is to be believed if he declares, "This bird was permitted to me by my master who taught me hunting," provided that this hunter is known to be an expert in these unclean species and their names.

16. As for a person who does not recognize them and is unfamiliar with their names, he should examine the following tokens specified by the Sages: A bird which seizes its food with its claws certainly belongs to these species and is therefore unclean; if it does not seize its food with its claws and has one of the following three tokens, it is deemed clean, namely, an extra talon, a *zefek* (crop), which is the same as the Scriptural *mur'ah,* or a craw that may be peeled by hand.

17. These tokens may be relied upon, because among all these forbidden species there are but two which do not seize their food with their claws, and have one of the aforementioned tokens, namely the bearded vulture and the osprey, and these two are not found in inhabited localities but only in the deserts and in the distant isles of the sea which are beyond human habitation.

18. If the craw may be peeled with a knife, but not by hand, and the bird has no other token, it is considered a doubtful case,

even if it does not seize its food with its claws. If the craw is hard and firmly attached, but when left in the sun becomes soft so that it may be peeled by hand, the bird is deemed permitted.

19. The Geonim have declared that they had a tradition to the effect that no decision may be rendered permitting a bird which has only one of these tokens, unless that token is that the craw may be peeled by hand. If the craw could not be peeled by hand, the bird was never declared permitted, even if it possessed a crop or an extra talon.

20. Any bird which parts its feet when a cord is stretched out for it to perch on, two claws on one side and two on the other, or which seizes its food in the air and eats it in the air, is deemed a bird of prey and is unclean. A fowl which flocks with unclean fowls and is similar to them is also deemed unclean.

21. The Torah permits eight species of locusts: the grasshopper; another species of grasshopper called *razbaniṯ;* the cricket; another species of cricket called *'arṣuḇya;* the common locust; another species of locust called "the vineyard bird"; the bald locust; and another species of bald locust called "the Jerusalemite *Yoḥana.*"

22. He who is expert in them and in their names may eat of them, and a hunter is to be believed in their case as in the case of birds. But he who is not expert in them must examine their tokens. They possess three tokens: Whichever has four legs and four wings which overlie most of the length of its body and most of its circumference, and has in addition two legs with which to leap, is deemed a clean species. Even if it has an elongated head and a tail, so long as it is known by the name of locust, it is clean.

23. If at present the locust has no wings or legs, or if its wings do not cover the greater part of the body, but it is known that it will grow them after some time when it has matured, it is deemed permitted immediately.

24. With fish there are but two tokens, fins and scales. The fin

is the organ with which it swims, and the scales form the covering over its whole body. Every fish which has scales necessarily has also fins. If it possesses none at the moment, but is known to possess them when fully grown, or if it has scales while it is in the sea, but sheds them when out of the water, it is deemed permitted. If its scales do not cover its whole body, it is still permitted. Even if it has only one scale or only one fin, it is deemed permitted.

CHAPTER II

1. From the general rule, *And every beast that parteth the hoof and hath the hoof cloven in two, and cheweth the cud among the beasts, that shall ye eat* (Deut. 14:6), it follows that any animal which does not chew the cud and has no cloven hoofs is forbidden, and a negative commandment which is deduced from a positive commandment has the same force as a positive commandment. With regard to the camel, pig, hare, and coney Scripture says, *Nevertheless, these shall ye not eat of them that only chew the cud or of them that only have the hoof cloven,* etc. (Deut. 14:7), from which you learn that they are prohibited by a negative commandment, even though they have one of the tokens of a clean animal. How much more so is it true, then, with regard to other unclean animals and beasts which have no token at all, that the prohibition against eating them derives from a negative commandment as well as from the positive commandment derived from the words *that shall ye eat.*

2. Therefore, whosoever eats a portion the size of an olive of the flesh of an unclean animal or beast is punishable by a flogging on the authority of the Torah. It is immaterial whether he eats of their flesh or of their fat, since in the case of unclean animals and beasts Scripture does not differentiate between flesh and fat.

3. Although Scripture says, *and man became the soul of a liv-*

ing creature (Gen. 2:8), man does not belong to the species of living creatures which have cloven hoofs; therefore, man is not forbidden by a negative commandment. However, he who eats human flesh or fat, whether of a living or a dead person, while not liable to a flogging, is guilty of violating a positive commandment, since Scripture enumerates the seven species of beasts of which it says, *These are the beasts which ye may eat* (Lev. 11:3), implying that whatever is not included among them may not be eaten, and a negative commandment which is deduced from a positive commandment has the same force as a positive commandment.

4. Whosoever eats an olive's bulk of the flesh of an unclean bird is punishable by a flogging on the authority of the Torah, as it is said, *And these ye shall have in abomination among the fowls, they shall not be eaten* (Lev. 11:13). In addition, he transgresses a positive commandment, as it is said, *Of all clean birds ye shall eat* (Deut. 14:11), implying that "of an unclean bird ye shall not eat." In the same way, he who eats an olive's bulk of an unclean fish is also liable to a flogging, as it is said, *and they shall be an abomination unto you, ye shall not eat of their flesh* (Lev. 11:11); moreover, he transgresses a positive commandment, since Scripture says, *whatsoever hath fins and scales shall ye eat* (Deut. 14:10), from which it follows that fish which have no fins and scales may not be eaten. Hence you learn that whosoever eats of unclean fish, animal, beast, or bird has both failed to fulfill a positive commandment and transgressed a negative one.

5. Unclean locusts are included in "winged creeping things," and whosoever eats an olive's bulk of a winged creeping thing is liable to a flogging, as it is said, *And all winged creeping things are unclean unto you, they shall not be eaten* (Deut. 14:19). What is a "winged creeping thing"? Creatures like flies, gnats, hornets, bees, and their like.

6. Whosoever eats an olive's bulk of the "creeping things of the earth" is likewise liable to a flogging, as it is said, *And every*

creeping thing that creepeth upon the earth is an abomination, it shall not be eaten (Lev. 11:41). What is a "creeping thing of the earth"? Creatures like snakes, scorpions, beetles, centipedes, and their like.

7. As for the eight creeping things which are mentioned in the Torah—*the weasel, the mouse, the great lizard . . . the gecko, the land crocodile, the lizard, the sand lizard, and the chameleon* (Lev. 11:29–30)—whosoever eats a lentil's bulk of their flesh is liable to a flogging. The minimum amount for liability for eating is in this case the same as the minimum amount for rendering unclean, and all of them may combine with one another to make up the lentil's bulk.

8. This rule refers to a person who eats of them after they are dead; if one cuts a limb from one of them while it is yet alive and eats it, he is not liable to a flogging unless it contains an olive's bulk of flesh, and they all combine to make up the olive's bulk. If he eats a complete limb of a creeping thing after its death, he is liable to a flogging if it is the size of a lentil.

9. Both the blood and the flesh of the eight creeping things combine to make up the size of a lentil, but only if the blood is still in the flesh. Similarly, the blood of a snake combines with its flesh to make up the bulk of an olive, and one is liable to a flogging if he eats it, since its flesh is not separated from its blood, even though the flesh itself does not render unclean. The same is true of all the other creeping things which do not render unclean.

10. If a person collects the blood of creeping things which has oozed out, and eats of it, he is liable to a flogging if it amounts to the bulk of an olive. That is, only if he has been cautioned against eating a creeping thing; if the warning was merely against eating blood, he is exempt, since the only blood which is forbidden is that of an animal, beast, or bird.

11. All these minimum amounts and their differentiations are rules given to Moses from Sinai.

12. Whosoever eats an olive's bulk of "a creeping thing of the water" is punishable by a flogging on the authority of the Torah, as it is said, *Ye shall not make yourselves abominable with any creeping thing which creepeth, neither shall ye make yourselves unclean with them* (Lev. 11:43), thus including in this negative commandment "creeping things of the earth," "winged creeping things," and "creeping things of the water." What is a "creeping thing of the water"? These are small creatures such as sea worms and water leeches, as well as the extraordinarily large creatures which are the beasts of the sea. The general rule is that whatever does not have the form of a fish, whether clean or unclean, such as seals, dolphins, frogs, and such like, is a "creeping thing of the water."

13. The species which originate in dust heaps and carcasses, such as maggots, worms, and their like, and which are born not through intercourse between male and female but out of putrefaction of dung, and its like, are called *creeping thing that moveth upon the earth* (Lev. 11:44). He who eats an olive's bulk of them is liable to a flogging, as it is said, *neither shall ye defile yourselves with any manner of creeping thing that moveth upon the earth* (*ibid.*), even though they do not multiply by breeding. On the other hand, *all creeping things that creep upon the earth* (Lev. 11:42) refers to such as procreate by intercourse between male and female.

14. In the case of such species as originate in fruit and food, the rule is that once they come out and reach the ground, even if they subsequently return inside the food, whosoever eats an olive's bulk of them is liable to a flogging, as it is said, *all creeping things that creep upon the earth* (Lev. 11:42), the import of which is to forbid those which come out *upon the earth*. If they do not come out, it is permitted to eat the fruit with the worm inside it.

15. This refers only to food which became wormy after it had been plucked from the soil. If it becomes wormy while still attached to the soil, the worm is forbidden, as though it had crawled

out to the ground, since it had originated upon the ground, and one is liable to a flogging on account of it. In case of doubt, the worm is likewise forbidden. Consequently, all species of fruit which are prone to become wormy while still attached to the soil should not be eaten without examination of their interior, lest there should be a worm in them. If, however, the fruit is kept for twelve months after being plucked, it may be eaten without examination, since a worm in fruit cannot survive for twelve months.

16. If the worm comes out into the air without touching the ground, or only part of its body reaches the ground, or if it drops out after its death, or is found on a pip inside, or comes out of one article of food and enters into another—all these are forbidden on account of the doubt involved, but no flogging is incurred because of them.

17. Worms found in the entrails of fish, or in the brain of an animal, or in the flesh, are forbidden. On the other hand, if salted fish become wormy, the worm within them is deemed permitted, since such fish are like fruit which had become wormy after being plucked, and which may be eaten together with the worm. The same applies to water in vessels which generates creeping things, and which may be drunk together with the creeping things, since Scripture says, *whatever hath fins and scales in the waters, in the seas, and in the rivers, them shall ye eat* (Lev. 11:9), meaning that in the waters, in the seas, and in the rivers you may eat creatures which have fins and scales, and may not eat those which do not have them. In vessels, however, whether these creatures do or do not have fins and scales, they are permitted to be eaten.

18. As regards creeping things of the water which originate in pits, ditches, and caves, since these waters are not flowing but are contained, they are like water in vessels, and the creeping things in them are permitted. One may bend down and drink, and need not restrain himself, even though in drinking he may swallow some of these minute creeping things.

19. This rule, however, refers only to creatures which have not left the place of their origin; once the creeping thing emerges, even if it subsequently returns to the vessel or to the pit, it is forbidden. If it crawls out upon the sides of the jug and then falls back into the water or into the beer, it is permitted. Similarly, if it crawls out upon the walls of the pit or of the cave and then returns to the water, it is also permitted.

20. If a person strains wine, vinegar, or beer and swallows the gnats, mosquitoes, or worms which he had strained out, he is liable to a flogging on account of "creeping things of the water" or "creeping winged things," even if he restores them to the vessel after straining them, since they had left their place of origin. But if he does not strain them, he may drink the liquid without hesitation, as we have explained.

21. That which we have said in this chapter about eating an olive's bulk refers to a person who eats an olive's bulk of a large creature, or combines part of one creature with part of another of its own species, so that all together he eats an olive's bulk. If he eats a whole unclean creature, even if it is smaller than a mustard seed, he is liable to a flogging on the authority of the Torah. It is immaterial whether he eats it dead or alive, and even if it putrefies and changes its form, once he eats it whole, he is liable to a flogging.

22. If an ant lacks but one of its legs, a person who eats it is not liable to a flogging unless it is the size of an olive. Therefore, whosoever eats a whole fly or a whole gnat, whether alive or dead, is liable to a flogging on account of "winged creeping things."

23. If a creature possesses the characteristics of a "winged creeping thing," a "creeping thing of the water," and "a creeping thing of the earth," all together—for example, if it has wings, walks on the ground like all creeping things, and breeds in the water—and a person eats of it, he is liable to a triple flogging. If in addition it belongs also to the species which originates in fruit, he is liable to a fourfold flogging. And if moreover it is of the species

which breed and multiply, he is liable to a fivefold flogging. If in addition to its belonging to the species of "winged creeping things," is also belongs to the class of unclean fowl, he is liable to a sixfold flogging, namely for unclean fowl, for a "winged creeping thing," for a "creeping thing on the earth," for a "creeping thing in the water," for "that which moves upon the earth," and for a worm in fruit, whether he eats it whole, or whether he eats an olive's bulk of it. Consequently, he who eats a flying ant which breeds in water is liable to a fivefold flogging.

24. If a person minces some ants and then adds to that which he had minced a whole ant, so that the total constitutes an olive's bulk, and then eats the mixture, he is liable to a sixfold flogging, five times for the whole ant, and once for eating an olive's bulk of the carcass of unclean creatures.

CHAPTER III

1. All food which is a product of any of the forbidden species whose consumption carries liability to flogging, is likewise forbidden to be eaten on the authority of the Torah. For example, the milk of unclean animals and beasts and the eggs of unclean fowl or fish, as it is said, *and the daughter of the ya'ănah* (Lev. 11:16), meaning its egg. The same applies to any other creature that is forbidden like the *ya'ănah,* and to everything else that is like an egg.

2. Human milk is permitted, even though human flesh is forbidden. We have already explained that human flesh is forbidden by a positive commandment.

3. Bees' and hornets' honey is permitted, since it is not exuded from their bodies; rather they collect it from the flowers into their mouths and then regurgitate it into the hive, in order that they may have it available for food during the winter.

4. Although human milk is permitted, the Sages have forbidden an adult to suckle it directly from the breast; the woman must first milk it into a vessel, and only then may the adult drink it. An adult who suckles from the breast is regarded as though he had sucked unclean matter, and is liable to the flogging prescribed for disobedience.

5. A suckling child may continue to suckle even for four or five years. But if it was weaned and went without suckling for three days or more, while in good health and not on account of illness, it may not resume suckling once again. This applies only if it was weaned after it had reached the age of twenty-four months; if weaned within this period, it may resume suckling until the expiration of twenty-four months, even if it had gone without for a month or two.

6. Although the milk of unclean cattle and the eggs of unclean birds are forbidden on the authority of the Torah, no liability to a flogging is incurred, since it is said, *Of their flesh ye shall not eat* (Lev. 11:11), meaning that a person is liable to a flogging on account of the flesh, but not on account of the egg or milk. He who eats of them is regarded as having eaten half the minimum amount which is forbidden by the Torah, for which he is therefore not liable to a flogging. But he is liable to the flogging prescribed for disobedience.

7. It would appear to me that whosoever eats the roe of an unclean fish which is found in its belly should be regarded as though he had eaten the entrails of unclean fish, and is liable to a flogging on the authority of the Torah. The same applies to the eggs of unclean birds which are still attached to the cluster, and which have not yet been separated and matured. Whosoever eats of them should be liable to a flogging, as though he had eaten of the bird's entrails.

8. If a person eats the egg of an unclean bird in which the embryo had already commenced to form, he is liable to a flogging on account of "winged creeping things"; if he eats the egg of a

clean bird whose embryo had begun to form, he is liable to a flogging prescribed for disobedience.

9. If a drop of coagulated blood is found upon the egg, the rule is as follows: If it is upon the white of the egg, a person may simply discard the drop and eat the remainder; if the blood is upon the yolk, the whole egg is forbidden. Infertile addled eggs may be eaten, if one is not fastidious.

10. A newborn chick may be eaten even before it has opened its eyes. The milk of an animal which has been rendered ṭĕrefah is forbidden, as it is considered to be the milk of an unclean animal. Similarly, the egg of a clean bird which has been rendered ṭĕrefah is deemed to be like the egg of an unclean bird, and is forbidden.

11. A chick hatched from the egg of a ṭĕrefah bird is permitted, so long as the species itself is not unclean. If the bird is doubtfully ṭĕrefah, all the eggs of the first clutch must be kept back. If it thereupon bears a second clutch and begins to lay them, the first batch of eggs is permitted, for had the bird been ṭĕrefah it would have laid no more eggs. If it lays no more eggs, the first batch is forbidden.

12. The milk of an unclean animal does not curdle and become thick like the milk of a clean animal. If the milk of an unclean animal is mixed with that of a clean animal, and is set, only the milk of the clean animal will become thick, while the milk of the unclean animal will come out with the whey of the cheese.

13. Consequently the rule should be that while milk in the possession of a heathen should be forbidden, as he might have mixed it with the milk of an unclean animal, the cheese of a heathen should be permitted, since the milk of an unclean animal cannot make cheese. In the time of the Sages of the Mishnah, however, they decreed a prohibition of heathen cheese as well, for the reason that the heathens set it with the membrane of the stomach of an animal slaughtered according to their own method, which is considered nĕḇelah. And should it be objected that the

membrane of the stomach is a minute quantity in proportion to the milk which is curdled by it, and that therefore it should be neutralized on account of its small quantity, the answer is that it is the membrane which curdles the milk into cheese, and seeing that it is the forbidden thing which causes the curdling, the whole mixture becomes forbidden, as will be explained in due course.

14. As for cheese which the heathens curdle with herbs or fruit juices, such as date brandy, whose presence can be detected in the cheese, some of the Geonim have ruled that it is forbidden, on the ground that the prohibitive decree had been issued against all heathen cheese, whether set with a forbidden or a permitted agent, as a precaution, seeing that the heathens usually curdle milk with forbidden matter.

15. Whosoever eats of heathen cheese, or drinks milk milked by a heathen not in the presence of an Israelite, is liable to the flogging prescribed for disobedience. As for heathen butter, some of the Geonim have permitted it, seeing that there is no decree against butter, and that the milk of unclean animals does not curdle. Other Geonim, however, have forbidden it, because of the drops of milk which remain in it, since the buttermilk does not mix with the butter in such a way as to become neutralized owing to its small quantity. And there is also the apprehension in the case of all heathen milk that it may have been mixed with the milk of unclean animals.

16. It would therefore appear to me that if a person buys butter from a heathen and boils it until the drops of milk disappear, it is permitted. Should it be argued that the milk has merely become mixed with the butter and both have been boiled together, the answer is that the milk has in any case become neutralized because of its minute quantity. However, butter boiled by heathens is forbidden, on account of having been boiled in heathen vessels, as will be explained.

17. If an Israelite is seated in the proximity of a herd owned by a heathen, and the heathen brings him milk from the herd, it

is permitted, even if the heathen has also unclean animals in his herd, and even if the Israelite does not actually see the heathen do the milking. That is, however, only if the Israelite could have seen him milking if he had stood up, since the heathen would in that case be afraid to milk an unclean animal, lest the Israelite should stand up and see him.

18. An egg that is round or pointed at both ends, or has the white inside the yolk, is certainly the egg of an unclean bird. If one end is pointed and the other rounded, and the yolk is inside the white, it may belong either to a clean or to an unclean bird. A person should therefore question the Israelite hunter who is selling the egg. If he says that it is the egg of a certain bird which he specifies by name, and if that bird is a clean one, he may be relied upon. But if he says that it is the egg of a clean bird without specifying it by name, he should not be relied upon.

19. Consequently a person should not purchase eggs from a heathen unless he recognizes them and has expert knowledge that they are the eggs of a specific bird which is clean. No apprehension need be felt that they may be the eggs of a bird which had been rendered ṭĕrefah or nĕḇelah. A person should not under any circumstances purchase beaten eggs from a heathen.

20. The eggs of fish have the same tokens as the eggs of birds. If both ends are rounded or pointed the egg is unclean; if one is round and the other pointed, a person should question the Israelite vendor. If he says, "I myself salted them, after having taken them out of a clean fish," a person may eat them on his assurance, but if he says merely that they are clean, he is not to be relied upon unless he is a man whose trustworthiness in adherence to the dietary laws has been established.

21. Similarly, a person should not purchase cheese or cuts of fish which have no tokens except from an Israelite whose trustworthiness in adherence to the dietary laws has been established. In the Land of Israel, however, when the majority of the inhabitants were Israelites, a person was permitted to purchase such

victuals from any Israelite there. Milk may be purchased from any Israelite anywhere.

22. If a person pickles unclean fish, the brine thereof is forbidden. The brine of unclean locusts, however, is permitted, since locusts have no fluid in their bodies. Brine should therefore not be purchased from a heathen, unless a clean fish is floating in it, even if it is only one fish.

23. If a heathen brings a crate full of open jugs of brine, and a single clean fish is floating in one of them, all are permitted. If the jugs are closed and he opens two in succession, and a clean fish is found in both, all are likewise permitted. The head and the spine of the fish, however, must still be preserved, so that a person may recognize it as a clean fish. Salted minced fish, called "hashed *ṭariṯ*," may therefore never be purchased from a heathen. If, however, the head and spine are recognizable, even though minced, it may be purchased from a heathen.

24. If a heathen brings a keg of fish cut up in such a way as to make it obvious that all of the pieces belong to one fish, should scales be found on one piece, all are deemed permitted.

CHAPTER IV

1. Whosoever eats one olive's bulk of the flesh of an animal, beast, or bird which had died of itself, is liable to a flogging, as it is said, *Ye shall not eat of anything that dieth of itself (nĕḇelah)* (Deut. 14:21); and whatever has not been slaughtered in accordance with the laws of šĕḥiṭah is regarded as though it had died of itself. In the Laws Concerning Šĕḥiṭah it will be explained what constitutes valid and invalid šĕḥiṭah.

2. The prohibition of nĕḇelah applies to clean species alone, since only they are fit for šĕḥiṭah, and had they been slaughtered in accordance with the laws of šĕḥiṭah they would have been

thereby permitted to be eaten. In respect to unclean species, however, in whose case šĕḥiṭah is useless, whether šĕḥiṭah is performed upon them, whether they had died a natural death, or whether a person cuts a limb from them while they are alive and eats it— liability to a flogging is incurred not on account of nĕḇelah or ṭĕrefah, but only because of eating the flesh of an unclean animal.

3. Whosoever eats a clean bird of any size alive is liable to a flogging for eating nĕḇelah. Even if the bird is less than an olive's bulk in size, he is liable to a flogging, seeing that he has eaten it whole. If, however, he eats it after it had died, he is not liable to a flogging unless he has eaten an olive's bulk. And even if there is not an olive's bulk of flesh in the whole bird, once the bird as a whole is the size of an olive's bulk, he is liable because of nĕḇelah.

4. Whosoever eats an olive's bulk of the flesh of a stillborn young of a clean animal is liable to a flogging on account of eating nĕḇelah. It is also forbidden to eat of a newborn young until the eighth night after its birth, since any young which has not lived for eight days is regarded as potentially stillborn, although a person is not liable to a flogging for it. If, however, it is known that the young had completed the requisite number of months in the womb—which is nine months for large cattle and five for small —before being born, it is permitted from the day of its birth.

5. The caul which emerges with the calf is forbidden to be eaten, but a person who eats it nevertheless is exempt, since it is not considered meat.

6. Whosoever eats an olive's bulk of the flesh of a clean animal, beast, or bird which has been rendered ṭĕrefah, is liable to a flogging, as it is said, *Any flesh that is torn of beasts (ṭĕrefah) in the field ye shall not eat; ye shall cast it to the dogs* (Exod. 22:30). This ṭĕrefah mentioned in Scripture refers to an animal torn by a beast of prey, such as a lion, a leopard, or their like. The same applies to a bird torn by a bird of prey, such as a falcon or its like. It cannot be said that this term applies only to cases where the beast of prey has not only torn the animal but killed it as well,

for if it had died it would have become nĕḇelah. Indeed, what difference does it make whether the animal had died a natural death, or whether a person smote it with a sword and slew it, or whether a lion mauled it and killed it? Perforce, then, the reference must be to cases where the animal is torn by the beast of prey, but does not die as a result of the mauling.

7. If, then, a torn beast which has not died as a result of the mauling is forbidden, it might be assumed therefrom that if a wolf comes forth and drags away a kid by its foot, tail, or ear, and someone forthwith chases the wolf and rescues the kid from its mouth, the kid should be forbidden, seeing that it is torn. That is why Scripture says expressly, *Any flesh that is torn of beasts in the field ye shall not eat; ye shall cast it to the dogs,* that is, it is not forbidden until it becomes fit only for a dog. Hence you learn that ṭĕrefah mentioned in the Torah refers to an animal so torn and crushed by a beast of prey that it is fatally wounded, although not yet dead. And even if a person anticipates its death and performs šĕḥiṭah upon it before it dies, it is still forbidden as ṭĕrefah, since it could not have continued to live as a result of the wound inflicted upon it.

8. From all this you learn that the Torah has forbidden, first, a dead animal—which is considered nĕḇelah—and, second, one which is bound to die as a result of its wounds, though not yet dead—which constitutes ṭĕrefah. And in exactly the same manner as in the case of the animal which had died—where no distinction is made between the causes of death, whether the animal had died of natural causes, or fell down to its death, or was strangled to death, or was torn and killed by a beast of prey—in the same way no distinction is made in the case of an animal which is about to die, whether a beast of prey had torn and crushed it, or the animal itself had fallen from a roof and had fractured most of its ribs, or had fallen and injured its organs, or was shot by an arrow and its heart or lungs were pierced, or contracted a disease which caused the perforation of its heart or lungs or brought about the fracture of most of its ribs, and so

forth. Once the animal is about to die, it is in every case considered ṭĕrefah, whether the cause is an act of man or an act of heaven. This being so, why does the Torah specify *torn?* The answer is that Scripture speaks in terms of what occurs most commonly. For if you should say that this is not so, you will then have to say that it refers only to an animal *torn . . . in the field,* and that if it was torn in a courtyard you would not forbid it! Hence you learn that Scripture does indeed speak only in terms of the most common occurrence.

9. The essence of this verse is therefore that an animal which is about to die on account of its wound, and cannot survive as a result of that wound, is forbidden. Hence the Sages have enunciated the general rule that every disease which, if it afflicts an animal, makes it impossible for that animal to survive renders it ṭĕrefah, and in the Laws Concerning Šĕḥiṭah it will be explained which diseases render an animal ṭĕrefah and which do not.

10. Similarly, if a person cuts some flesh from the living body of one of the clean animals, that flesh is deemed ṭĕrefah, and whosoever eats an olive's bulk of it is liable to a flogging for eating ṭĕrefah, since this flesh comes from an animal upon which no šĕḥiṭah has been performed, nor has it died. What difference does it make whether a beast of prey tears it, or a person cuts it with a knife, whether it is the whole animal, or only a part of it? Scripture declares *Any flesh that is torn of beasts in the field ye shall not eat,* implying that once the flesh has become "flesh in the field" it is deemed ṭĕrefah.

11. An animal which is sick as the result of natural enfeeblement and is about to die is permitted, since no fatal wound had developed in any of its vital organs, seeing that the Torah forbids only that which can be compared to an animal torn by a beast of prey, that is, it must have a wound from which it will surely die.

12. While such an animal is permitted, the greatest of the

Sages have nevertheless avoided eating an animal that was hastily slaughtered before natural death could set in, even if it still quivered at the conclusion of šĕḥiṭah. There is thus no prohibition attached to it, but he who prefers to be strict in this matter is praiseworthy.

13. If a person performs šĕḥiṭah upon an animal, beast, or bird and no blood issues therefrom, it is deemed permitted, and it cannot be said that it may have been dead before šĕḥiṭah. Similarly, if a person slaughters a healthy animal and it does not quiver, it is also permitted. An animal dangerously ill, however—that is one which, when stood up, cannot remain standing, though it may eat food like a healthy animal—which does not quiver when slaughtered, is considered nĕḇelah and makes one liable to a flogging. If it does quiver, it is permitted. The quivering must take place at the conclusion of šĕḥiṭah; it is of no effect if it occurs at the commencement thereof.

14. What is meant by quivering? In the case of small animals or large or small beasts, if it stretches its foreleg forward and pulls it back, or if it stretches its hind leg forward, even without pulling it back, or if it merely bends its hind leg—all these motions constitute quivering and the animal is permitted. If, however, the animal stretches out its foreleg but does not pull it back, the animal is forbidden, for that action is merely the sign of the departure of life. In the case of large animals, it is immaterial whether it is the foreleg or the hind leg, whether the animal stretches out the leg and does not bend it, or bends it and does not stretch it out—all this constitutes quivering and the animal is permitted. If, however, the animal stretches out neither foreleg nor hind leg, nor bends it at all, it is considered nĕḇelah. In the case of a bird, even if it flutters its eyelid or twitches its tail, this constitutes quivering.

15. If a person performs šĕḥiṭah upon a dangerously ill animal at night, so that he does not know whether it had quivered or not, it is considered doubtfully nĕḇelah, and is forbidden.

16. With the sole exception of things prohibited to the Nazirite, as will be explained in its proper place, things forbidden by the Torah do not combine with one another to make up the minimum requisite amount. Thus, were a person to take a little forbidden fat, a little blood, a little of the flesh of an unclean animal, a little of the flesh of a nĕḇelah, a little of the flesh of an unclean fish, and a little of the flesh of an unclean bird, and similarly of any other forbidden things, and combine them all to make up an olive's bulk, and then eat it, he would not be liable to a flogging, but would be considered as though he had eaten half the minimum requisite amount.

17. All the different kinds of nĕḇelah, however, do combine with one another, and so does nĕḇelah combine with ṭĕrefah. Similarly, all unclean animals and beasts combine with one another, but flesh which is nĕḇelah does not combine with the flesh of an unclean animal. Thus, were a person to take flesh from the nĕḇelah of an ox, the nĕḇelah of a deer, and the nĕḇelah of a cock, put them together, and eat an olive's bulk of the mixture, he would be liable to a flogging. Similarly, if he joined together half an olive's bulk of the flesh of a nĕḇelah of a clean animal with half an olive's bulk of a ṭĕrefah, or half an olive's bulk of the flesh of a nĕḇelah with half an olive's bulk of flesh from a living clean animal, and then ate it, he would also be liable to a flogging. Likewise, if he combined the flesh of a camel, a pig, and a hare, and ate an olive's bulk of it, he would again be liable to a flogging. Were he, however, to combine half an olive's bulk of the nĕḇelah of an ox with half an olive's bulk of the flesh of a camel, they would not combine to form the requisite olive's bulk, and so in similar instances. In like manner, the flesh of an unclean animal cannot combine with the flesh of an unclean bird or an unclean fish, since they belong to different categories, and each one of them is prohibited by a separate negative commandment, as we have explained. However, all unclean birds combine in the same manner as do all unclean animals and beasts. The general rule is that all things which are

forbidden by the same negative commandment do combine; such things as are prohibited by two separate commandments do not combine, with the sole exception of nĕbelah and ṭĕrefah, since ṭĕrefah is but the first stage of nĕḇelah.

18. Whosoever eats of the skin, the bones, the sinews, the horns, the hoofs, or the caul of a nĕḇelah, of a ṭĕrefah, or of unclean animals and beasts, or of the claws of birds—cut off at a point where the blood spurts forth—is exempt, even though this is forbidden, since these parts are unfit for human consumption and do not combine with flesh to form an olive's bulk.

19. The stomach of a nĕḇelah or of an unclean animal is permitted, since it is like any other part of the offal. It is therefore permitted to curdle cheese with the stomach of an animal slaughtered by a heathen or with the stomach of an unclean animal or beast. The membrane of the stomach, however, is like any other part of the entrails, and is forbidden to be eaten.

20. The skin in front of a donkey's face is permitted, since it is considered similar to dung and urine, which are permitted. Some kinds of skin, however, are regarded as flesh, and whosoever eats an olive's bulk of them is liable to a flogging, as though he had eaten an olive's bulk of flesh; that is, if he eats the skin while it is still tender.

21. The following kinds of skin are regarded as similar to flesh: human skin; the skin of the domesticated pig; the skin of the hump of a camel which has never borne a burden, or has not yet reached the stage of bearing a burden, so that its skin is still tender; the skin of the privy parts; the skin under the tail; the skin of a foetus; and the skin of the gecko, the land crocodile, the lizard, and the sand lizard. All these skins, when tender, are regarded in every respect as flesh, both as to the prohibition of eating and as to uncleanness.

22. With regard to the ox which has been stoned, Scripture says, *and its flesh shall not be eaten* (Exod. 21:28). How could

it be permissible to eat it after the ox has been stoned, seeing that it has become nĕḇelah? What the verse means to convey is that from the moment the ox has been sentenced to stoning, it becomes immediately prohibited and is regarded as an unclean animal. If therefore a person anticipates the carrying out of the sentence and performs valid ṣĕḥiṭah upon the ox, he is forbidden to derive any benefit from it, and if he eats an olive's bulk of its flesh he is liable to a flogging. So also, after the ox has been stoned, he may neither sell it nor give it to a dog or to a heathen. That is why Scripture says, *and its flesh shall not be eaten*. A person is allowed, however, to derive benefit from the dung of such an ox. If after sentence has been passed, it becomes known that the ox is not liable to stoning—for instance, if the witnesses in the case are found to have been guilty of collusion—it is to be released and may pasture with the flock. If the facts become known after the stoning has been carried out, a person is permitted to derive benefit from the carcass.

CHAPTER V

1. The Sages have learned by tradition that when the Torah says, *Thou shalt not eat the life with the flesh* (Deut. 12:23), its purpose is to forbid the eating of a limb cut from a living animal. And concerning such a limb the Holy One, blessed be He, said to Noah, *Only flesh with the life thereof, which is the blood thereof, shall ye not eat* (Gen. 9:4). This prohibition of eating a limb from a living animal applies only to clean animals, beasts, and birds, and not to unclean ones.

2. It is immaterial whether the limb consists of flesh, sinews, and bones, such as the fore and hind legs, or whether it has no bones, such as the tongue, the testicles, the spleen, the kidneys, the heart, and their like. The only difference is that an organ which has no bone is prohibited on account of a limb from a

living animal, whether a person cuts it off whole or in part, while in the case of a limb which has a bone, he is liable only if he removes it in its natural form, that is, including the flesh, bone, and sinews. If, however, he removes the flesh alone from that limb, he is liable on account of ṭĕrefah, as we have explained, and not on account of a limb from a living animal.

3. Whosoever eats an olive's bulk of a limb from a living animal is liable to a flogging, even if he eats a complete limb; so long as it is the size of an olive's bulk he is liable; if less, he is exempt. If he cuts from the limb in its natural form a piece consisting of an olive's bulk of flesh, bones, and sinews, and eats it, he is liable to a flogging, even though the flesh thereof is but a negligible quantity. But if, after plucking the limb from the living animal, he divides it and separates the flesh from the bones and sinews, he is not liable to a flogging, unless he eats an olive's bulk of the flesh alone; the bones and sinews do not combine to make up the olive's bulk, seeing that he had altered the limb's natural form.

4. If a person divides the limb and eats it in small pieces, he is liable only if there is an olive's bulk of flesh in any one piece; if not, he is exempt. If he takes an olive's bulk of the limb in its natural form, i.e. flesh, bone, and sinew, and eats it, even though it is divided into pieces inside his mouth before he swallows it, he is nevertheless liable to a flogging.

5. If a person plucks a limb from a living animal, and if as a result of this the animal becomes ṭĕrefah, and if he then eats the limb, he is liable to a twofold flogging, once for a limb from a living animal and once for ṭĕrefah, since both prohibitions become effective simultaneously. Similarly, if he plucks forbidden fat from a living animal and eats it, he is liable to be flogged twice, once on account of a limb from a living animal and again on account of forbidden fat. Should he pluck forbidden fat from an animal which is considered ṭĕrefah and eat it, he would be liable to a triple flogging.

6. Flesh dangling from an animal, or a dangling limb, if it cannot be restored so that it would become whole again, is forbidden, even if it does not become entirely separated until after šĕḥiṭah has been performed, although a person is not liable to a flogging for eating it. Should the animal die, the dangling portion is regarded as though it had become loose during the animal's life. One is therefore liable to a flogging on account of a limb from a living animal, if he eats it. But if the limb can be restored to the animal and made whole again, once šĕḥiṭah is performed upon the animal, it is deemed permitted.

7. If a person dislocates an animal's limb, or crushes or mashes it—for instance, if he crushes or detaches the testicles—the animal is not forbidden according to the Torah, since it still retains some life, and for that reason it does not putrefy. Nevertheless it is forbidden to eat of it, seeing that from ancient times all Israel have adopted the custom of refraining from eating of it, because it is equivalent to a limb from a living animal.

8. In the case of a fractured bone, if flesh or skin covers the major portion of the thickness of the fractured bone and the major portion of the circumference of the fracture, it is permitted. If the bone protrudes, that limb is forbidden. When therefore a person slaughters the animal or bird, he should cut the limb off at the fracture and discard it, the remainder of the animal being permitted. If the bone is fractured, and flesh covers the major portion thereof, but is lacerated or rotted, like the flesh which the surgeon scrapes away; or if the major portion of the flesh is distributed in more than one place; or if the flesh is perforated or slit; or if it is cut out like a ring; or if its upper layer has been scraped away so that only a film of flesh remains; or if the inner layer of the flesh on the fractured bone is so rotted that the flesh covering the bone does not touch it—in all these cases the decision should be to forbid the limb, until such time as the flesh heals. Whosoever eats from any of these is liable to the flogging prescribed for disobedience.

9. If a person inserts his hand into the abdomen of an animal

and severs the spleen, the kidneys, or their like, and leaving the severed portions inside, performs šěḥiṭah upon the animal, these severed portions are forbidden on account of a limb from a living animal, even if they remain within the abdomen. If, however, he severs a portion of the unborn young in the mother's womb, but does not take it out, and subsequently slaughters the mother, the severed portion or limb of the young is permitted, as long as it had not been taken out. If the young thrusts forth its fore or hind leg, that limb is in all circumstances forbidden, whether one cuts it off before šěḥiṭah is performed upon its mother, or after šěḥiṭah. And even if the young withdraws that limb back into its mother's womb, and the mother is subsequently slaughtered, or if the calf is born and lives for many years, that limb remains forbidden because of ṭěrefah, since all flesh which emerges from its original enclosure is forbidden as flesh separated from the living, as it is said, *and flesh in the field is ṭěrefah* (Exod. 22:30): that is, once it has emerged into the place which to it is like a "field," it is thereby rendered ṭěrefah, as we have explained.

10. If part of the limb emerges and part—even if only a minor portion of it—remains in its place within, only that portion which has emerged is forbidden, while the portion which remains within is permitted. If a person severs the portion of the limb which was exposed, after the young has pulled it back, and then slaughters the mother, only that portion which had been exposed is forbidden, and the rest of the limb is permitted. If the young does not pull back the limb and one cuts it off while it protrudes, whether he severs it before or after šěḥiṭah, the place of the cut is forbidden, that is the surface which is exposed to the air. Having severed that portion which had been exposed, one must therefore again cut off the exposed surface of the cut.

11. Any limb of an unborn young which emerges and which is severed before šěḥiṭah while it is outside, is regarded as a limb of a living animal, and one is liable to a flogging for eating it, even if the young dies before šěḥiṭah is performed. If the limb is severed after šěḥiṭah, however, he who eats of it is not liable

to a flogging, even if the young dies. If the animal dies and one subsequently severs the limb from the young and eats of it, he is liable to a flogging because of a limb of a living animal.

12. If an unborn young thrusts forth its limb with the result that the limb becomes forbidden, and then is born and turns out to be a female, it is forbidden to drink its milk because of the doubt, seeing that the milk derives from all of its organs; since it has one limb which is forbidden, the milk is regarded as a mixture of the milk of a ṭĕrefah animal with the milk of a clean animal.

13. If one slaughters a pregnant animal, and finds a foetus within it, the foetus, whether dead or alive, is permitted for consumption. And even the caul is permitted. If part of the caul emerges, and one then slaughters the animal, the rule is as follows: If the caul is attached to the young, the portion which has emerged is forbidden, but the remainder is permitted; if it is not attached, it is wholly forbidden, since there is the possibility that the foetus which was within the caul that had partly emerged has disappeared, while the caul of the foetus which was in fact found in the womb has also disappeared. Needless to say, if no foetus whatsoever is found in the womb, the whole caul is prohibited.

14. If a person finds a living young within the slaughtered mother—even if it is fully nine-months developed, and may possibly live—it does not require šĕḥiṭah, since the šĕḥiṭah of its mother has already validated it for consumption. Once, however, it sets its feet on the ground, it requires šĕḥiṭah.

15. If a person tears an animal open—without performing šĕḥiṭah—or performs šĕḥiṭah upon a ṭĕrefah animal, and finds inside it a nine-months live young, it requires šĕḥiṭah in order to validate it for consumption, since its mother's šĕḥiṭah is in this case useless for the young. If it is not fully nine-months developed, it is forbidden, even if it is alive in the womb of the ṭĕrefah mother, since it is like a limb of its mother. If a young thrusts

forth its head from the womb and then pulls it back, and if šĕḥiṭah is thereupon performed upon its mother, the mother's šĕḥiṭah is useless for the calf. It is regarded as having already been born, and therefore requires its own šĕḥiṭah.

CHAPTER VI

1. If a person consumes an olive's bulk of blood willfully, he is liable to extinction; if in error, he must bring a fixed sin offering. It is explicitly stated in the Torah that a person is liable only for the blood of animal, beast, or bird alone, whether they are clean or unclean, as it is said, *and ye shall eat no manner of blood, whether it be fowl or animal, in any of your dwellings* (Lev. 7:26), and beasts are included in the class of animals, since it is said, *These are the animals which ye may eat, the ox,* etc., *the hart, and the gazelle* (Deut. 14:4). For the blood of fish, locusts, insects, and creeping things, and for human blood, however, a person is not liable on account of the prohibition of blood. For this reason the blood of clean fishes and locusts is permitted to be consumed, even if one collects it in a vessel and drinks it. The blood of unclean locusts and fish is forbidden because it is a product of their bodies, like the milk of an unclean animal, while the blood of insects is like their flesh, as we have explained.

2. Human blood, once it has emerged, is forbidden on the authority of the Scribes, and one is liable on account of it to the flogging prescribed for disobedience. But if one's teeth are bleeding, the blood may be swallowed without hesitation. However, if one bites into a piece of bread and finds blood on the bread, he must scrape away the blood before eating the bread, since in this case the blood has already emerged.

3. Extinction is incurred only for blood which issues as a result of šĕḥiṭah, stabbing, or decapitation, as long as the blood retains its redness; for blood which accumulates in the heart; and for

the blood of bloodletting, as long as it flows freely. For the blood which spurts forth at the beginning of bloodletting, before the blood commences to flow freely, and for the blood which spurts forth at the end of the operation, when the flow is about to come to an end, one is not liable, and this blood is regarded as the blood of the organs, for life departs only with evenly flowing blood.

4. One is not liable to extinction for the last blood that oozes forth, or for blood of the organs, such as the spleen, the kidneys, or the testicles, or blood which invades the heart during šĕḥiṭah, or blood in the liver. Nevertheless, whosoever consumes an olive's bulk of it is liable to a flogging, as it is said, *and ye shall eat no manner of blood* (Lev. 7:26). As for the liability to extinction, it is said, *for the life of the flesh is in the blood* (Lev. 17:11), that is, one is not liable to extinction except on account of the blood with which the departure of life takes place.

5. The blood of a foetus found in the belly of an animal is regarded as similar to the blood of the young which has already been born. Consequently, one is liable to extinction only for the blood found accumulated in its heart, whereas the remainder of its blood is considered as blood of the organs.

6. Whether for roasting or for boiling, one must tear open the heart and remove its blood before salting it. Should a person cook the heart without opening it, he may open it after cooking, and it is then permitted. If, however, he eats it without opening it, he is not liable to extinction because of it. This, however, refers only to the heart of a bird which contains less than an olive's bulk of blood; for the heart of an animal one is liable to extinction, since it contains at least an olive's bulk of the heart's blood, for which extinction is incurred.

7. If the liver is cut open and thrown into vinegar or boiling water, so that it becomes bleached, it is then permitted to be cooked. But all Israel have long since adopted the custom of singeing it over the fire before cooking it, whether it is to be cooked alone or with other meat. It is similarly a widespread

custom not to cook or roast the brain before singeing it over the fire.

8. If one cooks a liver without singeing it over the fire or without scalding it in vinegar or boiling water, the whole dish is forbidden, both the liver itself and the victuals cooked with it. It is permitted, however, to roast liver and meat together on one spit, if the liver is placed below the meat. Nevertheless, if one disregards this rule and places the liver above the meat, he may still eat of it.

9. It is permitted to cook the spleen, even together with meat, since it does not consist of blood, but is merely flesh which resembles blood. Should one break the neck of an animal before its life has departed, the blood becomes absorbed in the organs, and it is forbidden to eat the meat raw, even if it is scalded. How then should one proceed? He should cut a piece, salt it thoroughly, and thereupon boil or roast it. We have already explained that if one performs šĕḥiṭah upon an animal, beast, or bird, and no blood comes forth, they are permitted.

10. Meat cannot be rid of its blood unless it is thoroughly salted and rinsed. How should one proceed? First, he should rinse the meat, and then salt it thoroughly and leave it in the salt for the time it takes to walk a mile. He should then rinse it well again until the water is entirely clear, and immediately thereafter cast it into boiling—not tepid—water, so that it would become bleached, and no more blood would emerge.

11. In salting meat a perforated vessel should be used, and salt which is as heavy as coarse sand, for salt which is as fine as flour is absorbed in the meat and does not extract the blood. It is also required to shake the salt off the meat before rinsing the latter.

12. All this applies only to meat which is to be boiled; meat for roasting needs merely to be salted and may be roasted imme-

diately thereafter. Should one desire to eat meat raw, he must first salt and rinse it thoroughly, after which he may eat of it. If a person scalds meat in vinegar, he may eat it raw, and may also drink the vinegar in which it was scalded, since vinegar does not extract the blood.

13. The vinegar in which meat has been scalded should not be used a second time for the same purpose. If a piece of meat becomes reddened while in the vinegar, both the meat and the vinegar are forbidden, unless the meat is thoroughly salted and then roasted. Meat which has become reddened, as well as the testicles of animals and beasts still in their scrotum, and the neck containing the jugular veins, all of which are full of blood, may be cooked if they are first cut open and properly salted. If a person does not cut them open but roasts them on a spit, placing the neck with the opening facing downwards, or if he grills them over the coals, they are permitted.

14. If one roasts the head of an animal in an oven or furnace, and suspends it so that the place where šĕḥiṭah was performed faces downwards, the head is permitted, since the blood oozes out. If it is suspended in such a manner that the place of šĕḥiṭah is on a side, the brain is forbidden, because in such a case the blood collects in it. The remainder of the meat, however, which is on the outer side of the bones is permitted. If the snout is left suspended downwards, it is permitted, provided that a straw or reed is inserted into it so that an aperture is left through which the blood can ooze out. If one does not do so, the brain is forbidden.

15. It is forbidden to place an empty vessel under meat which is being roasted, in order to receive the juice which drips from it, until all redness in it has disappeared. How then should one proceed? One should throw a little salt in the vessel, and leave the vessel there until the meat is fully roasted. The fat in the vessel which floats on the surface may then be taken, but the juice underneath it is forbidden.

16. It is permitted to eat bread upon which roast meat had been cut up, since that which the bread has absorbed is merely fat. If fish and birds are salted together, even if this is done in a perforated vessel, the fish is forbidden, since the flesh of fish is soft and absorbs the blood which emerges from the birds. Needless to say, the same applies to fish salted together with the flesh of animals or beasts.

17. If whole birds are stuffed with meat and eggs and are then boiled, they are forbidden, since the blood enters into the stuffing, even if a person first salts them thoroughly, and even if the meat stuffing is already boiled or roasted. If the birds are roasted, they are permitted, even if the meat inside is raw, and even if the aperture faces upwards.

18. If a person stuffs entrails in the same manner with roasted or boiled meat, or if he stuffs them with eggs and then boils or roasts them, they are permitted, since the entrails cannot be presumed to retain blood. The Geonim also have rendered a decision to the same effect.

19. If one covers birds with dough and roasts them, whether the birds are whole or cut up, the rule is as follows: If the paste is made with coarse meal, a person may eat of it, even if it turns red, since such paste is crumbly and permits the blood to emerge. If, on the other hand, the paste is made with flour from moistened wheat grain, it is permitted only if it remains as white as silver; otherwise it is forbidden. With regard to other kinds of meal, if the paste becomes red it is forbidden, and if not, it is permitted.

20. It is forbidden to cut hot food with a knife which was used to perform *šeḥiṭah*, unless the knife is first brought to a white heat, or sharpened on a whetstone, or thrust forcefully ten times into hard ground. If, however, a person does nevertheless cut hot food with it, that food is permitted. Similarly, one should not in the first instance cut radishes or other pungent foods with it. If one washes the knife or wipes it with a cloth, it is permitted to cut radishes and their like with it, but not hot food.

21. It is forever forbidden to eat hot food from a vessel in which meat had been salted, even if it is lined with lead, for the blood has already been absorbed by the earthenware.

CHAPTER VII

1. Whosoever eats an olive's bulk of forbidden fat willfully is liable to extinction; if in error, he must bring a fixed sin offering. The Torah declares explicitly that he is liable with respect to the fat of only three species of clean animals, as it is said, *Ye shall eat no fat of ox, or sheep, or goat* (Lev. 7:23). It is immaterial whether the fat is of an animal upon which šĕḥiṭah had been performed, or whether the animal is nĕḇelah or ṭĕrefah. In the case of other animals and of beasts, however, whether clean or unclean, their fat is considered the same as their flesh. Similarly, in the case of a stillborn young of these three species of clean animals, its fat is considered the same as its flesh, and whosoever eats an olive's bulk of its fat is liable to a flogging for eating nĕḇelah.

2. Whosoever eats of the fat of an animal which is nĕḇelah or ṭĕrefah is liable on account of eating forbidden fat, as well as on account of eating nĕḇelah or ṭĕrefah. Since the additional prohibition affecting the flesh, which was originally permitted, is now added to the prohibition of the fat, he is liable to be flogged twice.

3. If one performs šĕḥiṭah upon an animal and finds inside it an unborn young, the latter's fat is permitted, even if it is found alive, seeing that it is regarded as one of its mother's organs. If, however, it has completed its requisite number of months and is found alive, even if it had not yet set its feet on the ground and therefore does not require šĕḥiṭah, its fat is nevertheless forbidden, and one is liable to extinction on account of it. All the forbidden veins and membranes of it must be removed, as in the case of other animals.

4. If one inserts his hand into an animal's womb and cuts the fat from a completely developed young, and then draws it out, he is liable, for it is the same as if he had cut a piece of the fat of the mother itself, since the completion of the months of development has already caused the young's fat to become prohibited.

5. There are three kinds of fat for which one is liable to extinction: the fat upon the entrails, upon the two kidneys, and upon the flanks. The tail fat, however, is permitted. Although this tail fat, too, is called *ḥeleḇ,* it is so called only in connection with the sacrifices, just as the kidneys and the lobe above the liver are called ḥeleḇ in the same connection, and just as you say *"the ḥeleḇ of the land"* (Gen. 45:18), and *"the ḥeleḇ of kidneys of wheat"* (Deut. 32:14), which means "the choice produce of the land" and "the choice of kidneys of wheat." They are called ḥeleḇ because these portions of the sacrificial offering form part of the heave offering and were burned before the Divine Name, and there can be nothing more choice than that which is offered to Him. It is for this reason that it is stated in connection with the tithe heave offering, *when ye heave the ḥeleḇ thereof from it* (Num. 18:30).

6. The fat upon the omasum and the second stomach constitutes the fat of the entrails. Similarly, the fat which is at the joint of the thighs within constitutes the fat of the flanks, and one is liable to extinction on account of it. There is also upon the stomach a layer of fat curved like a bow, which is likewise forbidden, whereas the sinew which serves as the string of the bow is permitted. The sinews in the fat are also forbidden, but carry no extinction.

7. Fat covered by flesh is permitted, for Scripture has forbidden only that which is *upon the flanks* (Lev. 3:4), not that which is within the flanks. Similarly, it is only the fat upon the kidneys which is forbidden, not the fat inside the kidneys. Nevertheless, one should remove the white portion inside the kidneys, and

only thereafter eat them. There is, however, no need to scrape the spot further for it.

8. There is, at the base of an animal's loins, near the top of its flank, what appears like two cords of fat. While the animal is alive this fat appears to be upon the entrails, but after death flesh is joined to flesh and this fat becomes covered up, and cannot be seen unless one layer of flesh is separated from the other. Nevertheless, this fat is forbidden, since it does not constitute fat which is covered with flesh. Otherwise, wherever one finds fat under the flesh, and the flesh surrounds it on all sides, so that it cannot be seen until the flesh is torn open, that fat is permitted.

9. The fat of the heart and of the small entrails—meaning the twisting small bowels—is wholly permitted, and is like permitted fat. The only exception is the fat upon the upper part of the entrails next to the stomach, which is the beginning of the entrails. This fat must be scraped away, and that is what is referred to as the forbidden fat of the small bowels. Some of the Geonim, however, state that the "upper part of the entrails" which must be scraped away is the other end, whence the excreta emerge, that is, the end of the entrails.

10. There are in an animal's body forbidden veins and membranes, some of which are prohibited on account of fat, and some on account of blood. Such veins and membranes as are forbidden on account of blood must be removed before the meat is salted and boiled, as we have stated. If, however, the meat is already cut and salted, there is no need to remove them; nor need they be removed if the meat is roasted. As for sinews and membranes which are forbidden on account of fat, they must be removed from the flesh in any case, whether for boiling or roasting.

11. There are five such sinews in the flanks, three on the right flank and two on the left. Each of the three on the right branches out into two, and each of the two on the left branches out into three, and all are forbidden on account of fat. Similarly, the sinews of the spleen and of the kidneys are forbidden because of fat; and so are the membrane on the spleen, the one on the

flanks, and the one on the kidneys. Extinction is incurred for eating the membrane upon the convex side of the spleen; the remainder of this membrane, while forbidden, involves no liability to extinction.

12. There are two membranes upon the kidneys. The outer membrane involves extinction, in the same way as the fat upon the kidney. The inner membrane, however, is like all other membranes. And the sinews in them are forbidden, but without involving liability to extinction.

13. The veins of the heart, the foreleg, the tail, and the lower jaw on either side of the tongue; similarly, the fine veins inside the heart, which are as delicate as a spider's web and are intertwined with one another; the membrane on the brain inside the skull; and the membrane on the testicles—all these are forbidden on account of blood.

14. The testicles of a kid or lamb less than thirty days old may be cooked without peeling off the scrotum. After thirty days, should fine red veins appear in them, it is evident that the blood has begun to circulate in them, and they may not be boiled until they have been peeled, or cut open and salted, as we have explained. If, however, the red veins are not visible, they are permitted.

15. The entrails through which the food travels are presumed to hold no blood.

16. It would seem to me that the prohibition of all these veins and membranes rests on the authority of the Scribes. If, however, it is assumed that the prohibition is based on the authority of the Torah, being included in the interdict of *all fat* and *all blood* (Lev. 7:23, 26), one would still be liable only to the flogging prescribed for disobedience, since these things would be analogous to half the minimum quantity, which is forbidden by the Torah, but for which no flogging is incurred.

17. One may neither salt nor rinse fat together with meat, nor may one cut meat with a knife used to cut fats. Nor may

he rinse meat in a vessel in which he has rinsed fats. A butcher should therefore have three knives, one for performing šĕḥiṭah, one for cutting meat, and one for cutting fats.

18. In localities where it is the custom for the butcher to rinse the meat at his shop, he must have two separate vessels, one for rinsing meat and one for rinsing fats.

19. A butcher is forbidden to stretch the fat of the flanks over the meat in order to improve its appearance, for the membrane covering the fat is very thin and is liable to be crushed in the butcher's hand, with the result that the fat would ooze out and be absorbed into the meat. But although it is prohibited to do these things, yet they do not render the meat forbidden if one does them, nor is he liable to a flogging, but is merely to be instructed not to do it again.

20. Similarly, one may not salt meat before removing the forbidden membranes and veins, but if he has done so, he may remove them after the salting. Even if the sinew of the thigh vein is among them, he may still remove it after the salting, and may then cook the meat.

21. If a butcher customarily porges his meat, and a vein or a membrane is subsequently found in it, he is to be instructed and cautioned not to deal lightly with forbidden things. Should fat be found in the meat after his treatment, if it is the size of a barleycorn, he is to be removed from his position. If an olive's bulk of fat is found, even if distributed in several places, he is to be both flogged for disobedience and removed, seeing that the butcher is relied upon to remove all fat.

CHAPTER VIII

1. The prohibition of *the sinew of the thigh vein* (Gen. 32:33) obtains with clean animals and beasts, even if they are nĕḇelah

or ṭĕrefah. It obtains also with an unborn young and with animals consecrated for sacrifice, whether they are to be eaten or not, and it obtains both with the right and the left thigh. According to the Torah, only that portion which is upon the hollow of the thigh is forbidden, seeing that it says *upon the hollow of the thigh (ibid.)*. The remainder of the sinew, however, both that which is above the hollow and that which is below it, as well as the fat upon the sinew, is prohibited only on the authority of the Scribes. There are two such sinews, the inner one, next to the bone, which is forbidden by the Torah, and the upper one, the whole of which is prohibited on the authority of the Scribes.

2. Whosoever eats of the inner sinew of the thigh vein, namely of the portion which is upon the hollow of the thigh, is liable to a flogging. If he eats of its fat, or of the remaining portion of the sinew, or of any portion of the outer sinew, he is liable to the flogging prescribed for disobedience. The minimum amount which must be eaten for this liability is an olive's bulk, but if he eats the whole of that portion of the sinew which is upon the hollow of the thigh, he is liable to a flogging even if it amounts to less than an olive's bulk, since it is considered a separate entity.

3. If he eats an olive's bulk of the sinew on the right thigh and an olive's bulk of the sinew on the left thigh, or if he eats two whole sinews, even if they do not amount to an olive's bulk, he is liable to be flogged twice. In this wise, he is liable to a flogging for each individual sinew.

4. The prohibition of the sinew of the thigh vein does not apply to birds, since they have no hollow of the thigh, their thigh being elongated. Should a bird be found whose thigh is like that of an animal, that is with a hollow, the sinew of its thigh vein would be forbidden, though no flogging would be incurred for it. Similarly, in the case of an animal having a thigh which is elongated like that of a bird, the sinew would be forbidden, though again no flogging would be incurred for it.

5. Whosoever eats of the sinew of the thigh vein of an unclean animal or beast is exempt, since the prohibition does not apply to unclean animals, but only to an animal which is wholly permitted. Nor is it as though he had eaten of any other part of its body, since the sinews are not included with the flesh, as we have explained. But if he eats the fat upon the sinew, it is as though he had eaten of the animal's flesh.

6. Whosoever eats the sinew of the thigh vein of a nĕḇelah, a ṭĕrefah, or a burnt offering, is liable to be flogged twice, since the sinew is included in the prohibition of the rest of its body which would otherwise have been permitted, and now to this prohibition there has been added the other prohibition of the sinew itself.

7. Upon removal of the sinew of the thigh vein, the spot should be scraped after it, to make certain that no remnant of the vein has been left behind. The butcher is relied upon to remove the sinew, just as he is relied upon to remove the fat. One should not, however, purchase meat from any butcher unless he is an upright man, known for his observance of the dietary laws, that is known to slaughter for himself and sell his own meat, and to be trustworthy.

8. What was said above applies only outside the Land of Israel; in the Land of Israel, at such time as the Land belongs wholly to Israel, one may purchase meat from anyone.

9. In the case of a butcher who is relied upon to sell valid meat, if it is discovered that he has let nĕḇelah or ṭĕrefah pass out of his hand, he must refund the money to the purchasers, and in addition must be placed under a ban and removed from his position. Nor is there any remedy for him to enable him to sell meat again, unless he proceeds to a place where he is unknown, and there proves his integrity by restoring a lost article of considerable value which he has found, or unless, having performed šĕḥiṭah on his own confidence, he himself declares it ṭerefah and discards the carcass, despite the fact that a serious

loss is involved for him, in which case it may be considered certain that he has indeed repented, without any deceit.

10. If a person purchases meat and dispatches it by the hand of an unlearned Israelite, that Israelite may be relied upon with regard to it, and even though there can be no presumption in his case of strict observance of the dietary laws, one need not fear that he may have substituted other meat for it. For even the bondsmen and bondswomen of Israel may be trusted in this regard. This does not, however, apply to a heathen, since he may substitute other meat.

11. If there are ten shops, nine of which sell meat of šĕḥiṭah, while one sells meat of nĕḇelah, and if a person has purchased meat in one of them and does not know which shop it was, the meat is forbidden, since in the case of a fixed object the possibility one way or the other is assumed to be equal. If, however, meat is found abandoned in the market place, the rule follows the majority of the shops, according to the principle that whatever emerges is regarded as having emerged from the majority. Consequently if the majority of the vendors are heathens, the meat is forbidden; if they are Israelites, it is permitted.

12. Similarly, in the case of meat found in the possession of a heathen, when it is not known from whom he had purchased it, the rule is that if the meat vendors are Israelites, the meat is permitted. This is so according to the Torah, but the Sages have from ancient times forbidden all meat found either in the market place or in the possession of a heathen, even if all the slaughterers and all the vendors are Israelites. And not only this, but even if one buys meat and leaves it in his house, and loses sight of it, it is forbidden, unless it had a mark on it, or unless he is so familiar with its appearance that he can identify it with certainty, or unless it is wrapped up and sealed.

13. If one suspends a vessel filled with pieces of meat, and the vessel breaks so that the pieces of meat fall to the ground, and he then comes along and finds them, the rule is as follows: If

they have no mark, nor does he recognize them, the meat is forbidden, since it is possible that an animal or a creeping creature had dragged away the meat which was in the vessel, and that the meat now on the ground is other meat.

14. One is permitted to derive benefit from the sinew of the thigh vein. An Israelite is therefore permitted to send to a heathen a thigh with the sinew of the thigh vein still in place, and the whole thigh may be delivered in the presence of another Israelite. No apprehension need be felt that the other Israelite may eat of it before the sinew is removed, since its position is recognizable. For this reason, if the thigh is cut up, it may not be delivered to the heathen in the presence of the other Israelite before removing the sinew, lest the Israelite should eat of it.

15. Wherever the Torah says "thou shalt not eat," "ye shall not eat," "they shall not be eaten," or "it shall not be eaten," it includes the prohibition of both eating and benefit, unless it specifies to the contrary, as in the case of nĕḇelah, where it is said, *thou mayest give it to the stranger that is within thy gates, that he may eat it* (Deut. 14:21), or in the case of fat of which it is said, *it may be used for any other service* (Lev. 7:24), or unless it is interpreted in the Oral Law to the effect that the benefit of it is permitted, as in the case of insects, creeping things, blood, the limb of a living animal, and the sinew of the thigh vein, all of which are permitted for benefit by tradition, although they are forbidden for consumption.

16. In the case of all food the benefit of which is forbidden, if one derives benefit from it but does not eat of it—for instance if one sells it or makes a gift of it to a heathen, or gives it to dogs—he is not liable to be flogged on the authority of Scripture, although he is liable to the flogging prescribed for disobedience, and the money obtained for it is permitted. In the case of everything which is forbidden for consumption but permitted for benefit, even though one may benefit from it, he is forbidden to traffic in it or to employ forbidden things deliberately in his

handicraft, with the sole exception of forbidden fat, of which it is said, *it may be used for any other service*. Therefore, one should not traffic in nĕḇelah, ṭĕrefah, insects, or creeping things.

17. A hunter who accidentally traps unclean beasts, birds, or fish, or clean and unclean together, may sell them, but he should not deliberately engage in trapping unclean species. It is, however, permitted to trade in milk that was milked by a heathen, even without the supervision of an Israelite, as well as in heathen cheese, and similar merchandise.

18. The general rule is that it is forbidden to trade in such articles as are prohibited by the Torah, and it is permitted to trade in articles interdicted by the Scribes, regardless of whether they are forbidden on account of doubt or on account of certainty.

CHAPTER IX

1. It is forbidden, according to the Torah, to cook meat with milk, as well as to eat of the mixture, and it is also forbidden to benefit from it; it must be buried, and its ashes are forbidden like the ashes of everything which is liable to burial. Whosoever cooks an olive's bulk of both of them together is liable to a flogging, as it is said, *Thou shalt not seethe a ḳid in its mother's milḳ* (Exod. 23:19, 34:26; Deut. 14:21). Similarly, whosoever eats an olive's bulk of both of them, that is of meat and milk which have been cooked together, is liable to a flogging, even if he himself did not cook them.

2. The only reason why Scripture is silent with regard to the prohibition of eating meat and milk together is that it has already forbidden the cooking, that is, since the cooking thereof is forbidden, it is unnecessary to state that its consumption also is forbidden, in exactly the same way as Scripture is silent with regard to the prohibition of marrying one's daughter, having already forbidden the daughter's daughter.

3. According to the Torah, the prohibition applies only to the meat of a clean animal boiled in the milk of a clean animal, as it is said, *Thou shalt not seethe a kid in its mother's milk*. The word "kid" is used here in a general sense and includes the young of ox, sheep, and goat, except where Scripture specifically defines it and says, *a kid of the goats* (Gen. 37:17). "A kid" and "its mother's milk" are mentioned here only because Scripture speaks of the most common example. On the other hand, should one cook the meat of a clean animal in the milk of an unclean animal, or the meat of an unclean animal in the milk of a clean animal, the cooking would be permitted, and so would benefit therefrom, and the prohibition against eating it would not be on account of meat with milk.

4. Similarly, meat of beast and bird cooked in the milk of a beast or of an animal, is not forbidden to be eaten, according to the Torah, and for that reason both the cooking and the benefiting are permitted. The eating thereof is, however, forbidden on the authority of the Scribes, in order that people should not extend the permission to cover the Biblical prohibition of meat of animals with milk, and as a consequence eat the meat of a clean animal cooked in the milk of a clean animal, on the ground that the literal meaning of the verse forbids only a kid in its own mother's milk. That is why the Sages forbade all meat with milk.

5. It is permitted to eat fish and locusts cooked in milk, and if one performs šĕḥiṭah upon a bird and finds fully developed eggs inside it, the eggs may be eaten with milk.

6. One is not liable to a flogging for eating meat steamed in milk vapor, just as one is not liable if he cooks meat on the Sabbath in the hot springs of Tiberias, or in any similar manner. Likewise, if one cooks meat in whey, or in the milk of a dead animal, or in the milk of a male, or if he boils blood with milk, he is exempt and is not liable to be flogged on account of meat with milk. If, however, one cooks the meat of a dead animal, or forbidden fat, with milk, he is liable to be flogged for the

cooking, but not for the eating of meat with milk, since the prohibition of meat with milk cannot take effect upon the already existing prohibition of nĕḇelah or fat, inasmuch as the former is neither a comprehensive prohibition, nor does it introduce additional factors, nor is it a case of two prohibitions taking effect simultaneously.

7. Whosoever cooks a foetus in milk is liable, as is he who eats of it. But should he cook the caul, the hide, the sinews, the bones, or the soft base of the horns or hoofs in milk, he is exempt, as is he who eats of them.

8. If meat falls into milk, or milk is spilled upon meat, it is prohibited if the quantity is sufficient to impart a flavor. How is this to be determined? If a piece of meat falls into a vessel of boiling milk, a heathen should be requested to taste the dish. If he says that it tastes of meat, it is forbidden; if not, it is permitted, but the piece of meat itself is prohibited in any case. This applies only if the meat is extracted before it exudes the milk which it had absorbed; otherwise one must estimate whether there is one part of meat to at least sixty parts of milk, since the milk which had been absorbed in the meat and which had thereby become prohibited, has emerged and become mixed with the remainder of the milk.

9. If milk is spilled into a dish of meat, the piece of meat upon which the milk has fallen should be tasted. If it has no milk flavor, the whole dish is permitted. If the piece of meat tastes of milk, that piece is forbidden; for even if upon being squeezed it would lose the flavor of milk, seeing that it tastes of milk now, it has become prohibited. One should then estimate the size of that piece against the whole contents of the dish; if the several pieces of meat, plus the vegetables, the gravy, and the spices, are of such volume that this piece of meat constitutes not more than one-sixtieth of the total, only this piece is forbidden, while the remainder is permitted.

10. This applies only if one had not stirred the contents of the

pot at the beginning, at the time when the milk fell in, but only at the end, and had not covered it. If he had stirred it from beginning to end, or had covered it from the moment the milk fell in and kept it covered until cooking was completed, the decision depends on whether the milk has flavored the dish. Similarly, if the milk fell into the gravy or in the midst of the pieces of meat, and it is not known on which piece it fell, one should stir the whole contents of the pot until everything in it is again mixed; if the dish as a whole has a milky taste it is forbidden, if not, it is permitted. If no reliable heathen is available to taste it, the principle of one part in sixty takes effect, whether it is a case of meat falling into milk or milk falling into meat. If there is one in sixty, it is permitted; if the proportion is less, it is forbidden.

11. Milk may not be boiled in a pot in which meat had been previously cooked. If one does so nevertheless, the decision depends on whether the pot imparts a meaty flavor to the milk.

12. The udder is forbidden on the authority of the Scribes, although according to the Torah meat which is boiled in the milk obtained from an animal after šĕḥiṭah has been performed upon it is not forbidden, as we have explained. For this reason, if one tears open the udder and washes the milk out of it, the udder may be roasted and eaten. If he cuts it crosswise and rubs it against a wall until no milky moisture remains upon it, it is permitted to cook it with other meat. It is, however, forbidden to cook an unopened udder, whether of a calf which has never given milk or of a fully grown cow. If one disregards this prohibition and cooks the udder by itself, he is permitted to eat of it. If he cooks it with other meat, it is subject to the principle of one part in sixty, the udder being included in the count.

13. How so? If the bulk of the whole, including the udder, is sixty times that of the udder itself, the udder is forbidden and the remainder of the meat is permitted. If it is less than sixty, it is all forbidden. In either case, if the udder thereupon falls into another dish, it renders that dish prohibited and must be once again subjected to the principle of one in sixty, as in the first

instance. The reason is that the udder in itself, having been cooked, is considered as one forbidden piece of meat, and must be reckoned according to its volume after cooking, and not according to its volume at the time it fell into the dish.

14. It is forbidden to roast an udder which has been cut open on a spit above other meat. If one does so nevertheless, both are permitted.

15. A stomach cooked with the milk which is within it is permitted, since this milk is regarded not as milk, but as offal, it having undergone a change in the bowels.

16. It is forbidden to curdle cheese with the membrane of the stomach of an animal upon which šĕḥiṭah had been performed. If one does so curdle it, the cheese should be tasted; if it tastes of meat, it is forbidden; if not, it is permitted, since the curdling agent itself is permitted, being the stomach of an animal upon which šĕḥiṭah had been performed. The only prohibition applicable in this case is therefore that of meat with milk, which depends upon whether the membrane affects the flavor. If, however, one curdles milk with the membrane of the stomach of a nĕḇelah, a ṭĕrefah, or an unclean animal, the cheese is forbidden, not on account of meat with milk, but on account of nĕḇelah, since the curdling agent itself is prohibited. It is because of this apprehension that heathen-made cheese is forbidden, as we have explained.

17. Meat by itself is permitted, as is milk. It is only when the two become mixed together as a result of cooking that both are forbidden. This applies when both are cooked together, or when one of them, while hot, falls into the other which is also hot, or even when one of them while cold falls into the other which is hot. But if one of them, while hot, falls into the other which is cold, one need only pare away all the meat which came in contact with the milk and may then eat of the remainder. If cold falls into cold, he need merely wash the piece of meat and may then eat of it. It is therefore permitted to wrap meat and cheese in the same kerchief, as long as they do not touch each other,

but if they do touch one need but wash the meat and the cheese and may then eat of them.

18. Salted food which is so salty as to be inedible is regarded as equivalent to hot food. If, however, it is edible, like porridge, it is not regarded as equivalent to hot food.

19. If a bird upon which šĕḥiṭah has been performed falls into milk or porridge containing milk, the rule is as follows: If the bird is uncooked, one merely need wash it, and it is then permitted; if it is roasted, he must pare it. If the bird is in segments, or is well seasoned, and it then falls into milk or porridge, the bird is forbidden.

20. It is forbidden to set poultry and cheese together on a dining table, lest one should become habituated to transgression and eat one with the other, even though the prohibition of the flesh of birds with milk is based merely on the authority of the Scribes.

21. Two guests at an inn who are not acquainted with one another may eat at the same table, the one eating meat and the other cheese, since the one is not on such terms of familiarity with the other as to share his food with him.

22. Dough may not be kneaded with milk. If one does so knead it, all the bread baked therefrom is forbidden, lest he should become accustomed to transgression and eat this bread with meat. Nor may one grease an oven with tail fat; if he does so, all the bread is forbidden unless he heats the oven first, lest he should eat the bread with milk. If, however, he alters the appearance of the bread to make it recognizable, so that he would not eat either meat or milk with it, it is permitted.

23. Bread baked together with roast meat, and fish roasted with meat, may not be eaten with milk. If one cooks fish in a dish out of which he had eaten meat, he may eat that fish together with porridge.

24. If one cuts radishes or similar pungent things with a knife with which he had previously cut roast meat, he may not eat them

with porridge. In the case of cucumbers and melons, however, if one cuts them with a knife used previously to cut meat, he need merely scrape away the surface of the cut and may eat the remainder with milk.

25. One should not place a jug of salt side by side with a jug of milk sauce, since the salt would absorb moisture from it, with the result that he may later cook meat salted with this salt which is flavored with milk. One may, however, place a jug of vinegar by the side of a jug of milk sauce, since vinegar would not absorb moisture from it.

26. Having partaken first of cheese or milk, one may eat meat immediately thereafter. He must, however, wash his hands and cleanse his mouth between the cheese and the meat. With what should he cleanse his mouth? With bread, or by chewing fruit and swallowing it or spitting it out. One may employ any food for cleansing his mouth, with the exception of dates, flour, or vegetables, since these do not cleanse the mouth properly.

27. This applies only to the meat of animal or beast; one who eats poultry after milk or cheese need neither cleanse his mouth nor wash his hands.

28. If one eats meat first, whether the meat of animal or bird, he should not consume milk after it until the expiration of a period of time equal to the interval between one meal and the next, that is about six hours. This is on account of the fragments of meat which adhere in the interstices between the teeth and which are not removed by cleansing.

CHAPTER X

1. All the prohibitions mentioned hitherto refer to living creatures. There are, however, other interdicts in the Torah which apply to agricultural produce, to wit, the new produce of the

field, mixed seeds of the vineyard, untithed produce, and the fruit of the first three years.

2. What is meant by the new produce of the field? It applies only to the five species of grain of which the new harvest was forbidden to be eaten until the *'Omer* was offered up on the sixteenth day of Nisan, as it is said, *And ye shall eat neither bread, nor parched corn, nor fresh ears until this selfsame day* (Lev. 23:14). Whosoever ate an olive's bulk of the new corn before the 'Omer was offered up was liable to a flogging on the authority of the Torah. The prohibition obtains in every place and at all times, whether in the Land of Israel or outside, whether the Temple is in existence or not, except that during the existence of the Temple, once the 'Omer was offered up the new corn was immediately permitted in Jerusalem, while in distant places it was permitted only after midday, since the court was not likely to postpone it until after midday. When the Temple is not in existence the new corn is forbidden on the authority of the Torah for the whole of that day. At the present time, in places where people observe the festival for two days, the new corn is forbidden on the authority of the Scribes for the whole of the seventeenth day of Nisan until the evening.

3. Whosoever eats an olive's bulk of each, bread, parched corn, and fresh ears, before this day, is liable to a triple flogging, since it is said, *And ye shall eat neither bread, nor parched corn, nor fresh ears*. The Sages have learned by tradition that each one of these three is the subject of a separate negative commandment.

4. All produce which took root before the offering of the 'Omer, even if it did not ripen until after the offering, is allowed for consumption from the time that the 'Omer is offered up. Produce which took root after the 'Omer was offered up, even if sown before the offering of the 'Omer, is forbidden until the 'Omer of the following year is offered up. This rule applies on the authority of the Torah to all places and at all times.

5. In the case of wheat which took root after the 'Omer was

offered up, but which was harvested and the grain thereof sown, so that when the next 'Omer was subsequently offered up, it was still in the ground, it is doubtful whether that 'Omer renders the wheat permitted, because it is considered as though it were stored in a vessel; or whether it does not render the wheat permitted, since it has become nullified in the ground. Consequently if one harvests this wheat and eats of it, he is not liable to be flogged for transgression, though he is liable to the flogging prescribed for disobedience. Similarly, in the case of a spike of corn which had grown to a third of its full size before the 'Omer was offered up, if one uproots it and then transplants it after the 'Omer was offered up, and the spike increases in size, it is doubtful whether it should be forbidden because of the increase, until the following 'Omer is offered up, or whether it should be permitted, since it did take root before the 'Omer was offered up.

6. What is meant by mixed seeds of the vineyard? When any species of grain or vegetable is sown together with a vine, whether by an Israelite or by a heathen, whether it grows of its own accord or whether the vine is planted in the midst of the vegetable patch, both are forbidden for either consumption or benefit, as it is said, *Lest the whole fruit be forfeited, the seed which thou hast sown, and the increase of the vineyard* (Deut. 22:9); the meaning is, lest both should become forfeited and prohibited.

7. Whosoever eats an olive's bulk of mixed seeds of the vineyard, whether of the vegetables or of the grapes, is liable to a flogging on the authority of the Torah, and both combine to form the requisite minimum amount.

8. This applies only to seeds sown in the Land of Israel. Outside the Land, the prohibition of mixed seeds of the vineyard is based only on the authority of the Scribes. In the Laws Concerning Mixed Seeds it will be explained which species are forbidden on account of mixed seeds of the vineyard and which are not, as well as the manner in which they become forbidden, and the time when they become prohibited, and which become consecrated and which do not.

9. What is meant by *'Orlah*? If one plants a fruit tree, all the fruit produced by that tree for the first three years after the planting is forbidden, both for consumption and for benefit, as it is said, *Three years shall it be as forbidden unto you. It shall not be eaten* (Lev. 19:23); and whosoever eats an olive's bulk of it is liable to a flogging on the authority of the Torah.

10. This applies only to trees planted in the Land of Israel, as it is said, *And when ye shall come into the Land and shall have planted all manner of trees* (*ibid.*). With regard to 'Orlah outside the Land of Israel, however, it is a rule given to Moses from Sinai that 'Orlah definitely known to be such is forbidden, while doubtful 'Orlah is permitted. In the Laws Concerning the Second Tithe it will be explained which things are prohibited on account of 'Orlah and which are permitted.

11. Doubtful cases of 'Orlah and of mixed seeds of the vineyard are forbidden in the Land of Israel; in Syria, that is the territory conquered by David, they are permitted. How so? If there is a vineyard with 'Orlah, and grapes are sold outside of it, or if vegetables are sown in it, and vegetables are being sold outside of it, and it is uncertain whether the produce sold has come from this vineyard or from another, in Syria it would be permitted. Elsewhere, outside the Land, even if one sees the grapes brought out of a vineyard of 'Orlah, or vegetables brought out of a vineyard, he may purchase them, providing that he does not actually see the grapes of 'Orlah being cut or the vegetables being picked by hand.

12. A vineyard which is subject to doubt as to whether it is 'Orlah or mixed seeds, is forbidden in the Land of Israel and permitted in Syria, and, needless to say, also elsewhere outside the Land.

13. If a jar of wine is found concealed in an orchard of 'Orlah, the wine may not be drunk, but is permitted for benefit, since a thief would not hide a stolen article in the place whence he had stolen it. If grapes are found hidden there, they are forbidden, for fear that they might have been picked and hidden in the same place.

14. If an Israelite and a heathen who are partners in the planting stipulate at the time of entering into the partnership that the heathen would consume the fruit during the three years of 'Orlah, and the Israelite would eat the fruit of three permissible years as against the fruit of the years of 'Orlah, it is permitted. If they did not make this stipulation at the commencement of the partnership, it is forbidden. The former, however, is permitted only if they do not make a regular reckoning. How so? For instance, if an account is kept of how much fruit the heathen had eaten during the years of 'Orlah, so that the Israelite might eat the same amount of fruit in the permitted years, the arrangement is forbidden, since that would constitute an actual exchange of the fruit of 'Orlah for later fruit.

15. It would appear to me that the law of the fourth year's fruit of a young tree does not apply outside the Land of Israel, and that the fruit of the fourth year may be eaten without any redemption, since the prohibition outside the Land of Israel was decreed only with regard to 'Orlah. This may be proven by an argument *a priori*: If in Syria, where one is subject, according to the enactment of the Sages, to the law governing tithes and the Sabbatical year's produce, one is not liable for the fourth year's fruit of a young tree, as will be explained in the Laws Concerning the Second Tithe, then elsewhere outside the Land of Israel, where tithes and the seventh year do not apply, one is certainly not liable on account of fruit of the fourth year. In the Land of Israel, however, this law applies both while the Temple was in existence and after. Some of the Geonim have ruled that the fourth year's fruit of the vine alone must be redeemed outside the Land of Israel, after which it is permitted to be eaten, but there is no basis for this view.

16. In the Land of Israel the fruit of the fourth year is wholly forbidden until it is redeemed. In the Laws Concerning the Second Tithe the regulations governing their redemption, the law stipulating when they may be eaten, and the time when the count for 'Orlah and for the fourth year must begin, will be explained.

17. How are the fruits of the fourth year to be redeemed at the

present time? After one has gathered them he should recite the benediction, "Blessed art Thou, O Lord our God, King of the universe, who has sanctified us with His commandments and has commanded us concerning the redemption of the planting of the fourth year." He should then redeem them all, even if with only one *pĕruṭah,* and say further, "Behold, these are redeemed with this pĕruṭah." The coin should then be cast into the Dead Sea. Or else he must render them profane with a pĕruṭah's worth of other produce, and say, "Behold, all these fruits are rendered profane by this wheat," or "by this barley," as the case may be, and he must thereupon burn the wheat or barley, so that they would not become a snare for others. He may then eat all of the fruit.

18. Some of the Geonim have ruled that even after the fruits of the fourth year have been redeemed or rendered profane, one may not eat them until the fifth year has been ushered in, but there is no basis for this ruling. It would appear to me that this is a wrong decision based on an erroneous interpretation of the Scriptural verse, *And in the fifth year ye shall eat the fruit thereof* (Lev. 19:25). What this verse really means is that in the fifth year one may eat the fruit thereof without having to redeem it, like any other unconsecrated fruit. One should not pay any attention to this ruling.

19. What is meant by *Ṭeḇel?* Every food from which one is obligated to separate heave offerings and tithes is called Ṭeḇel, until such time as he separates them, and he is forbidden to eat of it, as it is said, *And they shall not profane the holy things of the children of Israel which they offer unto the Lord* (Lev. 22:15), meaning that they shall not regard as profane that which is still consecrated, since the holy things which have to be offered from it have not yet been offered. He who eats an olive's bulk of Ṭeḇel before he has separated the great heave offering or the heave offering of tithes, is punishable by death at the hand of heaven, as it is said, *And they shall not profane the holy things of the children of Israel . . . and so cause them to bear the iniquity that bringeth guilt* (*ibid.* 22:15,16).

20. If, however, one eats of produce from which the great heave offering and the heave offering of tithes have already been taken, but from which the ordinary tithes have not yet been separated, even if the poor man's tithe alone is still left in it, he is liable to a flogging on account of Ṭeḇel. No liability to death is incurred, however, since transgression involving death applies only to the great heave offering and the heave offering of tithes.

21. The explicit prohibition against eating Ṭeḇel from which tithes have not yet been taken is to be found in the general rule, *Thou mayest not eat within thy gates the tithe of thy corn,* etc. (Deut. 12:17). In the Laws Concerning Heave Offerings and Tithes it will be explained which things are liable to heave offering and tithes and which are exempt, which are liable on the authority of the Torah and which on the authority of the Scribes. Whosoever eats an olive's bulk of Ṭeḇel forbidden on the authority of the Scribes, or of the mixed seeds of the vineyard or 'Orlah outside the Land of Israel, is liable to the flogging prescribed for disobedience.

22. The juice which is extracted from the fruits of Ṭeḇel, from new produce, from sacred produce, from the spontaneous growth of the Sabbatical year, and from the mixed seeds of the vineyard and the fruits of 'Orlah, is forbidden like the fruits themselves, but one is not liable to a flogging on account of it, with the exception of the wine and oil of 'Orlah, and the wine of the mixed seeds of the vineyard, for which one is liable to a flogging, as he is liable for the olives and grapes themselves.

23. There are other prohibitions which apply to edible holy things, all being based on the authority of the Torah; for example, the prohibition of eating the heave offerings, first fruits, dough offerings, and second tithes. There are also prohibitions of consecrated things of the altar, such as *Piggul,* the remnant of sacrifices, and sacrifices which have become unclean; each of these will be explained in its appropriate place.

24. The minimum amount for the eating of which one is liable,

whether to a flogging or to extinction, is an olive's bulk. We have already explained the prohibition of leavened bread on Passover and the laws appertaining thereto in the Laws Concerning Leaven and Unleaven. The prohibition of food on the Day of Atonement, however, stands in a class by itself, while the prohibition of the produce of grapes to a Nazirite is not of universal application, and therefore the prohibition of each of these, their requisite minimum amounts, and the laws appertaining to them are explained in their appropriate places.

CHAPTER XI

1. Wine which has been used as a libation in idol worship is prohibited for benefit, and whosoever drinks the smallest quantity of it is liable to a flogging on the authority of the Torah. Similarly, whosoever eats of heathen offering, whatever the quantity, whether meat or fruit, or even salt and water, if he eats the smallest amount of it, he is liable to be flogged, as it is said, *Who did eat of the fat of their sacrifices, and drank the wine of their drink offerings* (Deut. 32:38).

2. Wine which has been poured out as a libation to an idol is considered the same as a sacrifice which has been offered up to it, and since the prohibition is concerned with idolatry, it involves no minimum requisite amount, as it is said, *And there shall cleave* NOUGHT *of the accursed thing to thy hand* (Deut. 13:18).

3. Heathen wine of which it is not known whether it has or has not been poured out as a libation, is called undefined heathen wine and is prohibited for benefit, just the same as wine used for libation, this rule being one of the enactments of the Scribes. Whosoever drinks a quarter of a *log̱* of such wine is liable to the flogging prescribed for disobedience.

4. Any wine touched by a heathen is forbidden, since he may have made a libation with it, seeing that the thoughts of an

idolater are generally directed towards idolatry. Hence you learn that the wine of an Israelite which is touched by a heathen becomes subject to the law governing undefined heathen wine, which is prohibited for benefit.

5. Wine touched by a heathen unintentionally or touched by a heathen child is forbidden for consumption, but allowed for benefit. Slaves acquired from a heathen, who have been circumcised and immersed immediately, are considered as no longer making libations, and wine touched by them is permitted for drinking, even though they have not yet habituated themselves to Israelite customs, and the mention of idolatry has not yet ceased issuing from their mouths.

6. In the case of male children of heathen bondswomen born in Israelite possession, who have been circumcised but not yet immersed, the rule is as follows: If they are adults, they render wine which they touch forbidden; if they are minors, they do not.

7. The wine of a resident stranger, that is one who has accepted the seven Noachian commandments, as we have explained, is forbidden for drinking but allowed for benefit. Wine may be left in his sole care, but may not be deposited with him as a pledge. Similarly, the wine of any Gentile who is not an idolater, such as a Moslem, is forbidden only for consumption but not for benefit; all the Geonim have so ruled. The undefined wine of those who worship idols, however, is forbidden for benefit.

8. Wherever in this connection it is stated that the wine is forbidden, if the non-Israelite on whose account the wine is rendered prohibited is an idolater, it is forbidden also for benefit; if he is not an idolater, it is prohibited for consumption only. Wherever a heathen is mentioned without further qualification, the reference is to an idolater.

9. Only such wine as is fit to be poured out upon the altar may be considered libation wine for idols. For this reason, when the Sages enacted the decree prohibiting undefined heathen wine, or any wine touched by a heathen and thereby rendered forbidden

for benefit, the decree was confined to wine fit for libation. Therefore, the boiled wine of an Israelite that was touched by a heathen is not forbidden, and one may drink it even from the same cup with the heathen. Wine mixed with water, however, and wine which has begun to ferment but is still potable, is prohibited if touched by a heathen.

10. The Geonim of the Maghrib have ruled that if a little honey or yeast is mixed with wine, the wine is no longer fit for the altar; consequently it is to be considered like boiled wine or beer, and unfit to be used as libation wine, and therefore one is permitted to drink it with a heathen.

11. When does heathen wine become forbidden? From the time when the heathen treads the grapes and draws off the wine. Even if it has not yet descended into the vat, but is still in the wine press, it is prohibited. For this reason one should not tread grapes in the wine press together with a heathen, for fear that he may touch the wine with his hand and render it libation wine, even if his hands are bound. Nor may one acquire from a heathen a press full of pressed grapes, even if the wine is still mixed with the grapeskins and pips, and has not yet descended into the vat.

12. If a heathen treads the grapes but does not touch them, while an Israelite stands over him and even pours the wine into the jug, the wine is forbidden for consumption.

13. Heathen wine vinegar is forbidden for benefit, since it had become libation wine before it became fermented. Should a heathen press grapes into a jug, no apprehension need be felt on account of libation wine, even if the juice flows over his hands. If after eating some grapes from a basket he throws the remaining one or two *sĕ'ah* of grapes into the wine press, he does not render the wine libation wine, even if some of it is sprinkled upon these grapes.

14. Heathen grapeskins and pips are forbidden for twelve months. After twelve months they are dry, with no moisture

remaining in them, and are therefore allowed to be eaten. Similarly, wine lees which have dried out after twelve months are permitted, since they then retain no odor of wine and are considered like dust and earth.

15. It is forbidden to pour wine into heathen wine skins and vessels which had contained their own wine, unless one first stores them for twelve months, or puts them into the fire so that the pitch on them becomes softened, or unless they are heated, or unless he puts water in them for three full days. He must pour out the water and change it three times, every twenty-four hours, for three days. It is immaterial whether the vessels are the heathen's property or were borrowed from an Israelite and then filled with heathen wine. If one pours wine into them before cleansing them, it is forbidden for consumption.

16. It is, however, allowed to pour beer, brine, or pickle into these vessels at once, without further ado. It is also permitted to put wine into them after the brine or pickle, since the salt draws out the heathen wine absorbed by the vessels.

17. If one purchases from a heathen new vessels which have not yet been lined with pitch, he may pour wine into them at once, and no apprehension need be felt that the heathen may have previously put libation wine in them. If the vessels are already pitched, he must wash them, even though they are new. Similarly, a vessel in which libation wine is put only momentarily, and not for extended storage, such as a ladle, funnel, etc., need merely be washed with water, and this suffices.

18. It is likewise forbidden to drink from an earthenware cup out of which a heathen had drunk wine. If, however, one rinses it three times in succession, it is permitted, since the deposit of wine in it is thus removed. That is, only if the cup is lined with lead, after the manner of potters, or if it is lined with pitch; if it is of pure earthenware it must be washed only once.

19. In the case of earthenware vessels lined with lead which were used for libation wine, the rule is as follows: If they are

white, red, or black, they are allowed; if green, they are forbidden, since these absorb liquids. If a portion of the earthenware is exposed, both white and green are prohibited, since they too are absorbent. It would appear to me that this rule applies only when the heathen wine was put in them for extended storage; if not, one need but rinse them and they are permitted, even if they are of pure earthenware.

20. A wine press of stone or wood in which a heathen had pressed grapes, or a wine press of stone which a heathen had pitched, but in which he had not yet trodden, must be scoured four times with water and ashes, whereupon it is permitted to be used for pressing. If there is still moisture in it, the ashes should be used before the water; if not, the water should be applied before the ashes.

21. In the case of a pitched stone press trodden by a heathen, or a pitched wooden press, even if not yet trodden by him, one must first peel off the pitch. If one leaves the press unused for twelve months or puts water in it for three full days, he need not peel off the pitch, since one should not be more stringent with a wine press than with vessels, and the instruction to peel off the pitch is meant only to make the press permitted for use immediately.

22. One is forbidden to tread immediately in a heathen earthenware wine press even if he peels off the pitch, unless he heats it in a fire until the pitch is loosened. If, however, he leaves it unused for twelve months or puts water in it for three full days, it is permitted, as we have explained above.

23. If a heathen wine strainer is made of hair, one need only wash it and may then strain with it; if it is made of wool, he must scour it with ashes and water four times, and leave it to dry, after which he may use it. If made of linen, he must keep it for twelve months, and if it has knots in it, he must untie them. The same applies to vessels made from rushes and palm leaves, and similar baskets in which wine is pressed; if they are tied together with cords, he must wash them, but if they are tightly interwoven,

he must scour them with ashes and water four times, dry them, and may then use them. If they are tied with flax, he must leave them unused for twelve months before using them, and if there are knots in them, he must untie them.

24. How does one cleanse the appurtenances of a wine press in which a heathen had trodden, in order that an Israelite might use them for treading? The planks, the troughs, and the posts supporting the pressing beam must be washed. The trusses, if of wicker or hemp, must be dried; if of shavings or rushes, they must be left unused for twelve months. If one wishes to make them permitted at once, he may scour them in boiling water, or soak them in olive water, or leave them under a spout of running water, or in a spring of flowing water, for twelve hours, and thereafter they are permitted.

25. During the time when all of the Land of Israel was in Israel's possession, people were permitted to buy wine from any Israelite without apprehension, while outside the Land they were not allowed to buy it except from a person who was known for his observance of the dietary laws. At the present time wine may not be bought anywhere except from a person known to observe the dietary laws. The same is true in the case of meat, cheese, and cuts of fish which have no tokens, as we have explained.

26. If one is a guest at the home of a householder, at whatever place or time, and the host places before him wine, meat, cheese, or cuts of fish, he is permitted to eat them, and he need not inquire as to the host's reliability, even if he is not closely acquainted with him, but knows only that he is an Israelite. If it is known that the host does not observe the dietary laws and is not particular in these matters, one should not be his guest. If the guest disregards this rule and does stay with this householder, he should not eat meat or drink wine on the host's assurance, unless a reliable man testifies to their permissibility for consumption.

CHAPTER XII

1. What constitutes the act of touching whereby a heathen renders wine forbidden? He must touch the wine itself—either with his hand or with any other organ of his body with which it is the custom to pour out heathen libations—and shake it. If after he stretches out his hand into the jug, someone seizes his hand before he withdraws it and holds it still, and the jug is thereupon opened from the bottom so that the wine which is below the level of his hand flows out, that wine is not forbidden. Similarly, should the heathen grasp an open vessel of wine and shake it, even if he does not elevate the vessel or touch the wine, it is forbidden.

2. If a heathen takes a vessel of wine, and having elevated it, pours out the wine, it is prohibited, even if he does not shake it, since the wine has emerged as a result of his action. If he lifts it, but neither shakes nor touches it, it is permitted.

3. If a heathen holds the vessel to the ground while an Israelite pours wine into it, the wine is permitted. If the heathen shakes the vessel, however, the wine is forbidden.

4. A heathen is permitted to carry a closed vessel of wine from one place to another, even though the wine is thereby shaken up, since this is not the customary manner of libation. If he carries a skin of wine from one place to another, holding the mouthpiece of the skin in his hand, the wine is permitted, whether the skin is full or partly empty, even though the wine is shaken up in the process. If he transports an open earthenware vessel full of wine, the wine is prohibited, since he may have touched it. If, however, the vessel is partly empty, the wine is permitted, unless he shakes it.

5. If a heathen touches wine unintentionally, it is permitted, but only for benefit. How so? For instance, if he falls upon a wine

skin, or if he stretches out his hand into a jug thinking that it contains oil, and it is found to contain wine.

6. If the wine comes forth as a result of the heathen's action, but without his intention, it is permitted even for consumption, so long as he does not touch it. How so? For instance, if he lifts up a vessel of wine and pours it into another vessel, thinking it to be beer or oil, it is permitted.

7. If a heathen enters a house or a shop in quest of wine, puts forth his hand while feeling around, and touches the wine, it is forbidden, since his intention was to obtain wine. Therefore, this cannot be regarded as unintentional touching.

8. If a jug is cracked lengthwise and a heathen quickly clasps it in his arms so that the shards should not come apart, the wine is permitted for benefit only. If the jug is cracked breadthwise and he holds down the upper part of it so that it should not fall off, the wine is permitted even for consumption, since the wine is not preserved through the heathen's action.

9. If a heathen falls into a winevat and is brought out dead, or if he measures the winevat with a stick, or knocks a fly or hornet from its surface with a stick, or beats with his hands upon a hot jug in order to cool it, or takes a jug and throws it into a pit in his anger—in all these cases the wine is permitted for benefit only. If the heathen is brought out alive, the wine is forbidden even for benefit.

10. If the jug has a bunghole on the side, and the bung drops out of it, and a heathen inserts his finger in the bunghole to prevent the wine from escaping, all the wine from the top of the jug to the level of the hole is forbidden, while that which is below the hole is permitted for consumption.

11. In the case of a curved siphon made of metal, glass, or similar material, one end of which is inserted in the jug while the other remains outside, the rule is as follows: If one sucks in the wine so that it begins to flow out in the usual manner, and a

heathen comes along and places his finger over the mouth of the siphon, thus preventing the wine from flowing, all the wine in the jug is rendered prohibited, since it would all have flowed out continuously were it not for his hand. Thus all of the wine may be considered as having remained in being through his action.

12. If one pours wine from one vessel into another containing heathen wine, all the wine in the upper vessel becomes forbidden, since the flowing column acts as a connector between the wine in the upper vessel and the wine in the lower one. For this reason, when one measures out wine for a heathen into the vessel which is in his hand, he should repeatedly break the flow or pour in short spurts, so that there should be no continuous flow to connect the two and thereby prohibit the wine left in the upper vessel.

13. One should not measure out wine to an Israelite through a funnel used to measure out wine to a heathen, if there are some drops retained on the rim at the tip of the funnel, unless he rinses and dries it. If he does not rinse it, the wine is forbidden.

14. In the case of a vessel which is full of wine and has a double spout, like the vessels used for washing the hands, if an Israelite holds it, sucking and drinking the wine from one spout, while a heathen does so from the other, it is permitted. That is, only if the Israelite ceases drawing while the heathen is still drinking, since at the moment when the heathen ceases drawing, the wine which is in his spout returns to the vessel and renders prohibited all the wine that remains in it, for that wine is considered to have remained in existence through the heathen's action.

15. If a heathen sucks wine from a jug through a siphon, all the wine in the jug becomes prohibited, for when he stops drinking the wine drawn up by him in the siphon falls back into the jug and renders everything in it forbidden.

16. If heathens are associated with an Israelite in transporting jars of wine from one place to another, and the Israelite walks behind them to watch them, the rule is as follows: Even if they

are as far as a mile ahead of him, the wine is permitted, since the fear of the Israelite is upon them and they are apt to say, "Now the Israelite may get ahead of us and see us." But if the Israelite says, "Go ahead, and I will follow you," once they are out of his sight long enough for them to open a jar and then stop it up again and dry it, all the wine is forbidden for drinking. If the time is less than this, the wine is permitted.

17. Similarly, should an Israelite leave a heathen in his shop, even if the former goes in and out of the shop all day, the wine is permitted. If, however, the Israelite informs the heathen that he is going away, and he tarries long enough for a jug to be opened, closed up, and dried, the wine is forbidden for drinking. So also, if an Israelite leaves his wine in a wagon or on a ship with a heathen, and goes to town to attend to his business, the wine is permitted. But if he informs the heathen that he is leaving, and tarries long enough for a jug to be opened, closed up, and dried, the wine is forbidden for drinking. All this applies only to stopped up jugs; in the case of open ones, even if the Israelite does not tarry, once he informs the heathen that he is leaving, the wine is forbidden.

18. If an Israelite who is eating with a heathen at the same table goes out, leaving open wine on the table and on the sideboard, the wine on the table is forbidden, while the wine on the sideboard is permitted. If before leaving he says to the heathen, "Pour out and drink," all the open wine in the house is forbidden.

19. If an Israelite who is drinking with a heathen hears the sound of prayer in the synagogue and leaves, even the open wine is permitted. For the heathen is apt to say, "Now he may be reminded of the wine and may return in haste, and find me touching his wine," and is therefore not likely to stir from his place; hence only the wine in front of him is forbidden.

20. If an Israelite and a heathen dwell together in the same courtyard, and they both come out in haste to see a wedding or a funeral procession, and the heathen returns first and closes the

door, and then the Israelite comes in after him, the open wine in the Israelite's home is still permitted; since the only reason why the heathen closed the door is that he believed that the Israelite had already re-entered his home and that no one had been left outside, for he thought that the Israelite had preceded him.

21. If an Israelite and a heathen have open jugs of wine in the same house, and the heathen enters the house and closes the door behind him, all the wine is forbidden. If, however, there is a window in the door, so that a person standing outside and looking through it can see what is in front of him, all the jugs opposite the window are permitted, while those on the sides are forbidden, since in the case of the former the heathen would be afraid that someone might see him.

22. Similarly, if a heathen, upon hearing a lion's roar or a similar sound, flees and hides among open jugs, the wine is permitted, since he is apt to say to himself, "Perhaps another Israelite person is hiding here, and will see mc if I touch the wine."

23. If an Israelite has open jugs stored in the wine cellar of an inn, and a heathen has other jugs in the same inn, and this heathen is discovered standing among the open jugs belonging to the Israelite, the rule is as follows: If he is confused when discovered, and behaves like a thief caught in the act, the wine is permitted for drinking, since on account of his fear and apprehension he would have had no leisure to render the Israelite's wine libation wine. If he does not behave like a thief caught in the act, but stands there confidently, the wine is forbidden. If a child is found among the jugs, all the wine is permitted regardless of the circumstances.

24. If a troop of soldiers enters a district, the rule is as follows: In times of peace, all the open jugs of wine in the shops are forbidden, while the closed ones are permitted; in times of war, if the troop marches right through the district and passes on, both are permitted, since the soldiers had no leisure to render the wine libation wine.

25. If a heathen is discovered standing by the side of a winevat, the rule is as follows: If he has a lien on the wine, it is forbidden, since he would feel free to handle it and would thus render it libation wine; if he has no lien on it, the wine is permitted for drinking.

26. If a heathen harlot is in the company of Israelite men, the wine is permitted, for the fear of them is upon her and she is not apt to handle the wine. In the case of an Israelite harlot in the company of heathens, even the wine in front of her in her own cup is forbidden, since they are apt to touch it without her knowledge.

27. If a heathen is found at a wine press, and there is enough wine moisture there to moisten the palm of one hand to such an extent that the moisture on that hand is sufficient to moisten the palm of the other hand, one must rinse the whole wine press and dry it. If the amount of moisture is less, he need only rinse it, and even this is an excessive precaution.

28. In the case of a jug of wine floating in a river, if it is found opposite a city the majority of whose inhabitants are Israelites, the wine is permitted for benefit; if opposite a city where the majority are heathens, it is forbidden.

29. If large vessels full of wine are found in a place where most of the wine merchants are Israelites, and these vessels are of the type used only by wine merchants to store wine, they are permitted for benefit. In the case of jugs of wine broken open by thieves, if the majority of the thieves in that city are Israelites, the wine is permitted for drinking; if not, it is prohibited.

CHAPTER XIII

1. If an Israelite purchases or rents a house in the courtyard of a heathen and uses it to store wine, the rule is as follows: If the

Israelite resides in that court, the wine is permitted, even if the door is left open, since the heathen would always be afraid to enter, for he would say to himself, "The Israelite may now suddenly come home and find me in his house." If the Israelite resides in another courtyard, he should not go out without locking the door, and the key and the seal should remain in his keeping; he need not, however, fear that the heathen may forge a key to the house.

2. If the Israelite goes out without locking the door, or if he locks it and leaves the key in the heathen's care, the wine is forbidden for drinking, for fear that the heathen may have entered and rendered the wine libation wine, since the Israelite is not there. If, however, the Israelite says to him, "Hold this key for me until I return," the wine is permitted, since the Israelite gave him charge only of the key, not of the house.

3. If a heathen hires an Israelite to press wine for him according to the rules of cleanness, so as to make it permitted to Israelites and to enable them to purchase it from him, the rule is as follows: If the wine is in the house of the heathen, and the Israelite who has charge of the wine dwells in that courtyard, the wine is permitted, even if the door is open and the Israelite comes and goes. If the Israelite in charge dwells in another courtyard, the wine is forbidden, even if the key and the seal are in the Israelite's care. For inasmuch as the wine belongs to the heathen and is in his possession, he would not be afraid to forge a key and enter the house, and might say, "Let come what may—even if they get to know about it, they can do no more than fail to buy the wine from me."

4. Even if the heathen gives a receipt in advance to the Israelite, stating that he had received from him the money against the sale of the wine, nevertheless, inasmuch as the Israelite cannot take it out of the heathen's possession until he actually pays him the money, the wine still belongs to the heathen, and is therefore forbidden, unless the Israelite supervisor resides in that courtyard. The supervisor, however, need not sit there and watch it con-

tinuously, but may go in and out, as we have explained, whether the wine is in the possession of the owner or in the possession of another heathen.

5. If this clean wine belonging to the heathen is located in a public domain, or in a house which opens into a public domain, where Israelites walk to and fro, the wine is permitted, since it has not yet entered the private domain of the heathen.

6. A refuse heap, a window, or a date palm, even one bearing no fruit, is regarded as equivalent to a public domain. If therefore a jug of wine is located there, and a heathen is found there also, he does not render the wine forbidden. A house opening into one of them is considered as though it were open into a public thoroughfare.

7. If a courtyard is divided off by a low partition, with a heathen on one side and an Israelite on the other; or if there are two roofs, that of the Israelite being higher than that of the heathen; or if the two roofs are even and are separated by a low partition, one need feel no apprehension that the wine might be rendered libation wine or be made unclean, even if the heathen can stretch out his hand and reach the part of the Israelite.

8. An Israelite is permitted to deposit his wine with a heathen in a closed vessel, but only on condition that it has two marks of identification, and that is what is called a seal within a seal. How so? If he closes the jug with a covering utensil which does not fit tightly, in the manner that all people normally close jugs, and plasters it with clay, this constitutes a single seal. If the covering utensil fits tightly in the jug and one plasters it over on top, that constitutes a seal within a seal. Similarly, if one ties up the mouth of a wine skin, it is considered one seal; if he inverts the mouthpiece of the wine skin inwards and then ties it up, this is considered a seal within a seal. So also any alteration which constitutes a change from the normal practice of closing is considered one seal, and the plastering or tying of it constitutes a second seal.

9. If an Israelite deposits wine with a heathen under only one seal, it is forbidden for drinking, but permitted for benefit, provided a separate corner is set aside for it.

10. Boiled wine, beer, wine mixed with other ingredients such as honey or oil, as well as vinegar, cheese, and milk, and in fact everything that becomes prohibited on the sole authority of the Scribes, if entrusted by an Israelite to a heathen, does not require two seals, one alone sufficing. But if he entrusts plain wine, meat, or unidentifiable cuts of fish to a heathen, two seals are necessary.

11. It would appear to me that in all instances where we have said in this connection that wine which is the property of Israelites is forbidden for drinking but permitted for use, because it came in contact with a heathen, the word "heathen" signifies one who actually worships idols. If it is a Gentile, that is a non-idolater, such as a Moslem, who unintentionally touches wine belonging to an Israelite, or beats upon the jug, the wine is permitted for drinking, and so in all similar cases.

12. If, however, an Israelite entrusts his wine to a resident stranger or sends it with him, and thereupon leaves him, or if the Israelite leaves his house open in the courtyard of a resident stranger, the wine is forbidden for drinking, since, in my judgment, the apprehension of possible forging or substitution applies equally to all heathens. Once the wine is in their keeping, it is in all circumstances forbidden for consumption.

13. There are certain things which in themselves are not prohibited on account of libation wine, but were nevertheless forbidden by the Sages in order to avoid the possibility of libation wine. They are as follows: A heathen may not pour water into wine held by an Israelite, lest he should come to pour the wine into the water; nor may a heathen carry grapes to the wine press, lest he should come to tread the grapes and touch the juice; nor may he assist an Israelite when the latter pours wine from one vessel to another, lest the Israelite should leave the first vessel in

the heathen's hand, with the result that the wine would be poured through the latter's action. If, however, the heathen does assist him, or pours the water into the wine, or brings the grapes, the wine is nevertheless permitted.

14. Similarly, a heathen is permitted to smell wine jugs belonging to Israelites, and an Israelite is allowed to smell jugs used for libation wine. There is no prohibition involved in it, since odor has no substance, seeing that it is not a tangible thing.

15. We have already explained that if an Israelite transgresses and sells an article which is forbidden for benefit, the money received for it is permitted, with the exception of money from the sale of idols, their appurtenances, and offerings made to them, as well as the wine poured out as libation to them. The Sages have ruled stringently also with regard to undefined wine, by rendering the money received for it forbidden, like the money received in payment for wine with which a libation was made to idols. Therefore, if a heathen hires an Israelite to work with him in making wine, the Israelite's wages are forbidden for benefit.

16. Similarly, if the heathen hires an ass or a ship from an Israelite to transport wine, the price of that hire is forbidden. If the heathen pays the Israelite in money, the Israelite should carry it away to be cast into the Dead Sea; if the payment is made in garments, articles, or produce, the Israelite should burn them and bury their ashes, so as to derive no benefit even from the latter.

17. If an Israelite hires out an ass to a heathen for riding and the heathen places vessels of wine upon it, the price of that hire is permitted. If the heathen hires the Israelite to smash jars of libation wine, his hire is permitted, and a blessing will come upon him for being instrumental in reducing abomination.

18. If a heathen hires an Israelite laborer and says to him, "Transport these hundred jugs of beer for one hundred *pĕruṭah,*" and one of the jugs is found to contain wine, the entire hire money is forbidden.

19. If, however, the heathen says to the Israelite, "Transport for me several jugs at the price of one pĕruṭah for each," and the Israelite transports them, and then it is found that among them are jugs of wine, the payment for the jugs of wine is forbidden, but the remainder of the wages is permitted.

20. If a heathen sends a jug of wine to Israelite craftsmen in lieu of wages, they are permitted to say to him, "Give us its value in money," but once the wine has come into their possession such an exchange is forbidden.

21. If a heathen who owes an Israelite a *mina* goes forth and sells an idol or some libation wine and then brings the money to the Israelite, the money is permitted; but if prior to selling the heathen says to the Israelite, "Wait until I have sold my idol," or "my libation wine, which I possess, and I will bring the money to you," the money realized is forbidden, even if the merchandise sold is undefined wine, since the Israelite would be interested in the preservation of this merchandise, so that he might be repaid from the proceeds of the sale.

22. Similarly, if a proselyte and a heathen who are partners decide to dissolve the partnership, the proselyte may not say to the heathen, "You take the idol and I will take the money, you the wine and I the produce," since the proselyte would be interested in the preservation of the former, so that he might take their equivalent in the latter. But if a proselyte and a heathen inherit from their heathen father, the proselyte may say to the heathen, "You take the idol and I will take the money, you the wine and I the oil." The Sages have made this alleviation in the case of the inheritance of a proselyte, so that he might not return to his former evil ways. Once this idol or this wine has come into the proselyte's possession, however, it becomes forbidden.

23. If an Israelite sells his wine to a heathen, the rule is as follows: If he has settled the purchase price, but has not yet measured out the wine, the money is permitted; for while the seller, having settled the price, regards the sale in his mind as

completed, the buyer acquires the purchase only when he takes possession of it. And since the wine does not become libation wine until the heathen touches it, the result is that at the moment of sale it is still permitted. If, however, the Israelite measures it out first, while the price is not yet settled, the purchase money is forbidden, since the matter is not yet settled in his mind, even though the heathen has already taken possession of the wine, with the result that when the heathen touched it the matter was not yet finished in the seller's mind, so that the wine became forbidden through contact with the heathen. It is therefore as though the Israelite had sold undefined heathen wine.

24. This applies only when the Israelite measures out the wine into his own vessels. If he measures it out into the heathen's vessel or even into his own vessel which the heathen is holding, he must take the money first and then measure out the wine. If he measures it out before taking the money, even though he has settled the price beforehand, the money is forbidden, since once the wine reaches the vessel it becomes forbidden as undefined heathen wine.

25. If an Israelite gives a *denar* to a heathen shopkeeper, and then says to his heathen workman, "Go forth and eat and drink at that shopkeeper's place, and I will settle the account with him," apprehension need be felt that the workman may drink wine, and it would be as though the employer had bought libation wine for the workman and had given it to him to drink. A comparable prohibition applies to the Sabbatical year. For instance, an Israelite might give a denar to an unlettered Israelite shopkeeper, and then say to his Israelite workman, "Go forth and have a meal at that shop, and I will settle the account with the shopkeeper"; should the workman thereupon eat untithed produce, the employer would be liable for making a forbidden arrangement.

26. If, however, he says to the workmen, "Go forth and eat and drink with this denar," or "Eat and drink on my account at this shopkeeper's place, and I will pay," even though he has

assumed thereby the indebtedness, seeing that the debt is not for a specified amount, it is permitted, and the employer need fear neither on account of libation wine, nor on account of the produce of the Sabbatical year, nor on account of tithes.

27. If the king allocates his wine to the people and collects from them whatever payment he desires for it, an Israelite may not say to a heathen, "Here, take these two hundred *zuz* and go in my stead to the king's treasury," so that the heathen would collect the wine which was allocated under the name of the Israelite, after paying the money for it to the king. He should rather say to him "Here, take these two hundred zuz and acquit me with the treasury."

28. If a heathen deliberately touches an Israelite's wine in order to cause him damage, it may be sold, but only to the heathen who has rendered it forbidden. For since the heathen's intention was to cause loss to the Israelite and to render his wine forbidden, it is the same as though the heathen had smashed or burned the Israelite's property, in which case he is liable to pay damages. Therefore the money which the Israelite receives for it from him is in fact damages, and not the proceeds of a sale.

CHAPTER XIV

1. The minimum quantity which must be consumed of all foods forbidden by the Torah, in order to incur flogging, extinction, or death at the hand of heaven, is the bulk of a medium-sized olive. We have already explained that a person who is liable to extinction or to death at the hand of heaven for eating forbidden food, is liable to a flogging.

2. This standard, like all standards, is a rule given to Moses from Sinai. Although it is forbidden by the Torah to eat the smallest amount of a prohibited article, flogging is incurred only

for eating an olive's bulk. If one eats a quantity less than an olive's bulk he is liable only to the flogging prescribed for disobedience.

3. The olive's bulk referred to excludes the amount remaining in the interstices between the teeth, but that which remains between palate and tongue combines with what one has swallowed, since his palate has already benefited from an olive's bulk. Even if he eats half an olive's bulk and throws it up, and then eats that same half an olive's bulk which he had thrown up, he is liable, since liability comes from the enjoyment by the palate of an olive's bulk of forbidden food.

4. If one leaves an olive's bulk of forbidden fat, nĕḇelah, Piggul, or remnant of a sacrifice, and their like, in the sun so that it shrinks, he is exempt if he eats it. If thereafter he leaves it in the rain and it swells up again to its original volume, he is liable to extinction or to a flogging. If it is at the outset less than an olive's bulk, but swells up to an olive's bulk, it is forbidden, but he is not liable to a flogging on account of it.

5. We have already explained that the prohibitions enumerated in the Torah do not combine with one another to make up an olive's bulk, with the exception of the meat of nĕḇelah which combines with the meat of ṭĕrefah, and of the things forbidden to a Nazirite, which will be explained in their proper place. The five species of grain, however, as well as their flour and dough, do combine to form an olive's bulk with regard to the prohibition of leaven on Passover, the prohibition of new produce before the offering of the 'Omer, and the prohibition of second tithes and heave offerings.

6. It would appear to me that whatever is liable to heave offering or to tithes combines to form an olive's bulk with regard to Ṭeḇel, since they all come under one category. To what may this be compared? To the nĕḇelah of an ox, the nĕḇelah of a sheep, and the nĕḇelah of a deer, which all combine to form an olive's bulk, as we have explained.

7. If one eats a large quantity of forbidden food, he is not liable to a separate punishment of flogging or extinction for each olive's bulk, but incurs only one liability for the whole meal. If, however, witnesses have cautioned him separately against each individual olive's bulk, he is liable for each separate warning, even though it is all one uninterrupted meal.

8. If one eats a barleycorn's or a mustard seed's bulk of one of the forbidden foods, and following a slight pause again eats a mustard seed's bulk, and so on, until he completes an olive's bulk, the rule is as follows: Whether he did it in error or deliberately, if the time taken from beginning to end was such as to permit the eating of three eggs, the amounts eaten combine together, and he is liable to extinction, a flogging, or a sacrifice, as though he had eaten an olive's bulk at one time. If, however, the time taken from beginning to end was longer than that—even if there was no actual pause, and he had eaten the several bulks of a mustard seed one after the other—once he has taken a longer time than what it takes to eat three eggs in order to complete the eating of the olive's bulk, they do not combine together, and he is exempt.

9. Similarly, if one drinks swallow by swallow a quarter of a *log̅* of undefined heathen wine, or if he makes a mush of leavened matter on Passover, or melts forbidden fat, and sips it little by little, or if he drinks blood in small quantities, the rule is as follows: If the time taken from beginning to end was such as to permit the drinking of a quarter of a log̅, the sips combine together; if not, they do not combine.

10. One is not liable on account of any of the forbidden foods unless he eats them in such a manner as to derive enjoyment from them, with the exception of meat with milk and the mixed produce of the vineyard, since the expression "eating" is not mentioned in their case. The prohibition of eating them is expressed in other terms, namely, "seething" and "forfeiture," in order to render them forbidden even when eaten in such a manner as to afford no enjoyment.

11. How so? If one melts fat and drinks it while hot so that it burns his palate, or if he eats it raw; or if he mixes bitter ingredients like gall and wormwood with libation wine or with a dish of nĕbelah, and then eats the bitter mixture; or if he eats forbidden food after it had putrefied so that it gives forth such a stench as to render it unfit for human consumption—he is exempt. If, however, he mixes something bitter with a dish of meat with milk, or with wine from a vineyard of mixed seeds, and consumes it, he is liable.

12. If one eats forbidden food playfully or unthinkingly, even though his intention is not directed towards eating, once he derives enjoyment from it he is as liable as though his intention had been directed towards eating. In the case of enjoyment which comes to a person against his will from any of the prohibited things, the rule is as follows: If he subsequently directs his mind to it, it is forbidden; if not, it is permitted.

13. Whosoever eats forbidden food merely to satisfy his appetite or because he happens to be hungry is liable. If, however, he is wandering in the wilderness and has nothing other than forbidden food to eat, it is permitted, because of the danger to life.

14. If a pregnant woman catches a whiff of forbidden food, such as the meat of sacrifice or swine's flesh, one may give her to eat of the gravy. If her craving is thereby appeased, well and good; if not, she should be given to eat of the meat, but less than the minimum amount. If she craves more, she may be fed more, until she is satisfied.

15. Similarly, if an invalid catches a whiff of something forbidden that has in it vinegar on anything else which stirs up a craving for it, the same rule applies as in the case of a pregnant woman.

16. If a person is seized with an attack of morbid hunger he may be given forbidden things to eat at once, until his eyes brighten. One should not go about searching for permitted food,

but should immediately give him whatever comes to hand. One should feed him first food less stringently forbidden, and if his eyes brighten, it should suffice; if not, one may then feed him food more stringently prohibited.

17. How so? If there are at hand Ṭeḇel and nĕḇelah, he should be fed nĕḇelah first, since the eating of Ṭeḇel carries the death penalty. If nĕḇelah and the spontaneous growth of the Sabbatical years are available, he should be fed first the spontaneous growth of the Sabbatical year, whose prohibition is based on the authority of the Scribes, as will be explained in the Laws Concerning the Sabbatical Year. If Ṭeḇel and the growth of the Sabbatical year are at hand, he should be fed the latter. In the case of Ṭeḇel and heave offering, if it is impossible to rectify the former, he should be fed Ṭeḇel, which has not the same degree of sanctity as heave offering. And so on, in a similar manner.

18. We have already explained that one prohibition cannot take legal hold where another already exists, unless both are coincidental, or the second introduces factors additional to the first, or is more comprehensive than the first. Hence it is possible for a person by eating one olive's bulk to become liable to a fivefold flogging, providing that he was warned about the five prohibitions involved in it all together. How so? Let us suppose that a man in a state of uncleanness eats an olive's bulk of the fat of the remnant of a sacrifice on the Day of Atonement; he would become liable to a flogging for each of the following: eating forbidden fat, eating of the remnant of a sacrifice, eating on the Day of Atonement, eating sacred things in a state of uncleanness, and deriving benefit from sacred things and misusing them.

19. Why then in this instance does one prohibition take hold when another already exists? The fat of this animal was originally forbidden for food but permitted for benefit. Once the animal was consecrated as a sacrifice, its fat became forbidden also for benefit, and since the prohibition of benefit is an added one, the prohibition of the use of the fat of consecrated things is thus

added on to the fat. Now the fat is still permitted for the altar, although forbidden to an ordinary person. When thereupon it becomes the remnant of a sacrifice, so that the prohibition for the altar is now added on to it, it also becomes additionally prohibited to the ordinary person. Furthermore, this man who ate it was originally permitted to eat the flesh of this animal but forbidden to eat its fat. Once he becomes unclean, he is prohibited to eat its flesh also, thus again an additional prohibition is added on to the fat. At this point the Day of Atonement comes along with its prohibition of all food, and since this prohibition extends to profane food as well, it is once more added on to this fat. The same applies to all similar instances.

CHAPTER XV

1. If a forbidden article becomes mixed with a permitted article, the rule is as follows: If it is of a different species, the mixture is forbidden so long as the prohibited article imparts to it a flavor of its own; if it is of the same species, so that its flavor cannot be detected, it becomes neutralized by the greater quantity.

2. How so? If some kidney fat falls into a dish of pounded beans and is completely dissolved, the beans should be tasted. If the flavor of the fat cannot be detected, both ingredients are deemed permitted. If the flavor of the fat is present, as well as its substance, both are deemed prohibited on the authority of the Torah; if the flavor of the fat is present but not its substance, both are deemed forbidden on the authority of the Scribes.

3. What is meant by its substance? For instance, if there is an olive's bulk of fat to each three eggs' bulk of the mixture, and one then eats three eggs' bulk of the mixture, he is liable to a flogging, since the amount eaten contained an olive's bulk of fat, so that both the flavor and the substance of the forbidden matter were present. If on the other hand he eats less than three eggs'

bulk, he is liable only to the flogging prescribed for disobedience, on the authority of the Scribes. Similarly, if there is less than an olive's bulk of fat to each three eggs' bulk of the mixture, even though the flavor of the fat is present, and he eats all of that dish, he is liable only to the flogging prescribed for disobedience.

4. If kidney fat falls into tail fat and the whole is dissolved, the rule is as follows: If the quantity of tail fat is twice as large as that of kidney fat, the entire mixture is permitted on the authority of the Torah; even if one cut of nĕḇelah becomes mixed with two cuts of an animal upon which šĕḥiṭah had been performed, the whole is permitted on the authority of the Torah. The whole mixture, however, is forbidden on the authority of the Scribes, unless the prohibited thing has lost its identity because of its extremely small quantity, so that it cannot be considered a thing of value whose substance remains in existence, as will be explained.

5. How great must the quantity of the admixture be for the forbidden matter to lose its identity because of its extremely small quantity? That depends upon the respective proportion which the Sages have specified: for some things it is one in sixty, for others one in a hundred, and for still others, one in two hundred.

6. From this you learn that for all things forbidden on the authority of the Torah, whether they involve flogging or extinction, or mere prohibition of benefit, if they become mixed with permitted food, the rule is as follows: If one species is mixed with another species, the mixture is forbidden if the prohibited component imparts a flavor of its own; if two similar species are mixed so that it is impossible to detect the flavor of the prohibited component, the proportion is one in sixty, one in one hundred, or one in two hundred, as the case may be. The sole exceptions are libation wine, because of the gravity of idolatry, and Ṭeḇel, seeing that it is possible to rectify it. For this reason when mixed with substances of the same species, the smallest quantity of them renders the mixture forbidden; when mixed with a substance of

another species, the mixture is prohibited if they impart a flavor, in the manner of all forbidden things.

7. How so? If the contents of several jugs of wine are spilled over one drop of libation wine, the entire mixture is forbidden, as will be explained. Similarly, if a cup of wine of Ṭebel becomes mixed with a jugful of valid wine, the whole quantity becomes Ṭebel, until the due heave offerings and tithes are separated from the mixture, as will be explained in its proper place.

8. Although the produce of the Sabbatical year, when mixed with its own species, should render the mixture forbidden whatever its amount, and when mixed with another species, should render the mixture forbidden if it imparts a flavor, it is not included in the prohibitions set forth in the Torah. The reason is that such a mixture is not forbidden, except that one must eat it all in the sanctity appertaining to produce of the Sabbatical year, as will be explained in its appropriate place.

9. Although leaven on Passover is prohibited by the Torah, it is likewise not included in these rules, because the mixture of leavened and unleavened matter is not forbidden for all time, since after Passover the entire mixture becomes permitted, as we have explained. For this reason the smallest quantity of leaven renders the mixture prohibited, whether it is mixed with its own species or with another species.

10. The same rule applies to new grain which becomes mixed with old grain before the 'Omer has been offered up, the smallest amount of new grain rendering the mixture forbidden, since it is capable of being rendered permissible, for after the offering of the 'Omer the whole mixture becomes permitted. The same applies to everything which is capable of being rendered permissible, even if its prohibition is based only on the authority of the Scribes. As an example, for a thing forbidden on account of *mukṣeh,* or because it came into being on a festival, the Sages have specified no minimum amount, so that even one part in many thousands cannot be neutralized, since there is a way in which it may be

rendered permitted. Similar examples are consecrated things, second tithes, and their like.

11. For 'Orlah, however, for the produce of a vineyard of mixed seeds, and for prohibited fat and blood, and their like, and also for heave offerings, the Sages have specified a minimum amount, since there is no way in which they may become permitted to everyone.

12. It would appear to me that even if something which has the capability of being rendered permissible becomes mixed with another species and does not impart a flavor, it should be permitted. For that which has the capability of being rendered permissible should not be subject to a more stringent rule than Ṭebel, which is likewise capable of being rectified, yet when mixed with another species is forbidden only if it imparts a flavor, as we have explained. As for leaven on Passover, the stringency concerning it need evoke no surprise, since Scripture says, *Ye shall eat* NOTHING *leavened* (Exod. 12:20), which is why the Sages have imposed greater restrictions upon it, as we have explained.

13. The folowing are the quantities which the Sages have specified: heave offering, heave offering of tithe, dough offering, and first fruits are neutralized one part in one hundred and one, after which the priest's share must be taken out of the mixture; they combine together with one another. Similarly, a piece of shewbread mixed with pieces of profane bread is neutralized one part in one hundred and one. How so? If one *sĕ'ah* of flour of one of these, or one sĕ'ah of all of them mixed, falls into a hundred sĕ'ah of profane flour, and the whole becomes intermingled, a person should take out from the total one sĕ'ah for the priest, equivalent to the sĕ'ah which fell in, and the remainder is permitted to everyone. If it falls into less than one hundred sĕ'ah, the whole mixture becomes the priest's share.

14. 'Orlah and the produce of a vineyard of mixed seeds become neutralized one part in two hundred and one, and combine together with one another; and no priest's share need be taken

out of the mixture. How so? If the fourth of a *log̱* of wine of 'Orlah or of a vineyard of mixed seeds, or a fourth consisting of both of them mixed, falls into two hundred fourths of permitted wine, the whole mixture is permitted and it is unnecessary to remove any priest's share at all. If it falls into less than two hundred, the whole is forbidden for benefit.

15. Why is it necessary to take out the priest's share of the heave offering and not of 'Orlah or of the produce of the vineyard of mixed seeds? Because the heave offering is priestly property. Hence any heave offering for which the priests do not care, such as the heave offering of *ḳělisin,* carobs, and Edomite barley, need not be taken out.

16. Why did the Sages double the proportion in the case of 'Orlah and the produce of a vineyard of mixed seeds? Because these are forbidden for benefit. And why did they rely upon the proportion of one to one hundred in the case of heave offering? Because the heave offering of the tithe is one part out of one hundred, and its presence in the mixture renders the whole hallowed, as it is said, *even the hallowed part thereof out of it* (Num. 18:29), which according to the Sages means: If that which has to be taken out of it returns to it, it renders it hallowed.

17. The proportion of all other things forbidden on the authority of the Torah, such as the flesh of insects and creeping things, fat, blood, and their like, is one to sixty. How so? If an olive's bulk of kidney fat falls into sixty times its volume of tail fat, the whole is permitted. Should it fall into less than sixty parts, the whole is forbidden. Similarly, if it is a barleycorn's bulk of fat, sixty barleycorns are required to neutralize it. The same ruling applies to all other prohibitions. If some fat of the sinew of the thigh vein falls into a pot of meat, its proportion is reckoned on the basis of one to sixty, but the fat itself is not included in the proportion, even though the fat of the sinew of the thigh vein is forbidden only on the authority of the Scribes, as we have explained. For since the sinew of the thigh vein is considered

an individual entity, the Sages have ruled stringently regarding it, just as if it had been forbidden in the Torah. Neither is the sinew itself included in the proportion, nor does it render anything forbidden, since sinews do not impart a flavor.

18. On the other hand, if an udder is cooked with meat, the proportion is one to sixty, including the udder, for since the udder is forbidden only on the authority of the Scribes, as we have explained, the Sages have ruled leniently with respect to its proportion.

19. In the case of a chick found in an egg which was boiled with permitted eggs, if there are sixty-one eggs apart from this one, the sixty-one are deemed permitted. Should there be only sixty apart from this one, all the eggs are forbidden, for inasmuch as the fruitful egg is a separate entity, the Sages have made a distinction with regard to it by adding to its proportion.

20. If, on the other hand, the egg of an unclean bird is boiled together with the eggs of a clean bird, it does not render them forbidden. If they are beaten up together, or if the contents of an egg of an unclean bird or of a ṭĕrefah bird are mixed with the contents of other eggs, the proportion is one to sixty.

21. Where did the Sages find support for the proportion of one to sixty? From the fact that the portion which is taken from the ram of the Nazirite's sacrifice, that is the shoulder, constitutes one sixtieth part of the rest of the ram, and when the whole ram is cooked this shoulder does not render it prohibited, as it is said, *and the priest shall take the shoulder of the ram when it is cooked* (Num. 7:19).

22. If one species becomes mixed with another species of the same kind, and also with a third and different ingredient—for instance, if kidney fat falls into a dish consisting of tail fat and pounded beans—and the whole becomes intermingled, forming one mass, the tail fat and the pounded beans are regarded as constituting a single substance, and the amount of kidney fat is

measured against the combined pounded beans and tail fat. If the proportion is one to sixty, the mixture is permitted, seeing that it is impossible in this instance to detect the flavor of the kidney fat.

23. The same rule applies to heave offerings which become mixed, for which the proportion is one to one hundred, and to the produce of a vineyard of mixed seeds or ʻOrlah, for which the proportion is one to two hundred.

24. In the case of all prohibited things, the proportion, whether it is one to sixty, one to one hundred, or one to two hundred, should be measured against everything contained in the pot, including the gravy and the spices and even the quantity absorbed by the pot itself after the forbidden article had fallen into it. This last need only be approximated, seeing that it cannot be determined accurately.

25. It is forbidden at the outset to neutralize articles prohibited on the authority of the Torah, but if one does so, they are permitted. Nevertheless, the Sages have penalized such a transgressor by making the whole mixture forbidden. It would appear to me, however, that since only a penalty is involved, the mixture should be forbidden solely to him who had transgressed and neutralized the prohibited article, while to others it should be permitted.

26. How so? If a *sĕʼah* of ʻOrlah falls into a hundred sĕʼah of permitted food, so that the whole becomes forbidden, one may not add another hundred sĕʼah, in order to raise the proportion to one to two hundred and one. But if one transgresses and does so, the whole mixture is permitted. A person may, however, at the outset neutralize an article prohibited only on the authority of the Scribes.

27. How so? If milk falls into a pot containing the flesh of fowl, so that it imparts a flavor to the dish, one may add the flesh of another fowl until the flavor of milk is neutralized, and so in all similar cases.

28. We have already explained that if a forbidden article imparts its flavor to a permitted article, the whole becomes prohibited. This applies, however, only where such an addition improves the permitted article; if the forbidden addition impairs the permitted article and spoils its taste, the article is permitted. That is, if the addition impairs the permitted article from beginning to end; if it spoils it at first but in the end improves it, or improves it at first and only subsequently spoils it, the article is prohibited.

29. Who should taste the mixture? In the case of heave offerings mixed with profane food, a priest should taste it. If the taste of the heave offerings is recognizable, the whole becomes the priest's share. In the Laws Concerning Heave Offerings the rule governing the priest's share will be explained.

30. In the case of meat with milk; of libation wine, the wine of 'Orlah, or the wine of a vineyard of mixed seeds which fell into honey; or of the flesh of creeping things and insects which is cooked with vegetables, and their like—in all these cases a heathen should taste the food and his word may be relied upon. If he says that no taste of the forbidden article is present, or that the taste is there but it is bad, so that the food has become spoiled, the whole mixture is permitted. That is, provided the flavor does not improve in the end, as we have explained. If a heathen is not available to taste the mixture, the proportion may be calculated against the respective standard, one to sixty, one to one hundred, or one to two hundred.

31. If a rodent falls into beer or vinegar, it is proportioned at one to sixty, since apprehension need be had that its flavor may improve the beer or the vinegar. But if it falls into wine, oil, or honey they are permitted, even if it imparts a flavor, for it is a spoiling flavor, since all these articles must have a fragrant odor, whereas the rodent causes them to have an unpleasant odor and ruins their flavor.

32. If a kid is roasted together with its fat, even the lobe of its

ear is forbidden for consumption, since the fat is absorbed by the organs, improving the flesh and imparting a flavor to it. For this reason, if the kid is so lean that it has only a little kidney fat or fat of the entrails, about one part of fat to sixty parts of flesh, one may peel the flesh and eat it until he reaches the fat. Similarly, if one roasts a leg with the sinew of the thigh vein still in it, he may peel the flesh and eat until he reaches the sinew, which he must then discard. Likewise, if he roasts a whole animal without removing its forbidden veins and membranes, he may peel the flesh and eat it, and upon reaching the forbidden part he may cut it out and discard it, for the sinews do not impart a flavor to be measured.

33. One should not roast in the same oven the flesh of an animal upon which šĕḥiṭah has been performed together with the flesh of a nĕḇelah or of an unclean animal, even if they do not touch one another. If, however, one does so roast them, it is deemed permitted, even if the forbidden portion is very fat and the permitted one lean. The reason is that odor alone does not render anything forbidden—only the actual flavor of a forbidden thing does so.

34. If salted meat of nĕḇelah is soaked with the meat of an animal upon which šĕḥiṭah had been performed, the latter is deemed forbidden, since the juice of the nĕḇelah becomes absorbed into the flesh of the animal upon which šĕḥiṭah had been performed, and it is impossible in this case to go by either the taste or the amount absorbed. Similarly, if salted unclean fish is soaked with unsalted clean fish, the latter is prohibited because of the brine which it has absorbed. If, however, the clean fish is salted and the unclean unsalted, the salted fish is not forbidden, for it is the unsalted which absorbs from the salted. If unclean fish is pickled with clean fish the whole is forbidden, unless the proportion of unclean fish to clean fish is less than one to two hundred.

CHAPTER XVI

1. All these proportions prescribed by the Sages in the case of a forbidden article mixed with a permitted article of its own species apply only when the forbidden article does not act as a souring or spicing agent, or when it is not a thing of value which remains as it is and does not become commingled and dissolved in the permitted article. If it does act as a souring or spicing agent, or is a thing of value, the smallest amount of it renders the mixture forbidden.

2. How so? If leaven from wheat of the heave offering falls into dough of profane wheat, and there is sufficient leaven to ferment the dough, the whole of the dough becomes the priest's share. Similarly, if spices of heave offering fall into a dish of profane food of the same species, and there is enough to spice the whole mixture, the whole becomes the priest's share. This is so even if the proportion of leaven or spice is no more than one part to a thousand. The same applies to leaven of the mixed seeds of a vineyard which falls into dough, or spices of 'Orlah which fall into a dish—the whole is forbidden for benefit.

3. Seven things are classified as articles of value, in that the smallest amount of them renders a mixture of their own species forbidden. They are these: crack-nuts, Badan pomegranates, sealed jugs, young beet shoots, cabbage stalks, Greek pumpkins, and home-baked loaves.

4. How so? If a Badan pomegranate which is 'Orlah becomes mixed with thousands of other pomegranates, the whole is forbidden for benefit. Likewise, if a sealed wine jug of 'Orlah or of a vineyard of mixed seeds becomes mixed with thousands of other sealed jugs, they are all forbidden for benefit. The same rule applies to the rest of the seven articles.

5. Similarly, if a cut of nĕḇelah or of an unclean animal, wild beast, bird, or fish becomes mixed with thousands of other cuts, the whole is forbidden until that cut is removed. Only after it has been removed may one proceed to apply the required proportion of one to sixty to what remains. For if that cut is not removed, the forbidden article remains unchanged in its original state, being a cut of value to the owner, since he would be honored by offering it to guests.

6. The same rule applies to a cut of meat mixed with milk, or to a cut of a profane animal slaughtered in the courtyard of the Temple. Since they are forbidden for benefit on the authority of the Scribes, as will be explained in the Laws Concerning Šĕḥiṭah, the smallest amount of them renders the whole mixture prohibited until they are removed. Similarly, in the case of the sinew of the thigh vein which is cooked with other sinews or with meat, if one can identify it, he should remove it, and the remainder is then permitted, since sinews do not impart a flavor. If, however, he cannot identify it, the whole mixture is forbidden, for since the sinew is regarded as a separate entity, it is a valued article and the smallest amount of it renders the mixture forbidden.

7. All living creatures are likewise classed as valued things and do not become neutralized. Consequently, if an ox sentenced to stoning becomes mixed with a thousand other oxen, or if a heifer whose neck was to be broken is mixed with a thousand heifers, or if the slaughtered bird of a leper's sacrifice is mixed with a thousand birds, or the first-born of an ass with a thousand asses, all are prohibited for benefit. Other things, however, even if customarily sold by number, are neutralized in their requisite proportion.

8. How so? If a bundle of vegetables from a vineyard of mixed seeds becomes intermingled with two hundred other bundles, or if a citron of 'Orlah becomes mixed with two hundred other citrons, the whole is permitted, and so in all similar cases.

9. It would appear to me that any article valued by the residents

of any particular place, as crack-nuts and Badan pomegranates were valued in the Land of Israel at that time, renders a mixture forbidden whatever its quantity, according to its importance in that locality at that time. The only reason that these particular seven articles were mentioned is because the smallest quantity of them renders a mixture prohibited anywhere. The same ruling applies to all similar things in other localities, and it is clear that all these prohibitions are based on the authority of the Scribes.

10. If one pomegranate from such a mixture falls in with two other Badan pomegranates, and one of these three then falls in with another batch of pomegranates, these last are permitted, since the pomegranate of the first mixture had already become neutralized in a greater quantity. But should a pomegranate of the first mixture fall in with a thousand others, all are forbidden, since an article is declared neutralized in a greater quantity in order to render it permitted only if a double doubt exists, that is, if a part of the second mixture falls into another place it does not render the new mixture prohibited; and so in all similar cases.

11. If the nuts which were rendered forbidden because of the one nut of 'Orlah among them are cracked, or if the pomegranates are shredded, or if the jugs are opened, or the pumpkins cut, or the loaves sliced after they had become forbidden, they become neutralized one part to two hundred and one. The same rule applies to a cut of nĕḇelah minced with other cuts so that they all resemble it—it becomes neutralized in sixty parts.

12. It is forbidden, however, to crack the nuts, or shred the pomegranates, or open the jugs, once they have become forbidden, in order to cause them to become neutralized in two hundred and one parts, for one is forbidden to neutralize a prohibited article in the first place, and if he does so, he is liable to a penalty whereby the article is rendered forbidden to him, as we have explained.

13. If leaven of a vineyard of mixed seeds, together with leaven of heave offering, falls into a batch of dough, and if both are

sufficient when combined—though not when separate—to leaven the dough, that dough is forbidden to an Israelite but allowed to a priest. Similarly, if condiments of heave offering and of a vineyard of mixed seeds fall into a dish, and when combined—but not when separate—are sufficient to flavor it, the dish is forbidden to an Israelite, since it has been seasoned with articles prohibited to him, although it is permitted to a priest.

14. Condiments of one species, but of two or three different categories, or of three species but of the same category, combine together to act as seasoning agents and render the mixture forbidden, and the same applies to leavening agents. How so? Since leaven of wheat and leaven of barley are both called leaven, they are regarded not as two separate species, but as one species, and are combined together in estimating the amount required to leaven a batch of wheaten dough, if the flavor of the combination is that of wheat, or a batch of barley dough, if the flavor of the combination is that of barley.

15. What is meant by one species with three categories? For example, in the case of water parsley, meadow parsley, and garden parsley, although each one of them belongs to a separate category, they are all of the same species and therefore combine together as far as seasoning is concerned.

16. If leaven of heave offering or of a vineyard of mixed seeds falls into a batch of dough already leavened, or if seasoning of heave offering, of ʻOrlah, or of a vineyard of mixed seeds falls into an already seasoned dish, the rule is as follows: If there is sufficient leaven to leaven the dough had it been unleavened, or sufficient seasoning to season the dish had it been unseasoned, the whole is forbidden. If there is not sufficient to season or to leaven, the leavening and seasoning are neutralized according to their proportions, heave offering one part to one hundred and one, and ʻOrlah and the produce of a vineyard of mixed seeds one part to two hundred and one.

17. Heave offering neutralizes ʻOrlah and the produce of a

vineyard of mixed seeds. How so? If a *sĕ'ah* of heave offering falls into ninety-nine sĕ'ah of profane food, and then half a sĕ'ah of 'Orlah or of the produce of a vineyard of mixed seeds falls into the mixture, no prohibition results either of 'Orlah or of the produce of a vineyard of mixed seeds, since they become neutralized one part to two hundred and one, even though part of the two hundred consists of heave offering.

18. Similarly, 'Orlah and the produce of a vineyard of mixed seeds neutralize heave offering. How so? If a hundred sĕ'ah of 'Orlah or of the produce of a vineyard of mixed seeds fall into twenty thousand sĕ'ah of profane food, the whole mixture amounting to twenty thousand and one hundred sĕ'ah, and if subsequently one sĕ'ah of heave offering falls into each one hundred sĕ'ah of the mixture, the whole mixture is permitted, since the heave offering becomes neutralized one part to one hundred and one, even though part of the hundred sĕ'ah which neutralizes it consists of 'Orlah or of the produce of a vineyard of mixed seeds, as the case may be.

19. Similarly, 'Orlah neutralizes the produce of a vineyard of mixed seeds, and vice versa; also, the produce of the vineyard of mixed seeds neutralizes the produce of the vineyard of mixed seeds, and 'Orlah neutralizes 'Orlah. How so? If two hundred sĕ'ah of 'Orlah or of the produce of a vineyard of mixed seeds fall into forty thousand sĕ'ah of profane food, and then into each two hundred sĕ'ah of the mixture there falls a sĕ'ah of 'Orlah or of the produce of a vineyard of mixed seeds, the whole mixture is permitted, for once the prohibited article which originally fell into it had become neutralized, the whole mixture became permitted profane food.

20. If a garment is dyed with dye made from shells of 'Orlah fruit, it must be burned; if it is mixed with others it is neutralized one part to two hundred and one. Similarly, food cooked with fire of shells from 'Orlah fruit, or bread baked with fire of shells of 'Orlah fruit or of the produce of a vineyard of mixed

seeds, must be burned, since the use made of these forbidden substances is evident in these articles. If they become mixed with others they are neutralized one part to two hundred and one.

21. Similarly, if a man has woven into a garment one *siṭ*'s length of thread dyed with dye made from shells of 'Orlah fruit, and does not know which thread it is, the dyed thread is neutralized one part to two hundred and one. If the ingredients of 'Orlah dye become mixed with the ingredients of permitted dye, they are neutralized one part to two hundred and one; but if forbidden liquid dye becomes mixed with permitted liquid dye, it is neutralized in a greater quantity of the latter.

22. If an oven is heated with shells of 'Orlah fruit or of the produce of a vineyard of mixed seeds, whether the oven is new or old, it must first be cooled, and then may be reheated with permitted fuel. If one bakes bread or any other victual in the oven before it is cooled, it is forbidden for benefit, since the improvement brought about in the bread or victual is due to the prohibited fuel. If he rakes out all the fire first and then cooks or bakes food in the heat of the oven, this is permitted, since the forbidden fuel has now disappeared.

23. If a potter fires plates, cups, dishes, or flasks in a fire made with shells of 'Orlah fruit, they are forbidden for benefit, since it is the fuel—which is forbidden for benefit—that has made them into new utensils.

24. Bread baked over live coals of 'Orlah wood is permitted, for once the wood has become coal its prohibited nature has disappeared, even though the coal is still burning. If a dish is cooked with shells of 'Orlah fruit or of the produce of a vineyard of mixed seeds, and then permitted fuel is added, the victual is forbidden, even though both fuels have contributed to its cooking, for while it was being cooked by the forbidden fuel, the permitted fuel had not yet been added, with the result that part of the cooking was done with permitted fuel and part with forbidden fuel.

25. If a sapling of 'Orlah is mixed with other saplings, or a garden bed of a vineyard of mixed seeds with other garden beds, one may in the first place pick from all of them. If the proportion is two hundred permitted saplings to one forbidden sapling, or two hundred permitted garden beds to one forbidden one, all that has been picked is permitted. If the proportion is less than this, all the picked produce is forbidden. Why then did the Sages permit one to pick in the first place? Would it not have been logical to forbid the whole until one first takes the trouble to remove the prohibited sapling or garden bed? The answer is that it is presumed that a person would not risk rendering his entire vineyard forbidden for the sake of one plant, and had he been aware of it, he surely would have removed it.

26. If one curdles milk with the sap of unripe 'Orlah figs, or with the stomach of an animal offered up to idols, or with vinegar made from libation wine, the resulting cheese is forbidden for benefit, even though this is a case of mixing two different species, and only a negligible quantity of the forbidden factor is used, for it is this factor—which is recognizable—that curdles the milk into cheese.

27. The rule is that the fruit of 'Orlah and the produce of a vineyard of mixed seeds must be burned, while their liquids must be buried, since it is impossible to burn liquids.

28. As we have said above, if the smallest quantity of libation wine is mixed with permitted wine, the whole is forbidden for benefit. When does this apply? When one pours the permitted wine upon a drop of libation wine. If he pours libation wine from a small jar into a vat of wine, should he even continue pouring all day, the libation wine becomes continuously neutralized. If, however, he pours from a jug, whether from the permitted to the forbidden or vice versa, the whole is prohibited, since the flow descending from the jug is a considerable one.

29. If undefined heathen wine becomes mixed with permitted wine, the smallest quantity renders the mixture forbidden for consumption, and one should sell it to a heathen, deduct the

value of the prohibited wine, and cast it into the Dead Sea, whereupon he may derive benefit from the remainder of the money. Similarly, if a jug of libation wine becomes mixed with jugs of permitted wine, the whole is forbidden for consumption but allowed for benefit. One should therefore, upon selling the entire mixture to a heathen, convey the value of that jug to the Dead Sea, and the same applies to a jug of undefined heathen wine.

30. If water is mixed with wine or vice versa, it depends upon whether it imparts a flavor, since it is mixed with a different species. When does this apply? When the permitted liquid falls into the forbidden. If the prohibited liquid falls into the permitted, it becomes continuously neutralized. That is, if one pours it in from a small jar, so that it pours out and descends in small quantities. But how can water be forbidden? If it is an object of worship or is used in idolatrous offerings.

31. If a ladle of water falls into a vat of wine, and subsequently libation wine falls into the mixture, the permitted wine should be regarded as though it were not there, and the water which fell in should be estimated against the libation wine. If it would have neutralized the flavor of that wine, the water overwhelms and neutralizes it, and the whole mixture is then allowed.

32. If libation wine falls upon grapes, they should be washed and are thereupon permitted for consumption. If the grapes are split open, the rule is as follows: If the wine, whether old or new, imparts a flavor to the grapes, they are forbidden for benefit; if not, they are allowed for consumption.

33. If libation wine falls upon figs, they are permitted, since wine spoils the flavor of figs.

34. If libation wine falls upon wheat, the latter is forbidden for food but allowed for benefit. One may not sell the wheat to a heathen, lest he should resell it to an Israelite. What then should one do? He should grind the wheat and bake it into bread, and then sell the bread to a heathen when no Israelite is present, so

that no Israelite would subsequently buy the bread from the heathen, since heathen bread is forbidden, as will be explained later. Why should the wheat not be tested to determine if a flavor has been imparted to it? Because wheat is absorbent and the wine is swallowed up by it.

35. If libation wine becomes fermented and falls into fermented beer, the smallest quantity of it renders the mixture forbidden, since it is of the same species, both being vinegar. If wine becomes mixed with vinegar, whether the vinegar falls into the wine or vice versa, an estimate should be made as to whether a flavor has been imparted.

CHAPTER XVII

1. If flesh of nĕḇelah or of abominable and creeping things is cooked in an earthenware pot, one may not cook the meat of an animal upon which šĕḥiṭah had been performed in that pot on that selfsame day. If one nevertheless cooks in it any kind of meat, the dish is forbidden; if he cooks another kind of eatable, it depends on whether it absorbs a flavor from the pot.

2. According to the Torah, such a pot is forbidden only on that same day, when the fat which has been absorbed in it has not yet spoiled. The Scribes, however, have ruled that one should not cook in that pot ever. For that reason one should never purchase from a heathen old earthenware vessels which have already been used for hot food, such as pots and plates, even if they are lead-glazed. If he nevertheless does acquire them and cooks in them, the dish is permitted from the second day onwards.

3. If one acquires from a heathen tableware of metal or glass which has never been used, it must be immersed in the water of an immersion pool, whereupon it may be used for eating and drinking. Utensils which have been used for cold substances, such as cups, flasks, and ladles, should be rinsed and immersed in an

immersion pool, and are thereupon permitted. Utensils which have been used for hot food, such as kettles, boilers, and water heaters, must be scalded and immersed and are then permitted. Utensils which have been used over an open fire, such as spits and gratings, must be made white-hot in a fire until the crust peels off, and then immersed, and are thereupon allowed.

4. How is scalding performed? A small kettle is placed inside a large kettle which is filled with water, so that it covers the small one, and is then brought to full boil. If the vessel to be scalded is large, one should make a lip of dough or clay around its rim, fill it with water above the rim, and bring it to a boil. In all cases, however, if the vessels are used before scalding, rinsing, or bringing to a white heat, as the case may be, or before immersing, they are permitted, since the fat absorbed in them imparts a spoiling flavor, as we have just explained.

5. This immersion which must be applied to tableware acquired from heathens before it may be used for eating and drinking has nothing to do with the Scriptural law of cleanness and uncleanness, but is based solely on the authority of the Scribes. There is an allusion to it, however, in the verse, *everything that may abide the fire, ye shall make go through the fire, and it shall be clean* (Num. 31:23). The Sages have learned by tradition that this refers only to the cleansing of vessels from heathen cooking, and not from uncleanness, since no uncleanness can be removed by fire. For all unclean things rise out of their uncleanness only through immersion, and uncleanness acquired through contact with a corpse is removed through sprinkling in addition to immersion. The only instance in which fire is referred to is the case of vessels used for heathen cooking, and since the verse says, *and it shall be clean,* the Sages reasoned that Scripture meant to imply an additional act of cleansing—i.e. immersion—after the passing through the fire, which frees the vessel from the effects of heathen cooking.

6. It is only table utensils made of metal which have been purchased from a heathen that are liable to this immersion. If one

borrows them from a heathen, or if a heathen deposits them as a pledge, one need only rinse, scald, or bring them to a white heat, as the case may be, and no immersion is required. Similarly, if one purchases wooden or stone utensils, he need only rinse or scald them, respectively. Likewise, there is no need to immerse earthenware vessels, but if they are lead-glazed they are regarded as though made of metal and must be immersed.

7. If one purchases a knife from a heathen, he must bring it to a white heat, or polish it on a suitable grindstone. If it is a good knife, free from pits, it is sufficient for him to insert it forcefully into hard ground ten times, and then he may eat cold food cut with it. If the knife is pitted, or if it is a good knife but he wishes to eat hot food cut with it or to perform šĕḥiṭah, he must bring it to a white heat or polish the whole of it. If he performs šĕḥiṭah with it before cleansing it, he must rinse the place of the incision; it is preferable, however, to peel off the outer layer of flesh instead.

8. One may not perform šĕḥiṭah with a knife used in slaughtering a ṭĕrefah animal, unless he rinses it first, even in cold water, or wipes it with a rag.

9. There are other things which the Sages have forbidden, these prohibitions, although without root in the Torah, having been decreed by them in order to keep the people away from heathens, so that Israelites might not mingle with them, lest such commingling should lead to intermarriage. These things are as follows: drinking with heathens, even in circumstances where no apprehension need be felt for libation wine; and eating their bread or cooked food, even where no concern need be had for heathen cooking utensils.

10. How so? One may not drink at a banquet with heathens, even if the beverage is boiled wine, which is not forbidden, or even if one drinks out of his own vessels. If, however, the majority of the company are Israelites, this is allowed. Nor may one drink heathen beer manufactured from dates, figs, and the like. This applies, however, only in the place where it is sold.

Should one bring this beer to his own house and drink it there, it is permitted, since the essence of the decree is merely to prevent an Israelite from dining with heathens.

11. It is permitted to drink apple wine, pomegranate wine, and their like in all circumstances, since the Sages did not extend the prohibition to uncommon things. Raisin wine, however, is considered wine and is liable to become libation wine.

12. Although the Sages forbade heathen bread, there are nevertheless localities where people exercise leniency in this matter and purchase bread from a heathen baker for lack of an Israelite baker, considering it permitted on the ground that it is a case of emergency. But for householder's bread, none of the authorities has ruled leniently in regard to it, since the essence of the prohibition is to prevent intermarriage, and if an Israelite should eat the bread of a heathen householder, he might dine with him also.

13. If a heathen fires an oven and an Israelite bakes bread in it; or if the Israelite fires the oven and the heathen bakes in it; or if the heathen both fires the oven and bakes the bread, and the Israelite comes along later and stirs the fire a little or damps it—in all these cases, inasmuch as the Israelite has participated in the baking of the bread, it is permitted. Indeed, even if the Israelite has done no more than cast one piece of firewood into the fire, he has thereby rendered permitted all the bread in the oven, since the purpose of this rule is merely to make clear that wholly heathen bread is forbidden.

14. If a heathen boils for an Israelite wine, milk, honey, quinces, or any similar food which is usually eaten raw, it is allowed, since the prohibition of heathen food extends only to those foods which are not ordinarily eaten raw, such as meat, unsalted fish, eggs, and vegetables. In the case of these foods, if the heathen cooks them from beginning to end and the Israelite does not participate in the cooking, they are forbidden because of heathen cooking.

15. This applies only to foods which might be served at the royal table to be eaten with bread, such as meat, eggs, fish, and their like. In the case of food which is not served at the royal table to be eaten with bread, such as lupines, it is permitted if cooked by a heathen, even though it is not eaten raw. The same applies in all similar instances. For the essence of the decree is to prevent intermarriage, in order that a heathen should not invite an Israelite to dine with him, and as a rule a man does not invite his friend to dine with him unless the food he serves consists of delicacies that might be served at the royal table to be eaten with bread.

16. Small fish salted by an Israelite or a heathen are regarded as partially cooked. If, therefore, a heathen roasts these fish after an Israelite had salted them, they are permitted, since food partially cooked by an Israelite, whether at the beginning or at the end, is allowed. For this reason, if a heathen leaves meat or a pot over the fire and an Israelite then turns the meat or stirs the contents of the pot, or if the Israelite leaves it over the fire and the heathen does the rest, the food is permitted.

17. Fish salted or fruits smoke-cured by a heathen until they are fit for consumption are permitted, since for the purposes of this decree salting is not regarded as the equivalent of boiling, nor smoking as the equivalent of cooking. Similarly, heathen parched corn is allowed, and was not forbidden by the Sages, seeing that one does not invite a friend to dine on parched corn.

18. If a heathen cooks peas, beans, lentils, and their like, for sale, they are forbidden because of heathen cooking in such localities where they are served at the royal table as a side dish. These foods are also prohibited everywhere on account of forbidden heathen vessels, since they might have been cooked with meat, or in a pot in which meat had been cooked. Similarly, spongy cakes fried by heathens in oil are also forbidden, because of heathen utensils.

19. If a heathen cooks some food unintentionally, it is per-

mitted. How so? For instance, should a heathen set fire to a meadow in order to burn off the grass, and should locusts in the grass be thereby roasted, they are permitted, even in a locality where they are served at the royal table as a side dish. Similarly, if he singes an animal's head in order to remove the hair, it is allowed to eat of the dangling flesh or of the ear tips which are roasted in the course of singeing.

20. If a heathen cooks figs, the rule is as follows: If they were sweet prior to cooking, they are permitted, but if they were bitter and became sweet through the cooking, they are forbidden. If the figs were bittersweet, they are likewise prohibited.

21. Roasted lentils, whether kneaded with water or with vinegar, are forbidden. Roasted wheat or barley, which is kneaded with water, is permitted.

22. Heathen oil is allowed, and he who forbids it stands guilty of grievous sin, since he thereby rebels against the decision of Rabbi Judah the Prince's court which declared it permitted. Even if the oil is boiled it is permitted. For oil cannot be forbidden either on account of heathen cooking, since it may be consumed raw, or because of the forbidden heathen vessels, seeing that meat spoils oil and imparts an unpleasant odor to it.

23. Similarly, if heathen honey is boiled, and sweetmeats are made with it, it is allowed, for the same reason.

24. If a pomace of dates belonging to a heathen is stewed, whether in a large or a small caldron, it is permitted, since stewing impairs its flavor. Similarly, pickled vegetables usually prepared without vinegar or wine, or pickled olives or locusts taken directly from the storehouse, are permitted. On the other hand, locusts and pickles over which wine is poured are forbidden. They are likewise forbidden if vinegar, or even fermented beer, is poured over them.

25. Why did the Sages forbid fermented heathen beer? Because

heathens put wine lees into it. For that reason, if it is taken directly from the storehouse, it is allowed.

26. In localities where the practice is to put wine into brine pickle, the latter is forbidden; but where wine is more expensive than brine pickle, it is permitted. This ruling applies in all similar cases where apprehension is felt that the heathen might have added forbidden matter to food, since no one would add an expensive ingredient to a cheap substance, because he would incur a loss thereby, while he would add a cheap ingredient to an expensive substance, since he would profit thereby.

27. If a minor eats one of the forbidden foods, or performs work on the Sabbath, the court is under no obligation to compel him to desist, since he is not of mature mind. This holds only when he does it of his own accord. It is, however, forbidden to feed him deliberately with such foods, or even with foods which are prohibited solely on the authority of the Scribes. Similarly, it is forbidden to habituate him to desecration of Sabbath and festival, even in such things as are prohibited merely because they are contrary to the spirit of Sabbath rest.

28. Although the court is under no obligation to compel a minor to desist from such matters, it is nevertheless incumbent upon his father to reprove him and make him refrain, in order to train him in sanctity and avoidance of sin, as it is said, *Train up a child in the way he should go,* etc. (Prov. 22:6).

29. The Sages have forbidden the consumption of food and drink of the kind that is revolting to most people, like food and drink contaminated with vomit, excrement, or putrid secretion, and their like. They have also forbidden eating and drinking out of filthy utensils which offend against one's natural fastidiousness, such as utensils used in the privy, the glass vessels used by barber-surgeons for bloodletting, and their like.

30. Similarly, the Sages forbade eating with grimy and dirty hands, or upon a soiled tablecloth, since all these things are in-

cluded in the verse, *ye shall not make yourselves abominable* (Lev. 11:43). He who eats such revolting foods is liable to the flogging prescribed for disobedience.

31. It is likewise forbidden to delay the normal evacuation of one's large or small orifices, and he who does so is counted among those who make themselves abominable, not to speak of the grave illnesses which he may thereby bring upon himself, thus endangering his life. Man should, on the contrary, accustom himself to bowel movements at regular times, so that he would not make himself offensive in the presence of people nor render himself abominable.

32. Indeed, he who is painstaking in these things gains exceeding sanctity and purity for his person, and purges his soul for the sake of the Holy One, blessed be He, as it is said, *ye shall therefore sanctify yourselves and be holy, for I am holy* (Lev. 11:44).

TREATISE III

LAWS CONCERNING ŠĔḤIṬAH

Involving Five Commandments,

Three Positive and Two Negative

To Wit

1. To eat meat only after šĕḥiṭah has been performed;
2. Not to perform šĕḥiṭah on a dam and its young on the selfsame day;
3. To cover up the blood of beast and bird;
4. Not to take the dam with its young;
5. To send away the dam if one takes it from off its young.

An exposition of these commandments is contained in the following chapters.

NOTE

In the list of the 613 commandments prefixed to the Code, those dealt with in the present treatise appear in the following order:

Positive commandments:

[1] 146. To eat meat only after šěḥiṭah has been performed, as it is said: *Then thou shalt kill of thy herd and of thy flock as I have commanded thee* (Deut. 12:21);

[3] 147. To cover up the blood of beast and bird, as it is said: *He shall pour out the blood thereof, and cover it with dust* (Lev. 17:13);

[5] 148. To send away the dam from the nest, as it is said: *Thou shalt in any wise let the dam go* (Deut. 22:7).

Negative commandments:

[2] 101. Not to perform šěḥiṭah on a dam and its young, as it is said: *Ye shall not kill it and its young both in one day* (Lev. 22:28);

[4] 306. Not to take the dam with its young, as it is said: *Thou shalt not take the dam with the young* (Deut. 22:6).

CHAPTER I

1. It is a positive commandment that whosoever wishes to eat of the flesh of a domestic animal, wild beast, or bird, must first perform šĕḥiṭah upon it, and only thereafter may he eat of it, as it is said, *and thou shalt kill of thy herd and of thy flock* (Deut. 12:21). Scripture also says with regard to a blemished firstling, *even as the roebuck and the hart is eaten, so shalt thou eat them* (*ibid.* v. 22). Thus you learn that a wild beast is in the same category as a domestic animal in respect to šĕḥiṭah. In regard to birds Scripture says, *And whatsoever man . . . that taketh in hunting any beast or bird that may be eaten, he shall pour out the blood thereof* (Lev. 17:13), which teaches that the slaughtering of a bird is to be performed in the same manner as the slaughtering of a beast. There is thus but one law of šĕḥiṭah applying to all of them.

2. For this reason whosoever performs šĕḥiṭah upon a domestic animal, wild beast, or bird must first recite the benediction, "Blessed art Thou, O Lord our God, King of the universe, who has sanctified us with His commandments and has commanded us concerning šĕḥiṭah"; but if he fails to recite the blessing, whether in error or willfully, the meat is nevertheless permitted. It is forbidden to eat of the meat of an animal upon which šĕḥiṭah has been performed as long as it continues to quiver, and whosoever eats of an animal before life is extinct transgresses a negative commandment, since this is included in the general prohibition, *ye shall not eat with the blood* (Lev. 19:26). He is, however, not liable to a flogging on account of it, and it is allowed to cut a portion from the animal after šĕḥiṭah has been performed but before life is extinct, provided that one salts the meat thoroughly, rinses it well, and leaves it until the animal is dead, after which he may eat of it.

3. Fish and locusts do not require šĕḥiṭah, and it is the gathering of them which renders them permitted for consumption. For as to fish, Scripture says, *If flocks and herds be slain for them, will they suffice for them, or if all the fish of the sea be gathered together for them?* (Num. 11:22). Thus the gathering of fish is made equivalent to the slaughtering of herds and flocks. As for locusts, it is said, *the gathering of the locust* (Isa. 33:4), implying that for them also the gathering alone suffices. For this reason, if fish die a natural death in the water they are permitted, and it is also allowed to eat live fish.

4. This method of slaughtering, which is mentioned in the Torah without definition, must needs be explained, in order to know upon what organ of the animal šĕḥiṭah is to be performed, what is the extent of šĕḥiṭah, with what instrument and when, where, and how it is to be performed, what things invalidate it, and who may perform it. All these matters are contained in the general commandment of the Torah, *then shalt thou kill of thy herd and thy flock as I have commanded thee, and thou shalt eat within thy gates* (Deut. 12:21), which means that Moses was commanded concerning all these matters orally, as in the case of the rest of the Oral Law, which is referred to as *commandment*, as we have explained in the Introduction to this work.

5. The place of šĕḥiṭah in a living animal is the throat, the whole of which is valid for this purpose. How so? In the gullet, it extends from the beginning of that place which, when severed, contracts, and as far as the point where it becomes hairy and begins to be broken up like the stomach. That is the place of šĕḥiṭah in the gullet.

6. If one performs šĕḥiṭah above this place, that is at what is called the wide part of the gullet, or below this place, that is from the point where the bowels commence downwards, the šĕḥiṭah is considered invalid. The measurement of the wide part of the gullet at the upper end, which is not valid for šĕḥiṭah, is in the case of a domestic animal or wild beast as much as one can grasp

in his two fingers, while in the case of a bird it depends upon its size. At the lower end, it extends as far as the crop.

7. What is the place for šěḥiṭah in the windpipe? It is from the thyroid cartilage downwards, as far as the top of the lobe of the lung when the animal stretches out its neck to pasture. That is the place for šěḥiṭah in the windpipe, and the part opposite that place on the outside is called the throat.

8. If the animal strains itself and stretches out its neck abnormally, or if the slaughterer forces these organs and stretches them upwards, and then, upon performing šěḥiṭah in the place of šěḥiṭah, that is in the throat, finds that it has been performed in the windpipe or in the gullet beyond the proper place of šěḥiṭah, it is deemed a doubtful case of něbelah.

9. The slaughterer should perform šěḥiṭah in the middle of the throat. If he performs it at the side, the šěḥiṭah is nevertheless considered valid. What should be the extent of šěḥiṭah? It should extend over both organs, the windpipe and the gullet. The preferable extent of šěḥiṭah is when it severs both of them, in either animal or bird, and this should be the slaughterer's aim. If he severs only the major part of one of the organs in a bird, or the major part of both organs in a domestic animal or wild beast, the šěḥiṭah is considered valid.

10. If, in the case of a domestic or wild animal, one severs all of one organ and only half of the other, the šěḥiṭah is invalid. Should one sever the major part of both organs, even if he exceeds the half by a mere hairsbreadth, it is valid. For once he has severed more than half of the organ, the excess over half, no matter how small, is enough to make it a major part.

11. If one severs half of each organ, even in the case of a bird, the šěḥiṭah is invalid. If the windpipe of a bird is split half open and the slaughterer then performs šěḥiṭah by extending the original cut a little further so as to cover more than half of the organ, whether he begins the šěḥiṭah at the uninjured part of the wind-

pipe and continues into the split part, or whether he inserts the knife into the cut and continues cutting so as to cover the greater part of the organ, the šěḥiṭah is valid.

12. Whosoever performs šěḥiṭah must examine the organs after the slaughtering has taken place. If he fails to undertake the examination, and the head is severed before he examines it, the carcass is considered něḇelah, even if the slaughterer is generally scrupulous and expert.

13. Every animal while alive is presumed to be forbidden, until it is known for a certainty that valid šěḥiṭah has been performed upon it.

14. With what instrument may šěḥiṭah be performed? With any, whether it is a metal knife, a flint, a piece of glass, the sharp outer shell of a reed stalk, or similar cutting things. That is, however, only if its edge is sharp and without notches. Should the edge have an indentation, even if the teeth of the indentation are exceedingly small, the šěḥiṭah is invalid.

15. If the teeth of the indentation run in one direction only, one should not perform šěḥiṭah with that instrument. If the slaughterer does, however, perform šěḥiṭah in the opposite direction, where the notches are not felt, the šěḥiṭah is regarded as valid.

16. How so? If when the knife is examined during the forward movement one does not feel any notches in it, but when examined during the reverse movement one does so, the rule is as follows: If the slaughterer performs šěḥiṭah with a forward movement only, and does not bring the knife back in a reverse movement, the šěḥiṭah is valid; should he follow with a reverse movement of the knife, the šěḥiṭah is invalid.

17. A knife whose edge is wavy like a snake but free from notches, may be used for šěḥiṭah in the first instance. A knife whose edge is smooth but not sharp, may also be used for šěḥiṭah, as long as it has no notches. Even if one works it to and fro all day long until šěḥiṭah is performed, that šěḥiṭah is valid.

18. In the case of a sharp knife which had been whetted, with the result that its edge is not smooth, but feels to the touch like the head of an ear of corn, which catches the finger, one may perform šĕḥiṭah with it, seeing that is has no notch.

19. If one plucks a reed or extracts a tooth, or cuts a flint or a toenail, and they are sharp and unnotched, one may perform šĕḥiṭah with them. But if he inserts them into the ground he should not perform šĕḥiṭah with them while they are stuck in the ground. If he does so, however, the šĕḥiṭah is valid.

20. If one performs šĕḥiṭah with them while they are still attached to their original place, as they were since the beginning of their creation, without uprooting them, the šĕḥiṭah is invalid, even if there are no notches in them.

21. If one takes an animal's jawbone with several sharp teeth still attached to it and performs šĕḥiṭah with it, it is invalid, since the teeth resemble a saw. Should the jawbone have only one tooth set in it, he may perform šĕḥiṭah with it in the first instance, even though the tooth is still attached to the jawbone.

22. If one brings a knife to a white heat in the fire and then performs šĕḥiṭah with it, the šĕḥiṭah is valid. In the case of a knife having one edge like a saw and the other even, one should not perform šĕḥiṭah with the even edge in the first instance, lest he should unintentionally perform šĕḥiṭah with the other edge, but if he does so nevertheless, the šĕḥiṭah is valid, seeing that he has in fact used the even edge.

23. A slaughterer must examine the edge of the knife and both sides of it. How is this examination to be performed? By drawing the knife to and fro first on the flesh of the finger and then on the fingernail along the three sides of the knife, that is, the edge and both sides, to make sure that there are no notches of any kind in it. Thereafter he may perform šĕḥiṭah.

24. The slaughterer must also examine the knife in similar fashion after šĕḥiṭah has been performed, since if he should dis-

cover a notch in it after šěḥiṭah, the result would be a doubtful case of nĕḇelah. For the knife may have become notched on the hide, so that when he performed šěḥiṭah on the organs, he might have done so with a notched knife. Consequently he who performs šěḥiṭah upon several animals or birds must examine the knife after each act of šěḥiṭah; should he fail to do so, and upon examining the knife at the conclusion discover that it is notched, all the animals slaughtered would have to be regarded as doubtful cases of nĕḇelah, including even the first.

25. If he examines the knife before šěḥiṭah but not after, then uses it to split bone, wood, or the like, and thereupon examines the knife and finds it notched, the šěḥiṭah is nevertheless valid, since the presumption is that the knife became notched when used on the hard material. Similarly, if one negligently fails to examine the knife following šěḥiṭah, or if the knife is lost prior to the examination, the šěḥiṭah is valid.

26. If a slaughterer fails to examine his šěḥiṭah knife in the presence of a Sage and then performs šěḥiṭah with it on his own confidence, the knife must be examined. If it is found in good condition and properly inspected, he should be put under a ban, because otherwise he would rely upon himself on another occasion, when the knife may happen to be notched, and perform šěḥiṭah with it. Should the knife be found notched, he should be removed from his post as well as put under a ban, and an announcement should be made to the effect that all meat slaughtered by him is ṭĕrefah.

27. What should be the length of the šěḥiṭah knife? Any length, providing that it is not so pointed as to pierce instead of cutting, as does the blade of a small knife or any similar instrument.

28. When may šěḥiṭah take place? At any time, day or night, as long as one has a torch with him, so that he can see what he is doing. If he performs it in the darkness, however, his šěḥiṭah is valid.

29. If one erroneously performs šĕḥiṭah on the Day of Atonement or on the Sabbath, the šĕḥiṭah is nevertheless valid, even though, had he done it deliberately, he would have been liable to death in the case of the Sabbath, or to a flogging in the case of the Day of Atonement.

CHAPTER II

1. It is permitted to perform šĕḥiṭah in any place, with the exception of the Temple court, where šĕḥiṭah was allowed to be performed solely upon animals consecrated for the altar. It was thus forbidden to slaughter profane animals in the Temple court, whether cattle, wild beast, or bird, and so indeed is it stated concerning "flesh of desire," *If the place which the Lord thy God shall choose to put His name there shall be too far from thee, then thou shalt kill of thy herd and of thy flock . . . and thou shalt eat within thy gates* (Deut. 12:21). Hence you learn that "flesh of desire" may be slaughtered only outside of "the place which the Lord has chosen."

2. Thus that which was slaughtered without the Temple precincts was permitted for consumption "within all the gates," but when a profane animal was slaughtered within the Temple court, although the meat was clean, it was forbidden for benefit, as in the case of meat with milk and the like. It was required to be buried and its ashes were forbidden, even if the animal was slaughtered for medicinal purposes, or to provide food for heathens or dogs. If, however, one slaughtered an animal in the Temple court by stabbing or hamstringing it, or if it was slaughtered there by a heathen, or if an Israelite slaughtered it and found it to be ṭĕrefah, or if one slaughtered unclean cattle, wild beasts, or birds in the Temple court—in all these cases the animal was permitted for benefit.

3. It was not only cattle and wild beasts which were forbidden

to be brought into the Temple courtyard, but any profane thing, even flesh of an animal upon which šĕḥiṭah had been performed, or produce, or bread. If one transgressed and brought them in, however, they were permitted to be consumed as they were. All these things were forbidden by tradition, and whosoever performed šĕḥiṭah upon profane animals in the Temple court, or ate an olive's bulk of flesh thus slaughtered, was liable to the flogging prescribed for disobedience.

4. If one said, "This animal shall be a peace offering, but its unborn calf shall be profane," and the mother was slaughtered in the Temple court, the calf was permitted for consumption, seeing that it was impossible for him to slaughter the calf separately "in a place far away."

5. One should not perform šĕḥiṭah in such a manner that the blood would fall into the sea or into a river, lest people should say that he is a water worshiper, since it would appear as though he were making an offering to the water. Nor should he slaughter into a vessel filled with water, lest people should say that he is slaughtering to the image which appears in the water. Nor should one slaughter in such a way that the blood would fall into a vessel or into a hollow, since that is the custom of idol worshipers. If, however, one does perform šĕḥiṭah in this wise, it is valid.

6. One may slaughter in such a wise that the blood would fall into a vessel full of muddy water, since no image would be visible therein. Similarly, one may slaughter in such a manner that the blood would fall outside a hollow, but would then flow into it. One should not do so, however, in the market place, lest he should thereby imitate the heretics. If he nevertheless slaughters into a hollow in the market place, it is forbidden to eat the meat of his šĕḥiṭah until he is questioned, lest he should indeed be a heretic. It is, however, permitted to slaughter over the side of a ship, so that the blood would flow down the side and into the sea. It is also permitted to slaughter over the outside of a vessel.

7. How is šĕḥiṭah to be performed? By stretching out the neck

of the animal and drawing the knife to and fro until šĕḥiṭah is completed. Whether the animal is in a recumbent position, or standing, with the slaughterer grasping the nape of its neck and performing šĕḥiṭah with the knife in his hand underneath, the šĕḥiṭah is valid.

8. If one thrusts the knife into a wall and draws the neck of the animal against it until šĕḥiṭah is performed, it is valid. That is, provided the neck of the animal is below and the knife above, for should the neck be above the knife, the sheer weight of the animal's body might so press upon the knife as to cause an incision to be made, without the back-and-forth movement of the knife, and this would not constitute šĕḥiṭah, as will be explained. For this reason, in the case of a bird, šĕḥiṭah is valid whether its neck is above the knife thrust into the wall or below it.

9. If one slaughters by drawing the knife forward only, without drawing it backward, or vice versa, the šĕḥiṭah is valid. If the knife is drawn repeatedly back and forth until the head is severed, the šĕḥiṭah is likewise valid. If the knife is drawn forward only, or backward only, and the head is severed by this movement alone, the rule is as follows: If the length of the knife is fully double the width of the neck of the animal which is being slaughtered, the šĕḥiṭah is valid; otherwise it is invalid. If one performs šĕḥiṭah upon two heads at once, it is valid.

10. If two men hold the knife—even if one holds one end and the other the opposite end—and they thus slaughter, the šĕḥiṭah is valid. Similarly, if two men hold two knives and slaughter simultaneously at two places in the neck, their šĕḥiṭah is valid. Even if one of them severs only the gullet, or the major portion of it, and the other, performing šĕḥiṭah at another point, severs the windpipe or the major part of it, the šĕḥiṭah is valid, even though a complete šĕḥiṭah is not performed in one place. Likewise, šĕḥiṭah performed in a slanting direction or as though with a strigil is valid.

11. Intention is not required for the slaughtering of profane

animals; even if one performs šĕḥiṭah absent-mindedly, or in play, or throws a knife in order to stick it in a wall, and the knife in its flight performs šĕḥiṭah, once šĕḥiṭah is accomplished correctly, in its proper place and to the proper extent, it is valid.

12. For this reason, should a deaf-mute, an imbecile, a minor, a drunkard whose mind is confused, or a person temporarily deranged perform šĕḥiṭah in the presence of other persons who observe that it was done according to regulation, it is valid. If, however, a knife is dropped and while falling performs šĕḥiṭah, it is invalid, even if it is performed properly, since Scripture says, *and thou shalt kill* (Deut. 12:21), implying that the slaughterer must be a human being, even if he had no intention of performing šĕḥiṭah.

13. If a knife is affixed to a wheel of stone or wood, and a person revolves the wheel, placing the neck of a bird or animal opposite the knife in such a position that with the revolution of the wheel šĕḥiṭah is performed, it is valid. If, however, the wheel revolves by water power, and the person merely places the creature's neck against it in such a way that šĕḥiṭah is performed, it is invalid. If the flow of water is released by a human being, so that the water flows by his action and causes the wheel to revolve, and šĕḥiṭah is performed with the wheel's revolution, it is valid, since it was caused by human action. This, however, applies only to the first revolution of the wheel which is due to human action, since from the second revolution onward the wheel is moved not by human action, but by the force of the flowing water.

14. If one slaughters in the name of mountains, hills, seas, rivers, or wildernesses, even though his intention is not to worship them, but merely to obtain a cure from illness or some similar boon connected with heathen superstitions, that šĕḥiṭah is invalid. If he slaughters in the name of the Planet of the Sea, or of the Planet of the Mountain, or of stars and planets, and the like, the meat is forbidden for benefit, like all idolatrous offerings.

15. If one performs šĕḥiṭah upon an animal for the purpose of sprinkling its blood or offering up its fat to idols, it is forbidden,

since the law of intention with regard to profane animals outside the Temple is derived from the law of intention with regard to consecrated animals within the Temple, and an intention such as this renders the latter invalid, as will be explained in the Laws Concerning Hallowed Offerings Rendered Unfit.

16. If one first performs šĕḥiṭah and then conceives the intention of sprinkling the blood or offering the fat to an idol, it is forbidden out of doubt, since apprehension need be felt that the end may be indicative of the nature of the beginning, and that it was with this intention that he had performed the slaughtering.

17. If one performs šĕḥiṭah upon an animal under the name of such consecrated animals as are offered up as freewill or votive offerings, it is invalid, since it is the same as if one had slaughtered consecrated animals outside the precincts of the Temple. If he performs šĕḥiṭah under the name of consecrated animals which are not offered as votive or freewill offerings, it is valid.

18. How so? If one were to slaughter under the name of a burnt offering, a peace offering, a thank offering, or a Paschal lamb, that šĕḥiṭah would be invalid. The reason why this applies also to the Paschal lamb is that insofar as he may set aside the Paschal lamb in any year whenever he so desires, it is similar to an offering which is offered as a votive or freewill offering. If he performs šĕḥiṭah under the name of a sin offering, an unconditional guilt offering, or a suspensive guilt offering, or under the name of a firstling, a tithe offering, or a heave offering, that šĕḥiṭah is valid.

19. If a person liable to a sin offering performs šĕḥiṭah and says, "This is under the name of my sin offering," that šĕḥiṭah is invalid. If having a sacrificial animal in his house he slaughters it and says, "This is under the name of the substitute for my sacrifice," that šĕḥiṭah is likewise invalid, since he has performed substitution with it.

20. If a woman slaughters under the name of the burnt offering due after childbirth, and says, "This is for my burnt offering,"

her šĕḥiṭah is valid, since the burnt offering of a woman after childbirth is not a votive or freewill offering, and she herself has not been delivered of a child that she should be liable to bring a burnt offering. Nor need apprehension be felt about the possibility that she may have had a stillborn child, since the fact that a woman has given birth to a stillborn child is bound to become known. But if one performs šĕḥiṭah under the name of the burnt offering of a Nazirite, even though he is not a Nazirite, that šĕḥiṭah is invalid, since Naziriteship is essentially a vow.

21. If two men take hold of a knife and slaughter, one of them having the intention of slaughtering under the name of something which renders šĕḥiṭah performed for that purpose invalid, while the other either has no intention whatsoever, or has an intention directed towards a thing which does not render the šĕḥiṭah invalid, that šĕḥiṭah is nevertheless invalid. Similarly, if they perform šĕḥiṭah one after the other, and one of them has the intention towards a forbidden thing, he renders the šĕḥiṭah invalid. This rule, however, applies only if the latter person is a partner in that animal; if not, he does not render the šĕḥiṭah forbidden. For an Israelite cannot render forbidden a thing which is not his, so that in such a case his intention can have no purpose other than to cause the owner distress.

22. If an Israelite slaughters for a heathen, that šĕḥiṭah is valid, whatever the intention of the heathen may have been, since what is to be taken into consideration is the intention of the slaughterer of the animal, not that of its owner. Consequently, if a heathen, even a minor, performs šĕḥiṭah for an Israelite, that šĕḥiṭah is nĕḇelah, as will be explained later.

CHAPTER III

1. Five things impair šĕḥiṭah, and the basic principle of the regulations of šĕḥiṭah is that one must be painstakingly careful

about each one of them. They are: pausing (*šĕhiyyah*), pressing (*dĕrasah*), digging (*ḥalaḏah*), misplacement (*hag̱ramah*), and wrenching (*'ik̦k̦ur*).

2. What is meant by "pausing"? If after one begins to perform šĕḥiṭah, he raises his hand before completing the act and pauses in the middle of it, whether in error, willfully, or accidentally, and then he or another person resumes šĕḥiṭah and completes it, the rule is that if he pauses long enough for the animal to be raised up, laid down, and slaughtered, the šĕḥiṭah is invalid; if less than this, it is valid.

3. In the case of a small animal the minimum duration of the pause is the time which it takes to raise, lay down, and slaughter a small animal. In the case of a large animal, it is the time which it takes to raise, lay down, and slaughter a large animal. In the case of a bird, the time is the same as for a small animal.

4. If one performs a small part of šĕḥiṭah, then pauses a little, then performs another small part of šĕḥiṭah and again pauses a while, and so on until šĕḥiṭah is completed, without pausing at any one time for the minimum duration—although all the short periods of pause, if added together, would amount to the minimum period of pausing—it is a doubtful case of nĕḇelah. Similarly, if the period of pause is sufficient to raise and lay down the animal and perform šĕḥiṭah only on the minor part of the organs, but not to perform a complete act of šĕḥiṭah, it is likewise a doubtful case of nĕḇelah.

5. In case one performs šĕḥiṭah upon the major part of one of the organs of a bird or of both organs of an animal, even if he then pauses half a day before he resumes and completes the severing of the organs, it is valid, for once he has performed šĕḥiṭah upon the required minimum extent of the organs, his subsequent cutting constitutes no more than the cutting of the flesh of an animal upon which šĕḥiṭah had already been fully performed.

6. If one performs šĕḥiṭah upon half or less of the windpipe alone, and then pauses for a considerable time, he may resume and

complete the šěḥiṭah, without anything affecting its validity. If, however, he performs šěḥiṭah upon the major part of the windpipe, or if he perforates the gullet to the smallest extent, and then pauses for the full minimum period of pausing, the šěḥiṭah is invalid, whether he resumes and completes the šěḥiṭah which he had commenced, or whether he performs a complete šěḥiṭah at another point of the neck. The reason is that if the major part of the windpipe of an animal or bird is severed, or if the gullet is perforated to the smallest extent, the animal is nĕḇelah and the subsequent šěḥiṭah can avail it nothing, as will be explained.

7. Thus it is clear that pausing cannot take place at all in the case of the windpipe of a bird, since if one performs šěḥiṭah upon the major part of the windpipe and then pauses, valid šěḥiṭah has already been performed, and when he resumes it, he is regarded merely as though he were cutting flesh; while if he performs šěḥiṭah on the small part of the windpipe and then pauses, he may resume the šěḥiṭah whenever he so desires, since a bird does not become forbidden as nĕḇelah unless the major part of the windpipe has been severed.

8. If one performs šěḥiṭah upon a bird and then pauses, and is not certain whether the gullet has become perforated or not, he should perform šěḥiṭah once more upon the windpipe alone at another point, and leave the bird until life is extinct. He should then examine the inside of the gullet, and if no drop of blood is visible upon it, it is certain that the gullet had not been perforated, and the šěḥiṭah is valid.

9. What is meant by "digging"? If one inserts the knife between the two organs, whether he thus severs the upper organ with an upward stroke, or the lower organ with a downward stroke, which is the manner of šěḥiṭah, it is invalid.

10. If one inserts the knife under the skin and performs šěḥiṭah in the proper manner upon the two organs, or inserts the knife under the matted wool of the neck, or spreads a strip of cloth over both the knife and the neck of the animal and then performs

šĕḥiṭah under the cloth—all these cases, since the knife is not visible, are doubtful cases of nĕbelah. Similarly, if one performs šĕḥiṭah upon the minor part of the organs under cover and then completes the šĕḥiṭah without cover, it is doubtful nĕbelah.

11. What is meant by "pressing"? If one smites with the knife upon the neck as one smites with a sword, and severs the organs at one stroke, without a to-and-fro movement, or if he rests the knife upon the neck of the animal and presses it down hard, so as to cut as one cuts a radish or a cucumber, until he severs the organs, it is invalid.

12. What is meant by "misplacement"? The performance of šĕḥiṭah upon the upper part of the windpipe, at a point which is not valid for šĕḥiṭah. There are two structures having the appearance of two grains of wheat at the upper extremity of the windpipe, in the great ring. If šĕḥiṭah is performed within these grains in such a way that any part of them is left above the cut, it is valid, since in that case one has performed šĕḥiṭah from the thyroid cartilage downwards, and that is a place which is valid for šĕḥiṭah. If one does not leave any part of these grains above the cut, but slaughters at a point above them, it constitutes misplacement and is invalid.

13. If one performs šĕḥiṭah upon the major part of one organ of a bird or upon the major part of both organs in an animal and then completes the šĕḥiṭah by pressing or misplacement, it is valid, since šĕḥiṭah has already been performed to a validating extent. If he performs misplacement on the first third and šĕḥiṭah on the remaining two thirds, it is also valid. If he cuts one third with šĕḥiṭah, one third with misplacement, and the last third with šĕḥiṭah, it is likewise valid. Should he perform misplacement on the first third, šĕḥiṭah on the second, and misplacement on the last, it is invalid. If he performs pressing or digging on the first third or the middle third, it is also invalid.

14. What is meant by "wrenching"? When the throat—which is the windpipe—or the gullet is wrenched loose and one or both

of them become dislocated before the completion of šĕḥiṭah. But if after performing šĕḥiṭah upon one organ of a bird, or on the major part of the organ, the second organ becomes dislocated, that šĕḥiṭah is valid.

15. If one of the organs of a bird becomes dislocated and thereafter šĕḥiṭah is performed on the other organ, it is invalid. If one performs šĕḥiṭah upon one organ, and then finds that the other is dislocated, and does not know whether the dislocation occurred before or after šĕḥiṭah, it is a doubtful case of nĕḇelah.

16. If the organ upon which šĕḥiṭah had been performed is found to be dislocated, the šĕḥiṭah is valid, since the organ certainly became displaced after šĕḥiṭah had been performed, for had it become displaced previously to šĕḥiṭah it would have been loose and šĕḥiṭah could not have been performed upon it.

17. This rule applies only if one does not grasp the organs in his hand while šĕḥiṭah is being performed, for otherwise it is possible for šĕḥiṭah to be performed after dislocation, and for this reason, if the organ is found to be both displaced and cut, it is a doubtful case of nĕḇelah.

18. Wherever the term "invalid" is applied to šĕḥiṭah, the animal involved is nĕḇelah, and should one eat an olive's bulk of it he is liable to a flogging for eating nĕḇelah, for only a valid šĕḥiṭah releases an animal from the state of nĕḇelah, as our master Moses—peace be upon him—has enjoined, and as we have explained. Every doubtful šĕḥiṭah results in doubtful nĕḇelah, and whosoever eats of it is liable to the flogging prescribed for disobedience.

19. An animal whose hip, together with its socket, is missing, so that when it lies down it is seen to be imperfect, is nĕḇelah. If the animal is split asunder, so that it is as though it had been severed in twain and divided into two bodies, šĕḥiṭah cannot avail it. Similarly, if its neck is fractured and most of the flesh round it torn, or if its back is torn down its length, like a fish, or

if the major part of the windpipe is severed, or if the gullet is perforated to the smallest extent in the place valid for šĕḥiṭah, it is nĕḇelah already during life, and šĕḥiṭah cannot avail it. Both animals and birds are in the same category in this respect.

20. The gullet has two membranes, the outer one red and the inner one white. If only one of them is perforated, the animal is valid; if both are perforated, even to the smallest extent, in the place valid for šĕḥiṭah, it is nĕḇelah. Whether šĕḥiṭah is performed at the point of the perforation, or at another point, it is of no avail. If both membranes are perforated, but the perforations are not opposite one another, it is likewise nĕḇelah.

21. If the gullet is perforated and a new membrane has been formed which closes up the perforation, the new membrane does not count and the gullet is regarded as though it were still perforated. If a thorn is found thrust into the gullet, it is doubtful nĕḇelah, for fear that the gullet may have become perforated and that a new membrane may have been formed over the perforation, which cannot therefore be detected. If, however, the thorn is found lying lengthwise in the gullet, no apprehension need be felt, since most nondomesticated animals habitually eat thorns.

22. The gullet may not be examined from the outside, but only from the inside. How should one proceed? One should turn it inside out to inspect it. If a drop of blood is found on it, it is certain that it has been perforated.

23. If the major part of the cavity of the windpipe is split open in the place valid for šĕḥiṭah, it is nĕḇelah, as it is also if it has a hole the size of an *'issar*. If it has a number of small perforations, the rule is as follows: If the perforations involve no loss of substance, they combine together when measured as to whether they cover the major part of the cavity of the windpipe; if they involve loss of substance, they combine together when measured as to whether they cover the area of an 'issar. Similarly, if a strip of flesh is missing, its length is added on towards the area of an 'issar. With regard to a bird, the rule is as follows: If the strip

or the area of the perforations which involve loss of substance, when rolled up and placed over the mouth of the windpipe, would cover the major part of it, it is nĕḇelah. If not, it is valid.

24. If the windpipe is pierced right through on both sides, so that an 'issar can be inserted through its breadth, it is nĕḇelah. If it is slit lengthwise, as long as the smallest amount is left at the top and at the bottom of the slit in the place valid for šĕḥiṭah, it is valid.

25. If a windpipe is found to be perforated and it is uncertain whether the perforation took place before or after šĕḥiṭah, another perforation should be made after šĕḥiṭah at another point, and the two perforations should then be compared. If they are similar, the šĕḥiṭah is valid. One may make comparisons, however, only between one large ring and another large ring, or between one small ring and another, but not between a large ring and a small one, or vice versa, for the whole windpipe consists of rings, and between each pair of large rings there is a smaller ring which is softer than these two.

CHAPTER IV

1. If an Israelite who does not know these five things which impair šĕḥiṭah, as well as the other laws regulating šĕḥiṭah which we have explained, slaughters privately, both he and everyone else are forbidden to eat of that šĕḥiṭah, since it is something which comes near to doubtful nĕḇelah, and whosoever eats an olive's bulk of it is liable to the flogging prescribed for disobedience.

2. Even if he had performed valid šĕḥiṭah in our presence on four or five occasions, and this subsequent šĕḥiṭah performed privately appears to be perfectly proper, it is nevertheless forbidden to eat of it. For since he does not know those things which impair šĕḥiṭah, he may have impaired this šĕḥiṭah unawares. For

instance, he may have paused, or pressed, or used a notched knife, and the like, unintentionally.

3. An Israelite who knows the regulations of šĕḥiṭah should nevertheless not slaughter privately in the first instance, until he has performed it on a number of occasions in the presence of a Sage and has thus become expert and dexterous. If, however, he does perform šĕḥiṭah for the first time privately, that šĕḥiṭah is valid.

4. The person who knows the regulations of šĕḥiṭah and had performed it in the presence of a Sage until he has become expert is called a professional, and all professionals may thereafter slaughter privately in the first instance. Even women and slaves may perform šĕḥiṭah in the first instance if they are professionals.

5. The šĕḥiṭah of a deaf-mute, an imbecile, a minor, or a drunkard whose mind is confused is invalid, since they lack understanding and may impair the šĕḥiṭah. Consequently if they slaughter in the presence of one who does know, and he sees that they perform šĕḥiṭah in a proper manner, their šĕḥiṭah is valid.

6. If a person unknown to us slaughters privately, he should be questioned. If he is found to know the essential rules of šĕḥiṭah, his šĕḥiṭah is valid.

7. If from afar off one observes an Israelite perform šĕḥiṭah and then go on his way, and it is unknown whether he is well versed in the laws of šĕḥiṭah or not, the šĕḥiṭah is valid. Similarly, if a person says to his messenger, "Go and perform šĕḥiṭah for me," and subsequently finds the animal slaughtered in the manner of šĕḥiṭah, but is not sure whether it was his messenger or someone else who had performed the šĕḥiṭah, it is valid, since the majority of those who have to do with šĕḥiṭah are professionals.

8. If one misses a kid or a chicken and subsequently finds them in a house slaughtered in the manner of šĕḥiṭah, they are permitted, since the majority of people who have to do with šĕḥiṭah are professionals. If, on the other hand, he finds them in a

market place, they are forbidden, for fear that they may have been rendered nĕḇelah and were therefore thrown away. Similarly, if he finds them in the dustbin of a house, they are forbidden.

9. If a professional slaughterer becomes mute, but is able to understand and hear, and his mind is sound, he may continue to perform šĕḥiṭah in the first instance. The same applies in case of deafness.

10. A blind man should not slaughter in the first instance, unless other people see him do so, but if he does perform šĕḥiṭah privately it is valid.

11. If a heathen—even a minor—performs šĕḥiṭah, even in the presence of an Israelite and with a perfect knife, his šĕḥiṭah is nĕḇelah, and whosoever eats of it is liable to a flogging on the authority of the Torah, as it is said, *and they call thee and thou eat of their slaughtering* (Exod. 34:15). Since Scripture warns us not to eat of their slaughtering, you learn that their slaughtering is forbidden, and cannot be compared to the šĕḥiṭah of an Israelite who does not know the rules of šĕḥiṭah.

12. The Sages have erected a further great barrier in this matter, by decreeing that even the šĕḥiṭah of a Gentile who is not an idolater is nĕḇelah.

13. If a heathen begins the šĕḥiṭah by severing a minor part of the organs and an Israelite then completes it, or if an Israelite commences it and a heathen completes it, the šĕḥiṭah is invalid, for the rule is that šĕḥiṭah must be valid from beginning to end. If, however, a heathen performs šĕḥiṭah on such a portion of the organs as does not render it nĕḇelah—for instance, on half of the windpipe only—and an Israelite finishes it, it is valid.

14. An apostate Israelite who deliberately transgresses against one of the Scriptural commandments, yet is an expert in šĕḥiṭah, may slaughter in the first instance, but an observant Israelite should first examine the knife, and then hand it to this apostate

to perform šĕḥiṭah with it, since the presumption is that he himself will not take the trouble to examine it. If, however, he is an apostate to such an extent as to be guilty of idolatry or public profanation of the Sabbath, or if he is an atheist, that is one who denies the authority of the Torah and of our master Moses, as we have explained in the Laws Concerning Repentance, he is regarded as a heathen and his šĕḥiṭah is nĕḇelah.

15. One who is invalidated as a witness because he is guilty of a Scriptural transgression, may perform šĕḥiṭah privately if he is an expert, on the ground that he will not relinquish that which is permitted in order to eat that which is forbidden, for this presumption obtains with regard to all Israelites, even the wicked ones among them.

16. The šĕḥiṭah of Sadducees and Boethusians and their disciples, and of all those who go astray after them and do not believe in the Oral Law, is forbidden; but if they slaughter in our presence, it is permitted. For the prohibition against their šĕḥiṭah is due to the fear that they will impair it, inasmuch as they do not believe in the traditional rules of šĕḥiṭah; hence they cannot be trusted when they say, "We did not impair it."

17. When the children of Israel were in the wilderness they were not enjoined concerning the performance of šĕḥiṭah upon unconsecrated animals, but were wont to stab or slaughter them, and then eat them like the heathens. They were commanded in the wilderness merely that whosoever wished to perform šĕḥiṭah should do so only with peace offerings, as it is said, *Whatsoever man there be of the House of Israel that ḳilleth an ox . . . and hath not brought it unto the door of the Tent of Meeting to present it as an offering unto the Lord . . . that man shall be cut off from among his people, to the end that the children of Israel may bring their sacrifices . . . and sacrifice them for sacrifices of peace offerings unto the Lord* (Lev. 17:3–5). But whosoever wished to stab animals in order to eat them in the wilderness was free to do so.

18. This procedure was not meant to apply to subsequent generations, but solely to the period when the Israelites were in the wilderness, during which time stabbing was allowed. They were there commanded that upon entering the Land of Israel stabbing would become forbidden and they might eat of unconsecrated animals only after šĕḥiṭah, which might be performed in any place in the world outside the Temple court, as it is said, *When the Lord thy God shall enlarge thy border . . . thou shalt kill of thy herd and thy flock, which the Lord hath given thee,* etc. (Deut. 12:20–21). This commandment is binding upon all generations, namely, that one should first perform šĕḥiṭah and only thereafter may he eat of the flesh.

CHAPTER V

1. We have already explained in the Laws Concerning Forbidden Foods that the ṭĕrefah ("torn") mentioned in the Torah refers to an animal about to die; the word ṭĕrefah is employed here only because Scripture speaks in terms of the most common occurrence, for instance, when the animal is torn by a lion or a similar beast of prey, and is left fatally injured, but not yet dead.

2. There are, however, in addition to this, diseases which, if they occur in an animal, render it ṭĕrefah, and the rules governing them were given to Moses from Sinai. Eight such categories of ṭĕrefah were communicated to Moses on Sinai, to wit: clawed (*dĕrusah*), perforated (*nĕkubah*), absent (*ḥăserah*), removed (*nĕṭulah*), split (*pĕsukah*), torn (*kĕru'ah*), fallen (*nĕfulah*), and fractured (*šĕburah*).

3. Although all of them are subject to rules given to Moses from Sinai, nevertheless since "clawed" is the only disease explicitly mentioned in the Torah the Sages were more stringent about it. Every doubtful case of clawing is therefore forbidden, while of the remaining seven kinds of ṭĕrefah there are doubtful cases which are permitted, as will be explained.

4. Clawing takes place when a lion or a similar beast of prey tears an animal and claws it with its forepaws, or when a hawk, an eagle, or the like attacks a bird with its talons. In the case of large domestic and wild animals clawing applies only to a lion, while in the case of small animals it applies to any beast of prey from a wolf upward. In the case of kids and lambs, even a cat, a fox, a marten, or the like may inflict clawing, and certainly so in the case of birds.

5. The hawk may claw even a bird larger than itself, but other birds of prey may claw only birds of their own size, but not larger than themselves.

6. A weasel may claw birds, while a dog cannot claw at all, whether the victim be a bird or an animal, domestic or wild. A hawk may claw a kid or a lamb, but only if its talons penetrate into the interior cavity of the animal's body.

7. Clawing can be inflicted only with the forepaw of the beast of prey; no concern need be had with respect to the hindpaw. It can be inflicted only with the claw, and no apprehension need be had of it being inflicted with the teeth, unless the beast bites through to the interior cavity of the animal's body, in which case an inspection should be made to determine whether one of the organs which, if pierced, would render the animal ṭĕrefah, has in fact been pierced. Clawing can also be inflicted only deliberately; hence if a beast of prey falls upon an animal in such a way that its claws happen to sink into it, this does not constitute clawing. Clawing can take place only while the beast of prey is alive; if it attacks and is then killed, while its paw is still upon its victim, so that its claws do not release the prey until after it is killed, no apprehension need be had about clawing.

8. What is the procedure in the case of clawing? Wherever we have said that apprehension need be had, the animal which has been attacked should be slaughtered and the whole of its interior cavity should be examined, from the foot of the leg to the skull. If it is found to be completely free of every kind of disability which would render an animal ṭĕrefah, and if no trace of claw-

ing is found within it, it is permitted. If such a mark of clawing is discovered, it is ṭĕrefah and therefore forbidden on the authority of the Torah.

9. What constitutes such a mark of clawing? When the flesh opposite the entrails has become reddened. If it is crushed, so that it resembles the flesh which the surgeon scrapes away from a wound, it is regarded as though it were missing, and the animal is likewise ṭĕrefah.

10. If the attacker has clawed the statutory organs of šĕḥiṭah, the animal is ṭĕrefah if they are reddened, and the smallest amount of such clawing renders it ṭĕrefah. Once the organs are reddened to the slightest degree as a result of the clawing, the animal is ṭĕrefah.

11. A doubtful case of clawing renders the animal forbidden until it is inspected in the same manner as a certain case of clawing. How so? If a lion makes its way among oxen, and a loose claw is found in the back of one of them, concern need be had that the lion may have clawed it, and it cannot be said that the ox might have rubbed itself against the wall. Similarly, if a fox or marten enters a chicken run and the beast remains silent while the chickens cackle, apprehension need be had that the beast may have clawed them. But if it growls while they cackle, it may be assumed that the birds do so merely in terror of its presence and its growling, and not because they are being clawed. Similarly, if it bites off the head of one of them, so that its rage is thereby assuaged, or if both remain silent, no fear need be felt, for had the beast harmed the birds they would have cackled.

12. If it is doubtful whether a beast of prey has entered the run or not, or if a beast is seen to enter and it is not known whether it is predatory or not, no fear need be felt. Similarly, if a bird enters a thicket of trees or rushes and emerges with its head or neck dripping blood, no apprehension need be had that it may have been clawed, and it may be assumed that it might have injured itself against the trees.

CHAPTER VI

1. What is meant by "perforated"? There are eleven organs of the body which, if perforated to their cavity to the slightest extent, render the animal ṭĕrefah, to wit: the wide part of the gullet, the membrane of the brain, the heart with its aorta, the gall bladder, the tube of the liver, the stomach, the maw, the omasum, the second stomach, the small bowels, and the lung with its tube.

2. We have already explained the extent of the wide part of the gullet, namely, that it is the part of the gullet which is not valid for šĕḥiṭah, above the gullet itself. If it is perforated to its cavity to the smallest extent, it is ṭĕrefah.

3. The brain has two membranes. If only the upper one, next to the bone, is perforated, the animal is permitted; if the lower one, next to the brain, is perforated, it is ṭĕrefah. Where the brain begins to lead off to the spine, that is beyond the bean-like structures which are the beginning of the nape of the neck, a different law applies to the membrane: if it is perforated beyond these bean-like structures, the animal is permitted.

4. If the brain itself is perforated or crushed, but the membrane remains intact, the animal is valid. If the brain gushes out like water or flows like melted wax, it is ṭĕrefah.

5. If the heart is pierced as far as the chambers thereof, whether as far as the large chamber on the left or the small one on the right, the animal is ṭĕrefah. If only the flesh of the heart is pierced, but the perforation does not penetrate inside the chamber, it is permitted. The aorta, that is the large artery which leads from the heart to the lungs, is like the heart: if it is perforated to the smallest extent into its cavity, it is ṭĕrefah.

6. If the gall bladder is pierced, but the perforation is com-

pletely closed by the liver, the animal is permitted. If the perforation is not so closed, even if it lies quite close to the liver, it is ṭĕrefah.

7. In case a kernel is found in the gall bladder, the rule is as follows: If it is shaped like a date stone which has no sharp point, the animal is permitted; if it has a sharp point like the kernel of an olive, it is forbidden, since the stone must have pierced the gall bladder when it entered, and the reason that the perforation is no longer visible is that the top of the wound has become covered with a crust.

8. If any one of the tubes of the liver, that is its veins in which the blood originates, is pierced to the slightest extent, it is ṭĕrefah. Consequently if a needle is found in dissecting the liver, the rule is as follows: If it is a large needle, with sharp end pointing inwards, it is certain that the needle must have pierced the tubes when it entered. If, on the other hand, the rounded head is found pointing inwards, the assumption is that the needle must have entered by way of the arteries, and the animal is permitted.

9. If the needle is small, the animal is ṭĕrefah, since both ends of the needle being sharp, it must certainly have pierced the tubes; if it is found in the large artery of the liver, that is the wide tube in the center through which food enters the liver, the animal is permitted. If the flesh of the liver is infested with worms, the animal is also permitted.

10. If the stomach is pierced and clean fat closes the perforation, the animal is permitted. Similarly, in every case of perforation of the flesh, if the perforation is closed by flesh or fat which is allowed for consumption, it is permitted. The exceptions are the following: the fat of the heart; the membrane which covers the whole heart; the diaphragm in the middle of the abdomen which separates the digestive organs from the respiratory ones—it is that part which has to be torn open before the lungs can be seen, and which is called the membrane of the liver; the white area in the center of the liver; and the fat of the last entrail which

is among these organs. These do not shield a perforation, since they are firm, and if a perforation is closed by one of them, it is not regarded as sealed. The fat of a wild beast, whose corresponding fat in a domestic animal is forbidden, cannot act as a sealing agent, even though the fat itself is allowed for consumption.

11. If the maw is pierced, it is ṭĕrefah, and there is nothing which can seal it, since the fat which is upon it is forbidden. Similarly, in the case of the omasum and the second stomach, if one of them is perforated outwards, it is ṭĕrefah; but if the perforation in the one opens into the cavity of the other, the animal is permitted.

12. If a needle is found in the fleshy part of the second stomach on one side, the animal is permitted. If the needle has pierced a hole right through to the cavity of the second stomach, and a drop of blood is found at the point of the perforation, the animal is ṭĕrefah, since the perforation had certainly taken place before šĕḥiṭah. If no blood is visible at the point of the perforation, the animal is permitted, since the needle had certainly been forced through after šĕḥiṭah, and only then had pierced the flesh.

13. If an animal had been fed something which pierces the bowels, such as drops of asafoetida or the like, it is ṭĕrefah, since such a substance is certain to cause a perforation. If the animal remains alive for three days, and it is doubtful whether or not a perforation has taken place, each of the entrails in which food waste circulates—i.e. those which are called the small bowels—must be inspected, and if found perforated the animal is ṭĕrefah. Some of these small bowels wind and twist one within the other in a circle like a coiled snake, and are called the coils of the ileum. If one of these is pierced through into the other, it is permitted, since the other shields it.

14. If the bowels are pierced and secretion closes the perforation, the animal is ṭĕrefah, since secretion cannot form a permanent closure. If a wolf, a dog, or a similar beast drags away the entrails and abandons them, and they are then found perforated,

the perforation may be ascribed to the beast, and the animal is permitted. It cannot be said that the beast might have pierced the bowels exactly at a point previously perforated. If they are found pierced and it is unknown whether the perforation took place before or after šĕḥiṭah, another perforation should be made and the two should be compared. If the previous perforation is like the later one, the animal is valid, but if there is a difference between them, the first perforation must have taken place before šĕḥiṭah and the animal is ṭĕrefah. If the doubtful perforation had been manipulated by human hands, it is necessary to manipulate the perforation with which it is to be compared in a similar manner, and only then may they be compared.

15. If the bowels protrude but are not pierced, the animal is allowed, but if they become twisted—even if not perforated—it is ṭĕrefah, since it is impossible to restore them as they were once they have become twisted, and an animal with twisted bowels cannot survive.

16. If the last bowel, which is straight and without a curve—that is the one from which the excreta emerge through the anus, and which is joined to the roots of the thighs and is called the rectum—is pierced to the smallest extent, it is ṭĕrefah, like the rest of the bowels. This is true, however, only if it is pierced into the cavity of the belly; if the perforation is at the place where the bowel adheres to the thighs, it is permitted. Even if the whole part joined to the thigh is missing, it is still permitted, as long as there remains of it, in the case of an ox, a length of about four fingers.

17. A bird has neither maw nor omasum nor second stomach, but has corresponding to them the crop and the craw. All cases of ṭĕrefah are identical in domestic animal, wild beast, and bird; therefore, if the roof of a bird's crop is pierced to the smallest extent, it is ṭĕrefah. What is meant by the roof of the crop? It is that part which is drawn after the gullet when the bird extends its neck. If the remaining part of the crop is pierced, the bird is allowed.

18. The craw has two sacs. The outer one is red like flesh, and the inner one is white like skin. If only one is pierced, and not the other, the bird is permitted, so long as both of them are not perforated, even to the smallest extent. Even if both are pierced but not opposite one another, the bird is still allowed.

19. The spleen is not among the organs which render the animal ṭĕrefah if they are perforated to any extent whatsoever, and consequently the Sages did not include it among such organs. Perforation of the spleen must be of a certain minimum size, which is not equal throughout, in order to render the animal ṭĕrefah. How so? One end of the spleen is thick and the other thin—like the shape of the tongue. If the thick top part is pierced right through, the animal is ṭĕrefah. If it is not pierced right through, and the remaining lower layer of it is at least as thick as a gold *denar,* it is permitted; if less than that remains, it is regarded as though it were pierced right through, and is therefore ṭĕrefah. If the thin part of the spleen is pierced, the animal is permitted.

20. In the case of every organ concerning which the Sages have declared that when it is perforated to the smallest extent it renders the animal ṭĕrefah, if that organ is missing in its entirety the animal is also ṭĕrefah. It is immaterial whether the organ has been removed as a result of disease or by hand, or whether the animal was born without that organ. Similarly, if it was born with two such organs, it is likewise ṭĕrefah, since duplication of an organ is in this respect considered equivalent to the complete removal of that organ. How so? If one of the bowels, or the gall bladder, or any similar organ is missing, whether in a bird or an animal, it is ṭĕrefah. Similarly, if two gall bladders or two such bowels are found, it is also ṭĕrefah, and so in all similar instances. But if the spleen is removed, or if two spleens are found, the animal is permitted, since the spleen is not included among such organs.

21. The duplicate bowel which renders the animal ṭĕrefah must be duplicated from beginning to end, so that there are two

bowels side by side from beginning to end, like the paired entrails of a bird; or else the extra bowel must issue from the first bowel like a branch arising from a stalk and separated from it, both in bird and in animal. If, however, it rejoins the first bowel further on and becomes one with it at both ends, so that the two are separated only in the middle, the animal is allowed, for this does not constitute a case of duplicate organs.

CHAPTER VII

1. The lung has two membranes. If one of them is perforated, but not the other, the animal is permitted. If both of them are perforated, it is ṭĕrefah. Even if the whole of the outer membrane had peeled off and disappeared, it is permitted. If the windpipe is perforated to the smallest extent, from the level of the chest downwards—that is the lower portion of the windpipe which is not valid for šĕḥiṭah—it is ṭĕrefah.

2. If after one has begun to perform šĕḥiṭah upon the windpipe, and has severed the whole windpipe, the lung is pierced, and if he thereupon completes the šĕḥiṭah, the animal is ṭĕrefah, seeing that the lung was perforated before the completion of šĕḥiṭah. The same applies in all similar cases.

3. If one of the arteries of the lung is perforated, the animal is ṭĕrefah, even if the perforation opens into the other artery. If a lung is perforated and a membrane has formed over the perforation so as to close it, it is not a valid closure. If the main lobe of the lung is perforated—even if the flank of the animal closes the perforation—it is ṭĕrefah. If the lung is perforated at the point where the lobes are articulated—that is, the part upon which the animal lies—it is valid.

4. This latter rule, however, applies only where flesh acts as the closing agent of the perforation in the lobes; if the perfora-

tion is next to a bone, the bone does not form a valid shield. If the perforation of the lobes adheres to both bone and flesh, the animal is permitted.

5. If the main lobe of the lung is found to adhere to the flank, whether it has developed growths or not, apprehension need be felt that the lung may have become perforated. How is one to proceed? The lung should be detached from the flank, and care should be taken that it does not become perforated in the process. If it is found to be perforated, and a wound is found upon the flank opposite the perforation, the perforation may be ascribed to the wound and it may be assumed that the lung became perforated after šĕḥiṭah, when it was detached from the wound. If there is no wound upon the flank, it is certain that the perforation must have come about in the lung before šĕḥiṭah, and the animal is therefore ṭĕrefah.

6. If a section of the lung, no matter how small, is found to be obstructed, so that air does not enter into it and it does not inflate, the lung is regarded as if it were perforated and is ṭĕrefah. How is it to be examined? The part which does not inflate when the lung is inflated should be torn open. If fluid is found therein, the animal is permitted, since it is the fluid which had prevented the air from entering. If no fluid is found, a little saliva, a straw, a feather, or the like should be placed upon it, and the lung should then be inflated. If the saliva, straw, or feather moves, the lung is valid; if not, it is ṭĕrefah, since no air has entered into the obstructed section.

7. If the sound of escaping air is heard when the lung is inflated, and the place whence the sound comes is visible, saliva, a straw, or the like should be placed upon it. If it moves, it is certain that the lung is perforated and is ṭĕrefah. If the place cannot be detected, the lung should be placed in tepid water and inflated. If the water bubbles, it is ṭĕrefah. If not, it is certain that only the inner membrane was perforated and that the air passes between the two membranes, and this is the cause of the hissing sound which is heard when the lung is inflated.

8. Let this be a fundamental principle for you: Any lung which when inflated in tepid water does not cause the water to bubble, is free from any perforation.

9. If the lung empties itself like a ladle, but its upper membrane is whole and free from any perforation, the rule is as follows: If the arteries are still in their place and have not decayed, the animal is valid. If even one artery is in a state of decomposition, it is ṭĕrefah. How should one proceed? The lung should be perforated and the contents thereof should be poured into a vessel lined with lead or the like. If white threads are visible in the liquid, it is certain that the arteries have decomposed, and the animal is ṭĕrefah. If not, it is merely the flesh of the lung which has decomposed, and the animal is valid.

10. If swellings are found upon the lung, the rule is as follows: If they are filled with air or clear liquid, or with secretion which has the viscosity of honey or the like, or with secretion which is dry and hard, even as stone, it is permitted. If, however, it is found to be full of malodorous secretion, or malodorous or turbid liquid, it is ṭĕrefah. When the secretion is extracted and examined, the artery under it should be examined at the same time. If it is found to be perforated, the animal is ṭĕrefah.

11. If two adjoining swellings are found upon the lung, it is ṭĕrefah, since it is highly probable that there is a perforation between them, and there is no possible way of examining them. If there is only one swelling, but it appears as though it might be two, one of the two halves should be perforated. If the contents of the other half flow into it, the whole is one swelling, and the animal is permitted; if not, it is ṭĕrefah.

12. If a lung is decayed, it is ṭĕrefah. How so? For instance, if it appears to be whole, but when suspended breaks up and falls down piece by piece. If the lung is found to be perforated in a place where the hand of the slaughterer had manipulated it, it is permitted, since the perforation may be ascribed to this manipulation and it may be said that the perforation was caused by the

slaughterer's hand after šĕḥiṭah. If the perforation is found in another place, and it is uncertain whether it occurred before or after šĕḥiṭah, another perforation should be made and the two compared, in the same manner as is done with the bowels.

13. No comparison may be made between the lung of a small animal and the lung of a large animal, but only between the lungs of two small animals or two large animals. If a perforation is found in one of the swellings, the animal is ṭĕrefah, for it cannot be said, "Let us perforate another swelling and compare them," since a comparison is not decisive in such a case.

14. If a needle is found in the lung, the lung should be inflated. If no air escapes, it is certain that the needle had entered by way of the arteries and did not pierce the lung. If the lung has been cut up before it could be inflated and a needle is found in it, the animal is forbidden, since it is probable that the needle had pierced the lung as it entered.

15. If a worm in the lung had bored its way out and emerged, so that the lung has thus been perforated by the worm, the animal is permitted, since the presumption is that the worm had bored its way out and emerged after šĕḥiṭah.

[15A]. Another factor is color. In the case of some colors, if the normal color of the organ has changed to one of these invalidating colors, the organ is regarded as though it were perforated, for flesh whose normal color has changed to that color is regarded as dead flesh, as though the original flesh whose appearance has thus been changed had ceased to exist. And indeed Scripture says, *and there be live raw flesh in the rising . . . but whensoever live flesh appeareth* (Lev. 13:10, 14), from which it may be concluded that the remainder of the flesh which has changed its color is not live flesh.

16. If the color of the whole lung or of only a part of it has changed, the rule is as follows: If it has changed to a valid color —even if the whole lung has undergone this change—the animal

is permitted. If it has changed to an invalidating color, be it even to the smallest extent, the animal is ṭĕrefah, since an invalidating color is regarded as equivalent to a perforation, as we have just explained.

17. There are five invalidating colors in the lung, to wit: black like ink, yellow like cuscuta, the color of egg yolk, the color of bastard saffron, and the color of flesh. Bastard saffron is the dye used in dyeing garments, which is the color of hair that is reddish and tending toward yellow.

18. If the lung is found to be the color of dried palm branches, it should be declared forbidden on account of doubt, since its color is near to an invalidating color. None of these colors may be declared invalidating until the lung is inflated and massaged by hand. If it is thereby restored to a valid color, the animal is permitted. If the color remains unchanged, the animal is forbidden.

19. There are four valid colors, to wit: black as stibium, green as grass, red, and the color of the liver. Even if the whole lung is patched and spotted with these four colors, it is permitted.

20. If a bird falls into fire with the result that its heart, its liver, or its craw becomes green, or its entrails turn red, to the smallest extent, it is ṭĕrefah, since in a bird normally yellow organs which become red, or vice versa, as a result of fire, are regarded as though they had been removed, and the bird is therefore ṭĕrefah. This applies only if the organ retains this color after it has been boiled a little and massaged.

21. Any bird whose liver is found to be of the same color as the entrails, or whose entrails have changed color and retain their changed appearance even after boiling and massaging, as we have just explained, is certain to have fallen into fire which scorched its entrails, and is therefore ṭĕrefah. Indeed, even if the entrails of a bird are found to be unchanged, but change color when boiled, so that yellow organs become red, or red become yellow, it is

likewise certain that it had fallen into fire which scorched its entrails, and it too is ṭĕrefah. Similarly, if the outer skin of the gullet is found to be white and the inner red, in both animal and bird, the gullet is regarded as though it were nonexistent, and the creature is therefore ṭĕrefah.

CHAPTER VIII

1. What is meant by "absent"? There are two organs which render the animal ṭĕrefah if ought is absent from their number, to wit, the lung and the legs. The lung has five lobes. When it is suspended from the hand as one faces the front of the lung, there are three lobes on the right and two on the left. In addition, there is on the right a piece which looks like a small ear. It is not in line with the lobes, and lies within a special small pouch. This small ear is called *warda* ("rose"), because it resembles a rose. It is not included in the number of lobes, and consequently, should no "rose" be found, the animal remains permitted. In fact, such is its nature that it occurs in some animals and not in others. Should it be found to be perforated, however, even if its pouch closes the perforation, the animal is ṭĕrefah.

2. If any of the requisite number of lobes are absent, so that there is only one on the left or only two on the right, the animal is ṭĕrefah. If, however, there are two on the right, and also this "rose," the animal is still permitted.

3. If the number of lobes is reversed, so that there are three on the left and two on the right, not counting the "rose," or if the "rose" is located with the three lobes on the left side, the animal is ṭĕrefah, since one lobe is absent on the right side.

4. If the number of lobes exceeds the normal complement and the additional lobe is in line with the other lobes, or in front of the lung, that is facing the heart, the animal is permitted. If,

however, it is situated on the back of the lung, that is facing the ribs, it is ṭĕrefah, since an additional lobe is reckoned as equivalent to an absent lobe. It must, however, be at least the size of a myrtle leaf; should it be smaller than that, it is not regarded as a lobe and the animal is permitted.

5. If one lobe is found adhering to the adjacent lobe, the animal is permitted; if the adhering lobes are not in consecutive order, for instance if the first lobe adheres to the third, the animal is ṭĕrefah.

6. If two lobes have the appearance of one lobe, and not of two lobes adhering to one another, the rule is as follows: If there is a gap between them the size of a myrtle leaf, whether at their root, or in the middle, or at the end, so that it is evident that they are in fact two lobes adhering to one another, the animal is permitted; otherwise, this is regarded as a case of an absent lobe and the animal is ṭĕrefah.

7. If the whole lung consists of two solid parts, without any articulation of the lobes, the animal is ṭĕrefah. Similarly, if the body of the lung is defective—even if there is no perforation—it is regarded as a case of an incomplete number of lobes, and the animal is ṭĕrefah. Consequently, if a portion of it, no matter how small, is found to be so dry that it can be scraped off with the fingernail, the lung is regarded as defective, and the animal is ṭĕrefah.

8. If the lung is found to be puffed up like the root of a dried palm, it must be declared forbidden because of doubt, seeing that there is an unusual addition to its body, and it is conceivable that an addition to the body of the lung might be regarded as equivalent to an absent portion, as has been stated with reference to the number of lobes.

9. In the case of an animal which had been so frightened that its lung has become shrunken and has almost dried up, the rule is as follows: If the fright was caused by an act of heaven—for

instance, if the animal had heard thunder, or had seen flashes of lightning, or the like—it is permitted. If the fright was caused by an act of man—for instance, if another animal was slaughtered before it, and the like—the shrunken lung is regarded as though it were defective, and the animal is ṭĕrefah.

10. How is the lung to be examined in such a case? It should be placed in water for twenty-four hours. If in winter, the water should be tepid, and should be contained in a vessel through whose sides it cannot evaporate or leak, so that it would not cool quickly. If in summer, the water should be cold and should be contained in a vessel through whose sides it can evaporate, so that it would remain cool. If the lung then returns to its normal state, the fright was caused by an act of heaven, and the animal is permitted; if not, the fright was caused by an act of man, and the animal is ṭĕrefah.

11. An animal born with a hind leg missing is ṭĕrefah. Similarly, one born with an extra hind leg is also ṭĕrefah, since every addition to an organ is regarded as equivalent to the absence of that organ. On the other hand, should it have three forelegs or only one foreleg, it is permitted. Therefore, if a foreleg is amputated, the animal remains permitted. If a hind leg is amputated from the joint upwards, the animal is ṭĕrefah; from the joint downwards, it is permitted. To which joint does this refer? To the joint which is the end of the thigh, that is the joint nearest the body.

12. In case the bone is fractured above the knee joint, if all of it, or the major portion of it, protrudes, it is considered as though it had been amputated and had fallen off, and the animal is ṭĕrefah. Should flesh or skin cover the major part of the thickness and circumference of the fractured bone, the animal is permitted, even if part of the fractured bone had fallen off and is no longer there. The soft sinews are not regarded as flesh in this respect.

13. The "meeting of the sinews" in domestic animal and wild beast is located above the ankle, where the butchers hang up the

animal. It consists of three white sinews, one thick and two thin. At the point of their beginning they are hard and white, but gradually the whiteness recedes and the sinews begin to redden and become soft. This is called the meeting of the sinews, and in an ox its length is approximately sixteen fingerbreadths.

14. In a bird there are sixteen such sinews. They begin at the lower bone of the leg, from the extra talon, and extend to the end of the leg where it becomes scaly.

15. If the hind leg of an animal is severed at the point of the meeting of the sinews, it is ṭĕrefah. One should not be puzzled and say, "How can it be that if the leg is severed above the meeting of the sinews, so that it is severed above the upper joint, as we have explained, the animal is permitted, while if it is severed below the meeting of the sinews, it is forbidden?" For with regard to those things which render an animal ṭĕrefah, the deciding factor is that if an organ is severed in one place the animal can survive, whereas if it is severed in another place the animal is bound to die. In this case, the animal is forbidden not because the leg has been severed at the particular place, but because the sinews have been severed, and this severing of them is included in the list of things which render the animal ṭĕrefah, as will be explained.

16. What is meant by "removed"? There are three organs which, if removed, render the animal ṭĕrefah, even though the law of perforation or defectiveness does not apply to them. They are: the meeting of the sinews, the liver, and the upper jaw.

17. We have already explained that the only reason that an animal or a bird whose leg has been severed at the meeting of the sinews is ṭĕrefah, is the severing of these sinews. Consequently if the sinews alone are severed but the leg itself remains whole, it is also ṭĕrefah, seeing that the sinews have been removed.

18. If the thick sinew alone is severed in an animal, it is permitted, since the other two sinews remain intact. If the two slen-

der ones are severed, it is likewise permitted, since the thick one is larger than these two, so that only the minor portion of the meeting of the sinews has been removed, not the whole of it. If the major part of each sinew is severed, the animal is ṭĕrefah. Needless to say, if all of them are completely severed or removed, the animal is also ṭĕrefah.

19. In the case of a bird, even if the major part of only one of the sixteen sinews is severed, it is ṭĕrefah.

20. If the wings of a bird are fractured, it is permitted, just as is an animal whose forelegs are severed.

21. If the whole of the liver has been removed, the animal is ṭĕrefah. If an olive's bulk of it remains at the point where the liver is suspended, and another olive's bulk at the place of the gall bladder, it is permitted. If the liver is torn but remains attached to its membrane, it is permitted. If both the part where it is suspended and the part at the gall bladder have been removed, the animal is ṭĕrefah, even if the remainder of it is present.

22. We have just stated that if an olive's bulk of the liver remains at the place where the liver is suspended and another olive's bulk at the place of the gall bladder, it is valid. However, if this remainder is scattered, a little here and a little there, or is ragged, or elongated like a thong, a doubt arises concerning it; in such a case, it would appear to me that it is forbidden.

23. If the upper jaw is removed, the animal is ṭĕrefah; if the lower jaw is removed, that is, if it is detached as far as the place of the organs of the neck, without tearing the latter, it is permitted.

24. In the case of every organ concerning which it was stated that if it is absent the animal is ṭĕrefah, the same is true also if that organ has been removed. On the other hand, in the case of an organ concerning which it was stated that if it has been removed it is ṭĕrefah, the animal becomes forbidden only if that organ is cut off; if the animal was born with that organ absent,

it is permitted. For otherwise the effect would be that "absent" and "removed" would mean the same thing. And as for every organ concerning which it was stated that if it has been removed the animal is permitted, it is self-evident that if that organ had been absent since birth and had never been created, the animal is certainly permitted.

25. An animal whose maternal organ—that is its womb—or whose kidneys have been removed, is permitted. Consequently if it was born with only one kidney, or with three, it is also permitted. Similarly, if the kidney is perforated, the animal is likewise permitted.

26. Although an animal whose kidney is absent or has been removed is permitted, nevertheless, if the kidney is exceedingly small, it is ṭĕrefah. In a small animal an exceedingly small kidney means one the size of a pea, and in a large animal the size of a grape. Similarly, if the kidney is afflicted with disease—that is, if its flesh is like dead flesh which has putrefied after several days, so that if one grasps it at one end it disintegrates and falls to the ground—and if this disease has progressed as far as the white matter inside the kidney, the animal is ṭĕrefah. Likewise, if secretion—even if not malodorous—or turbid or malodorous liquid is found in the kidney, it is ṭĕrefah; if clear liquid is found in it, the animal is permitted.

CHAPTER IX

1. What is meant by "split"? If the membrane which covers the marrow of the spinal cord is split, the animal is ṭĕrefah, providing that the major part of its circumference is so split. If the membrane is cracked lengthwise or is perforated, the animal is permitted. Similarly, if the spine is fractured but the spinal cord is not split, or if the marrow inside the spinal cord is crushed and loose, the animal is permitted, as long as the membrane remains whole.

2. If the marrow has become liquefied and flows like water or melted wax, so that when the spinal cord is set up in an erect position it does not remain standing, the animal is ṭĕrefah. If it cannot stand up solely on account of its weight, the animal is doubtfully ṭĕrefah.

3. How far does the spinal cord extend? It begins beyond the two "beans" which are at the beginning of the nape of the neck and extends as far as the end of the second branching-off, so that beyond it there is only the third branching-off which is adjacent to the beginning of the fat-tail.

4. These three branchings-off are three bones attached to one another below the vertebrae of the spine. The spinal cord in a bird extends as far as between the wings. Below these points one need not take into consideration the cord as it extends further down, whether its membrane is split, or the marrow liquefied.

5. What is meant by "torn"? If the flesh which covers the major part of the maw—that is that part of the belly where the maw will protrude if the belly is torn open—is torn, the animal is ṭĕrefah. Even if the tear does not extend right through to the maw itself, so that it is not visible, once the major part of the thickness of this flesh is torn or removed, the animal is ṭĕrefah. What must be the minimum extent of the tear to render it ṭĕrefah? In its length, one handbreadth, but in the case of a small animal, if the major part of the flesh which covers the maw is torn lengthwise, it is ṭĕrefah, even if the tear is less than a handbreadth long, seeing that the major part of the flesh is torn.

6. If this flesh is pierced circularly or longitudinally, the rule is as follows: If the hole is larger than a *sela'*, that is, if it will just receive three date stones held closely together, the animal is ṭĕrefah. For if a hole of this size is stretched out, it will amount to a handbreadth.

7. If the whole of the hide of an animal has been flayed, whether by human hand or as a result of disease, so that the flesh is not covered by skin, it is ṭĕrefah. Such an animal is called

gĕluḏah ("flayed"). If, however, a sela''s breadth of hide remains along the entire length of the spine, upon the navel, and on the main portions of the limbs, the animal is permitted. If a sela''s breadth has been removed from the whole length of the spine, the navel, or the main portions of the limbs, but the rest of the skin is intact, the case is doubtful, but it would appear to me that the animal is permitted.

8. What is meant by "fallen"? If an animal falls from a height of ten handbreadths or more and one of its organs is crushed, the animal is ṭĕrefah. What constitutes crushing? When the organ is so shattered and injured by the fall that its form and appearance are impaired. Even if the organ is neither perforated, nor split, nor fractured, the animal is still ṭĕrefah. Similarly, if the animal is struck by a stone or stick with the result that one of the organs is shattered, it is also ṭĕrefah. To which organs does this apply? To those within the cavity of the body.

9. If an animal, having fallen down from a roof, gets up and walks about, no apprehension need be felt for crushed organs. If, however, it gets up on its legs but cannot walk, apprehension need be had. If it has jumped down of its own accord, no concern need be felt. If one leaves the animal on high ground and later finds it below, no apprehension need be had that it may have fallen.

10. If rams gore one another, no apprehension need be had for crushed organs, unless the animals fall to the ground. Similarly, if an animal drags its legs, no apprehension need be had that its organs may have been crushed or its spinal cord split.

11. If thieves engaged in stealing sheep throw them over the stable wall, no concern need be had for crushed organs, since thieves usually throw them in such a manner as to cause no fracture. If, however, the thieves return the sheep by throwing them back into the stable, the rule is as follows: If they do so out of fear, apprehension need be had for crushed organs; if out of repentance, no apprehension need be had, since their inten-

tion is certain to be to return the sheep in good condition and they would be careful when throwing them back.

12. When an ox is thrown down for slaughter, even if it falls so heavily as to make a loud thud, no apprehension need be had for crushed organs, since the ox digs in its hoofs and holds fast until it reaches the ground.

13. If an animal is smitten on the head and the blow glances off towards the tail, or if it is smitten on the tail and the blow glances off towards the head, even if the club hits the entire length of the spine, no apprehension need be had for crushed organs. If, however, the club is knobby, or if its tip hits part of the spine, apprehension need be had for crushed organs; the same is true if the blow is struck against the breadth of the spine.

14. If a bird is dashed against a hard object, such as a compact heap of wheat, or a basket of almonds, and the like, apprehension need be had for crushing of organs. If it is dashed against a soft object, such as a folded garment, straw, ashes, or the like, no apprehension need be had.

15. If its wings became stuck with lime when the bird was trapped and it threw itself about, the rule is as follows: If the bird was held by one wing only, no apprehension need be had for crushed organs; if it was held by both wings and it thrashed its body about, apprehension need be had.

16. If a bird strikes the surface of the water with force, the rule is as follows: If thereupon it swims upstream against the current for a distance equal to the length of its body, no apprehension need be had for crushed organs. If it swims downstream with the current, apprehension need be had, seeing that it may be simply carried by the current. If it outdistances a piece of straw or chaff floating on the water, it is proof that it is swimming by its own power and no apprehension need be had.

17. Wherever we have said that no apprehension need be had, the meaning is that the animal may be slaughtered immediately,

and no examination is required to see whether any of its organs have been crushed. And wherever we have said that concern need be had, it is to be understood that if the animal is slaughtered, one must undertake a thorough examination of the whole bodily cavity, from skull to thigh. If one of the causes of ṭĕrefah which we have enumerated is found, or if one of the inner organs is crushed and its form impaired, the animal is ṭĕrefah. Even if it is one of the organs which, had it been removed, would not have caused the animal to become invalid, such as the spleen and the kidneys, it would in this case render it ṭĕrefah. The sole exception is the womb; if it is found crushed, the animal is nevertheless permitted.

18. The organs of the throat need not be examined in this respect, since they cannot be crushed by a fall.

19. If an animal falls from a roof and does not regain its feet, it may not be slaughtered until after twenty-four hours. If the animal is slaughtered within this period, it is ṭĕrefah. And when šĕḥiṭah is performed after the twenty-four hours, the animal must be examined, as we have explained.

20. Similarly, if one steps on a bird with his foot—or if an animal treads on it—or hurls it against a wall, and it quivers, there must be a delay of twenty-four hours before it may be slaughtered, whereupon it must be examined in the manner which we have explained.

21. If the major portion of the organs of the throat is loose, the animal is ṭĕrefah, even if this was not caused by a fall. The same is true if they are folded over, since they are not fit for šĕḥiṭah. If, however, the major part of the wide portion of the gullet is separated from the jaw, the animal is nevertheless permitted, since the wide part of the gullet is not valid for šĕḥiṭah, as we have explained.

CHAPTER X

1. What is meant by "fractured"? The fracture of the greater part of the animal's ribs. There are eleven ribs on either flank of an animal; if six on one side and six on the other are fractured, or all eleven on one side and one on the other, it is ṭĕrefah. That is, however, if the fracture is located in the half-rib which is toward the spine.

2. However, if six ribs on either side are fractured, the animal is ṭĕrefah only if they are the large ribs which contain marrow; otherwise, even though the fractured ribs constitute a major part of the ribs, and even though the fractures are toward the spine, the animal is nevertheless permitted. Similarly, if most of the ribs are wrenched from their sockets, it is also ṭĕrefah. Even if only one rib is wrenched from its socket together with half of the vertebra in which the rib is set, it is ṭĕrefah. Likewise, if one vertebra is wrenched from the spinal column—even one of those which are situated below the flanks, where there are no ribs—the animal is ṭĕrefah.

3. If an animal's thigh is dislocated from its original place, so that it is out of its socket, and the sinews—that is, the cords on the socket bone which proceed to the male bone and hold it—are eaten away, it is ṭĕrefah. If the sinews are not eaten away, the animal is permitted.

4. Similarly, in the case of a bird, if its thigh is dislocated, it is ṭĕrefah. If the wing is dislocated from its socket, apprehension need be had that the lung may have been perforated, and one must therefore examine the bird before consuming it. If the foreleg of an animal is dislocated from its socket, however, it is permitted, and there is no need for apprehension.

5. If a piece the size of a *sela'* is missing from the skull of a domestic animal or wild beast, it is ṭĕrefah, even if the membrane

is not perforated. If the skull is perforated with a number of holes involving loss of bone, they all combine together to make up the size of a sela‘.

6. If the major portion of the length or of the circumference of the skull is crushed, the animal is ṭĕrefah, even if the membrane is intact and no portion of the skull bone is missing. If the greater part of its length is crushed, but the greater part of the circumference is whole, or vice versa, it is a doubtful case of ṭĕrefah, but it would appear to me that it should be forbidden.

7. If the skull bone of a water bird, such as a goose, is perforated, it is ṭĕrefah, even if the membrane of the brain is not pierced, since the membrane of a waterfowl is soft. If a land bird is struck on the head by a weasel, or strikes against stone or wood, one should place his hand next to the perforation and press down, or put his hand into the bird's mouth and press upwards. If the brain then protrudes through the perforation, it is certain that the membrane has been perforated and the bird is ṭĕrefah; if not, it is permitted.

8. If an animal is seized with congestion of the blood, or is suffocated with smoke, or is chilled, or if it has eaten a poison fatal to animals, or has drunk foul water, it is permitted. If it has eaten a poison fatal to human beings, or was bitten by a snake, and the like, it is permitted insofar as ṭĕrefah is concerned, but is forbidden on account of danger to human life.

9. The various forms of ṭĕrefah which have been enumerated and which may be found in domestic animals or wild beasts, when listed one by one, number seventy in all. They are as follows, in the order in which they have been explained in this treatise:

1. Clawing by a beast or bird of prey.
2. Perforation of the wide part of the gullet.
3. Perforation of the membrane of the brain.
4. Decay of the brain itself.
5. Perforation of the heart itself, right through to its cavity.

6. Perforation of the tube of the heart.
7. Perforation of the gall bladder.
8. Perforation of the tubes of the liver.
9. Perforation of the stomach.
10. Perforation of the maw.
11. Perforation of the omasum.
12. Perforation of the second stomach.
13. Perforation of the bowels.
14. Extrusion and inversion of the bowels.
15. Perforation of the spleen at its thick part.
16. Absence of gall bladder.
17. Two gall bladders.
18. Absence of the stomach.
19. Two stomachs.
20. Absence of the maw.
21. Two maws.
22. Absence of the omasum.
23. Two omasa.
24. Absence of the second stomach.
25. Two second stomachs.
26. Absence of one of the bowels.
27. Two bowels.
28. Perforation of the lung.
29. Perforation of the windpipe below the place which is valid for šĕḥiṭah.
30. Perforation of one of the tubes of the lung, even if the perforation opens into another tube.
31. Obstruction of part of the lung.
32. Decomposition of one of the tubes of the lung.
33. Malodorous secretion in the lung.
34. Malodorous fluid in the lung.
35. Turbid, though not malodorous, fluid in the lung.
36. Decomposition of the lung.
37. Discoloration of the lung.
38. Discoloration of the gullet.
39. Absence of some of the lobes of the lung.

40. Transposition of the lobes of the lung.
41. Additional lobe on the top of the lung.
42. Adhesion of one lobe to another not in their normal order.
43. A lung without lobar articulation.
44. Absence of a portion of the lung.
45. Withering of a portion of the lung.
46. Inflated and stiff lung.
47. Shrivelled lung in an animal frightened by man.
48. Absence of a hind leg, whether from birth or as the result of amputation.
49. Additional hind leg.
50. Removal of the meeting of the sinews.
51. Removal of the liver.
52. Removal of the upper jaw.
53. Excessive shrinkage of the kidney.
54. Affected kidney.
55. Kidney full of secretion.
56. Turbid, though not malodorous, fluid in the kidney.
57. Malodorous fluid in the kidney.
58. Splitting of the spinal column.
59. Crushing and decomposition of the marrow of the spinal column.
60. Laceration of most of the flesh covering the maw.
61. Peeling of the hide.
62. Crushing of organs as the result of a fall.
63. Detachment of the organs of the throat.
64. Fracture of the majority of the ribs.
65. Wrenching of the majority of the ribs from their sockets.
66. A rib wrenched from its socket together with its vertebra.
67. Wrenching of a vertebra from its socket.
68. Dislocation of the thigh from its socket.
69. Absence of a piece the size of a *sela'* from the skull.
70. Crushed and battered skull.

10. Every one of these seventy defects which render the animal or beast forbidden on account of ṭĕrefah has already been ex-

plained, each in accordance with its regulations. If any of these defects is found in a bird, in such organs as are common to both fowl and beast, the rule governing it is the same for both, with the exception of the defects of the kidney, the spleen, and the lobes of the lung. The reason, in the case of the lung, is that a bird does not have articulated lobes, like a beast, and even if they are found, their number is not constant. As regards a bird's spleen, it is round like a grape, quite dissimilar to the spleen of an animal. And since the Sages did not enumerate the causes for ṭĕrefah in a beast's kidney and spleen, thus failing to indicate that these defects would apply also to birds, no minimum size has consequently been laid down for the shrinkage of a bird's kidney, and similar cases.

11. There are two causes of ṭĕrefah in a bird which are additional to those in an animal, even though the animal has these same organs. They are, discoloration of the entrails due to fire, and perforation of the skull of a water bird.

12. One may not under any circumstances add to this list of causes of ṭĕrefah, for in the case of any other defect in an animal, beast, or bird, beyond those which the Sages of former generations have enumerated, and to which the contemporary Israelite courts of law have given their assent, it is possible for the animal to go on living, even if our own medical knowledge assures us that it cannot eventually survive.

13. Conversely, as regards the defects which the Sages have enumerated, concerning which they have said that they render the animal ṭĕrefah, even if it should appear from our present knowledge of medicine that some of them are not fatal and that the animal can survive them, one must go only by what the Sages have enumerated, as it is said, *according to the law which* THEY *shall teach thee* (Deut. 17:11).

14. Any slaughterer who is versed in these causes of ṭĕrefah and is known to be an observant Israelite, may himself perform šĕḥiṭah and the subsequent examination, and sell the meat, and

there should be no reason for apprehension, since the evidence of only one witness is acceptable in ritual matters, regardless of whether he stands to profit personally from his evidence or not. And we have already explained that nowadays one should not purchase meat from a butcher who performs both šĕḥiṭah and examination himself, whether outside or inside the Land of Israel, unless he is a professional. If ṭĕrefah meat issues from his hand, he should be banned and removed from office, and the only way in which he can regain his validity is to betake himself to a place where he is not known, and there restore to its owner a lost article of considerable value, or declare an animal of substantial value ṭĕrefah, to his own loss.

CHAPTER XI

1. For any animal or bird concerning which a doubtful case of ṭĕrefah has arisen—for instance, if an animal has fallen from a height and cannot walk, or if it has been clawed by a beast and it is not known whether the flesh opposite the bowels has reddened or not, or if its skull has been crushed and it is not known whether the major or the minor part of it is crushed, and similar instances—the rule is as follows: If it is a male animal and remains alive for twelve months, it may be presumed to be as free of injury as any other animal. In the case of a female, it is regarded as uninjured if it subsequently gives birth. If it is a male bird, one must wait twelve months; if a female bird, until it lays all the eggs of the first brood, and then bears the second brood of eggs and lays them.

2. It is forbidden to sell an animal which is thus doubtfully ṭĕrefah to a heathen during this period of waiting, since he may resell it to an Israelite.

3. All domestic animals, wild beasts, and birds are under the presumption of being in good health, and there is no need to be

apprehensive that they might have a defect which would render them ṭĕrefah. Consequently when valid šĕḥiṭah has been performed upon them they need not be examined to see whether they have one of the defects which would render them ṭĕrefah; rather, they are presumed to be permitted, unless something is found in them which gives cause for apprehension, whereupon that thing alone need be examined.

4. How so? For instance, if a bird's wing is dislocated, the lung must be examined to see whether it has been perforated; if an animal falls from a height, it must be examined to see whether any organs have been crushed; if the skull is battered, the membrane of the brain must be examined to find out whether it has been perforated; if a thorn, an arrow, a spear, or the like has pierced the creature through to the bodily cavity, apprehension need be had and the whole cavity must be examined to see if one of the organs whose perforation renders the animal ṭĕrefah has been perforated. And so in all similar instances.

5. Consequently if the lung has developed growths or adhesions, which latter are like threads suspended from it to the flank, the heart, or the membrane of the liver, apprehension need be had for a perforation and it must be examined. Similarly, if a swelling full of secretion is found on it, apprehension need be had that the artery underneath it may have been perforated, and it must therefore be examined.

6. On this basis it would logically follow that if a lung is found to have suspended adhesions like threads which extend from the main lobe of the lung to the flank, the heart, or the membrane of the liver, one should cut the adhesion, remove the lung, and inflate it in warm water. If it is found to be perforated the animal should be ṭĕrefah, but if the water does not bubble, indicating that the lung is free from any perforation, the animal should be permitted, since this adhesion does not mark the place of a perforation, or it may be that only the outer membrane is perforated. But we have never found anyone who had rendered a decision

to this effect, nor have we heard of any place where such a procedure is followed.

7. Therefore, notwithstanding that this procedure would appear to be justified according to the words of the Sages of the Talmud, the general custom in Israel is as follows: After šĕḥiṭah has been performed upon the domestic or wild animal, the membrane of the liver is torn open and the lung is examined *in situ*. If no suspended adhesion is found; or if the adhesion extends from one of the lobes of the lung to the flesh at a point where the lung rests when the animal lies down, whether it be the flesh between the ribs, or the flesh of the breast; or if the adhesion is found to extend from one lobe to the other in consecutive order, or from the main lobe to one of the adjacent lobes—in all these cases the animal is declared permitted.

8. If, however, the thread proceeds from the main lobe of the lung to any other point it may extend to, even if it is no more than a hairsbreadth thick, the animal is declared forbidden.

9. Similarly, if a thread proceeds from the lung to the heart, or to the membrane of the liver, or to the pericardium, or to the "rose," whether it proceeds from the main lobe of the lung or from a lesser lobe, even if it is no thicker than a hairsbreadth, the animal is declared forbidden. Likewise, if the "rose" is found to be adhering to its sac, or if a thread proceeds from it to its sac, it is declared forbidden. If a thread proceeds from one lobe to another not adjacent to it, the animal is also declared forbidden.

10. There are localities where the custom obtains that if an adhesion is found from one of the lobes to the flesh and also to the bone of the ribs, and it adheres to both of them, the animal is declared forbidden. My revered father belonged to those who declared it forbidden, while I am of those who declare it permitted. In a few places an animal is declared permitted even if the thread adheres only to the bone, but I consider it forbidden.

11. There are also places where it is customary to inflate the

lung to see whether it has been perforated, but in most places the custom is not to inflate it, so long as nothing has occurred to give rise to any apprehension on that account. In Spain and in the Maghrib we have never inflated a lung unless something was found which gave rise to such apprehension.

12. None of this is a matter of law, but only of custom, as we have explained. And we have never heard of anyone who required the examination of a bird unless something was found in it which gave rise to apprehension.

13. If someone performs šĕḥiṭah upon an animal and tears open the belly, but before he can examine the lung a dog or a heathen comes along and carries it away, the animal is nevertheless permitted. It cannot be said that the lung may have been perforated or have had adhesions, since it cannot be presumed to have a defect; rather, the presumption is that it is permitted until something which renders it ṭĕrefah becomes known. Just as no apprehension need be had in similar circumstances concerning the membrane of the brain, the spine, or the like, so also no apprehension need be had concerning a lung which has been lost. Nor can there be any accepted custom in this case, since there can be no custom about a thing which is not of common occurrence.

14. If a heathen or an Israelite comes along and merely pulls out the lung before it can be examined, the lung, seeing that it remains on hand, must be inflated, even though it is not known whether there were growths upon it or not. This inflation is necessary only out of regard for the general custom.

15. There are places where, in case loose adhesions are found suspended from the lung, the animal is declared forbidden, even though the adhesions are not connected with the flank or with any other place. Such a practice entails great loss and waste of Israelite money. At no time did such a custom obtain in France or Spain, nor has it been heard of in the Maghrib. There is therefore no valid reason to observe this custom; the lung should

merely be inflated, and if it is found free of any perforation, the animal is permitted.

CHAPTER XII

1. If one performs šěḥiṭah upon a mother and its young on the selfsame day, the flesh is permitted to be eaten, but the slaughterer is liable to a flogging, as it is said, *Ye shall not kill it and its young both in one day* (Lev. 22:28). The flogging is due only for performing šěḥiṭah upon the second animal. Consequently if one person performs šěḥiṭah upon one of the two animals, and another person then comes along and performs šěḥiṭah upon the other animal, the other person alone is liable to a flogging.

2. The prohibition of *it and its young* obtains for all time, in all places, both for unconsecrated and consecrated animals, whether the latter belong to the class of consecrated animals which may be eaten, or to the class of consecrated animals which may not be eaten. Consequently if the person who performed šěḥiṭah upon the first animal did so in the Temple court, and the person who performed it upon the second animal did so outside, or if the former performed it outside the Temple court and the latter within the court, whether both animals were unconsecrated or consecrated, or one was unconsecrated and the other consecrated, he who performed šěḥiṭah upon the second animal was liable to a flogging on account of *it and its young*.

3. The prohibition of *it and its young* obtains solely with regard to šěḥiṭah, as it is said, *ye shall not kill (tišḥăṭu) it;* that is the prohibition obtains only when šěḥiṭah is performed upon both animals. If the slaughterer stabs the first animal, or if it becomes nĕḇelah in his hand, it is permitted to perform šěḥiṭah upon the second animal; similarly, if he slaughters the first animal and then stabs the second animal, or it becomes nĕḇelah in his hand, he is exempt.

4. If a deaf-mute, an imbecile, or a minor performs šĕḥiṭah privately upon one of the two animals, it is permitted to slaughter the second animal, since their šĕḥiṭah is not regarded as a valid šĕḥiṭah at all.

5. If one performs šĕḥiṭah upon the first animal and it turns out to be a doubtful case of nĕḇelah, it is forbidden to slaughter the second animal. If, however, he does slaughter it, he is not liable to a flogging.

6. A šĕḥiṭah whose product is not valid for consumption is nevertheless regarded as šĕḥiṭah. Consequently if the first slaughterer performed šĕḥiṭah upon an unconsecrated animal in the Temple court, an animal which was ṭĕrefah, an ox which had been condemned to stoning, a heifer whose neck was to be broken, or a Red Heifer, or if he slaughtered for the purpose of idolatry, and then another person came along and performed šĕḥiṭah upon the second animal, this other person was liable to a flogging. Similarly, if the first person slaughtered the first animal and another person then came along and slaughtered the second animal, which was an unconsecrated animal in the Temple court, an ox condemned to stoning, a heifer whose neck was to be broken, or a Red Heifer, he was liable to a flogging.

7. If one slaughters for purposes of idolatry, he is not liable on account of *it and its young,* since he is already liable to the graver penalty of death. But if he was cautioned only concerning *it and its young,* and not about idolatry, he is liable to no more than a flogging.

8. The prohibition of *it and its young* obtains only in respect to a clean domestic animal, as it is said, *whether it be cow or ewe, ye shall not kill it and its young both in one day* (Lev. 22:28). It obtains also for crossbreeds. How so? If a male deer is mated with a she-goat and one slaughters the goat and its young, he is liable to a flogging. But if a male goat is mated with a doe, although it is forbidden to slaughter it and its young, if one does so, he is not liable to a flogging, seeing that the Torah has forbidden a cow and its young, not a doe and its young.

9. In case the offspring of this doe is a female and later gives birth to young, if one slaughters the daughter and its offspring, he is liable to a flogging. Similarly, in the case of a crossbreed which is the issue of a species of sheep and a species of goat, whether from a ram with a she-goat, or a he-goat with a ewe, he is liable to a flogging on account of *it and its young*.

10. It is permitted to slaughter a pregnant animal, since the unborn young is regarded as a limb of its mother. If, however, the unborn young emerges alive after šĕḥiṭah and sets its feet on the ground, it may not be slaughtered on the same day, although if one does so he is not liable to a flogging.

11. The prohibition of *it and its young* applies to the female parent only, since it is certain that the young is its offspring. If, however, the sire is known for a certainty, one should not slaughter both sire and young on the same day. If one does so nevertheless, he is not liable to a flogging, since it is still doubtful whether or not the prohibition applies to the male parent also.

12. If one slaughters a cow and then two of its calves on the same day, he is liable to a twofold flogging. If he first slaughters the calves and then the dam, he is liable to be flogged only once. If he slaughters the cow and its daughter, and then the daughter's calf, he is liable to a double flogging. If he slaughters the cow and the daughter's calf, and then the daughter itself, only a single flogging is incurred, whether he or another person performs šĕḥiṭah upon the daughter.

13. If two individuals purchase two animals, dam and young, and seek a legal decision in the case, the answer is that the person who made the earlier purchase should have the right to perform šĕḥiṭah first, while the second should wait until the morrow. But if the second person anticipates the first and slaughters his own animal, he has gained the advantage, and it is the first person who must wait until the morrow.

14. At four seasons of the year the seller of an animal must

inform the purchaser in case he has already sold its dam or its young, whichever it may be, to another person for the purpose of šĕḥiṭah, so that the latter purchaser would wait and not slaughter his animal until the morrow. These occasions are: the eve of the last day of the Feast of Tabernacles, the eve of the first day of the Festival of Passover, the eve of Pentecost, and the eve of New Year.

15. When does this apply? When the seller sees that the purchaser of the latter animal is in a hurry to acquire it, and it is late in the day, so that the presumption is that he will slaughter it at once. If, however, the day is still young, there is no need to inform him, for he may not slaughter until the morrow.

16. If one sells the dam to a bridegroom and its young to the bride, he must inform them of it, since it is certain that they will slaughter both animals on the same day, and so in all similar cases.

17. In the *one day* mentioned in connection with *it and its young,* the day follows the night. How so? If one has slaughtered the first animal on Tuesday evening, he should not slaughter the second until Wednesday evening. Similarly, if he has slaughtered the first one on Wednesday afternoon, before twilight, he may slaughter the second on Wednesday evening. If he has slaughtered the first one at twilight on Wednesday evening, he should not slaughter the second one until Thursday evening, but if he does nevertheless perform šĕḥiṭah during the day on Thursday, he is not liable to a flogging.

CHAPTER XIII

1. If one takes a dam with its young and performs šĕḥiṭah upon the dam, the flesh is permitted for consumption, but he is liable to a flogging for slaughtering the dam, as it is said, *Thou shalt not take the dam with the young* (Deut. 22:6). Similarly,

if it dies before he lets it go, he is liable to a flogging, but if he lets it go alive after having taken it, he is exempt.

2. The same rule applies to any negative commandment the transgression of which may be rectified by the subsequent performance of the pertinent positive commandment. It is one's duty in such a case to fulfill this positive commandment, and if he fails to do so, he is liable to a flogging.

3. If someone else comes along, snatches the dam from his hand, and sets it free, or if the dam escapes from his hand against his will, he is nevertheless liable to a flogging, since Scripture says, *Thou shalt in any wise let the dam go* (*ibid.* 22:7). He is therefore not exempt from liability until he himself sets it free of his own accord. In this case, he has not fulfilled this positive commandment to set it free, which would have rectified his transgression.

4. If one takes the dam with its young and clips its wings so that it cannot fly, and then sets it free, he is liable to the flogging prescribed for disobedience. He should moreover be compelled to keep the dam with him until its wings have grown again and then release it. If it dies prior to this, or escapes and is gone, he is still liable to a flogging, seeing that he has not fulfilled the pertinent positive commandment.

5. How should he set the dam free? He should grasp it by its wings and send it flying. If he sends it off and it returns, and he again sends it off and it again returns—even if it happens four or five times—he is still obligated to send it away, since Scripture says, *Thou shalt in any wise let the dam go.*

6. If one says, "I intend to take the dam and set the young free," he is nevertheless bound to send away the dam also, as it is said, *Thou shalt in any wise let the dam go.*

7. If one takes the young and then restores them to the nest, and after that the dam returns and sits upon them, he is not obligated to send her away again. If he sets the dam free, and

then recaptures it, it is permitted, for the Torah forbids its capture only when it is unable to fly away because it is hovering over its young to protect them from being taken, as it is said, *and the dam [is] sitting on the young* (*ibid.* 22:6). If, therefore, he lets it go from his control and then catches it again, it is permitted.

8. The law of releasing the dam applies only to a clean bird which is not domesticated, such as doves in a cote or in an attic, or birds which have nested in an orchard, as it is said, *if a bird's nest chance to be before thee* (*ibid.*). Domesticated birds, such as geese, chickens, and doves which nest in the house, do not come under the obligation to release the dam.

9. If the young are already flying about, so that they have no more need of their dam, or if the eggs are addled, one is not obligated to release the dam. If the young are tĕrefah, they are regarded as equivalent to addled eggs, and one is again not bound to release the dam.

10. If a male bird is found sitting in a nest, one is not obligated to release it. If an unclean bird is found sitting on the eggs of a clean bird, or a clean bird on the eggs of an unclean bird, one is again not obligated to release it.

11. If a clean bird is sitting on the eggs of another clean species, one is obligated to release it, but if he does not, he is not liable to a flogging. If the dam is ṭĕrefah, he must release it.

12. If one performs šĕḥiṭah upon the minor part of the organs while the dam is in the nest, before removing her, he must release her; but if he does not do so, he is not liable to a flogging.

13. If the dam is fluttering about with her wings touching the nest, he must release her; if they do not touch, he is not obligated to do so. If a piece of cloth or feathers act as an interposition between her wings and the nest, he must likewise release the dam, but if he fails to do so, he is not liable to a flogging.

14. If there are two layers of eggs and the dam's wings touch

the upper layer, or if it is sitting upon addled eggs with fertile eggs underneath them, or if one dam is sitting on top of another, or if a male bird is sitting in the nest and the dam is sitting on the male bird, one may not take the dam. If he does take her, he should release her, but if he does not do so, he is not liable to a flogging.

15. If the dam is sitting in the midst of young or eggs but without touching them, one need not release her. The same applies also if she is sitting at the side of the nest with her wings touching only the side.

16. If the dam is perched on two branches of a tree with the nest between, an estimate should be made whether the dam would fall into the nest if the branches were removed; if she would, she must be released.

17. If the dam is sitting on only one chick or only one egg, she must be released. If a nest is found on the surface of the water or upon a living animal, the dam must likewise be released. The only reason why Scripture speaks of "young" and "eggs" in the plural, and of *in any tree or on the ground* (Deut. 22:6), is because it generally speaks of things as they commonly occur.

18. It is forbidden to take possession of the eggs as long as the dam is sitting on them. Consequently if she is sitting on eggs or young in one's own attic or dovecote, they are not regarded as domesticated, and the fact that the courtyard belongs to him does not give him possession of the eggs or young. Just as he cannot transfer ownership of these eggs to others, so his courtyard cannot give him title to them, and consequently he must release the dam.

19. It is forbidden to take the dam with the young even for the purpose of using them for the purification rites of a leper, in fulfillment of a Scriptural commandment. If he does take them, he must release the dam. If he fails to do so, he is liable to a flogging, since a positive commandment cannot override a positive commandment and a negative commandment together, while

a positive commandment and a negative commandment together do override a positive commandment.

20. If one had consecrated a bird to the upkeep of the Temple and it flew away from his hand, and if he, being able to recognize it, subsequently found it sitting on young or on eggs, he had to take the entire contents of the nest and bring it to the treasurer of the Temple, since the law of releasing the dam did not apply to consecrated birds, for Scripture says, *but the young thou mayest take unto thyself* (Deut. 22:7), and these could not be taken "unto thyself."

21. If a bird has killed a man, one is exempt from releasing it, since the law requires it to be brought to court for judgment.

CHAPTER XIV

1. It is a positive commandment to cover up the blood which issues from the šĕḥiṭah of a clean beast or bird, as it is said, *And whatsoever man . . . that taketh in hunting any beast or bird that may be eaten, he shall pour out the blood thereof, and cover it with dust* (Lev. 17:13). Consequently before covering up the blood, one must recite the benediction, "Blessed art Thou, O Lord our God, King of the universe, who has sanctified us with His commandments and has commanded us concerning the covering up of the blood."

2. The commandment to cover up the blood applies to both domesticated and nondomesticated animals, since the words *that taketh in hunting* have been used by Scripture merely because this is the common occurrence. The commandment applies to unconsecrated animals but not to consecrated ones, whether they be consecrated for the altar or for the upkeep of the Temple. If one transgressed and performed šĕḥiṭah upon these, he was not obligated to cover up their blood.

3. If one first slaughters a beast or a bird and then consecrates it, or if he consecrates the blood only, he must cover it up.

4. A crossbreed which is the issue of a domestic animal and a wild beast, or a creature concerning which it is doubtful whether it is a domestic animal or a wild beast, must have its blood covered up, but no benediction need be recited. If one slaughters on the Sabbath for the sake of an invalid, he must cover up the blood after the expiration of the Sabbath. Similarly, if one slaughters a doubtful animal or a crossbreed on a festival, he must cover up its blood at the conclusion of the festival.

5. If one slaughters both birds and beasts in one place, he need recite only one benediction and perform only one act of covering up the blood for all.

6. If blood becomes mixed with water, but still retains the appearance of blood, it must be covered up; if not, it need not be covered up. If blood is mixed with wine or with the blood of a domestic animal, the added fluid is regarded as though it were water. If under such an assumption it is possible that the mixture would have retained the appearance of blood, in which case one would have been obliged to cover it up—had the added fluid been the same amount of water—one must cover it all up; if not, no covering up is required.

7. If the blood, after having been covered up, becomes again uncovered, one need not cover it up once more. If the wind covers it up, one need not cover it up at all; but if it subsequently becomes uncovered, one must cover it up again.

8. Blood which has spurted out or blood on the slaughtering knife must be covered up if there is no other blood with which to fulfill the commandment of covering it up.

9. If after slaughtering the blood becomes absorbed in the ground, the rule is as follows: If it leaves a recognizable trace, it must be covered up; if not, is is regarded as though the wind had covered it up, and one need not cover it up again.

10. It is only blood issuing from such šĕḥiṭah as renders the animal fit for consumption that must be covered up, since it is said, *that may be eaten* (Lev. 17:13). Consequently, if one slaughters an animal and finds it to be ṭĕrefah, or if one slaughtered an unconsecrated animal in the Temple court, or a beast or bird condemned to be stoned, or if he slaughters an animal and it becomes nĕḇelah in his hand, he is exempt from the duty to cover up the blood. Similarly, if a deaf-mute, an imbecile, or a minor slaughters privately, one need not cover up the blood from their šĕḥiṭah.

11. With what may the blood be covered up? With earth dust, lime, gypsum, fine manure, sand so fine that the potter need not pulverize it further, ground stone and shard, fine hacheled flax, fine sawdust, brick dust, or powdered potter's or sealing clay, since all these may be regarded as species of dust. If, however, one inverts a vessel over the blood, or covers it with stones, that does not constitute covering up, seeing that Scripture says *with dust* (Lev. 17:13).

12. Consequently one may not cover up blood with coarse manure or coarse sand, or with flour, bran, coarse bran, or metal filings, since these are not species of dust. Gold dust alone is an exception and blood may be covered with it, since Scripture calls it dust, as it is said, *and it hath dust of gold* (Job 28:6), and also, *until it (the gold) was fine as dust* (Deut. 9:21).

13. One may cover up the blood with coal dust—that is furnace ashes—stibium, dust of chiseled millstones, and ashes, whether wood ashes or the ashes of burned garments, or even ashes of burned meat, since it is written, *from the ashes of the burning of the sin offering* (Num. 19:17). It is also permitted to cover up blood with the ashes of an apostate city.

14. Whosoever performs šĕḥiṭah must first spread dust underneath, then slaughter over it, and thereupon cover up the blood with more dust; he should not slaughter into a vessel and then cover up the blood with dust.

15. It is he who performs šĕḥiṭah who should also perform the covering up of the blood, as it is said, HE *shall . . . cover it with dust*. If he does not cover it up and another man sees it, the latter must cover it up, since this is a separate commandment whose fulfillment does not depend solely upon the person who performs šĕḥiṭah.

16. When one performs the commandment of covering up the blood, he should do it not with his foot, but with his hand, or with a knife or utensil, so as not to conduct the performance of the commandment in a contemptuous manner, thus treating God's commandments with scorn. For reverence is due not to the commandments themselves, but to Him who had issued them, blessed be He, and had delivered us from groping in the darkness by making the commandments a lamp to straighten out the crooked places and a light to teach us the paths of uprightness. And so indeed Scripture says, *Thy word is a lamp unto my feet, and a light unto my path* (Ps. 119:105).

ABBREVIATIONS

Tractates of Mishnah, Tosefta, and Talmud

Ab—*'Abot*
Ar—*'Ărakin*
AZ—*'Abodah Zarah*
BB—*Baba Batra*
Bek—*Běkorot*
Ber—*Běrakot*
Beṣ—*Beṣah*
Bik—*Bikkurim*
BḲ—*Baba Ḳamma*
BM—*Baba Měṣi'a*
Dem—*Demai*
Ed—*'Eduyyot*
Er—*'Erubin*
Ger—*Gerim*
Giṭ—*Giṭṭin*
Ḥag—*Ḥăgigah*
Ḥal—*Ḥallah*
Hor—*Horayot*
Ḥul—*Ḥullin*
Kel—*Kelim*
Ker—*Kěritot*
Ket—*Kětubbot*
Ḳid—*Ḳiddušin*
Kil—*Kil'ayim*
Ma—*Ma'áśěrot*
Mak—*Makkot*
Me—*Mě'ilah*
Meg—*Měgillah*
Men—*Měnahot*
MSh—*Ma'ăśer Šeni*
Naz—*Nazir*
Ned—*Nědarim*
Neg—*Něga'im*
Nid—*Niddah*
Or—*'Orlah*
Pes—*Pěsuḥim*
RH—*Roš haš-Šanah*
Sanh—*Sanhedrin*
Shab—*Šabbat*
Shebi—*Šěbi'it*
Shebu—*Šěbu'ot*
Sheḳ—*Šěḳalim*
Soṭ—*Soṭah*
Suk—*Sukkah*
Ta—*Ta'ănit*
Tem—*Těmurah*
Ter—*Těrumot*
Ṭoh—*Ṭŏharot*
Uḳ—*'Uḳsin*
Yad—*Yadayim*
Yeb—*Yěbamot*
Yoma—*Yoma*
Zab—*Zabim*
Zeb—*Zěbuḥim*

B. prefixed to the name of a tractate indicates a reference to the Babylonian Talmud; P. indicates a reference to the Palestinian (Jerusalemite) Talmud; and Tos a reference to the Tosefta. Otherwise the reference is to a tractate of the Mishnah.

Other Sources and Commentaries

Alfasi—*Hălaḵot* (by R. Isaac Alfasi [al-Fāsī, 1013–1103])

ARN—'Aḇot dĕ-Rabbi Nathan

'*Aruḵ—Sefer he-'aruḵ* (dictionary, by Nathan ben Jehiel [d. 1106])

Ben-Yehudah—E. Ben-Yehudah, *Millon hal-lašon ha-'iḇrit* (*Thesaurus totius hebraitatis*), Berlin and Jerusalem, 1908–1959

BY—*Beṯ Yosef* (commentary on the *Ṭurim* of Jacob ben Asher, by Joseph Caro [1488–1575])

Danby—*The Mishnah*, trans. Herbert Danby, Oxford, 1933

DER—Dereḵ 'Ereṣ Rabbah

DM—*Darḵe Mošeh* (commentary on the *Ṭurim* of Jacob ben Asher, by Moses Isserles [d. 1572])

Eccl. R.—Midrash Rabbah on Ecclesiastes

Exod. R.—Midrash Rabbah on Exodus

Geonica—L. Ginzberg, *Geonica*, New York, 1909

Ḥemdah gĕnuzah—Ḥemdah gĕnuzah (collection of Gaonic responsa), ed. Z. W. Wolfensohn, Jerusalem, 1863

HG—*Hălaḵot gĕdolot* (ascribed to Simeon Kayyara [9th century]); (H), ed. I. Hildesheimer, Berlin, 1888–92; (T), ed. A.S. Traub, Warsaw, 1874

HP—*Hălaḵot pĕsuḵot* (ascribed to Yehudai Gaon [8th century]), ed. S.D. Sassoon, Jerusalem, 1950

'*Iṭṭur—Sefer ha-'iṭṭur* (by R. Isaac ben Abba Mari [12th century]), Wilno, 1874

Jastrow—M. Jastrow, *A Dictionary of the Targumim, the Talmud Babli and Yerushalmi, and the Midrashic Literature* [photo-offset edition], New York and Berlin, 1926

KM—*Kesef Mišneh* (commentary on the Code, by Joseph Caro [1488–1575])

Lev. R.—Midrash Rabbah on Leviticus

Lewysohn—L. Lewysohn, *Die Zoologie des Talmuds*, Frankfurt am Main, 1858

LhR—*Lĕšonot ha-RaMBaM* (Part 5 of the Responsa of David Ibn Abi Zimra [16th century]), Warsaw, 1882

LM—*Leḥem Mišneh* (commentary on the Code, by Abraham Ḥiyya di Boton [d. 1588])

Löw—I. Löw, *Die Flora der Juden*, Wien and Leipzig, 1924–34

LṬ—*Leḵaḥ ṭoḇ* (by Tobiah ben Eliezer [11th century]), ed. S. Buber, Wilno, 1880–84

MdRŠ—Mĕkilta dĕ-Rabbi Šim'on, ed. D. Hoffmann, Frankfurt am Main, 1905

Mek—Mĕkilta

MhM—*Mirkeḇet ham-Mišneh* (notes on the Code, by Solomon Chelm [d. 1781])

MiM—Midrash Mishle

MM—*Maggiḏ Mišneh* (commentary on the Code, by Vidal de Tolosa [14th century])

MN—*Moreh nĕḇukim* (by Maimonides)

MO—*Migdal 'oz* (commentary on the Code, by Shem-Tob ben Abraham [14th century])

MT—Midrash Tanna'im on Deuteronomy, ed. D. Hoffmann, Berlin, 1908–09

OhG—*'Oṣar hag-gĕ'onim*, ed. B.M. Lewin, Haifa and Jerusalem, 1928–43

Oxford MS.—Codex Can. Or. 78 in the Bodleian Library (Neubauer 568)

PhM—*Peruš ham-Mišnah* (Maimonides' commentary on the Mishnah)

Preuss—J. Preuss, *Biblisch-talmudische Medizin, 3. unveränderte Auflage,* Berlin, 1923

PRK—Pĕsikta dĕ-Raḇ Kăhana, ed. S. Buber, Lyck, 1868

R.—Rabbi

RABD—*Haśśaḡot* (critical notes on the Code, by R. Abraham ben David of Posquières [1125–1198])

Rashi—R. Solomon ben Isaac of Troyes [1040–1105], author of commentaries on the Hebrew Bible and on the Babylonian Talmud

SER—Seder 'Eliyahu Rabbah (ed. M. Friedmann)

ShE—*Sefer ha-'eškol* (by Abraham ben Isaac of Narbonne [12th century]); (A), ed. B.H. Auerbach, Halberstadt, 1867–69; (B) ed. Ch. Albeck, Jerusalem, 1935–38

ShM—*Sefer ham-miṣwot* (by Maimonides), ed. Ch. Heller, Petrikau, 1914

Sif Deut.—Sifre on Deuteronomy

Sif Lev.—Sifra (on Leviticus)

Sif Num.—Sifre on Numbers

SMG—*Sefer miṣwot gaḏol* (by Moses ben Jacob of Coucy [13th century])

Song R.—Midrash Rabbah on the Song of Songs

ŠRA— *Šĕ'eltot* (by Aḥai Gaon [8th century]), ed. Wilno, 1861–67

ŠT—Ša'ăre tĕšuḇah (Gaonic responsa), ed. D. Luria, Leipzig, 1858

ŠYD—*Šulḥan 'aruḵ Yoreh de'ah* (by Joseph Caro [1488–1575])

Tanḥ—Midrash Tanḥuma, ed. S. Buber, Wilno, 1885

ThB—*Toraṯ hab-bayiṯ* (by Solomon ibn Adret [1235–1310]), Berlin, 1762

ThR—*Tĕšuḇoṯ ha-RaMBaM* (responsa, by Maimonides), ed. A. Freimann, Jerusalem, 1934

ṬOḤ—*Ṭur 'Oraḥ Ḥayyim* (by Jacob ben Asher [1269–1343])

Tosafoṯ—Tosafoṯ (critical and explanatory glosses to the Talmud, by the successors of Rashi)

ṬYD—*Ṭur Yoreh de'ah* (by Jacob ben Asher [1269–1343])

TYṬ—*Tosafoṯ Yom Ṭoḇ* (by Yom Ṭob Lipmann Heller [1579–1654])

YJS—Yale Judaica Series

YšŠ—*Yam šel Šĕlomoh* (by Solomon Luria [d. 1573])

NOTES

Cross-references consisting of four numbers indicate passages found in the Code outside the present volume, the numbers referring, respectively, to the Book, the Treatise, the Chapter and the Section where the passage in question occurs.

Treatise I: Forbidden Intercourse

Chapter I

1. "forbidden unions"—see IV, 1, i, 5 ff.

"extinction"—Hebrew *ḳareṯ,* literally "cutting off," as in the proof-verse cited. It means ultimate extermination at the hands of heaven; *see* Glossary.

"both of them"—Sif Lev. 18:29; B. BḲ 32a, and Rashi *ad loc.*

"fixed sin offering"—Ker 1:2; cf. IX, IV, i, 4 (YJS, *4,* 97). It is a general rule that where kareṯ is prescribed for an act committed wantonly, a sin offering must be brought if the act was committed in error.

2. Mak 1:9.

3. "Even if," etc.—disagreeing with the dictum of R. Jose ben Judah, B. Mak 6b, that a scholar may not plead ignorance of the law. Cf. also Eccl. R. 1, and XIV, 1, xii, 2 (YJS, *3,* 34).

4. Sanh 7:1.

"The following incur death by stoning"—Sanh 7:4.

5. Sanh 9:1 (different order); B. *ibid.* 76b; cf. XIV, 1, xv, 11 (YJS, *3,* 44).

6. "strangulation"—Sanh 11:1.

"the daughter of a priest"—*ibid.* 9:1.

"If she is a betrothed maiden"—B. Sanh 50b.

"wherever the Torah says"—B. Sanh 53a; even though this particular verse says *that they die.*

7. "extinction only"—Ker 1:1.

"Consequently"—B. Mak 13a–b.

8. Mak 3:1.

"by a negative commandment"—without the penalty of extinction; see IV, 1, i, 7.

"both he and she must be flogged"—Ker 2:4.

"the secondary degrees"—see IV, 1, i, 6; LhR 2126.

"flogged for disobedience, on the authority of the Scribes"—the court has authority to prescribe a flogging even where it is not required by Biblical law; Naz 4:3, P. Ḳid 4:6, and cf. ShM, p. 23.

"at its discretion"—B. Sanh 46a.

9. Sif Deut. 22:26; IV, III, ii, 4.

"cannot be applied to the man"—B. Yeḇ 53b. According to MM, this holds true even if he is forced to cohabit with her on pain of death, since erection is still impossible without his own intention, Cf. I, i, v, 4.

"A woman who is subjected to duress," etc.—B. Keṯ 51b.

10. Yeḇ 6:1; P. *ibid.*

mĕʿareh—the literal meaning of the verse quoted is "he hath uncovered her fountain"; *mĕʿareh* therefore means "he who uncovers."

"*gomer*"—"he who completes."

"And whether . . . in a normal or abnormal manner"—B. Hor 4a, Sanh 33b. Throughout the whole of this section references to natural and unnatural intercourse are enclosed within brackets in the printed text, since some authorities regard them as later additions. They occur, however, in the Oxford MS; see note to iii, 15, and xxi, 9.

"in a recumbent," etc.—cf. B. Sanh 37b, 38a; Yeḇ 59b.

11. B. Sheḇu 18a.

"a born eunuch"—contrasted with one who has been castrated.

"But he does debar the woman"—B. Soṭ 26b; Yeḇ 8:4.

"from eating of the heave offering"—a woman who has intercourse with a man forbidden to her is thereby rendered a "harlot" (cf. below, xviii, 1) who is debarred from marrying into the priesthood and is therefore forbidden to eat of the heave offering, the priestly portion. Cf. VII, iii, vi, 7.

12. "believing it to be licit"—B. Sanh 62b; for example, thinking that he was having intercourse with his wife, and it turned out to be his sister (MM).

"had no intention"—LhR 2125.

"or for the secondary degrees of propinquity"—MM, following RABD, omits this sentence, since it is a well established rule that there is no punishment for unintentional transgression of a negative commandment.

"a dead woman"—B. Yeḇ 55b.

"a fatal disease"—B. Sanh 78a.

"still alive," etc.—B. Sanh 120b.

"the windpipe and the gullet"—in which case the animal is bound to die. Cf. below, iii, i, and B. Ḥul 121b.

13. Nid 5:4–5

"not regarded as intercourse"—PhM *ad loc.;* Nid 45a.

14. Sanh 7:4; B. *ibid.* 55a; PhM *ad loc.* (for a general discussion of all such abnormalities).

"active . . . passive"—B. Ker 3a.

"both are exempt"—B. Sanh 54b.

15. B. Yeḇ 81a–83b. The hermaphrodite ('androḡinos, ἀνδρόγυνος) shows the characteristics of both sexes, while the *ṭumṭum's* sexual parts are so overgrown that it is impossible to determine his sex. Cf. IV, i, ii, 25; LhR 2127.

16. Sanh 7:4.

"Regardless," etc.—B. BḲ 54b; AZ 22b, 23a.

"Nor does Scripture differentiate"—B. Sanh 54b.

"whether he has connection," etc.—B. Sanh 55a.

17. Nid 5:4–5.

"the animal must be stoned"—the reason for this is explained in Sif Lev. 20:15, Sanh 7:4, and B. *ibid.* 55b, thus: While the animal itself cannot be held to blame, yet for reasons of public policy it must be destroyed, for if left alive it would serve as a constant reminder to the public of the unnatural act in which it was instrumental, and of the fact that neither participant was punished.

"If she is three years old," etc.—P. Sanh 7:7.

18. B. Sanh 55b.

"In any of the cases"—Nid 5:5, Yeb̠ 6:1, Ker 2:6.

"as we have explained"—in the first occurrence, above, Sec. 13; in the second, Sec. 9.

19. B. Mak 7a; B. BM 91a; Alfasi's decision, Yeb̠ Chap. 2.

20. B. Ḳid 80a.

"it happened"—B. Ḳid 80a.

"the son who curses"—Exod. 21:17; P. Ḳid 4:10 is the source for this proof, but quotes Exod. 21:15, *he that smiteth his father.*

21. P. Ḳid 4:10; B. BB 167b.

22. B. Ḳid 80a; Ket̠ 72a.

"a man who suspects his wife"—P. Soṭ 6:2 (and the commentaries *ad loc.*).

"with a harlot"—see below, Chap. xvii.

"was already presumed to be a harlot"—because of her husband's suspicion that she may have committed adultery. Valid testimony requires two witnesses. In this case, the sole available witness merely establishes the fact that testimony exists, and credence is given to him only because he is supported by the common presumption. Variant reading: "For although the root of testimony cannot be established by only one witness," etc.; the sense remains the same.

23. B. Ḳid 63b–64a.

Chapter II

1. B. Sanh 53a.

"from . . . betrothal"—cf. IV, 1, i.

"the wife of his brother who left no son by her"—is subject to levirate marriage (*yibbum*) or release (*ḥăliṣah*); cf. Deut. 25:5–10; the rule refers to any issue, either male or female.

"If he has intercourse"—B. Yeb̠ 32a; Sanh 7:4.

"near kin"—cf. Lev. 18:6.

"simultaneously"—cf. below, xvii, 8.

2. B. Sanh 53a–54a; LhR 2128.

"His brother's wife"—B. Yeb̠ 55a.

"as we have explained"—IV, 1, i, 6.

"A sister, whether on the father's . . . side," etc.—B. Mak 5b.

3. "The daughter of one's father's wife"—B. Yeb̠ 22b.

"his sister on the father's side"—i.e. his half-sister.

"If on the other hand, his father had married a woman"—B. Soṭ 43b.

"this daughter"—i.e. his step-sister. Sif Lev. 20:17.

"inasmuch as she is designated as his *sister*"—referring to a half-sister, B. Yeb̠ 22b.

4. B. Yeb̠ 22b.

"wedded to his father"—and born out of that wedlock.

5. B. Yeb̠ 54b; Mak 14a.

"Similarly," etc.—this sentence has been accidentally omitted in the Oxford MS.

6. Sanh 9:1; B. *ibid.* 76a.

"even though the Torah does not say, 'Thou shalt not uncover the nakedness of thy daughter' "—cf. ShM, negative commandment 336. Cf. also below, II, ix, 2, and note thereto; B. Ker. 5a, and Rashi *ad loc.*

"is silent"—i.e. had no need to say anything, since it stands to reason that if the granddaughter is forbidden, the daughter surely is also forbidden.

7. B. Yeb̲ 95a; Naz 12a; DER Chap. 1, and the commentary *ad loc.*

"both . . . by burning"—B. Sanh 76b.

8. B. Sanh 76b; P. Yeb̲ 10:6.

"and they"—Maimonides follows the view of R. 'Ăḳib̲a that *they* refers to the wife and her kinswoman. Since R. 'Ăḳib̲a says that after the wife's death burning is not incurred, but the kinswoman is merely prohibited, Maimonides interprets this prohibition as involving only extinction.

9. Lev. 18:18; B. Yeb̲ 9b, 96a; 54b–55a.

10. B. Yeb̲ 95a.

"seven women"—the six mentioned in Sec. 7, and the wife's sister mentioned in Sec. 9.

"the Laws Concerning Divorce"—IV, II, x, 9.

11. Yeb̲ 11:1; B. *ibid.* 97a, 97b.

"suspected"—B. Yeb̲ 26a.

"If, however, he has married"—Tos Yeb̲ 4:5.

12. B. Ḳid 12b; B. Yeb̲ 52a. Maimonides derives this law from the incident referred to. Cf. also B. Yeb̲ 95a; P. *ibid.* 10:6.

13. Yeb̲ 11:1; B. *ibid.* 97a.

14. "as we have explained"—above, Sec. 3.

"He is also permitted to marry the wife of his brother's son"—P. Yeb̲. 1:1, 11:4; Alfasi, Yeb̲ Chap. 2; DER 1.

"He may moreover marry a woman and her sister's daughter"—Ker 3:6.

"meritorious deed"—B. Yeb̲ 62b; Sanh 76b, and Rashi *ad loc.*

Chapter III

1. B. Ḳid 19a; cf. B. Yeb̲ 112b, 113a.

"with the wife of a deaf-mute," etc.—all the following cases, excepting the person of doubtful sex and the hermaphrodite, with whom betrothal is of doubtful validity, are instances of marriage valid in rabbinical, but not Biblical, law. Cf. IV, I, iv, 9 ff.

2. Nid 5:4.

"Laws Concerning the Unfaithful Wife"—IV, v, ii, 3 (cf. Num. 5:11 ff.).

"she has reached the age when she may exercise the right of refusal"—Hebrew *mi'un.* If a minor given in marriage by her father was divorced or widowed during her minority and then remarried while still a minor, she was, upon coming of age, permitted to leave her husband, in case she conceived an aversion for him, without the formality of a divorce, but merely by exercising the right of refusal. Cf. IV, II, xi, 1 ff.; B. Yeb̲ 107a. Mi'un, however, was abolished in the 15th century (cf. YšŠ to Yeb̲ 13:17; DM, *'Eb̲en ha-'ezer,* 155).

"a priest"—cf. below, Chap. xvii–xviii.

3. B. Sanh 50b, 89a.

"bastard"—a child born out of incest; see below, Chap. xv.

"Temple bondsman"—Nathin, i.e. a descendant of the Gibeonites; Josh. 9:27. Cf. B. Yeb 78b.

4. Sanh 7:9.

"maiden"—Hebrew *na'ărah,* which refers to a girl between the ages of twelve years and twelve years and six months, cf. Nid 5:6, 7, and Deut. 22:23 ff. for the law.

"If she has attained maturity—i.e. is older than twelve years and six months.

"even if her father"—Ket 4:5.

"while on the way"—MT 142.

5. B. Sanh 66b.

"if a betrothed maiden"—according to Lev. 21:9 she must be burned; but cf. the discussion in B. Sanh 50a–b (Maimonides accepts the view of the Sages).

6. Sanh 7:9; B. *ibid.* 66b.

7. Ket 4:3 mentions only a proselyte; according to MM, Maimonides rightly includes the manumitted bondswoman also.

8. B. Ket 45a. Maimonides follows here Alfasi in making this novel distinction between the maiden who has not yet left her father's authority, and the one who has already done so.

"as we have explained"—above, Sec. 4.

"three kinds," etc.—B. Ket 44b and 45a.

9. *Ibid.* 44b, and Alfasi.

"If she had committed adultery," etc.—MT 142.

10. *Ibid.* 45a, and MO *ad loc.*

"the Place of Stoning"—a special place some distance from the court house; cf. Sanh 6:1.

11. Ket 4:3; B. *ibid.* 45b.

"the Place of Stoning"—MT 141.

12. B. Yeb 34a.

"the Laws Concerning Sin Committed through Error"—IX, IV, iv, 1 (YJS, 4, 96).

"as will be explained"—below, xvii, 9–10.

"more than one"—literally, "many."

13. Ker 2:5; B. *ibid.* 11a.

"the Laws Concerning Matrimony"—IV, I, iv, 16.

14. Ker 2:5.

15. Ker 2:4; B. *ibid.* 11a; Yeb 55a.

"*a lying of seed*"—i.e. in a normal manner which could lead to conception of offspring.

"two ways"—i.e. natural and unnatural. The words from "Similarly" to "unnaturally," and "that there are two ways," have been expunged from the Oxford MS.

16. Ker 2:4; B. *ibid.* 11a.

"upon him"—the Yemenite MSS have "upon them."

17. B. Sanh 69a. Maimonides bases this interpretation on the fact that the Talmud, *loc. cit.,* does not say that, conversely, when the man is not liable to a sacrifice, she is not liable to a flogging (MM).

Chapter IV

1. B. Yeḇ 54a; Nid 1:1; B. *ibid.*, 32a.
"even if she is a minor"—Nid 5:3; Sif Lev. 15:19.
2. Lev. 12:2–5; Sif Lev 12:2; B. Yeḇ 74b, and Tosafoṯ *ad loc.;* B. Ker 7b.
"a woman having a flux"—i.e. one who has a flow of blood outside her menstrual period.
3. B. Shab 54b; Nid 35b.
"the general rule"—an almost exact quotation from a Gaonic interpretation (OhG, IV, *Ḥăgigah,* p. 9); SER 16, and Friedmann's note 21.
4. Nid 4:3; B. *ibid.* 34a.
5. B. Nid 35b.
6. B. Yoma 6a; Pes 90b.
"on the eighth night"—i.e. in the evening of the seventh day, the Hebrew twenty-four hours beginning with sunset.
"as we have explained"—above, Sec. 2.
7. B. Nid 67b.
"misled"—into thinking that she was having her immersion on the seventh day.
"another menstruant"—the Talmud, *ibid.*, says "her daughter."
8. B. Nid 67b.
9. Nid 2:4; B. *ibid.* 15a ff., 11a; Keṯ 72a.
10. B. Keṯ 22a–b.
11. B. Sheḇu 17b and 18a.
12–13. B. Sheḇu 18b.
12. B. Nid 63b.
14. Nid 2:1 and 4.
15. B. Nid 17a.
16. Nid 1:7, 2:1; B. *ibid.* 11b, 12b.
"aged"—past the age of menstruation.
17. Nid 2:4; B. *ibid.* 16b.
18. Nid 8:4; B. *ibid.* 57b.
"blood is found"—the assumption is that she had examined the rag, and thinking it spotless placed it under the pillow, but when she later examined it again she discovered the spot.
19. B. Nid 14a.
20–21. B. Nid 65b, 66a; Keṯ 72a.
22. B. Nid 66a.
"the . . . edge folded over"—to eliminate the original sharp edge.
"Laws Concerning Matrimony"—cf. IV, 1, xxv, 7 ff.

Chapter V

1. B. Ker 8b.
"through a mishap"—B. Nid 36b, 20b.
"jumped from place to place," etc.—Zaḇ 2:2; B. Nid 11a.

"irrespective of the amount"—B. Nid 40a.

"mustard seed"—Nid 5:2.

2. Nid 5:1; B. *ibid.* 41b.

"between the glands"—P. Yeḇ 6:1; B. Nid 41b. According to Preuss, p. 136, "glands" refers to the *labia.*

"in her flesh"—i.e. the issue is still in her flesh; cf. Sec. 16.

3. Nid 2:5.

"The whole neck"—"whole" seems redundant. Cf. Preuss, p. 134.

4. Cf. PhM to Nid 2:5, where Maimonides gives his interpretation of this Mishnah based on his knowledge and experience in anatomy. His interpretation agrees with neither the Talmud nor other explanations.

"the Sages call this orifice 'the passage' "—B. Nid 17b.

5. Nid 2:5; B. *ibid.* 17b.

"as will be explained"—below, vii, 5.

"if he entered the Temple"—a person is liable to bring an offering for entering the Temple while in a state of ritual uncleanness, and heave offerings and hallowed things which come into contact with an unclean person must be burned. Cf. VIII, III, iii (YJS, *12,* 92 ff.).

6–7. Nid 2:6.

6. "viscous"—for this meaning of *sĕmiḳah,* see ṬYD 188, 1, and Ben Yehudah, *s.v.*

7. "like bright crocus"—*ḳeren* is so explained by Maimonides himself, PhM to Nid 2:6; cf. also Nid 2:7, Tos Nid 3:11. According to Löw (II, 11), however, the correct translation is "like the horn of the crocus."

8–10. Nid 2:7; B. *ibid.* 19a ff.

8. "Sikhnin"—in Galilee.

10. "Sharon"—the coastal plain of Palestine.

"A woman's statement," etc.—B. Nid 20b.

11–12. B. Nid 20b and 21a.

11. *"mina"*—100 *zuz,* the zuz being about 3½ grams.

"loḡ"—the volume of six eggs.

13. Nid 3:1.

14. B. Nid 21b and 22b. Maimonides apparently had here the reading *ḳĕru'ah,* "torn," whereas our text of the Gemara has *ḳorĕ'ah,* "he tears it" (MM). Cf. the same reading in Sec. 13, where Maimonides has "torn open," in order to differ with the view of R. Simeon ben Yoḥai in B. Nid 21b. Cf. MM and MO, *ad loc.*

15. Nid 3:2.

"insect"—literally, "abominable thing."

16. B. Nid 21b.

17. Nid 9:1.

"a sensation"—such as a woman feels at the onset of menstruation. Cf. below, viii, 2.

"rectum"—for the meaning of *ḥalḥoleṯ* see Preuss, p. 106.

18. Nid 10:1; B. *ibid.* 55a.

19. Nid 10:1.

"a maiden"—between the ages of twelve and twelve and a half.

"onset of menstruation"—cf. P. Ber 2:6.

"An adult woman"—above 12 years and 6 months; B. Nid 64b. For the reason why night and not day is designated, and why a virgin is given four days, cf. PhM to Nid 10:1. Night is specified because the Sages disapproved of intercourse in daytime as contrary to decency; a virgin is given four days because it was customary for a virgin to be married on a Wednesday (cf. Keṯ 1:1), which would give her the rest of that week.

20–24. B. Nid 64b ff.

25. "If a man has intercourse with a virgin"—B. Nid 64b.

"with a child"—B. Nid 45a. As in all such regulations relating to girls who have not yet reached sexual maturity—always bearing in mind that in the East women mature earlier than in the West—the jurist is concerned merely with the particular legal aspect that he is discussing at the moment. In general, the Sages strongly disapproved of sexual contact with immature females, for many reasons, including the basic rule that the primary purpose of sexual intercourse is the propagation of the species.

Chapter VI

1. B. Nid 35b.

2–3. B. Nid 72b.

3. "a rule given to Moses from Sinai"—defined by Maimonides himself (ThR 166; cf. Introduction to PhM) as any law which is not explicitly stated in Scripture, and has not been cited by the Sages as being implied in Scripture, but has been transmitted by them as having been revealed to Moses at Mount Sinai. Other authorities have disagreed with this definition. Cf. Jair Bacharach, *Ḥawwoṯ Ya'ir*, 192.

4–7. All these laws are derived from B. Nid 72b and 73a. For the normal count of menstrual and clean periods Maimonides' source is Alfasi, Sheḇu, *Hilḵoṯ Nid*, 3b (ed. Wilno); cf. MM, *ad loc.*, who quotes Nahmanides to B. Nid 54a (summarized by R. Nissim, *ad loc.*). Cf. also the excursus ascribed to Sherira Gaon, Tanḥ (regular recension), end of section *Mĕṣora'*.

6. "as will be explained"—below, vii, 2.

7. "she who awaits"—explained below, Sec. 9 ff.

"days"—B. Keṯ 75a; Sif Lev 15:25.

8. Meḡ 1:7; B. *ibid.* 8a–b; Nid 72b.

9–12. B. Nid 72a.

9. "If she has no flow during the night"—B. Meḡ 20a.

11. "two turtle doves"—cf. Lev. 15:29. B. Pes 90b.

12. "during . . . her uncleanness"—in which case the immersion is of no avail, having taken place at an improper time.

13. Nid 10:8.

"in suspense"—in such a case of doubt she should have been particularly careful not to risk transgression, and should have abstained from intercourse.

14. B Nid 67b.

15. B. Nid 33a.

16. B. Nid 33a and b, 42a. Cf. X, v, v, 11 ff. (YJS, *8*, 272).

"If she has a flow"—B. Nid 72b.

"as we have explained"—above, Sec. 1 ff.

17–18. Nid 10:8.

17. *"upon* (Hebrew *'al*) *the time of her impurity"*—the English translations render "beyond the time of her impurity," which is actually the interpretation given here by Maimonides.

"that upon which they sit or lie"—cf. Lev. 15:4.

19. Nid 6:14; B. *ibid.* 53b ff.

"out of doubt"—since twilight is regarded as forming part of both the preceding and the following day, it is uncertain whether she had the flow on the seventh or on the eighth day of her period.

"three successive days"—assuming that the twilight was part of the following (eighth) day, in which case she would become a woman with flux. On the other hand, it is also possible that the moment of the flow at twilight fell within the preceding (seventh) day, so that there were only two consecutive days (the ninth and tenth), in which case she would not be adjudged a woman with flux.

20. Nid 10:2; B. *ibid.* 68b.

21–22. *Ibid.;* B. *ibid.* 68b and 7b.

23. B. Nid 54b; Naz 29a.

"which must not be eaten"—since it is a doubtful case; cf. Rashi *ad loc.*

"in its proper place"—IX, v, i, 6 (YJS, *4,* 157).

Chapter VII

1. Nid 4:6; B. *ibid.* 36b.

"but not if it is stillborn"—B. Nid 38b.

2. B. Nid 36b, 7b.

3. B. Nid 36b.

4. *Ibid.,* and 21a, 54b.

"since the day of delivery immediately followed travail"—i.e. there must be pain immediately preceding the birth.

"and the nature of the issue of the miscarriage is not known," etc.—i.e. it is not clear whether it is a recognizable foetus or just a clot of blood. Cf. KM *ad loc.*

5. B. Nid 35b, 37a.

"the blood of purification"—cf. Lev. 12:4.

"the offering of a woman with flux"—cf. IX, v, i, 3 (YJS, *4,* 155 f.)

6. This is an elaboration of the previous Section.

"as will be explained"—below, xi, 14. B. Nid 54a.

7. Nid 4:3, B. *ibid.* 35b.

8. *Ibid.* The seven days of cleanness are ordained in Scripture, and upon their expiration render the woman ready for immersion and subsequent cleanness. Hence they cannot lawfully be counted as days of menstruation or flux, simply because they were followed by a flow of blood. The blood in itself, however, is unclean and therefore renders the woman unclean, hence she must immerse herself to rid herself of this specific uncleanness, without waiting another seven days of cleanness.

9. Nid 4:6.

"days of fulfillment"—cf. Lev. 12:6; and IX, v, i, 5 (YJS, *4,* 156).

"Even if they are twins"—cf. B. Ker 9b–10a.

10. B. Nid 37a.

11. B. Nid 54b, 37b. Cf. above, note to vi, 4–7.

12. B. Nid 38a.

"at twilight"—Nid 6:14.

"perchance it was night"—seeing that twilight may be part of either the preceding or the following day.

13. "We have already explained"—above, iv, 6.

14. B. Nid 54a.

"on alternate days"—excluding the nights.

"on four nights only"—a period of 18 days is assumed here in the case of a woman whose flow is not continuous, but takes place on alternate days. Such a woman is incapable of becoming a woman with flux, since her flow never continues for the required three consecutive days; she can only become a menstruant. But inasmuch as 11 days must elapse between one menstrual period and the next, she cannot be adjudged menstruant again until 18 days have elapsed since the onset of her previous menstrual period. Now after the expiration of the seven statutory days of uncleanness (although she had a flow on only four of them, the first, third, fifth, and seventh), during which she was forbidden to have sexual contact, she may have intercourse on the eighth, night and day. On the ninth she is unclean, and must await her day of cleanness on the tenth. On the following night, that of the eleventh, she may have intercourse, which makes her unclean on the following day, still the eleventh, and makes the twelfth the corresponding day of cleanness, with intercourse permitted the following night, of the thirteenth. And so forth, making in all four nights (the eleventh, thirteenth, fifteenth, and seventeenth), in addition to the statutory night and day of the eighth ordained in Scripture. Cf. MM, KM, and TYṬ to Nid 6:14.

15–24. These sections are a detailed analysis of B. Nid 54a.

16. "she may never have intercourse again"—the schedule here is as follows:

Seven-day menstrual period:

1st–3rd day—she has a flow;

4th–6th day—she has none;

7th day—she has a flow;

8th–9th day—she has a flow (to complete her customary three-day flow);

10th day—she has no flow, but must await the day against the preceding two days (8th–9th) of flow;

11th–12th day—she may have intercourse;

13th–15th day—she has a flow and must therefore be adjudged a woman with flux, since the statutory 11 days between two menstrual periods have not yet elapsed. She must consequently observe a 7-day period of cleanness; but since she is constitutionally unable to avoid a flow for a period longer than three days, she can never rid herself of her status as a woman with flux, and thus can never again be permitted to have intercourse.

The same reasoning applies to the following paragraphs.

21. " 'She may have intercourse for a quarter of her days' "—B. Nid 54a. According to Nahmanides and R. Nissim, *ad loc.,* this contradicts the calculation given above, vi, 4–7.

Chapter VIII

1. Nid 1:2 and 9:8.
2. Nid 9:8.
3. "We have already explained"—see above, iv, 12–13, 16.
4. Nid 9:10.
5–6. B. Nid 11a. The reading is according to the emendation of MM; cf. B. Nid 64a.
6. "on the seventeenth thereof"—the Oxford MS has "the eighteenth."
7–8. B. Nid 64a. Cf. Tos Nid 9:3–4.
9. B. Nid 11a, 39b, 68b. Once a menstrual period has begun, the following seven days are covered by the Scriptural command and must be counted as such, provided the flow continues, confirming the fact of menstruation. Hence the period cannot be fixed anywhere in the middle of these seven days. If, however, the flow is not continuous, thus throwing a doubt upon the fact of menstruation, the period may be fixed anywhere within these seven days when no flow appears upon that particular occasion (cf. MhM *ad loc.*, I, 77a).
"on those days of her menstruation"—or her flux.
10. Cf. above, vi, 6.
11. Nid 2:1; 3:7.
12–14. The leniency of Secs. 12–14 is due to Maimonides' decision that the uncleanness of fixed periods is of rabbinic and not Biblical sanction; cf. below, Sec. 14, and PhM, introd. to Ṭoh (ed. Derenbourg, p. 10); PhM to Nid 4:7.
12. B. Nid 16a.
13. "as will be explained"—see X, iv, iii, 7 (YJS, *8*, 216).
"retroactively"—B. Nid 6a.
"clean"—*ibid,* 16a.
14. "as will be explained"—see X, iv, iii, 9 (YJS, *8*, 217).
15. Nid 2:1.
16. Ar 2:1; B. *ibid.* 8a–b.
17–22. An elaboration of the law in Sec. 6, derived from the Talmudic passage quoted, and summed up in Sec. 22.
22. "eighteen"—literally, "seventeen."

Chapter IX

1. B. Nid 57b.
"as we have explained"—above, v, 2.
"as we have explained"—above, v, 5.
2. Nid 8:1–3; B. *ibid.* 5a, 58a.
3. Nid 1:1.
"as we have explained"—above, viii, 13.
"a bloodstain . . . upsets her normal count"—Nid 6:13.
4. Nid 1:1, 3; B. *ibid.* 4b.
"When is a woman considered pregnant?"—Nid 1:4; B. *ibid.* 8b; P. *ibid.* 1:3.
5. Nid 1:4, 5; B. *ibid.* 8b, 9a; P. *ibid.* 1:5.

"In the case of a virgin"—B. Nid 10b.

6. Nid 8:1; B. *ibid.* 57b.

"the stain's square area"—Neḡ 6:1.

"several drops"—B. Nid 59a. The combined area of the drops may not be counted towards the required minimum size, but the area of elongated stains may be so counted.

7. Nid 9:3; B. *ibid.* 60b.

"mixed manure and earth"—cf. PhM to Kel 10:1, and Hai Gaon to *ibid.*

"Even if she examines the ground"—B. Nid 59b.

"colored garments"—B. Nid 61b. A bloodstain is clearly visible against a white background, and much less so against a colored one.

8. Nid 8:1; B. *ibid.* 57b–58a.

"touch things automatically"—literally, "are busily occupied."

9. B. Nid 59a.

10–11. Nid 8:1.

12. Nid 6:13; B. *ibid.* 52b.

13–14. B. Nid 52b.

15. B. Nid 53b.

16–18. An elaboration, in the usual style of Maimonides, of the principle enunciated in Sec. 15.

19–28. Nid 8:2, 3; B. *ibid.* 57b–59a.

19. Cf. MM, *ad loc.;* and BY to ṬYD 190 (quoting Ibn Adret's interpretation).

21. "from the girdle upwards"—cf. R. Nissim to B. Nid 57b.

26. *"sela'"*—a coin equal in value to two shekels.

27. "red blood . . . black blood"—i.e. blood of lighter or darker red; cf. Preuss, p. 144.

28. "a woman need have no anxiety concerning bloodstains"—since swine grub in refuse and scatter blood in all directions.

29. Nid 9:3; B. *ibid.* 60a.

30–31. B. Nid 58a.

32–35. Nid 9:4–5; B. *ibid.* 59b ff.

33. "is past the menopause"—literally "is an old woman."

36–37. Nid 9:6.

37. "potash"—this is the modern Hebrew interpretation of the word *'ašlaḡ*. Danby (p. 108, n. 17) translates it 'lion's leaf." The etymology and original meaning of the word are unknown. Maimonides himself (PhM *ad loc.*) interpreted it as "soap" (Arabic *ṣābūn*).

38. Nid 9:7; B. *ibid.* 62a ff.

39. Cf. below, xi, 3.

"in this chapter"—above, Secs. 12–18.

"as we have explained"—above, Sec. 2.

Chapter X

1. Nid 3:7; Sif Lev 12:2; P. Pes 2:1.

2. *Ibid.;* Nid 3:3.

"articulated foetus"—*mĕrukkam,* literally "woven," i.e. articulated, with recognizable joints; cf. Preuss, p. 482, and see the next Section.

3. "At the beginning"—cf. B. Nid 25a–b; Tos *ibid.* 4:10.

"two eyeballs of a fly"—so Rashi *ad loc.;* Jastrow translates "two drippings."

"the mouth is open"—*paṭuaḥ* (as in P. Nid 3:3); Tos and B. have *maṭuaḥ*, "stretched," which seems more logical.

4. Nid 3:3.

"worm-shaped"—so interpreted by Maimonides, PhM to Nid 3:3; another interpretation is "varicolored," cf. B. Nid 24b, and Rashi *ad loc.*

5. Nid 5:1; B. *ibid.* 40a, 41a.

"from its mother's side"—presumably by way of Caesarean section. Cf. Preuss, p. 492 ff.

6. Nid 3:5; B. *ibid.* 28a, 29a.

7. B. Nid 28a.

8. Nid 3:2; B. *ibid.* 21 ff.

9. B. Nid 23b.

10. B. Nid 24b. Maimonides' view of the whole subject of human monster births is fully explained in PhM to Nid 3:2.

"one eye"—*ibid.* 23b.

11. B. Nid 23b, 24a (cf. 28a); Tos Nid 4:5; B. Nid 18a.

12. Nid 3:3; B. *ibid.* 25b.

13. B. Nid 26a.

"the caul"—*šilya,* so explained also in PhM to Nid 3:4 (see P. Nid 3:3; Lev. R. 14); this is divergent from the Talmudic interpretation of the word as the placenta. Cf. Preuss, p. 462.

14–15. B. Nid 24b ff.

15. "If part of the caul emerges"—B. BḲ 11a–b.

16. B. Nid 26b, 27a.

"double birth"—of a male and a female child. Cf. Rashi *ad loc.*

"had also dissolved"—in other words, it may be that there were two births, and that the foetus of the first and the caul of the second had dissolved, leaving only the foetus of the second and the caul of the first.

17. B. Nid 21; cf. above, v, 13.

18. Nid 3:5.

19. Nid 3:6; B. *ibid.* 29a.

20–21. This follows from the general rules which Maimonides has elaborated in Chapters vi–vii.

21. B. Nid 30b.

Chapter XI

1. "the law of the Torah"—cf. Alfasi, Shebu, Hilkot Nid 3b (ed. Wilno).

"Great Court"—or "the Great Beth-Din," i.e. the Sanhedrin. See XIV, III, i, 1 (YJS, *3,* 138).

"between blood and blood"—Sif *ad loc.;* B. Nid 19a; Sanh 87a.

2. "as we have explained"—above, iv, 4.

"before . . . ten days old," etc.—Nid 5:3; B. Nid 32a.

3. B. Nid 20b, 66a; Alfasi, Shebu, Hilkot Nid 2. Cf. R. Asher to Nid 10:6 (end).

4. B. Nid 67b; cf. commentary by the disciples of R. Jonah to Alfasi, Ber 5, 21b–22a (ed. Wilno).

"as we have explained"—above, iv, 8.

5–6. For the Gaonic source see *Ḥemdah gĕnuzah,* 68; Mordecai ben Hillel, *Rab̲ Mordĕk̲ay,* to Nid, 738.

5. "as we have explained"—above, vii, 5.

"the custom"—Alfasi, Shebu, *Hilk̲ot̲ Nid* 4a (ed. Wilno).

"Iraq"—literally "Šin'ar," cf. Gen. 11:2, 9.

"Palestine"—literally, 'the Land of Desire," with reference to Jer. 3:19 and Ezek. 20:6. Tanḥ *Mišpaṭim* 17.

"the Maghrib"—*Ma'ărab̲,* "the West," the regular Arab name for the North-Western littoral of Africa.

6. Cf. HG(H), p. 625.

"as we have explained"—above, vii, 7.

7. Cf. ShE(A), I, 90; SMG, negative commandment 111; Jacob Tam, *Sefer hay-yašar,* Nid, 155 (and the commentary, ed. Epstein, *ad loc.*).

8–11. B. Nid 66a.

10. "If . . . she is marrying a scholar"—B. Yeb̲ 37b.

11–13. The difference is due to the fact that the voluntary stringency was adopted only with regard to the actual appearance of blood.

11. "as we have explained"—Chap. ix.

14. Tanḥ Lev. 15:25.

15. For the Gaonic source cf. ŠT, fol. 18, no. 173; *Geonica, 2,* 153 (no. 576), and 146.

"Minim"—(sing. *"Min"*) the name used in the Talmud for persons who went their own way in deviation from traditional law and became to some extent heretics.

"Sadducees"—the term, as used in medieval Jewish literature, generally refers to the Karaites. For the Karaite law governing a woman delivered of a child, cf. Aaron ben Elijah, *Gan 'ed̲en,* 114a; and the references quoted in *Geonica, 2,* 204.

16. Cf. above, iv, 3. B. Er 4b.

"A woman"—Oxford MS: "A menstruant."

"in the Laws Concerning Immersion Pools"—X, VIII (YJS, *8,* 495 ff.).

17. B. Nid 67b.

18–19. ThR 99.

18. B. Shab̲ 13a–b.

"as we have explained"—above, Sec. 16.

19. B. Ket̲ 61a. This is repeated almost verbatim from IV, I, xxi, 8.

"A woman is permitted"—B. Shab 64b.

Chapter XII

1. B. AZ 36b.

"neither shalt thou," etc.—Maimonides interprets this verse in accordance with ŠRA, III, 68–69; cf. the commentary *ad loc.,* and B. Ḳid 68b.

"heathen"—literally "one who worships stars and planets," i.e. an idolater.

"the seven Canaanitish nations"—with whom intermarriage is expressly forbidden by Scripture, Deut. 7:3.

2. B. Ber 58a; Sanh 82a.

"If he has a continuous . . . relationship"—B. AZ 36b; cf. PhM to Shab 1:4 (no. 17).

3. B. Tem 29b; cf. B. Ḳid 21b.

"she cannot be betrothed to him"—a priest is forbidden to marry a harlot, Lev. 21:7.

4. B. AZ 36b.

"ten or more"—B. Sanh 74b.

"zealots"—B. Sanh 82a.

"a rule given to Moses"—see above, note to vi, 3.

"Phinehas and Zimri"—Num. 25:1–8.

5–6. B. Sanh 82a.

5. "resident stranger"—see xiv, 7.

6. "post-Mosaic Scripture"—literally "tradition," i.e. the Bible excluding the Pentateuch.

"the tents of Jacob"—that is, the halls of learning.

7. B. Yeḇ 23a; Sif Deut. 18:10; P. Sanh 9:7 (P. goes on to say that the Sages disapproved of zealots, and even of the action of Phinehas). Cf. XIII, v, i, 7 (YJS, 2, 262).

9. B. Sanh 57b.

10. This deduction by Maimonides from Scripture, whereby he extends the rule to minors, has no Talmudic authority. The parallel of an animal cited by him is found in B. Sanh 55b. As MM points out, B. Yeḇ 60b explicitly states that the verse refers to women of mature age, whether or not they had "known man by lying with him." Moreover, since no death penalty may be imposed in the Dispersion, this rule, like all similar rules, is of purely academic import and does not apply to actual practice. It must also be remembered that the entire discussion deals with heathens, i.e. worshipers of plural gods.

11. B. Sanh 58b. The laws concerning immersion of slaves are detailed below, xiii, 11 ff.

"Consequently"—B. Yeḇ 100b.

12. "as we have explained"—see iii, 13 ff.

13. B. Yeḇ 100b, 23a. Cf. Lev. R. 9, 25.

"Onkelos"—a proselyte who became a Sage (end of the first century). He is the author of the translation of the Pentateuch into Aramaic, the Targum Onkelos (B. Meḡ 3a). Although he rarely departs from literal translation, he renders this verse thus: "A woman of the daughters of Israel shall not marry a male slave, nor shall a man of the sons of Israel marry a slave woman."

14. This is a natural deduction from B. Sanh 82a.

15–16. Derived from Yeḇ 11:5.

15. "If the Israelite child is the owner of the slave child"—so Oxford MS.

"to enter the congregation"—that is, to marry an Israelite woman.

16. Cf. B. Ḳid 76a.

17. B. Yeḇ 47b. Cf. B. Giṭ 82a.

18–19. Yeḇ 8:3; B. *ibid.* 76b, 77a.

19. Cf. P. Yeḇ 8:3.

20. B. Yeḇ 78a, where a controversy is mentioned as to whether the status of the child follows that of the father or that of the mother. Maimonides rules that the status of both father and mother should be considered, and since one of the parents is of the first generation, the child is of the second (and not of the third, following the other parent). Cf. MM *ad loc.;* Abraham ben Moses ben Maimon, Responsa, 125.

21. B. Yeḇ 78b–79a.

22. *Ibid.;* Rashi *ad loc.* Cf. B. Ḳid 68b, 77a; P. Ket̲ 3:1, and *Mar'eh hap-panim, ad loc.;* P. Ḳid 4:1.

23–24. *Ibid.*

24. "the seven sons of Saul"—2 Sam. 21:4–9.

25. Yad̲ 4:4 (cf. SMG, negative commandment 116); B. Sanh 96b (cf. R. Shimshon on Yad̲ 4:4); Tos Yad̲ 2:17; B. Ber 28a; Tos Ḳid 5:4.

"are not the original Egyptians"—literally "are other men."

"an Ethiopian"—Maimonides, living in Egypt, where Ethiopians were plentiful, includes them, although they are not mentioned in Scripture in this connection.

Chapter XIII

1. MdRŠ, p. 97; B. Ker 9a; Ger 2:5; Abraham ben Moses ben Maimon, Responsa, 126.

2. Exod. R. 19.

"they all had abandoned . . . circumcision"—PRK, p. 52a, and Buber's notes thereto.

"with the exception of . . . Levi"—Sif Num. 9:5. Cf. Rashi to Deut. 33:9 and Josh. 5:5.

3. *"sanctify them"*—by immersion, B. Yeḇ 46b.

4–5. See above, note to Sec. 1.

6. B. Yeḇ 46a and b; P. *ibid.* 8:1.

"Sabbath," etc.—when no sessions of the court are held; P. Er 4:5.

7. B. Ket̲ 11a.

"a privilege"—"it is permitted to confer a boon upon a person without his knowledge" (Er 7:11).

"a pregnant woman"—B. Yeḇ 78a.

"If the proselyte immerses himself privately"—B. Yeḇ 47a.

"If he comes forth and declares"—B. Yeḇ 46b.

8. B. Yeḇ 47a.

"invalidating his children's status"—see Tosafot̲ to B. Yeḇ 47a, *s.v. ne'ĕman.*

9. B. Yeḇ 47a; P. Ḳid 3:12; Alfasi Yeḇ 4 (p. 30); B. Yeḇ 45b.

"separating the heave offering"—see VII, III, iii. Although the duty of separating the *ḥallah* (priest's share) is obligatory on both men and women, it came to be regarded as the prerogative of women. Cf. B. Ket̲ 72a; ŠYD 328, 3, and *Bet̲ Hillel, ad loc.*

10. Cf. B. Pes 3b. See Ger 4; MO *ad loc.,* and the sources quoted there.

"a higher standard"—cf. below, xv, 21. In the Land of Israel all people were presumed to be Israelites. Outside of the Land this presumption could not obtain in the case of an individual who was not of Israelite origin, consequently it was incumbent upon him to bring proof of his having become a proselyte in the proper manner, before he was allowed to marry an Israelite woman. "I say" indicates that the following explanation of the purpose of this regulation is Maimonides' own. Cf. RABD and MM *ad loc.*

11. B. Yeḇ 45b, 46a.

"Consequently"—if the master wishes to retain the slave in his possession.

12. B. Yeḇ 47b, 48a.

"whereby"—so Oxford MS (*šebbah*).

13. B. Yeḇ 47b.

"interposition"—between the body and the water, rendering the immersion invalid.

14. B. Yeḇ 24b, 47a, 76b; see also below, note to Sec. 16.

"the beloved of the Lord"—"Jedidiah," 2 Sam. 12:25.

"the yoke of the Torah"—a metaphorical expression signifying the total of the divine commandments which are voluntarily and joyfully accepted by the believer. B. Yeḇ 47a.

15. A harmonizing of two contradictory statements in B. Yeḇ 76b and 79a (MM). Cf. P. Ḳid 4:1.

"laymen"—not an authorized court.

16. P. Sanh 2:6; Song R. 1, 10 (Solomon); P. Soṭ 1:8; Num. R. 9, 25 (Samson); B. Shab 56b.

"Scripture"—Judg. 14:3, 1 Kings 11:4.

17. B. Yeḇ 47b, 24b.

"to return to him his lost property"—it is a Scriptural obligation (Deut. 22:3) to restore a lost article to its Israelite owner; in the case of an idolater, the obligation is only moral (B. Ket 15b).

18. B. Yeḇ 109b, 47b; Ḳid 70b. Several explanations are offered by the Tosaṭoṯ (*ad loc.*): proselytes are apt to be insufficiently careful in observing the commandments, and Israelites might be misled by them into doing likewise; Scripture demands that proselytes be treated with utmost kindness and consideration, a requirement to which Israelites, owing to natural human failings, might not measure up fully; proselytes sometimes turn out to be even more observant than Israelites, thus causing the latter to be punished by Heaven for not attaining the same heights of piety.

"a scab upon the skin"—so Oxford MS.; the printed text has "the plague of leprosy."

"golden calf"—Exod. 32; Exod. R. 42.

"Kibroth Hattaavah—Num. 11:34.

"trials"—Num. 14:22.

"the mixed multitude"—Num. 11:4, interpreted as meaning proselytes; see Targum Jonathan to Num. 11:4, and Sif Num. 11:3–4.

Chapter XIV

1–5. B. Yeḇ 47a–b.

"righteous proselytes"—in contradistinction to "the proselytes of lions" (2 Kings 17:25), who go over to Judaism for an ulterior motive.

2. "gleanings . . . poor man's tithe"—i.e. one's duties toward the poor. See Lev. 19:9–10; Deut. 14:29.

"poor man's tithe"—so B. Yeb̲ 47b and Oxford MS; the printed text has "second tithe," which is obviously a scribal error.

5. "all heathen," etc.—Tanḥ to Deut. 29:9.

"for him"—so Oxford MS.

"he should be left to go on his way"—Ger 1:2.

"If he is already circumcised"—B. Shab 135a.

"blood of the covenant"—from the genital organ.

6. B. Yeb̲ 46b, 47b. Cf. Aaron Peraḥiah, *Paraḥ maṭṭeh 'Ahăron* (Amsterdam, 1703), II, 90 (no. 51).

"in the presence of the court"—the attending women make her sit down in the water up to her neck, this being a preliminary preparation, and not the immersion itself, which must be witnessed by the court. Thereupon the members of the court enter and observe her sitting in the water, after which she must rise and go down once more into the water, this now constituting the statutory act of immersion. But for reasons of public decency, the moment she begins to rise, the judges must turn around and commence departing thence, while she completes the act of immersion behind their backs.

7. B. AZ 64b; XIV, v, viii, 11 (YJS, *3*, 230); PhM to Ḥul 7:6; B. BḲ 38a.

"descendants of Noah"—i.e. the human race.

"pious individuals of the nations of the world"—who "have a portion in the world to come" (Tos Sanh 13:1).

"Laws Concerning Idolaters"—I, v, x, 6.

8. B. Ar 29a; Beḳ 30b; Tos Demai 2:5.

9. B. Yeb̲ 48a and b.

"Why do you come?"—see above, Sec. 1.

"at such time as the law of the Jubilee is in force"—so that he would go free in the year of Jubilee (Lev. 25:47 ff.). Cf. P. Yeb̲ 8:1.

10. B. Sanh 57b, 58a.

"Laws Concerning Kings and Wars"—XIV, v, ix, 5 ff. (YJS, *3*, 232–233).

11. B. Yeb̲ 22a, 97b.

12. B. Yeb̲ 22a.

"According to the Torah"—since the Scriptural law of incest is taken to apply only to Israelites.

"a proselyte"—so B. *ibid.* and the MSS; the printed text has "heathen."

13. B. Yeb̲ 97b ff.

14. B. Yeb̲ 97b.

"conceived while their mother was a non-Israelite"—literally, "not in sanctity."

"after their mother had become a proselyte"—literally, "in sanctity."

15. B. Yeb̲ 98b.

"as we have explained"—above, Sec. 13.

16. B. Yeb̲ 22a.

"secondary degrees"—See IV, 1, i, 6.

17. B. Sanh 58b; P. Yeb̲ 11:2.

18. When Maimonides says "it would appear to me" (cf. xii, 10, and below) he states his own deduction. B. Yeb̲ 45a; see MO *ad loc.*

19. B Yeb̲ 97b; Tem 30a; MdRŠ to Exod. 21:4.
"as cattle"—B. Yeb̲ 98a.

Chapter XV

1. Yeb̲ 4:13.
"except by a menstruant"—B. Yeb̲ 49b.
"whether by force or by consent"—B. Hag̃ 9b–10a; cf. HP, p. 142.
"both male and female"—Yeb̲ 8:3.

2. B. Ḳid 78a. See MM for Maimonides' own reply to the question of the Sages of Lunel concerning this passage; cf. ThR 152; his son's, R. Abraham's, reply, in his *Birḳat̲ 'Ab̲raham* (ed. Goldberg), 43.
"he is not liable to a flogging on account of bastardy"—so Oxford MS.
"as will be explained"—below, xvii, 3.
"If a man remarries"—B. Yeb̲ 11b.
"forbidden union"—although such a remarriage is prohibited (Deut. 24:4), it does not belong to the forbidden unions.

3–5. B. Yeb̲ 45b; cf. Solomon ibn Adret's novella *ad loc.*

3. B. Ḳid 66b.

4. B. Ḳid 69a.

6. P. Ḳid 3:13; B. Yeb̲ 78b; Ḳid 66b, 67a.

7. B. Ḳid 72b; 73a, 67b.

8–9. B. Ḳid 75a.

10. Ḳid 4:3; Yeb̲ 10:1.
"as we have explained"—above, Sec. 1.

11. B. Ḳid 74a.
"such as she could not lawfully marry"—so Oxford MS (*pĕsulin lah*).

12. P. Ket̲ 1:9; B. Ḳid 73a, 69a.
"Nathin"—see above, xii, 23.
"*šĕt̲uḳi*" (pl. *šĕt̲uḳim*)—literally, "one who stands silent (regarding his parentage)."

13. Ḳid 4:1.

14. B. Kid 74a. Cf. Responsa of Isaac ben Sheshet Perfet, 41.
"It would appear to me"—cf. above, note to xiv, 18; Responsa of Alfasi, 38.
"as we have explained"—above, Sec. 12.

15. Ḳid 4:8; B. *ibid*. 78b; Yeb̲ 47a.
"the father is not to be believed"—otherwise his statement would make his grandchildren also illegitimate.

16. Ḳid 4:8; B. Yeb̲ 47a.
"the son of a divorcée" etc.—in which case he is disqualified for the priesthood; see below, Chap. xix.

17. B. Yeb̲ 69b; Ket̲ 13b, 14a.
"a betrothed maiden"—is regarded as a married woman, although the marriage has not yet been consummated.
"legitimate"—for the priesthood.

18. B. Yeb̲ 70a.

19. "in this matter"—so Oxford MS (*bĕ-dab̲ar zeh*). Since the husband can-

not prove that her statement is false, the case comes under the rule stated above, Sec. 3, to the effect that a child born of a union between an Israelite woman and a heathen or slave is valid.

"twelve months"—B. Yeb̠ 80b; Preuss, p. 444.

20. B. Soṭ 27a.

"If she is excessively dissolute"—i.e. if most of her intercourse is not with her husband.

21. B. Ḳid 73a.

22. Ḳid 4:3.

23. Ḳid 4:3; B. *ibid.* 73a, 74a.

"marry proselytes"—cf. above, Sec. 7.

24. Cf. above, Sec. 7.

25–26. B. Ket̠ 15b; Mak 2:7 (and PhM *ad loc.*); B. Yoma 84b.

25. "was not executed for it"—cf. MhM (I, 14a–b) to II, 1, ii, 20. Since Jewish law is not obligatory upon non-Jews, the capital punishment imposed by Scripture for manslaughter is taken to apply only where the victim is an Israelite, whereas the foundling in this case may really be of heathen descent. Moreover, the rule given here is of purely academic interest, since the slaying of a non-Jew would come under the jurisdiction of the non-Jewish authorities anyway.

26. P. Yeb̠ 8:1.

"If the court," etc.—see above, xiii, 7.

"lost articles must be restored"—cf. above, note to xiii, 17.

"to clear away a pile of debris"—which must be done for an Israelite. B. Sanh 72b, Ket̠ 15b. See also ThR 61, and KM to III, 1, ii, 20.

"With respect to civil damages"—BḲ 3:11. In other words, he has all the rights and privileges of an Israelite.

27–29. Cf. above, note to xiv, 18. In the passage B. Ket̠ 15b the possibility of his marriage being certainly valid is not included.

27. "as we have explained"—above, Sec. 23.

29. "and our Sages have said"—B. Yeb̠ 37b.

"were to do this"—i.e. expose his daughter to prostitution.

30–32. B. Ḳid 73b.

31. "salted," etc.—cf. Preuss, pp. 467 ff.

33. Ḳid 4:3; and above, Sec. 7.

Chapter XVI

1. Yeb̠ 8:2; B. *ibid.* 76a.

2. P. Yeb̠ 8:2; B. *ibid.* 76a.

3–4. Yeb̠ 8:2; B. *ibid.* 75b; PhM to Yeb̠ 8:1.

5. B. Yeb̠ 76a.

6. B. Yeb̠ 75b.

7. B. Yeb̠ 75a.

8. B. Yeb̠ 76a.

9. B. Yeb̠ 75b. Cf. PhM to Yeb̠ 8:2; for the explanation of the seeming contradiction see Responsa of Jacob Berab, 2.

10–11. Sif Lev. 22:24; Tos Mak 5:6.

10. "or unclean"—B. Haḡ 14b.

"continues the process of castration"—B. Shab 111a.

11. "a female"—Sif Lev. 22:24. While the castration of females is thus theoretically lawful (since only men are presumed to be subject to the Biblical command to be fruitful and multiply), it was never actually practiced to any traceable extent; cf. Preuss, p. 438.

12. B. Shab 110b.

"A woman is permitted"—Tos Yeb̲ 8:4.

"sets a dog"—Sanh 9:1; cf. B. BḲ 24b. While legally he is not punishable, the suggested flogging for disobedience indicates the Sages' feeling that morally he is guilty.

13. B. BM 90b; ThR 139.

Chapter XVII

1. Lev. 21:14.

"Israelites of priestly descent"—it is a question of descent, and not of priestly function.

"a harlot"—see below, Chap. xviii.

"a profaned woman"—see below, Chap. xix.

"Whether he is a High Priest"—Sif Lev. 21:14; B. Hor 12b.

"a High Priest installed," etc.—for the first three categories see Meḡ 1:9, and Rashi *ad loc.* The oil used in anointing high priests since the time of Moses is said to have ceased by the time of King Josiah, and subsequently high priests were installed merely by investiture with the additional eight high priestly vestments (cf. Yoma 7:8; PhM to Meḡ 1:9). If the officiating High Priest became temporarily unfit for office because of ritual uncleanness, a substitute High Priest replaced him until such time as the former was again fit to resume his duties.

"the priest anointed as the chaplain of the army"—Deut. 20:2; Soṭ 8:1.

2. B. Ḳid 78a; Abraham ben Moses ben Maimon, *Birḵaṯ 'Aḇraham,* 43.

"taḵe"—i.e. "take in marriage"; cf. B. Ḳid 2a.

3–4. B. Ḳid 78a.

5. B. Ker 10b.

"as we have explained"—above, iii, 14.

6. B. Tem 29b. See above, xii, 3.

7. B. Yeb̲ 24a.

"for disobedience"—B. Mak 13a, and Tosafoṯ *ad loc.*

8. B. Ker 14a–b.

9–10. B. Ḳid 77a.

"the sequence . . . is different"—e.g., if she becomes profaned before she is divorced, in which case the rule in Sec. 8 does not apply.

11. B. Ḳid 77a; Yeb̲ 6:4.

12. Yeb̲ 2:3; 6:4; B. *ibid.* 20a.

"If she becomes subject"—i.e., if she is left as the childless widow of his brother.

"betrothed her to himself by a verbal declaration"—Sif Lev. 21:14; B. Yeb̲ 59a.

"If . . . he had betrothed any other widow"—Sif Lev. 21:14.

13. Yeb̲ 6:4; B. *ibid.* 61b.

"virgin maiden"—Sif Lev. 21:14; a girl between the ages of 12 years and 12 years and 6 months.

"He may never marry two wives"—see MO; B. Yeb̲ 59a (and Rashi *ad loc.*). Cf. B. Yoma 13a.

14. Yeb̲ 6:4; and B. *ibid.* 59a–b.

"she is permitted"—the rule is purely theoretical, on the ground that intercourse with an animal does not come under the heading of harlotry; since such intercourse is punishable scripturally by stoning, the High Priest could not marry the guilty girl anyway. Cf. below, xviii, 1.

15–16. B. Yeb̲ 60a.

17–18. B. Yeb̲ 59a.

18. "right of refusal"—cf. above, iii, 3, and note; Yeb̲ 13:2.

"as we have explained"—IV, II, xi, 16.

"is not . . . invalidated"—Yeb̲ 4:1.

19. B. Giṭ 81a.

20. See IV, II, x, 20; B. Giṭ 89a.

21. B. Giṭ 89a.

"transgression against Israelite custom"—cf. Ket̲ 7:6, where examples are given: a woman who leaves her home with her hair disheveled, spins in the market place (thus exposing her bare arms to strangers), speaks to everyone she meets, curses her husband's father to his—the husband's—face, and is immodestly loud voiced. Cf. also IV, I, xxiv, 12.

Chapter XVIII

1. B. Yeb̲ 68a, 61a; Ḳid 77b; PhM to Ḳid 4:6; B. Ḳid 67a; TYṬ to Yeb̲ 6:5. As Maimonides explains here, and below, in Sec. 5, the term "harlot" in this legal usage has nothing to do with immorality, but signifies a woman who is legally unfit to marry an Israelite or a priest, whether or not the cause of disability is of her own doing.

"an unfit priest"—a priest's son born out of wedlock.

"if a woman has intercourse"—B. Yeb̲ 59b.

"not . . . rendered a harlot"—B. Yeb̲ 60a.

2. Sif Lev. 22:12; Yeb̲ 6:5; B. *ibid.* 61b; P. *ibid.* 6:3.

3. Yeb̲ 6:5; B. *ibid.* 61b, 68a.

"a slave"—so MSS and editio princeps; omitted in the later editions.

"Ammonite," etc.—see above, Chap. xii.

"levirate marriage"—i.e. with a priest.

4. B. Yeb̲ 85a; P. *ibid* 5:4; 2:8.

"as we have explained"—IV, III, vi, 7.

5. "as will be explained"—below, xix, 16.

"as we have said"—above, Sec. 1.

6. B. Yeb̲ 56b; Ket̲ 14b.

7. B. Yeb̲ 56b.

"*neither she be taken in the act*"—the preceding portion of the verse reads, *and it be hid from the eyes of her husband, she being defiled secretly, and there be no witness against her.*

8. B. Ned̲ 90b; Soṭ 6a; Ḳid 66a.

"had set her eyes upon another man"—and wishes to be divorced in order to marry him.

9. B. Ned 90b.

"in the same manner as a person who declares," etc.—in which case it is in all circumstances forbidden to the person who makes the declaration.

10–11. B. Ket 9a.

10. "as we have explained"—above, Sec. 7.

12. B. Soṭ 28a; cf. IV, v, i–ii.

"If a man suspects"—the Scriptural ritual of the curse-causing water is set forth in Num. 5:11 ff. Its use was discontinued in the first century of the Christian era (cf. Soṭ 9:9).

13. Ket 1:9; B. *ibid.* 14a.

"a man of legitimate status"—so that the resulting child would have the same status, and would not be deemed a bastard.

14. B. Ket 14a ff.

"at a crossroads," etc.—i.e. publicly.

15. B. Ket 15a.

"in the case of a fixed object," etc.—cf. below, II, viii, 11, and note thereto.

16. Derived from B. Ket 15a; MM.

17. Ket 2:5, 9; B. *ibid.* 27b, 23a.

18. B. Ket 27b; B. BḲ 114b.

"and talking in his innocence," etc.—so Oxford MS, reading *wĕ-hayah* for *u-bĕnah,* and omitting *'ăni wĕ-'immi.*

19. Ket 2:9; B. *ibid.* 27b.

"in his own behalf"—since the effect of his testimony is to permit him to continue to live with his wife.

20. B. Ket 36b.

21. Ket 2:5; B. *ibid.* 23b.

"since the mouth that forbids," etc.—the only evidence that she was taken captive is her own statement.

22. Ket 2:5; B. *ibid.* 23a.

"the captor enters"—i.e. enters the courtroom where her case is being considered.

23. B. Ket 23b; Ḳid 12a–b.

24. Ḳid 3:8.

25. B. Ket 27b.

26–29. Ket 2:9; B. *ibid.* 27a.

26. "as we have explained"—above, Sec. 17.

30. Ket 2:9; B. *ibid.* 26b.

"as we have explained"—above, Sec. 19.

Chapter XIX

1. Sif Lev. 21:14–15; B. Ḳid 77a.

"profaned woman"—a woman whose marriage to a priest is unlawful, or the female issue of such a marriage; the term is again purely legal, and has nothing to do with moral, or even social, degradation.

2. Yeḇ 6:1.
"This applies"—cf. above, i, 13.
3. "a non-virgin"—B. Yeḇ 59a.
"widowed or divorced"—Yeḇ 6:3; B. *ibid.* 59a.
"even if she is found in fact to be still a virgin"—since it is physically possible for intercourse to take place with only partial loss of the tokens of virginity, or none at all.
4. Yeḇ 6:4; P. Ḳid 4:6; cf. above, xvii, 14–15.
5. B. Ḳid 77b.
"as we have explained"—above, xviii, 1.
"the child is . . . valid"—B. Yeḇ 49b.
6. Yeḇ 2:5; B. Ḳid 78a.
"with a menstruant"—Sif Lev 21:14; B. Yeḇ 60a.
7. B. Yeḇ 100b; Rashi *ad loc.;* B. Ḳid 77a.
8. B. Yeḇ 85a; P. *ibid.* 5:4, 9:4.
"We have already explained"—above, xvii, 7.
9. B. Keṯ 14a.
10. Yeḇ 11:5; B. Soṭ 6a; Yeḇ 100b; Sanh 5b; Sif Lev. 21:1.
11. B. Ḳid 73a.
"as we have explained"—above, Sec. 6.
12. B. Yeḇ 57a; Ḳid 4:7.
13. Sif Lev. 21:14; B. Yeḇ 77a; Keṯ 77a.
"as we have explained"—above, xviii, 3.
14. Ḳid 4:6.
15–16. Ḳid 4:1.
15. "not his mother's house"—B. BB 109b.
17. B. Ḳid 76b, 70a; Yeḇ 79a.
"Nevertheless, should you see"—B. Ḳid 71b.
"at the beginning"—Josh. Chap. 9.
18. Ḳid 4:4 (cf. PhM *ad loc.*); B. *ibid.* 76b.
19. Ḳid 4:4.
"intermingling," etc.—P. Ḳid 4:4.
20–21. B. Ḳid 76b.
22. B. Keṯ 14b.
"as we have explained"—above, Secs. 18–19.
23. Eḏ 8:3; B. Ḳid 75a.
"as we have explained"—above, xviii, 1.

Chapter XX

1. ThR 352. B. Keṯ 24b, 25a; Ḳid 76a.
"Heave offering and dough offering"—see VII, ii.
2. Ḳid 4:5.
"the Great Court"—the Sanhedrin during the period of the Temple.
3. B. Keṯ 25a.
"not of only a part of it"—cf. ShM, p. xv, n. 23.
"Similarly, heave offering," etc.—B. Yeḇ 82a.

4. "If witnesses"—so Oxford MS, omitting "two," found in the printed text and in MM.

"eating of the heave offering"—cf. B. Ket̲ 24b. The reason is that the penalty for an unauthorized person is death, hence it may be assumed that if the eater had not been a genuine priest, he would not have exposed himself to so grave a risk. Cf. MM.

"may not be elevated"—B. Ket̲ 25a–b.

"the priestly benediction"—literally, "the raising of the hands," Num. 6:22–26.

"first to the reading of the Torah"—a privilege of the priest, B. Giṭ 59b.

"on the evidence of a single witness"—Ket̲ 2:8, and TYṬ *ad loc.;* B. *ibid.* 23b; P. *ibid.* 2:7, and the commentaries thereto.

5. B. Ket̲ 25b.

"that he is his son"—i.e. his son by a marriage that is valid for a priest.

6. Ḳid 4:10.

7–8. Ḳid 4:11; B. *ibid.* 79b.

9. B. Ket̲ 24b.

10. B. Ket̲ 25b.

"to be presumed a priest"—i.e. a present-day priest, but not one of proven genealogy.

11. Ket̲ 2:7; B. *ibid.* 24a.

"and a Levite was called up after him"—if there is no priest in the synagogue, an Israelite may be called up instead, but he may not be followed by a Levite.

12. B. Ket̲ 26a.

13. Ket̲ 2:8 requires at least one witness. Cf. P. Naz 8:1.

"Nevertheless, he thereby renders himself forbidden"—in accordance with the principle "he has made it forbidden to himself."

14. B. Ket̲ 26a; BḲ 114b.

"immersed me"—an immersion was required to free one's self from uncleanness before the heave offering could be eaten; cf. Ber 1:1.

"Rabbi Judah han-Naśi' "—the compiler of the Mishnah (135–210).

15. Deduced from B. Ket̲ 26a; Ket̲ 2:10.

16. B. Ket̲ 26a, and Rashi *ad loc.;* in this case the general rule of following the majority of witnesses (in case the negative witnesses should outnumber the positive ones) is inoperative, since the original presumption is taken as primary proof, which is made unassailable by the testimony of the two favorable witnesses.

17. Yeḇ 11:7.

"seven months"—according to the Talmud (B. Yeḇ 42a; cf. Preuss, p. 456), the minimum age for a viable foetus is six months and a day. This is referred to as "seven months," but it naturally requires a three months waiting period.

18. Yeḇ 11:7.

"he may attend the watches"—the priests were divided into 24 watches, each one of which did duty for one week every six months. Cf. Ta 2:6.

19–20. B. Yeḇ 100b.

Chapter XXI

1. Sif Lev. 18:6 and 19; B. Shab 13b; Yeb̲ 55a; Exod. R. 16.
2. Ab̲ 3:13; B. Shab 62b, 64b; cf. PhM to Sanh 7:4; ThR 163.
"at a woman's little finger"—B. Ber 24a.
"the singing . . . or . . . her hair"—Maimonides apparently interprets the passages in B. Ber 24a, "(listening to) the (singing) voice of a woman is an act of forbidden union," and "(looking at) the hair of a woman is an act of forbidden union," to mean, "it is forbidden to listen to the singing voice or to look at the hair of a woman if intercourse with her would constitute an act of forbidden union."
3. B. Ḳid 41a; B. AZ 61a; PhM to Sanh 7:4.
4. B. Ned̲ 20a; Shab 13a.
5. B. Ḳid 70a; P. Ket̲ 5:6.
"A man may not inquire," etc.—what is meant is a married woman; the inquiry should be made of her husband.
6. B. Shab 13a; cf. B. AZ 17a.
7. Ḳid 4:12; B. *ibid.* 80b, 81b.
"if she is married"—but is still underage and continues living with her parents.
8. Sif Lev. 18:3; B. Yeb̲ 76a, 55b.
"they are not forbidden for the priesthood"—B. Yeb̲ 76a.
9. B. Ned̲ 20b.
"to no purpose"—B. Nid 13a.
"the Laws Concerning Knowledge"—I, III, V, 4–5.
10. B. Shab 86a, and Rashi *ad loc.;* B. Nid 16b; Beṣ 22a.
"Sabbath"—when it is forbidden to extinguish the light.
"the way of sanctity"—B. Ned̲ 20b.
11. B. Shab 152a; Ber 22a.
12–13. B. Ned̲ 20b.
13. "or seduces a man," etc.—the literal meaning of the text is "the man who seduces a woman," etc., but the context makes it clear that this passage deals with acts of wantonness forbidden to a woman, and not to a man, and the mention of Rachel and Leah later on is an obvious reference to Gen. 29:23, where Leah substituted herself for Rachel and deceived Jacob.
"become separated"—cf. Ezek. 20:38, and the Targum, and Ḳimḥi's commentary thereto.
14. B. Sanh 46a.
"by an act of intercourse"—B. Yeb̲ 52a; Ḳid 12b, in spite of Ḳid 1:1.
15. B. Ket̲ 65a.
"Similarly"—B. BB 98b; Ḳid 12b.
"nor . . . enter a bathhouse"—B. Pes 51a.
16. B. Pes 51a.
17. Ket̲ 7:6.
"nor should a woman walk"—B. Sanh 19a, and Rashi *ad loc.*
18. B. Nid 13a, 14b; Yeb̲ 34b; cf. Sec. 9, above.
"a minor"—B. Ḳid 41a.

"masturbators"—see LhR 1551 (177).

19. B. Nid 13b; Ḳid 30b; cf. ARN, Chap. 20 (YJS, *10,* 94–5).

"and back"—adding *wĕ-yašuḇ,* with the Oxford MS.

"sleep on his back"—B. Ber 13b; Nid 14a.

20. B. AZ 20b.

"Animal breeders"—B. BM 91a.

21. B. Mak 20a; BB 57b; AZ 20b.

"he is even forbidden," etc.—B. AZ 20b, which reads "brightly colored" (*ṣeḇa'*) as does the Oxford MS, instead of "woolen" (*ṣemer*) of the printed text. Having seen the woman wearing these fine clothes before, they would remind him of her enhanced beauty and lead him to unchaste thoughts.

22. B. Ber 61a; Ḳid 81a.

"A man is forbidden to pass by"—B. AZ 17a.

23. B. Nid 13a–b.

24. B. Shab 118b, 53b; PhM to Sanh 7:4.

"One of the early pietists"—R. Jose, called "a pious man" (*ḥasiḏ,* Aḇ 2:11) by his teacher, R. Joḥanan ben Zakkai; cf. Soṭ 9:15, where he is described as "of the small remnants of the pious ones."

25. B. Yeḇ 62b; Sanh 76b.

"and thou shalt think," etc.—this is evidently how Maimonides understood this verse in this particular context.

26. B. Yeḇ 61b, 62b; Sanh 76b; Tos Yeḇ 8:4; B. Yeḇ 44a.

"a barren woman"—see IV, I, xv, 7.

"a woman, on the other hand, may," etc.—Yeḇ 6:6; cf. IV, I, xv, 2.

27. B. Keṯ 27b, 28a.

28. B. Yeḇ 37b. See IV, II, x, 21.

29. B. Yeḇ 37b. Cf. ThR 155.

30–31. B. Yeḇ 64b; PhM to Beḳ 7:5.

31. "she need not be divorced"—see ThR 170; Responsa of Solomon ibn Adret, III, 364; and of Isaac ben Sheshet Perfet, 241.

"An unlettered Israelite"—B. Pes 49a–b.

32. B. Pes 49b.

Chapter XXII

1. Ḳid 4:12; B. *ibid.* 80b.

"If a bride"—B. Keṯ 4a.

2. B. Ḳid 82a.

"the greatest among the Sages"—B. Ḳid 81b: "Abaye, Rab Sheshet, and others."

"on the authority of tradition"—B. Ḳid 80b and AZ 36b say that it is Scriptural. Cf. Responsa of Solomon ibn Adret, I, 587.

3. B. Sanh 21a; AZ 36b.

"Amnon and Tamar"—2 Sam. Chap. 13.

"Shammai and Hillel"—the last of the "pairs" and the founders of the two Tannaitic schools (first century).

"the flogging," etc.—B. Ḳid 81a.

4. Ḳid 4:12; B. AZ 25b.
5–6. B. AZ 15b; AZ 2:1.
6. ThR 139.
"we have already explained"—above, xiv, 10.
7. B. AZ 22b.
8. Ḳid 4:12; B. *ibid.* 80b.
"One woman should not be alone"—LhR 1571 (207).
"whose business"—Ḳid 4:14.
9. B. Ḳid 81b.
10. Deduced from B. Ḳid 82b; cf. B. Sanh 55b.
11. Tos Bik 2:3; cf. KM, and Responsa of Menahem Azariah Fano, 130.
12. B. Ḳid 81a.
13. Ḳid 4:13; B. *ibid.* 83a; ThR 169, 182.
14. B. Sanh 19a.
15. P. Ket̲ 1:8; B. Nid 30b.
"an administrator"—B. Ber 63a.
16. B. AZ 22b.
"Nor should a woman"—B. BM 71a; cf. XII, v, ix, 6 (YJS, *5*, 280).
17. Hag̃ 2:1; B. *ibid.* 11b.
18. Sif Num. 11:10; B. Shab 130a; and Rashi to Num. 11:10.
19. B. Hag̃ 11b; Yoma 75a.
"have declared also"—B. BB 165a.
20. B. Ḳid 81b.
"The greatest of our Sages"—R. Meir and R. Tarfon.
21. Ab̲ 3:14.
"Nor should a man"—B. Yeb̲ 62b.
"But above all this"—B. Ḳid 30b.
"a heart devoid of wisdom"—MiM 24.
"and of wisdom"—B. Er 54b.

Treatise II: Forbidden Foods

Chapter I

1. Sif Lev. 11:3; B. Ḥul 66b (for fish). In ShM, positive commandments 149–152, Maimonides quotes the verses from which all this is derived. Cf. LM.

"animals, beasts"—Scripture differentiates between *běhemah,* domesticated cattle, here called animals, and *ḥayyah,* beast of chase, here referred to as beasts.

2. Ḥul 3:6; B. *ibid.* 59a.

"with the sole exception of the camel"—Maimonides, following the wording of the Talmud, omits the coney and the hare, Lev. 11:5–6. See MhM *ad loc.*

3. B. Ḥul 59a.

"end of the tail"—*ḳanfe ha-'uḳaṣ,* as in B. Ḥul 59a (also in Alfasi and HG), where Rashi seems to have read *taḥat̲ ha-'uḳaṣ,* "under the tail." On the meaning of *'uḳaṣ* in this context see *'Aruḳ,* Jastrow, and Ben Yehudah.

"crosswise"—literally "warp and woof," some muscles running one way, and some the other.

"wild ass"—cf. Job 39:5.

4. Beḵ 1:2.

"This . . . applies only"—B. Beḵ 24a.

5. Beḵ 1:2; B. *ibid.* 7b.

6. B. Ḥul 60b; cf. B. Nid 24a.

"the 'cloven'"—in the Hebrew, the term "cloven" is given here twice, expressed by two different words, and Maimonides takes the second "cloven" to be explanatory—"that is, a cloven animal." In the parallel verse, Lev. 11:4, the second "cloven" does not occur.

7. B. Ḥul 69a–b.

8. B. Ḥul 63b; 80a.

"the wild ox and the buffalo"—Kil 8:6, and PhM *ad loc.;* P. Kil 8:4. See Farḥi, *Kaftor wa-feraḥ,* Chap. 58 (ed. Edelman, 124a). The word rendered here "buffalo" (*mĕri'*) is usually translated "fattened cattle."

9. Lev. 7:23 for fat, and 17:13 for covering of blood.

"the fat"—distinction must be made between *ḥeleḇ,* usually abdominal fat, which is forbidden, and *šuman,* the fat of the forepart of the animal, which is permitted. Cf. below, Chap. vii.

10. B. Ḥul 59b.

12. "The wild ox"—cf. above, Sec. 8.

"the oryx"—B. Ḥul 59b; cf. Lewysohn, p. 114.

"Whenever one is in doubt"—B. Ḥul 79b.

13. B. Ḥul 79b, 132a.

"ḳoy"—a kind of bearded antelope; cf. Lewysohn, p. 115 ff.

"An animal," etc.—B. Beḵ 7a.

14. Ḥul 3:6; B. *ibid.* 61a ff., 63a–b; MhM *ad loc.;* LhR 1565 (201).

"since Scripture says . . . *after its ḳind"*—this phrase is generally interpreted to indicate another species of the same bird.

15. B. Ḥul 63b.

16. Ḥul 3:6; MhM *ad loc.*

"which is the same"—for the Scriptural term *mur'ah* (Lev. 1:16), the Talmud employs the term *zefeḳ.*

17. B. Ḥul 62a.

"and in the . . . isles"—so Oxford MS.

18. B. Ḥul 62b.

19. *Geonica, 2,* 111, 118, 120; ShE (A) III, 65; ṬYD 82, and Caro's commentary *ad loc.*

20. Ḥul 3:6; PhM *ad loc.*

"A fowl which flocks"—B. Ḥul 65a.

21–22. Ḥul 3:7; B. *ibid.* 65a–b, Shab 90a.

23. B. Ḥul 65a.

24. Ḥul 3:7; B AZ 39a.

"Every fish"—Nid 6:9; B. *ibid.* 51b.

"If it possesses none"—B. Ḥul 66a.

"only one scale," etc.—Sif Lev. 11:9.

Chapter II

1. Sif Deut. 14:6.

"has the same force as a positive commandment"—on this principle cf. ShM, negative commandment 172; MM and LM to III, 1, xx, 14.

"How much more so"—Sif Lev. 11:4.

2. B. Yoma 80a; Ḥul 102a, 117a.

"Scripture does not differentiate"—Ḥul 8:6.

3. Sif Lev. 11:4, and *Ḳorban 'Ahăron, ad loc.* Cf. B. Keṯ 60a, and ***Šiṭṭah*** *mĕḳubbeṣeṯ, ad loc.;* R. Nissim to Alfasi, *ad loc.;* Responsa of Solomon ibn Adret, I, 364; Elijah of Lublin, *Yaḏ 'Eliyahu,* 45.

"*the soul of a living creature*"—in Hebrew *nefeš ḥayyah,* usually translated "living soul," with *ḥayyah* being taken for the adjective "living," rather than the substantive "living creature, animal." The meaning is that since man was created in the image of God and was endowed with a soul representing God's breath, the prohibition of eating human flesh did not have to be included in the rule covering the consumption of animal flesh. Rather, cannibalism is prohibited directly by the inferred rule that flesh not expressly permitted by Scripture is *ipso facto* forbidden. Cf. below, iii, 2; SER 15.

4. Sif Lev. 11:13.

"a positive commandment" (first occurrence)—MT, *I*, 74 (to Deut. 14:11); ShM, positive commandment 150; cf. Sif Deut. 14:20.

"he who eats . . . an unclean fish"—B. Ḥul 66b.

"a positive commandment" (third occurrence)—Sif Deut. 14:6.

5. Sif Lev. 11:20.

6. B. Ḥul 67b.

7. B. Me 16b.

"The minimum amount," etc.—generally, the minimum for liability for eating forbidden food is an olive's bulk. In this case, this minimum is reduced to a lentil's bulk, in order to make it the same as the minimum for uncleanness.

8. Me 4:3; B. *ibid.* 16b, 17a.

9. Me 4:3.

"Similarly, the blood of a snake"—B. Ker 4b.

10. B. Ker 21b.

11. B. Er 4a; Suk 6a.

12. "Whosoever eats . . . of a 'creeping thing of the water' "—B. Mak 16b; for the applicability of the proof verse given here see MM.

13. Sif Lev. 11:44. It was commonly accepted that maggots are the product of putrefaction; cf. B. Ḥul 67b. The Biblical verbs "move" and "creep" were understood as referring to two different species, the former to creatures multiplying by spontaneous generation in decaying matter, the latter to creatures born out of union between the sexes.

14–20. B. Ḥul 67a–b.

15. "a worm . . . cannot survive for twelve months"—B. Ḥul 58a.

17. B. Ḥul 66b.

20. "as we have explained"—above, Sec. 17.

21. Mak 3:2; B. Ḥul 102b.

"in this chapter"—Secs. 5, 6, 12.

22. B. Naz 51b.

23. B. Mak 16b; ShM, negative commandment 179; MO and MhM *ad loc.;* Alexander Schorr, *Tĕḇu'oṯ Šor,* 13, 2.

24. B. Mak 16b; KM and LM *ad loc.*

Chapter III

1. Bek̠ 1:2; B. Ḥul 64b.

"the daughter of the ya'ănah"—a literal rendering of the Hebrew term, which is usually translated *the ostrich;* here *ya'ănah* alone is taken to be the name of the bird, while *daughter* is taken to mean its egg.

2. Cf. above, ii, 3, and below, Sec. 4.

3. Mak 6:4; B. Bek̠ 7b.

4–5. B. Keṯ 60a.

4. "unclean matter"—so the Gemara (*šek̠eṣ*); the text has *šereṣ,* "unclean reptile."

5. "while in good health and not on account of illness"—P. Keṯ 5:6; P. Nid 1:4.

6. B. Ḥul 64a; Yoma 74a.

"flogging . . . for disobedience"—III, iii, ii, 3 (YJS, *14,* 260).

7. Cf. B. Beṣ 7a; AZ 40a.

8. B. Ḥul 64a.

9–10. B. Ḥul 64b.

10. "The milk of an animal which has been rendered ṭĕrefah"—Ḥul 8:5.

"the egg of a clean bird"—Eḏ 5:1.

11. B. Tem 31a.

"If the bird is doubtfully ṭĕrefah"—B. Ḥul 57b, 58a.

12. AZ 2:6; B. *ibid.* 35b.

13. AZ 2:5; B. *ibid.* 35a.

"as will be explained"—see below, ix, 16.

14. ŠT 23b (no. 247).

15. ŠT 19b (no. 188); *Geonica, 2,* 153 (no. 575); B. M. Lewin, *'Oṣar ḥilluf minhağim,* I, 26.

16. Cf. LM; Solomon ibn Adret, Responsa, I, 110.

"as will be explained"—below, xvii, 2.

17. AZ 2:7; B. *ibid.* 39b.

18. B. Ḥul 64a.

19. Cf. B. Ḥul 63b. On the controversy connected with this rule cf. MM.

"A person should not . . . purchase beaten eggs"—B. Ḥul 64a.

20. B. Ḥul 63b, 64a.

21. B. AZ 39b says they may not be bought "in Syria," which Maimonides takes to mean "outside of the Land of Israel"; MM.

22. B. AZ 40a.

"The brine of unclean locusts"—Ter 10:9; Eḏ 7:2, and PhM *ad loc.*

"unless a clean fish is floating in it"—AZ 2:6.

23. B. AZ 40a.

"hashed *ṭariṯ*"—AZ 2:6.

24. B. AZ 40a.

Chapter IV

1. Ḥul 2:4.
"In the Laws Concerning Šĕḥiṭah—below, III, iii.
2. B. Ḥul 100b; LhR 1570 (206).
3. B. Ḥul 102b. Cf. MhM.
4. B. Ḥul 75a.
"It is also forbidden to eat of a new born calf"—B. Shab 135b, 136a.
"nine months," etc.—B. Beḵ 8a.
5. Ḥul 4:7.
"The caul"—*šilya;* see above, note to I, x, 13.
6. B. Ḥul 102b.
"This ṭĕrefah"—Meḵ 22:30.
7. Ḥul 3:1.
"until it becomes fit only for a dog"—MdRŠ, p. 153.
8. Meḵ 22:30.
9. Ḥul 3:1.
"in the Laws Concerning Šĕḥiṭah"—below, III, v ff.
10. B. Ḥul 102b.
"of one of the clean animals"—B. Ḥul 102a.
"flesh in the field"—that is, detached from the animal.
11. Ḥul 2:6.
12. B. Ḥul 37b.
13. Ḥul 2:5.
"An animal dangerously ill"—B. Ḥul 37b.
"The quivering"—B. Ḥul 38a, following the decision of Alfasi.
14. B. Ḥul 38b.
"large or small beasts"—B. AZ 16b.
15. Ḥul 2:6; BY to ṬYD 17.
16. B. Me 16a; Sif Lev. 17:10.
"the Nazirite"—cf. VI, III, v, 3 (YJS, *15,* 138), based on Naz 6:1.
17. Me 4:4; Tos. *ibid.* 1:29; B. *ibid.* 16a.
"as we have explained"—above, Chap. 2.
18. Ḥul 9:1.
"where the blood spurts forth"—B. Ḥul 121a; PhM to Ḥul 9:1.
19. B. Ḥul 116b; cf. MM for the variant readings.
20–21. B. Beḵ 7b; Ḥul 9:2; B. *ibid.* 122b.
20. "The skin in front of a donkey's face"—a membrane like a caul covering the young animal's face at birth (cf. Rashi *ad loc.*).
22. B. Ḳid 56b.
"and its flesh shall not be eaten"—Meḵ 21:28; B. Pes 22b, and below, viii, 15.
"the dung of such an ox"—B. AZ 34b.
"If after sentence has been passed," etc.—Ker 6:2.

Chapter V

1. B. Ḥul 101b, 102a–b; Sanh 59a.
2. B. Ḥul 103a. Cf. MhM for the objections raised to this rule.
   "as we have explained"—above, iv, 10.
3. B. Ḥul 102a, 103b.
   "if . . . he divides it"—P. Naz 6:1.
4. B. Ḥul 103b; MhM *ad loc.*
5. B. Ḥul 103a. Cf. LM for the objections raised to this rule.
6. B. Ḥul 73b–74a.
   "Should the animal die"—B. Ḥul 74a.
7. B. Ḥul 93a–b.
   "from ancient times"—B. Ḥul 93b.
8. B. Ḥul 76b, 77a. Cf. Responsa of Levi ibn Ḥabib, 83.
9. B. Ḥul 55a.
   "even if they remain within the abdomen"—B. Ḥul 69a.
   "If the young thrusts forth its fore or hind leg"—Ḥul 4:4.
   "and flesh in the field"—the verse is here translated in accordance with the deduction made from it.
   "once it has emerged"—B. Ḥul 68a.
   "which to it is like 'a field' "—that is, out of its normal bounds; MdRŠ, p. 153.
   "as we have explained"—above, iv, 10.
10. B. Ḥul 68a–b; and Alfasi *ad loc.*
11. Ḥul 4:4; B. *ibid.* 73a. Cf. MhM.
12. B. Ḥul 69a.
13. Ḥul 4:5.
   "even the caul"—Ḥul 4:7; PhM *ad loc.*
   "if it is not attached"—B. Ḥul 77b.
14. Ḥul 4:5; B. *ibid.* 75b.
15. Ḥul 4:5.
   "If it is not fully nine-months developed"—Ḥul 4:4.
   "thrusts forth its head"—Ḥul 4:1.

Chapter VI

1. Ker 1:2, for the general rule that where willful transgression incurs extinction, if one commits the transgression in error he is liable to a sin offering; Ker 5:1, for the specific prohibition of blood of animals and birds and the permissibility of blood of fishes and locusts (cf. also MM, and Responsa of David ibn Abi Zimra, IV, 1119 [46]).

   "the hart, and the gazelle"—are "beasts" (cf. i, 8), but are here referred to as "animals."

   "insects . . . creeping things . . . human blood"—B. Ker 21b. For the prohibition of human blood see the next Section.

   "as we have explained"—above, ii, 10.

2. B. Ker 22a; Ket 60a.
"if one's teeth are bleeding"—that is, if one's gums are bleeding.

3–4. Ker 5:1.

3. "stabbing"—according to B. Ḥul 17a, the children of Israel were permitted during their sojourn in the wilderness to eat the flesh of animals killed by stabbing.

5. Ḥul 4:5; B. *ibid.* 74b.

6. Ḥul 8:3; B. *ibid.* 109b; PhM *ad loc.;* B. Pes 74b.
"salting it"—see below, Sec. 10 ff.
"the heart of a bird"—B. Ker 22a.

7. B. Ḥul 111a.
"all Israel have long since adopted the custom"—Alfasi *ad loc.*

8. B. Ḥul 111a; PhM to Ter 10:11.
"the whole dish is forbidden"—unless it is neutralized as detailed in Chap. xv.

9. B. Ḥul 111a.
"since it does not consist of blood"—although it is the color of blood.
"Should one break the neck"—B. Ḥul 113a.
"We have already explained"—above, iv, 13.

10–11. B. Ḥul 113a; Solomon ibn Adret, Responsa, III, 251.

10. "the time it takes to walk a mile"—i.e. 18 minutes; a day's journey is taken to be 40 miles, covered in 18 x 40 minutes, or 12 hours of daytime (YJS, *14,* 517).
"boiling—not tepid—water"—see ŠRA 68, and Berlin's commentary, no. 13; *Geonica, 2,* 92.

12. B. Men 21a, according to the reading "and so with regard to roasting," where our version has "and so with regard to cooking." See Tosafot *ad loc.*
"to eat meat raw"—B. Ḥul 33a.
"If a person scalds meat"—B. Pes 74b.

13. B. Pes 74b; Ḥul 93b.

14. B. Ḥul 93b, and Alfasi *ad loc.*
"the head is permitted"—HG(H), p. 559.

15. B. Ḥul 112a–b.

16. B. Ḥul 112b.

17. B. Pes 74a; Alfasi, Ḥul Chap. 7; Berlin's commentary to ŠRA 68, no. 13. For a differing view cf. *Geonica, 2,* 92, 90.

18. B. Ḥul 113a. Cf. OhG, III, 85.

19. B. Pes 74a–b.
"flour from moistened wheat grain"—fine flour was made from grain moistened before grinding (cf. B. Pes 40a).

20. Ḥul 111b, 8b; LhR 1607 (244), 1604 (241).

21. B. Ḥul 111b.
"even if it is lined with lead"—that is an earthenware vessel, since vessels of metal can be cleansed; see below, xvii, 1–2.

Chapter VII

1. See note to vi, 1.
"The Torah declares explicitly"—see i, 8–9. This forbidden fat will henceforth be referred to as "fat."

"In the case of other animals"—Sif Lev. 7:23; Ḥul 8:6.

"Similarly, in the case of a stillborn young"—B. Ḥul 75a.

2. B. Ḥul 37a–b.

"Since the additional prohibition . . . is now added"—Cf. above, 1, xvii, 8. While the animal was alive its flesh was permitted, while its fat was forbidden. After it was rendered nĕbelah or ṭĕrefah, the new prohibition of the flesh was added to the prohibition of the fat.

3. Ḥul 4:5; B. *ibid.* 92b; MhM *ad loc.;* LhR 1559 (195).

"veins"—Hebrew *ḥuṭin,* literally "threads," used in the Talmud to designate both veins and sinews. In the following translation, "veins" is used where both veins and sinews are meant, or where the mention of blood indicates that the meaning is blood vessels. "Sinew" is used where the qualifying word "fat" in the context shows that what is meant is not a blood vessel.

4. B. Ḥul 75a.

5. B. Ḥul 93a, 117a. Cf. Lev. 3:3–4.

"ḥeleḇ"—generally rendered "forbidden fat." Maimonides points out that in this case, as in the other verses quoted, the word ḥeleḇ has the alternate meaning of "choice."

"just as the kidneys and the lobe above the liver"—Lev. 3:4.

"and there can be nothing more choice than that which is offered to Him"—so Oxford MS (*yoṯer min ham-muram*).

6. "Similarly, the fat which is at the joint"—ŠRA 68, and Berlin's commentary, no. 6; HG(H), p. 549; Alfasi, Ḥul Chap. 7.

"There is also upon the stomach," etc.—B. Ḥul 49b.

"The sinews in the fat"—B. Ḥul 92b.

7. "Fat covered by flesh," etc.—B. Ḥul 93a, and Alfasi.

8. B. Ḥul 93a; ThR 76.

9. B. Ḥul 49b, for fat of the heart; B. Ḥul 93a, for the entrails.

"Some of the Geonim," etc.—cf. R. Ḥananeel, as mentioned in MM *ad loc.,* and BY to ṬYD 64.

10–13. B. Ḥul 93a.

10. "as we have stated"—above, vi, 10.

11. "the convex side"—Hebrew *daḏ,* literally "nipple"; cf. Preuss, p. 112.

14. B. Ḥul 93b.

15. B. Ḥul 113a; ThR 96.

16. Maimonides bases himself on the fact that these veins and membranes, while serving as conduits for fluid blood, do not in themselves contain enough blood to amount to the statutory minimum, and therefore are not regarded as forbidden because of blood (cf. MM).

17–19. B. Ḥul 97b, 8b.

20. B. Ḥul 97b.

"the sinew of the thigh vein"—see below, Chap. viii.

21. B. Ḥul 93b.

"porges the meat"—by removing the veins and membranes.

"the butcher is relied upon"—by his customers; Ḥul 7:1; B. *ibid.* 93b.

Chapter VIII

1. Ḥul 7:1.
"clean animals"—Ḥul 7:6.
"even if they are nĕḇelah or ṭĕrefah"—B. Ḥul 100b, 101a.
"whether they are to be eaten," etc.—B. Ḥul 90a.
"The remainder of the sinew," etc.—B. Ḥul 96a.
"as well as the fat upon the sinew," etc.—B. Ḥul 92b.
"There are two such sinews," etc.—B. Ḥul 93b.

2. Ḥul 7:3.
"If he eats of its fat"—Ḥul 7:1.
"since it is considered a separate entity"—literally "creature"; B. Ḥul 96a.

3. Ḥul 7:3; B. *ibid.* 96b.
"flogged twice"—literally "flogged eighty strokes," i.e. double the statutory forty lashes which constitute a single flogging.

4. Ḥul 7:1; B. *ibid.* 92b.

5. Ḥul 7:6.
"as we have explained"—above, iv, 18.

6. B. Ḥul 101a.

7. B. Ḥul 92b.
"The butcher is relied upon"—B. Ḥul 93b, amending Ḥul 7:1.
"One should not, however, purchase meat," etc.—cf. B. AZ 39b; P. *ibid.* 2:9; above, iii, 20–21.

8. Cf. above, iii, 21.

9. Beḵ 5:6.
"Nor is there any remedy"—B. Sanh 25a; KM to XIV, II, xii, 9; MhM *ad loc.*

10. B. Ḥul 6b states that one need have no apprehension of substitution.
"bondsmen and bondswomen"—who have been circumcised and immersed as slaves, and who are therefore differentiated from heathens; MM. Cf. above, I, xii, 11.

11. B. Ḥul 95a.
"in the case of a fixed object the possibility one way or the other is assumed to be equal"—B. Keṯ 15a derives this rule from Deut. 19:11. This is in contradistinction to the rule that "whatever emerges is regarded as having emerged from the majority." Since the purchaser had gone into only one shop (the "fixed object"), the chance of it having been the single shop which sells meat of nĕḇelah is regarded as equal to the chance of it having been one of the nine shops selling meat of šĕḥiṭah, and it is therefore regarded as a fifty-fifty chance. Once, however, the meat is found outside the shops (thus having "emerged"), the chance of it having come from a shop selling meat of šĕḥiṭah is regarded as nine to one.

12. "This is so according to the Torah"—whereby the rule follows the majority of meat vendors; P. Sheḳ 7:2; B. Ḥul 95a–b.
"loses sight of it"—that is, it is not continuously under the eye of an Israelite. Cf. MhM *ad loc.*

13. B. Ḥul 95b; Beṣ 40a.

14. B. Pes 22a.

"An Israelite is therefore permitted"—Ḥul 7:2; B. *ibid.* 94a.

15. B. Pes 21b; BḲ 41a.

16. B. Pes 24b; P. Or 3:1.

"the money obtained for it is permitted"—Ḳid 2:9; B. *ibid.* 58a.

"everything which is forbidden," etc.—Shebi 7:3.

17. Shebi 7:4.

"It is . . . permitted to trade"—Tos Shebi 5:9.

18. P. Shebi 7:1.

Chapter IX

1. Meḵ 23:19; B. Ḳid 57b; Ḥul 115b.

"it must be buried," etc.—Tem 7:4.

"liable to burial"—because it is forbidden for benefit.

"an olive's bulk of both of them"—B. Ḥul 108b.

"which have been cooked together"—the Scriptural prohibition refers specifically to cooking ("seething"), and it is therefore only for cooking that flogging is explicitly incurred.

2. Targum Jonathan Deut. 14:21.

"in exactly the same way"—cf. LM, who quotes ShM, negative commandment 187. Cf. also above, 1, ii, 6, and note thereto; PhM to Ker 3:4; KM to X, 1, i, 2.

3. Ḥul 8:4; B. *ibid.* 113b, 114a; LhR 1382 (9).

"and 'its mother's milk' "—so Oxford MS.

"not . . . on account of meat with milk"—but on account of eating the milk or meat of an unclean animal.

4. Ḥul 8:1; B. *ibid.* 104a.

"the literal meaning of the verse," etc.—that is, if one were to confine himself to the letter of Scripture, the prohibition would be limited to nothing other than a kid seethed in its own mother's milk.

5. Ḥul 8:1.

"fully developed eggs"—B. Beṣ 6b; quoted in Alfasi, Ḥul Chap. 8.

6. P. Neḏ 6:1.

"the hot springs of Tiberias"—B. Shab 40b; cf. III, 1, ix, 3 (YJS, *14*, 48).

"or in any similar manner"—which does not constitute regular cooking.

"Likewise, if one cooks," etc.—B. Ḥul 113b, 114a.

"the milk of a male"—an abnormal male with excessively developed breasts may exude milk; so Rashi to Ḥul 113b.

"the meat of a dead animal"—cf. LhR 1608 (245).

"inasmuch as the former is neither," etc.—cf. above, 1, xviii, 8. Only where these three varieties of prohibition apply is it possible for a person to be doubly liable for one and the same transgression. Cf. also PhM to Ker 3:4 for a definition of these varieties.

7. B. Ḥul 113b; Ḥul 9:1; B. *ibid.* 121a.

8–10. Ḥul 8:3; B. *ibid.* 108a–b, 97a.

8. "one part . . . to . . . sixty"—for details see below, Chap. xv.

9. "should be tasted"—by a heathen, as in the preceding case.

10. "in the midst of"—so Oxford MS (*lĕ-ṯoḵ*).

11. B. Ḥul 111b.

12. Ḥul 8:3; B. *ibid.* 109b.

"as we have explained"—above, Sec. 6.

13. B. Ḥul 97b.

14. B. Ḥul 111a.

"above other meat"—since the milk from the udder may ooze out and become absorbed in the meat below.

15–16. B. Ḥul 116b.

16. "heathen-made cheese"—B. AZ 35a.

"as we have explained"—above, iii, 13.

17. B. Ḥul 108a; Pes 75b, 76a.

"It is therefore permitted to wrap meat"—Ḥul 8:2.

18. B. Ḥul 112a.

"porridge"—Hebrew *ḵutaḥ,* "a preserve consisting of sour milk, bread crusts, and salt" (Jastrow).

19. B. Ḥul 112a.

"well seasoned"—seasoning opens up the pores of the flesh and makes it absorb the milk more readily.

20. Ḥul 8:1.

21. Ḥul 8:2; B. *ibid.* 107b.

22. B. Pes 36a, quoted by Alfasi, Ḥul Chap. 8.; B. BM 91a.

"If, however, he alters the appearance"—B. Pes 36a.

23. B. Pes 76b, quoted by Alfasi, Ḥul Chap. 7.

"fish in a dish"—B. Ḥul 111b.

24. B. Ḥul 111b, 112a.

"cucumbers or melons"—which are nonpungent vegetables and do not absorb meat juice except on the surface of the cut.

25. B. Ḥul 112a.

"milk sauce"—Hebrew *ḵamaḵ,* "A Persian sauce of milk, curdled milk, etc." (Jastrow).

26. B. Ḥul 105a.

"wash his hands and cleanse his mouth"—B. Ḥul 104b, 105a.

27. B. Ḥul 104b.

"need neither cleanse his mouth," etc.—Rashi to B. Ḥul 104b explains that poultry meat does not adhere to the hands or to the back of the mouth.

28. B. Ḥul 105a (where no number of hours is given); Alfasi (who specifies six hours).

Chapter X

1. Cf. Ḳid 1:9.

"the new produce"—*'Orlah;* all these are explained later on.

2. Ḥal 1:1 (cf. TYṬ and Elijah of Wilno *ad loc.* for the variant readings); B. Ker 5a.

"five species of grain"—wheat, barley, spelt, oats, and rye.

"*'Omer*"—a measure of barley offered at the Temple on that day.

"in every place"—Or 3:9; PhM *ad loc.;* B. Men 68b.

"in distant places"—Men 10:5; PhM *ad loc;* B. *ibid.* 68a–b.

"When the Temple is not in existence," etc.—Men 10:5.

"for the whole of that day"—cf. B. Suk 41a–b.

"At the present time," etc.—B. Men 68b.

"in places"—i.e. in the Dispersion.

3. B. Ker 5a; ShM, principle 9 and negative commandments 189-191; ThR 368.

4. B. Men 70a, 71a.

5. B. BM 56b; Men 69b, according to the interpretation of Rashi *ad loc.* Cf. MhM *ad loc.*

"as though it were stored in a vessel"—i.e. as harvested produce in storage.

"it has become nullified in the ground"—i.e. it is to be considered as still in the ground and having not yet taken root (cf. KM).

6. Kel 8:1; P. Ḳid 1:8. Cf. MhM *ad loc.* In this Section Maimonides confines himself to the prohibition of eating. The details of the Laws Concerning Mixed Seeds of the Vineyard are found in VII, 1, v–vii.

"the meaning is"—cf. B. Ḳid 56b.

7. B. Pes 25a.

8. Or 3:9.

"it will be explained"—see note to Sec. 6, above.

9. Or 1:2; P. *ibid.*

"for benefit"—B. Ḳid 56b.

10. Or 3:9; B. Ḳid 39a.

"Laws Concerning the Second Tithe"—VII, v, ix–x.

11. Or 3:9; B. Ḳid 38b; ThR 141; MhM *ad loc.*

"the territory conquered by David"—this territory was regarded as the fruit of individual conquest, as opposed to national conquest, and has a lesser degree of sanctity. Cf. B. Giṭ 8b.

"in Syria it would be permitted"—despite the probability that the grapes or the vegetables came from the vineyard outside which they are sold.

12. The previous Section speaks of a vineyard which is certainly 'Orlah or diverse seeds, but the doubt is whether the produce sold came from that vineyard. In this Section the field itself is doubtful 'Orlah. The source is the same as in Sec. 11.

13. B. BB 24a; MhM *ad loc.*

14. B. AZ 22a; MhM *ad loc.*

15. "the fourth year's fruit"—Lev. 19:24; Solomon ibn Adret, Responsa, III, 231.

"in Syria"—see VII, v, ix, 1.

"In the Land of Israel"—MSh 5:2; B. Beẓ 5a.

"Some of the Geonim"—cf. ŚRA 100, and Berlin's commentary *ad loc.;* Solomon ibn Adret to B. BḲ 69a; *idem,* Responsa ascribed to Naḥmanides, 156; KM *ad loc.*

16. MSh 5:1–2; B. Ber 35a.

"In the Laws Concerning the Second Tithe"—VII, v, ix.

17. MSh 5:4 gives the regulations for their redemption while the Temple was in existence.

"at the present time"—when there is no Temple.

"with only one *pĕruṭah*"—B. Ar 29a.
"into the Dead Sea"—see B. Pes 27a.
"with a pĕruṭah's worth"—B. Ar 29a.

18. HG(T), p. 32; HG(H), p. 644, n. 81; ŠRA 100.
19. "He who eats an olive's bulk of Ṭeb̲el"—Mak 3:2.
"the great heave offering"—see VII, III, i.
"the heave offering of tithes"—see VII, III, ii.
"is punishable by death"—Sif Lev. 22:16; B. Sanh 83a.
20. B. Mak 16b.
"ordinary tithes"—see VII, IV, i.
"poor man's tithe"—in the third and sixth years, the poor man's tithe took the place of the second tithe which in other years had to be eaten by the owner in Jerusalem. Cf. Deut. 14:28 ff., 26:12.
21. B. Mak 16b.
"In the Laws Concerning Heave Offerings and Tithes"—see VII, III–IV.
22. Ter 11:3; B. Ḥul 120b; MhM *ad loc.*
"spontaneous growth of the Sabbatical year"—see Lev. 25:5.
23. Cf. Mak 3:1.
"Piggul"—"a sacrifice rejectable in consequence of an improper intention in the mind of the officiating priest" (Jastrow).
"remnant of sacrifices"—left over after the time appointed for eating them.
"in its appropriate place"—heave offerings: VII, III; first fruits: VII, VI, i–iv; dough offering: VII, VI, v–viii; second tithe: VII, V; Piggul: VIII, VII, xiii–xviii (YJS, *12,* 350–379); remnant of sacrifices: VIII, VII, xix, 7 (YJS, *12,* 381); sacrifices which have become unclean: VIII, VII, xix, 1 (YJS, *12,* 379).
24. Ker 1:1; Mak 3:15.
"Laws Concerning Leaven," etc.—III, V (YJS, *14,* 321 ff.).
"The prohibition of food on the Day of Atonement"—III, III, ii (YJS, *14,* 259 ff.).
"in a class by itself"—since it is a prohibition of all food whatsoever.
"Nazirite"—see VI, III, i.

Chapter XI

1. AZ 2:3; B. *ibid.* 29b; ŠRA 162, and Berlin's commentary; MhM *ad loc.*
"heathen offering"—B. AZ 32b.
"salt and water"—B. AZ 51b.
"the smallest amount"—AZ 5:8–9.
2. B. AZ 29b, 73a.
"NOUGHT"—that is not even the smallest possible amount. Cf. P. AZ 2:4.
3. B. AZ 31a, 36b.
"log̃"—a liquid measure, equivalent to the volume of six eggs.
4. B. AZ 58a, 59b; Ḥul 13a.
5. B. AZ 57a; cf. ŠT 252.
"circumcised and immersed"—cf. above, I, xii, 11.
6. B. AZ 57a; cf. ŠT 254; Abraham ben Moses ben Maimon, Responsa, 61.
7. B. AZ 64b.

"the seven Noachian commandments"—XIV, v, ix, 1 (YJS, *3,* 230–231).

"as we have explained"—cf. above, 1, xiv, 7.

"as a pledge"—since he will regard it as his own.

"all the Geonim have so ruled"—*Ḥemdah gĕnuzah,* 114; *Tĕšuḇoṯ gĕ'onim ḳadmonim* of Joseph Bonfils (ed. Cassel), 46; cf. ThR 369, and note to line 14.

8. This is a summary of the regulations already detailed.

9. B. AZ 30a.

"boiled wine"—cf. ŠT 258.

"and one may drink it"—Rashi *ad loc.*

10. "The Geonim of the Maghrib"—ThR 382; cf. *Hağahoṯ 'Ašeri* to B. AZ 30a; KM *ad loc.* Cf. III, 1, xxix, 14 (YJS, *14,* 189). The Maghrib is the western portion of the North African littoral.

"no longer fit for the altar"—cf. Lev. 2:11.

11. AZ 4:8; B. *ibid.* 55b.

12. B. AZ 56b, 57a.

13. AZ 2:3; ŠT 260.

"Should a heathen press grapes"—Tos AZ 7:4.

"If after eating some grapes"—Tos Ṭoh 11:9; AZ 7:5; ṬYD 125, and BY *ad loc.*

"sĕ'ah"—a liquid measure equivalent to one third of an ephah.

"even if some of it is sprinkled"—*mĕnattez* (so Oxford MS); the heathen's intention was to throw in the additional grapes, not to pour the juice; hence the sprinkling of the juice already in the press upon the newly added grapes was accidental, and cannot therefore be considered as intentional libation on the heathen's part.

14. AZ 2:3; B. *ibid.* 34a.

"no odor of wine"—i.e. no resemblance to wine.

15. AZ 2:3–4; B. *ibid.* 33a–b, 34b; cf. ŠT 261.

"If one pours wine"—B. AZ 29b.

16. B. AZ 22b; Solomon ibn Adret, Responsa ascribed to Nahmanides, 159.

"draws out"—so editio princeps (Rome, before 1480), *šoṯan;* the Oxford MS and the printed text have "burns," *śorfan.*

17. B. AZ 33a; P. *ibid.* 2:4.

"Similarly," etc.—B. AZ 74b.

18. B. AZ 33b and Rashi *ad loc.;* ThR 93; MhM *ad loc.;* LhR 1382(9).

"three times in succession," etc.—for the variant readings in this passage and the different interpretations of the ruling see KM, and BY to ṬYD 135. The reason given in BY is that lined cups retain more of the wine than pure earthenware cups.

19. B. AZ 33b.

"If a portion . . . is exposed"—cf. also B. Keṯ 107b.

"It would appear to me"—this follows from the whole trend of the discussion in B. AZ 33b.

20–21. AZ 5:11; B. *ibid.* 74b.

20. "four times"—B. AZ 75a.

22. AZ 5:11.

"unless he heats it"—B. AZ 34b.

23–24. B. AZ 75a.

23. "and leave it to dry"—reading *u-mannihah,* with the editio princeps.

24. "the posts"—(Hebrew *lulabin*) so *'Aruk;* Rashi interprets it as "twigs used as brooms."

"trusses"—baskets in which the wine is pressed. The term is usually applied to olive presses; see Ṭoh 10:8; Ma 1:7.

25. B. AZ 39b; Solomon ibn Adret, Responsa, I, 405.

"who was known for his observance"—cf. ŚT 254.

"The same is true in the case of meat," etc.—see above, iii, 21; viii, 7–8; MhM *ad loc.*

26. B. AZ 39b.

"a householder"—as distinct from an innkeeper.

"at whatever place or time"—that is, in or out of the Land of Israel, and regardless of whether it is or is not in Israel's possession.

"If it is known"—cf. Tos Demai 3.

"on the host's assurance"—that it has been prepared in accordance with dietary law.

Chapter XII

1. B. AZ 59b; MhM *ad loc.*

"or with any other organ of his body," etc.—cf. above, xi, 11.

"Similarly," etc.—B. AZ 57b, 60a.

2. B. Giṭ 52b.

3–4. B. AZ 60a.

4. "this is not the customary manner of libation"—but rather accidental shaking in the process of carrying.

"an open earthenware vessel"—the important point is that it is open, not that it is earthenware, which makes no difference.

5. B. AZ 57a.

"or if he stretches out his hand"—B. AZ 58a.

6. B. AZ 58a–b.

7. B. AZ 56b, 57b, 58a.

8. B. AZ 60a–b. In the first case, the heathen in grasping the cracked halves of the jug causes the wine to shake; in the second case his hand merely presses the upper part of the jug upon the lower part to close the crack, without causing any shaking of the wine. Cf. ThB 135b.

9. AZ 4:10; B. *ibid.* 60b; P. *ibid.* 4:11.

10. B. AZ 59b.

11. B. AZ 72b.

12. B. AZ 72b, in accordance with the statement in 72a that a flowing column constitutes a connector in the case of libation wine; MhM *ad loc.*

13. AZ 5:7; B. *ibid.* 74b; P. *ibid.* 5:10; and ThB 148a.

14. B. AZ 72b; cf. Responsa of Solomon ibn Adret, I, 712.

15. B. AZ 58a.

16. AZ 5:3.

"as far as a mile"—B. AZ 69a.

" 'Now the Israelite may get ahead of us,' " etc.—Cf. B. Ḥag̃ 20b.

17. AZ 5:4.

18. AZ 5:5.

"sideboard"—PhM *ad loc.*

19–23. B. AZ 70a.

24. AZ 5:6; B. *ibid.* 71a.

25. AZ 4:10; B. *ibid.* 60b.

"since he would feel free to handle it"—for he would regard it as ultimately his own.

26. B. AZ 69b, 70a.

27. B. AZ 60b.

"to moisten the palm of one hand," etc.—cf. III, III, iii, 4 (YJS, *14*, 263); Hai Gaon's commentary to Kel 8:3; PhM to Kel 8:3 and 10:8.

28–29. B. BB 24a.

28. "permitted . . . forbidden"—in each case it is regarded as coming from the majority.

29. "jugs of wine broken open by thieves," etc.—B. AZ 70a.

Chapter XIII

1. B. AZ 61a–b.

2. B. AZ 70b; MhM *ad loc.* In the former case no mention is made of the Israelite's return. In the latter case the Israelite stipulates that he will return, which is presumed to make the heathen apprehensive of being caught in the act if he should abuse his trust.

3. AZ 4:12; PhM *ad loc.*; B. *ibid.* 61a–b.

"comes and goes"—and does not have the wine under his constant supervision.

4. AZ 4:12.

5. AZ 4:11.

6. B. AZ 61a. The heathen is not likely to tamper with the wine, for fear that an Israelite standing on top of the heap, at the window, or in the upper branches of the tree, might see him.

7. B. AZ 70b.

"a low partition"—*mĕsifas;* Rashi explains it to mean a low partition; the *'Aruḵ* describes it as a hollow wall pierced by windows.

8–9. B. AZ 31a.

10. B. AZ 29b, 30a, 39b.

11. Cf. ShE (B) II, 77 (quoting responsum by R. Naḥshon Gaon).

"beats upon the jug"—to cool it, cf. above, xii, 9.

12. B. AZ 64b. Cf. above, xi, 7.

"forging"—of seals or keys.

13. B. AZ 58b, 59a.

"nor may he assist an Israelite"—B. AZ 72b.

"the wine is nevertheless permitted"—since this is merely an excessive precaution.

14. B. AZ 66b.

15. AZ 5:1; B. *ibid.* 62b.

"We have already explained"—above, viii, 16; xi, 1; IV, 1, v, 2.

16–17. AZ 5:1; B. *ibid.* 62b.

16. "into the Dead Sea"—cf. B. Pes 27a.

17. "to smash jars"—B. AZ 63b. Presumably the jars and their contents have deteriorated and become unusable.

18. AZ 5:1; B. *ibid.* 65a.

"and one of the jugs is found to contain wine"—cf. ṬYD 133 and BY *ad loc.*

19. B. AZ 65a.

20. AZ 5:7; LhR 1576 (212).

21. B. AZ 64a.

"mina"—one hundred *denar.*

22. B. AZ 64a; Ḳid 17b; PhM to Demai 6:10.

"this alleviation"—scripturally, the proselyte, considered the same as a newborn child (cf. above, I, xiv, 11), is no longer related to his heathen father and therefore has no right to his estate; nevertheless, as a concession to him, he was permitted to retain this right.

"it becomes forbidden"—i.e. he cannot offer to exchange the idol for money, oil, etc.

23. AZ 5:7; B. *ibid.* 71a–b. Cf. XII, 1, iii (YJS, *5,* 11 ff.).

24. B. AZ 71a.

25–26. B. AZ 63a–b.

25. "an unlettered Israelite shopkeeper"—who may be suspected of dealing in the produce of the Sabbatical year and in untithed produce.

27. B. AZ 71a. Maimonides follows some of the Geonim in this interpretation, quoted by ThB, p. 139a. See *Mar'eh hap-panim* to P. Demai 6:8. In the former case, the Israelite actually authorizes the heathen messenger to purchase the wine for him; in the latter case, he merely instructs the messenger to pay his tax for him, without reference to the wine which will be given out by the king's treasury upon payment of the tax.

28. B. AZ 59b.

Chapter XIV

1. B. Yoma 80a.

"medium-sized"—Kel 17:8.

"We have already explained"—above, ii, 2; vii, 1; I, i, 7.

2. B. Yoma 80a; Ber 41a–b; PhM to Kel 17:12.

"Although it is forbidden by the Torah," etc.—B. Yoma 73b; cf. III, III, ii, 3 (YJS, *14,* 260).

3. B. Ḥul 103b.

"from an olive's bulk"—the combined amounts are presumed to make an olive's bulk.

"an olive's bulk of forbidden food"—i.e., having been swallowed twice, the same half an olive's bulk is counted twice, making a full olive's bulk.

4. Ṭoh 3:4; PhM *ad loc.*

5. "We have already explained"—above, iv, 16–17.

"will be explained"—VI, III, iii.

"The five species of grain," etc.—Ḥal 1:1; B. Men 70a–b.

6. "It would appear to me"—according to B. AZ 66a, things belonging to the same category combine in the manner described by Maimonides. For the combining of the něbelah of ox, sheep, and deer, see above, iv, 17; MhM *ad loc.*

"as we have explained"—above, iv, 17.

7. Naz 6:4.

8. Cf. Ker 3:3; B. *ibid.* 13a; Pes 44a.

"three eggs"—according to the view in B. Er 83a, this is the volume of half a loaf given in the Mishnah.

9. Tos Yoma 5:3. Ker 3:3 gives the same standards for solid foods and liquids. B. Yoma 80a, however, accords with the view of Maimonides. Cf. III, III, ii, 4 (YJS, *14,* 260), and LM *ad loc.*

10. B. Pes 24b, 25a.

"any of the forbidden foods," etc.—see I, i, v, 8.

"seething"—Exod. 23:19, 34:26; Deut. 14:21.

"forfeiture"—cf. above, x, 6, and note.

11. "after it had putrefied"—B. AZ 67b; cf. above, ii, 21.

12. B. Sanh 62b. Cf. IX, iv, ii, 7 (YJS, *4,* 100).

"against his will"—B. Pes 25b.

13. B. Keṯ 19a: "Nothing comes before the saving of life except idolatry, incest, and the shedding of blood."

14. Yoma 8:5; B. *ibid.* 82a. It was commonly accepted that the cravings of a pregnant woman must be satisfied, because her life depends on it. Cf. B. Ker 13a.

15. B. Keṯ 61a–b.

16. Yoma 8:6; KM *ad loc.*

17. "as will be explained"—VII, vi, iv, 2.

"to rectify the former"—by removing the tithes and the heave offering; B. Yoma 83a.

18. "We have already explained"—above, i, xvii, 8.

"Hence it is possible," etc.—Ker 3:4.

19. Cf. PhM to Ker 3:4.

Chapter XV

1. B. Zeḇ 79a; Levi ibn Ḥabib, Responsa, 88.

2. "tasted"—by a heathen. Cf. below, Sec. 30.

"as well as its substance"—B. AZ 67a–b.

3. B. Pes 44a; AZ 67a.

4. Ḥul 7:5; B. *ibid.* 99b–100a, 97b. Cf. Responsa of Jacob Berab, 35.

"kidney fat . . . tail fat"—both are of the same species; kidney fat is forbidden, while tail fat is permitted; cf. above, vii, 4.

"as will be explained"—below, Chap. xvi.

6. B. AZ 73b; Ḥul 97a–b; MhM I, 77–78; Abraham ben Moses ben Maimon, Responsa, 128. The details of this Section are given in the Sections which follow.

"and Ṭeḇel," etc.—B. Ned 58a.

"it is possible to rectify it"—by removing the tithes and heave offerings.

7. "as will be explained"—cf. below, xvi, 28.

"Similarly, if a cup of wine of Ṭeb̲el"—B. AZ 73b.

"as will be explained in its proper place"—VII, IV, viii, 2.

8. Shebi 7:7; B. Neḏ 58a. Maimonides explains why the produce of the Sabbatical year is not included in Sec. 7, above. Although logically the rule governing mixtures should apply also to Sabbatical produce, Scripture does not expressly so apply it. Hence such mixtures are not prohibited, but since they contain Sabbatical produce they must be eaten in the sanctity prescribed for the consumption of this produce.

"as will be explained"—cf. VII, VII, v–viii.

9. B. Pes 30a, 29b.

"in these rules"—concerning libation wine and Ṭeb̲el, since ultimately the whole mixture becomes automatically permitted.

"as will be explained"—III, v, i, 6 (YJS, *14,* 325).

10. P. Neḏ 6:4; B. *ibid.* 58a.

"The same applies to everything"—B. Beṣ 4a.

"muḳṣeh"—literally "set apart," something which is forbidden for use on Sabbath and festivals because it is considered not utilizable on these days. It is a purely rabbinical prohibition; cf. B. Shab 44a.

"came into being on a festival"—Beṣ 1:1; B. *ibid.* 4a.

"consecrated things"—which can be redeemed.

"second tithes"—which are permitted to be eaten in Jerusalem.

11. "*'Orlah* . . . the produce of a vineyard of mixed seeds"—see above, Chap. x.

"prohibited fat and blood"—see above, Chap. vi–vii.

"heave offerings"—see above, x, 23, and note.

12. Cf. P. Neḏ 6:4; Alfasi, Ḥul Chap. 7; Solomon ibn Adret, Responsa, I, 500.

"as we have explained"—above, Sec. 6.

"need evoke no surprise"—that the smallest amount of leaven renders the mixture prohibited.

"NOTHING *leavened*"—i.e. not even the smallest amount, however large the admixture of unleavened matter. Cf. B. Pes 43a.

"as we have explained"—above, Sec. 9.

13. Or 2:1; PhM and TYṬ *ad loc.*

"Similarly, a piece of shewbread"—P. Or 2:1; MhM *ad loc.*

14. Or 2:1.

"If it falls into less than two hundred"—MO *ad loc.*

15. P. Or 2:1, Cf. VII, III, xiii, 1.

"ḳĕlisin"—the meaning is uncertain. Maimonides says it is a kind of fig; Rashi, a kind of pea or bean; according to others, it is the fruit of the Judas tree. Danby renders it "acorns." Löw (II, 391 ff.) identifies it with licorice. See Ter 11:4 and Uḳ 1:6. All these things are forbidden to non-priests, but their value to the priests was regarded as negligible.

16. Sif Num. 18:29; P. Or 2:1; PhM *ad loc.*

"If that which has to be taken out of it returns to it, it renders it hallowed"—quoted from P. Or 2:1, which adds: "and how much is it? one part out of one hundred"; i.e., if one particle of heave offering after being taken out of one hundred particles of produce falls back into the ninety-nine particles, the entire one hundred particles become hallowed.

17. B. Ḥul 98a, 97a; Alfasi, Ḥul Chap. 7.
"as we have explained"—above, viii, 1.
"an individual entity"—see above, viii, 2.
"sinews do not impart a flavor"—B. Ḥul 89b.

18. B. Ḥul 97b.
"as we have explained"—above, ix, 12–13.

19. B. Ḥul 98a. Cf. Abraham ben Moses ben Maimon, Responsa, 129. An egg containing a chick is forbidden, even if laid by a clean bird.

20. B. Ḥul 98a.
"it does not render them forbidden"—since they are unbroken in their shells.
"the contents of an egg"—i.e. a broken egg; cf. KM.

21. B. Ḥul 98a–b.

22–23. Maimonides deduces these laws from the various standards which he has set forth.

24. B. Ḥul 97b.

25. Ter 5:9; B. Beṣ 4b.
"It would appear to me"—cf. III, I, vi, 23 (YJS, *14*, 39).

26. "is permitted"—presumably (cf. Sec. 25) to others only, not to the transgressor himself.
"A person may . . . at the outset"—B. Beṣ 4b.

27. "flesh of fowl"—with milk, is subject to a rabbinical prohibition only; cf. above, ix, 4.

28. "We have already explained"—above, xiv, 11.
"spoils its taste"—B. AZ 67b; PhM to AZ 5:2.

29. B. Ḥul 97a, and Rashi *ad loc.*
"In the Laws Concerning Heave Offerings"—VII, III, xiii.

30. B. Ḥul 97b.

31. B. AZ 68b, 69a.
"a rodent"—literally "a mouse"; what is meant is not the domestic mouse or rat, but the field rodents whose flesh was esteemed by heathens as a delicacy, or, as the Gemara *loc. cit.* puts it, "was served at the king's table."
"since apprehension," etc.—cf. Alfasi.

32. B. Ḥul 96b–97a.

33. B. Pes 76b; Alfasi, Ḥul Chap. 7.

34. B. Ḥul 112b.
"Similarly, if salted unclean fish," etc.—B. Ḥul 113a; Solomon ibn Adret, Responsa, I, 392.
"If unclean fish is pickled," etc.—Ter 10:8; MhM *ad loc.; Mar'eh hap-panim* to P. Ter 10:5.

Chapter XVI

1. Or 2:4,6; 3:7. Cf. below, Sec. 3, 7–9.

2. Or 2:8; B. Ḥul 99b.

3. Or 3:7. As Maimonides points out in Sec. 9, these seven articles are merely examples of things which were regarded as of special value in Palestine in those times. Maimonides enumerates them exactly as they are listed in the Mishnah.

"Badan"—a Samaritan place near Nablus, noted for its pomegranates; cf. Löw, *3*, 85 f.

4. MhM *ad loc.*

5. Ḥul 7:5; B. *ibid.* 100a. Since the cut is fit to be offered to a guest, it is subject to the same rule as governs a thing of value.

6. AZ 5:9; PhM to BḲ 7:2; see also XI, II, ii, 8 (YJS, *9*, 65).

"Laws Concerning Šĕḥiṭah"—below, III, ii, 1–3.

"Similarly, in the case of the sinew," etc.—Ḥul 7:5.

"separate entity"—above, viii, 2.

7. Zeḇ 8:1; B. *ibid.* 73a; AZ 5:9.

"an ox sentenced to stoning"—Exod. 21:28.

"a heifer whose neck was to be broken"—in expiation of an unsolved murder, Deut. 21:4.

"a leper's sacrifice"—Lev. 14:4–7.

"the first-born of an ass"—Exod. 13:13.

"even if customarily sold by number"—B. Beṣ 3b.

9. See note to Sec. 3, above. LM *ad loc.*

10. B. Yeḇ 81b; Zeḇ 74a. Cf. I, IV, vii, 10, and MhM *ad loc.*

"from such a mixture"—of one Badan pomegranate and a thousand other pomegranates (see above, Sec. 4); cf. R. David ibn Abi Zimra *ad loc.*

11. Or 3:8. In all these cases they lose the characteristic which renders them articles of value.

12. See above, XV, 25.

13. Or 2:14–15.

"but allowed to a priest"—since heave offering is permitted to him, and there is not sufficient of the other leaven to cause leavening.

14. Or 2:10; PhM *ad loc.;* B. AZ 66a; Rashi *ad loc.*

15. "water parsley, meadow parsley, and garden parsley"—cf. P. Shebi 9:1.

16. Or 2:9, 11; B. AZ 68a.

17–19. Or 2:2–3; PhM and MhM *ad loc.*

20. Or 3:1, 4.

"must be burned"—dyeing and cooking make a significant change in the article, hence they are regarded in the same light as leavening and seasoning.

21. Or 3:2.

"one *siṭ*'s length"—cf. III, I, ix, 7 (YJS, *14*, 49); PhM to Or 3:2.

"If the ingredients of 'Orlah dye"—P. Or 3:1.

22. Or 3:5; B. Pes 26b. Cf. I, IV, vii, 13.

23. B. Pes 27a.

24. B. Pes 26b, 27a.

"even though both fuels have contributed"—since the rule is that if each one of two factors, one permitted and the other forbidden, contributes, the result is forbidden; B. Pes 27a.

25. Or 1:6; P. *ibid.* 1:4; PhM *ad loc.* Cf. B. Giṭ 54b.

26. Or 1:7; AZ 2:5; B. *ibid.* 35a. Cf. above, xi, 13.

27. Tem 7:5.

28. B. AZ 73a; MhM *ad loc.*

"As we have said above"—xv, 7.

"a small jar"—Hebrew *ṣilṣul,* for which B. AZ 73a has *ṣirṣur,* "a stone vessel containing a strainer and having an indented (comb-like) rim; a sort of cooler" (Jastrow).

29. AZ 5:10; B. *ibid.* 74a.
"into the Dead Sea"—AZ 3:9; I, iv, vii, 9, and LM *ad loc.*

30. AZ 5:8; B. *ibid.* 73a.

31. B. AZ 73a.

32. AZ 5:2; B. *ibid.* 66a.

33. AZ 5:2; on the various readings in this passage of the Mishnah cf. Tosafoṯ to B. AZ 65b.

34. B. AZ 65b; MhM *ad loc.*
"as will be explained"—below, xvii, 9, 12.

35. B. AZ 66a.

Chapter XVII

1. B. AZ 67b, 75b.

2. B. AZ 75b, 76a.

3. AZ 5:12; B. *ibid.* 75b, 76a. The general rule is that a utensil may be cleansed only by being subjected to the same heat as was applied to it while prohibited food was cooked in it.

4. B. AZ 76a–b.

5. B. AZ 75b; LM *ad loc.*

6. B. AZ 75b; KM *ad loc.*

7. AZ 5:12; B. *ibid.* 76b; Ḥul 8b.
"pits"—Hebrew *pĕḡimoṯ,* which may mean either pits (in the blade of the knife) or notches (in the cutting edge); B. AZ 76b, however, has *gumoṯ,* "pits, furrows" (and so does the Oxford MS); the pits may contain an accumulation of hardened fat which would not be removed by thrusting the knife into hard ground.
"ten times"—P. AZ 5:15 requires three times.
"If he performs šĕḥiṭah," etc.—B. Ḥul 8b, and decision of Alfasi.

8. B. Ḥul 8b.

9. "drinking with heathens"—B. AZ 8a, 31b.
"eating their bread," etc.—AZ 2:6; PhM *ad loc.*

10. B. AZ 8a.
"the majority of the company are Israelites"—B. AZ 30a; MhM *ad loc.*
"beer"—B. AZ 31b.

11. B. AZ 40b; BB 97b.

12. "Although the Sages forbade heathen bread"—AZ 2:6.
"there are . . . localities"—B. AZ 38b.
"considering it permitted"—so Oxford MS, *wĕ-heḵširuha;* the editio princeps has *u-ḵĕšerah.* The printed text has *ubaś-śadeh,* "and in the field," cf. B. AZ 35b.

13. B. AZ 38b.

14–16. B. AZ 38a.

15. "it is permitted"—B. AZ 59a.

17–18. B. AZ 38b.

19. B. AZ 38a.
"of the dangling flesh," etc.—cf. above, vi, 7.
20. B. AZ 38b.
"If they were sweet"—in which case, since they may be eaten raw, cooking does not render them forbidden; cf. Sec. 14.
"became sweet"—so Oxford MS, *u-mittĕḵom.*
21. B. AZ 38b. Wheat and barley were never kneaded with vinegar, hence there was no danger of libation wine.
22. AZ 2:6; B. *ibid.* 38b.
"grievous sin"—P. Shab 1:4; P. AZ 2:8.
23. AZ 2:7.
24. B. AZ 38b; Solomon ibn Adret, Responsa, III, 246.
"Similarly, pickled vegetables"—AZ 2:7.
"pickled . . . locusts"—B. AZ 40b.
25. B. AZ 32a.
26. B. AZ 34b.
27. B. Yeḇ 114a; Shab 90b. Cf. B. Er 40b.
"Similarly," etc.—cf. III, I, xxiv, 11 (YJS, *14,* 161), which seemingly does not agree with the statement made here. See MM and KM *ad loc.,* and BY to ṬOḤ 343.
28. B. Naz 29a. Cf. Exod. R. 1:1; SER, Chap. 13 (65–66).
"and avoidance of sin"—so Oxford MS (*ubi-pĕrišuṯ*).
29. B. Mak 16b; Shab 90b; cf. ARN 26 (YJS, *10,* 112).
"revolting"—Oxford MS has *ḳaṣah* for *ḳehah* in the printed text.
30. B. Ber 53b; Ḥul 105b.
31. B. Mak 16b; Beḳ 44b; Ber 62a; and I, II, iv, 1.
32. Cf. B. Ber 53b; ShM, principle 4.

Treatise III: Šĕḥiṭah

Chapter I

1. B. Ḥul 27b, 28a; ShM, positive commandments 146–147; MhM *ad loc.*
"thou shalt ḳill of thy herd"—Hebrew *wĕ-zaḇaḥta,* a term signifying sacrificial slaughtering.
2. "concerning šĕḥiṭah"—B. Pes 7b; P. Ber 9:3; without specifying the species slaughtered, since the same law applies to all.
"the meat is nevertheless permitted"—since the omission of a blessing does not render a ceremony invalid; B. Ber 15a; HG(H), p. 510.
"It is forbidden," etc.—B. Ḥul 117b.
"He is . . . not liable to a flogging"—no flogging is incurred for transgression of a comprehensive prohibtion, B. Sanh 63a; ShM, principle 9.
"it is allowed to cut a portion from the animal"—B. Ḥul 33a; by this time the animal has completely lost consciousness.
3. B. Ḥul 27b.
"locusts"—B. Ker 21b.

"As for locusts, it is said"—for the pertinence of the Scriptural verse quoted by Maimonides see ThB 56a, and MM. For the varying interpretations of Isa. 33:4 cf. Targum and Ḳimḥi versus Rashi.

"live fish"—Tos Ter 9:6; other authorities forbid it as an abomination; cf. MM.

4. B. Ḥul 27a, 28a.

"commandment"—the word *commandment* in Exod. 24:12 is regarded as referring to the Oral Law, in contradistinction to the word *law* in the same verse which is taken to refer to the Written Law; B. Ber 5a.

5. B. Ḥul 27b.

"the whole of which"—Ḥul 1:4.

"In the gullet"—B. Ḥul 43b.

"as far as the point," etc.—B. Ḥul 44a; HG(H), p. 517; Alfasi, Ḥul Chap. 3.

"broken up"—into folds.

6. B. Ḥul 43b, 44a, 56b.

"wide part of the gullet"—i.e. the pharynx.

"in his two fingers"—HG(H), p. 517; Alfasi, Ḥul Chap. 3.

"it depends upon its size"—cf. B. Ḥul 43b; BY to ṬYD 20.

7. B. Ḥul 19a, 45a.

8. B. Ḥul 45a. See MM and KM.

9. Ḥul 1:4.

"If he severs," etc.—Ḥul 2:1.

10. Ḥul 2:1.

11. B. Ḥul 28a–b, 19b.

"If the windpipe of a bird is split half open"—B. Ḥul 29a.

12. B. Ḥul 9a.

"scrupulous and expert"—literally, "alert and speedy."

13. B. Ḥul 9a. The Talmudic passage continues: "Once it has been slaughtered, it is under the presumption of being valid, until it is known what has rendered it ṭĕrefah." Cf. xi, 3 and 13.

14. Ḥul 1:2; B. *ibid.* 16b.

15–16. B. Ḥul 17b.

17. B. Ḥul 32a.

"but not sharp"—yet sharp enough to cut, although less efficiently than with a properly sharpened knife, since no knife free from notches is so dull as to be useless for cutting; cf. MM.

"all day long"—assuming that he can do it without stopping at all.

18. B. Ḥul 17b.

19. Tos Ḥul 1:6; B. Ḥul 15b, 16a, and decision of Alfasi.

"tooth . . . toenail"—of an animal; ŠYD 6, 2.

20. B. Ḥul 16b.

21. B. Ḥul 18a.

"a saw"—literally "a sickle"; in this context, an instrument combining a knife and a saw; cf. Sec. 22.

22. B. Ḥul 8a; LhR 1543(169).

"to a white heat . . . valid"—for a variant reading, "invalid," see KM.

"the other even"—Ḥul 1:2, and Rashi *ad loc.;* B. *ibid.* 15b.

23. B. Ḥul 17b.

24. B. Ḥul 10a.

"even the first"—since the knife may have become notched on the hide, before the first šĕḥiṭah.

25. B. Ḥul 10b.

26. B. Ḥul 17b, 18a; I, III, vi, 14 (item 20 in the list of those liable to be put under a ban). In the first instance, an apology and a promise to transgress no more cancels the ban and entitles the slaughterer to resume his occupation. In the second instance, like the slaughterer convicted of dispensing ṭĕrefah meat (cf. above, II, viii, 9), he must prove by positive acts of repentance that he is fit to be permitted to slaughter again. Cf. ŠRA 92, and commentary thereto.

"otherwise he would rely upon himself," etc.—in B. Ḥul 10b the reason given is disrespect for the Sage; cf. the detailed discussion in Alexander Schorr, *Tĕḇu'oṯ Šor,* 18, 35.

27. Ḥul 2:3; B. *ibid.* 31a.

"the blade of a small knife"—literally "the tip of a small *'izmel"*; on the various uses of the 'izmel cf. *'Aruḳ, s.v.* (ed. Kohut, I, 52–53; and p. xxxix, where the *'Or zaru'a* is quoted, to the effect that the 'izmel was provided with "horns," i.e. guards (cf. B. Ḥul 31a), to ensure that the blade would only puncture and not make a cut).

28. B. Ḥul 13b, 17a.

29. Ḥul 1:1; B. *ibid.* 15a. Cf. III, I, vi, 23 (YJS, *14,* 39).

Chapter II

1. Sif Deut. 12:21; B. Ḳid 57b; MhM *ad loc.*

"flesh of desire"—referred to in Deut. 12:20: flesh of animals intended for human consumption, and not for offering upon the altar.

"Hence you learn," etc.—that is, "thou shalt kill far from (i.e. outside) the place which the Lord has chosen (i.e. the Temple)"; cf. Sec. 2.

2. B. Ḳid 57b; MhM *ad loc.;* Tos Ḥul 2:14–15.

"It was required to be buried"—Tem 7:4; B. *ibid.* 34a.

"by stabbing"—according to B. Ḥul 17a, animals killed by stabbing were permitted to the children of Israel in the wilderness; cf. below, IV, 17. All the instances which follow are not regarded as constituting šĕḥiṭah.

"or if an Israelite," etc.—B. Ḳid 58a; Ḥul 85b.

3. B. BB 81b.

"they were permitted to be consumed"—B. Ḥul 85b.

"All these things," etc.—B. Pes 21b; PhM to Ḳid 2:9; XI, II, ii, 8 (YJS, *9,* 65).

4. B. Tem 11b.

5. Ḥul 2:9; B. *ibid.* 41b; PhM *ad loc.*

6. B. Ḥul 41b.

"should . . . imitate the heretics"—who slaughter in this manner. The Hebrew word for "imitate" is *yĕḥaḳḳeh;* the Gemara connects this word with the Biblical injunction not to follow the laws (or customs, Hebrew *ḥoḳ*) of the heathen, and Rashi accordingly interprets this passage as "lest he should confirm the heretics in their laws." Danby follows Rashi.

"over the side of a ship"—Ḥul 2:9.

7–8. B. Ḥul 16b. MM *ad loc.*

8. "as will be explained"—below, iii, 11.

"in the case of a bird"—whose body weighs but little.

9. Ḥul 2:3; B. *ibid.* 31a.

10. Ḥul 2:2.

"Similarly, if two men," etc.—B. Ḥul 30a–b; ŠRA 124, and Berlin's commentary, no. 14.

"as though with a strigil"—B. Ḥul 19b.

11. B. Ḥul 12b; 31a; cf. 30b.

12. Ḥul 1:1, for deaf-mute, imbecile, and minor. Cf. below, iv, 5.

"a drunkard"—cf. Tos Ter 3:1; B. Er 65a.

"If, however, a knife is dropped"—Ḥul 2:3.

"a human being"—Tos Ḥul 1:1.

13. B. Ḥul 16a.

14. Ḥul 2:8; B. *ibid.* 40a; R. Nissim to Alfasi *ad loc.*

"that šĕḥiṭah is invalid"—but the meat is permitted for benefit, since mountains and hills in themselves are not idols (B. AZ 45a).

"the Planet of the Sea," etc.—i.e. the Spirit of the Sea (cf. Rashi, quoted by KM), which can be worshiped as an idol.

15. B. Ḥul 39b.

"is derived," etc.—B. Ḥul 39a.

"as will be explained"—VIII, vii, xv, 10 (YJS, *12,* 361f.).

16. B. Ḥul 39b.

17–18. Ḥul 2:10. For the various offerings see VIII, v (YJS, *12,* 163 ff.)

17. "as if one had slaughtered consecrated animals"—since he can render them consecrated by making a freewill offering of them.

18. "this applies also to the Paschal lamb"—B. Ḥul 41b.

19. B. Ḥul 41b; Tem 5:5; IX, vi, ii, 1 (YJS, *4,* 179–80); The animal slaughtered was not designated beforehand for that specific sacrifice; hence, when the person slaughtered it under the name of that sacrifice, he was actually offering a substitute (cf. Lev. 27:10) for the proper sacrificial animal.

20. B. Ḥul 41b. MM *ad loc.*

"If a woman"—who has not borne a child (cf. further on). Women may perform šĕḥiṭah; cf. below, iv, 4, and note thereto.

"the burnt offering due after childbirth"—Lev. 12:6.

"the burnt offering of a Nazirite"—Num. 6:14.

"a vow"—Num. 6:2.

21. Ḥul 2:8, 10; B. *ibid.* 40a, 41a.

"For an Israelite cannot render forbidden," etc.—B. Ḥul 40b.

22. Ḥul 2:7; LM *ad loc.*

"as will be explained"—iv, 11. It should be pointed out, however, that whereas here the indicated reason is that the intention of the heathen is suspect, in iv, 11 the reason is adduced that it may bring about undue familiarity.

Chapter III

1. B. Ḥul 9a.
2. Ḥul 2:3; B. *ibid.* 32a; KM *ad loc.*
3. B. Ḥul 32a.
"In the case of a bird," etc.—for the source and interpretation of this rule see KM and ThB 24a.
4. B. Ḥul 32a; MhM, I, *ad loc.*
5. Tos. Ḥul 2:2; B. *ibid.* 28a.
6. B. Ḥul 28a.
"as will be explained"—below, Sec. 22–23.
8. B. Ḥul 28a.
9. Ḥul 2:4; B. *ibid.* 30b, 20b.
10. B. Ḥul 30b.
11. Ḥul 2:3.
12. B. Ḥul 19a.
"the great ring"—the cricoid cartilage.
13. B. Ḥul 19a; MM and KM *ad loc.*
14. B. Ḥul 28a, 44a; HG(H), p. 512; ThR 87.
15–17. B. Ḥul 54a.
16. B. Shab 128b.
18. Ḥul 2:4.
"as we have explained"—above, i, 1 and 4.
19. B. Ḥul 21a. Cf. ThR 91.
"If the animal is split asunder"—so Oxford MS (as in B. Ḥul 21a).
"Similarly, if its neck is fractured"—B. Ḥul 20b.
"like a fish"—B. Ḥul 21a.
"or if the major part . . . perforated"—B. Ḥul 32b.
"and birds"—B. Ḥul 56a.
20–21. B. Ḥul 43a.
20. "the point of the perforation"—B. Ḥul 11b.
21. "If a thorn," etc.—B. Ḥul 43a–b.
22. B. Ḥul 43a–b.
23. B. Ḥul 44a–b.
"If it has a number of small perforations," etc.—B. Ḥul 45a.
"they combine"—that is, their sizes are added to one another.
24. B. Ḥul 45a; MhM *ad loc.*
25. B. Ḥul 50a.

Chapter IV

1–2. B. Ḥul 9a.
3. B. Ḥul 3b.
4. "Even women and slaves"—Zeḇ 3:1. For women as slaughterers see C. Duschinsky's article in *Orient and Occident, Gaster Anniversary Volume* (London 1936), pp. 96–106. The slaves are those who have been immersed and became proselytes; see above, I, xii, 11.

5. Ḥul 1:1; B. *ibid.* 86a; cf. above, ii, 12.

"a drunkard"—cf. ThB 8b.

6–7. B. Ḥul 12a.

8. B. Ḥul 12a; LhR 1562(198).

9. Ter 1:2; PhM *ad loc.*

"he may continue to perform šĕḥiṭah"—even though he can no longer pronounce the appropriate blessing; cf. above, i, 2.

10. Ḥul 1:1; B. *ibid.* 13b.

11. Ḥul 1:1, and Rashi *ad loc.;* B. *ibid.* 13a.

12. B. Ḥul 13a, which points out that the thoughts of a heathen in such matters are not normally directed towards idolatry, in which case the regulation of the preceding Section should not apply. The Sages, however, have adopted a stringent view ("have erected a barrier"). Cf. above, ii, 22; and see Shabbethai Kohen to ŠYD 2, 2 for variant readings.

13. B. Ḥul 29b.

14. B. Ḥul 4a–b.

"an apostate to such an extent as to be guilty of idolatry or public profanation of the Sabbath"—and therefore regarded as a transgressor against the whole of Judaism, B. Ḥul 5a.

"an atheist"—so Oxford MS and editio princeps (*min*); the editions have "Epicurean."

"as we have explained in the Laws Concerning Repentance"—I, v, iii, 7–9 (see also PhM to Ḥul 1:2); according to the definitions given there, the text here should perhaps read "an atheist, or one who denies the authority of the Torah."

15. Cf. B. Ḥul 4a, which states that a deliberate transgressor may perform šĕḥiṭah if someone hands him a proper knife, since "he will not discard that which is permitted in order to eat that which is forbidden." A man invalidated as a witness is regarded by Maimonides as less than a deliberate transgressor. For a definition of witnesses invalidated because of transgression see XIV, II, x (YJS, *3,* 102 ff.).

16. B. Ḥul 3a.

"Sadducees and Boethusians"—the Boethusians are always coupled with the Sadducees in Talmudic literature as sects who denied the validity of the Oral Law; they took their names from Zadok and Boethus, disciples of Antigonus of Socho who rejected his teaching (Ab̲ 1:3). Cf. ARN Chap. 5 (YJS, *10,* 39). Maimonides has in mind the contemporary Karaites who in medieval Jewish literature are often called Sadducees. Cf. MM, and above, I, xi, 15 (and notes thereto).

17–18. B. Ḥul 17a.

Chapter V

1. "Laws Concerning Forbidden Foods"—above, II, iv, 6–9.

2. B. Ḥul 43a.

3. B. Ḥul 53a.

"'clawed' is . . . explicitly mentioned in the Torah"—i.e., ṭĕrefah as used in Scripture is understood to mean torn with claws; cf. above, II, iv, 6.

4. Ḥul 3:1; B. *ibid.* 52b.

5–7. B. Ḥul 53a.
6. B. Ḥul 52b.
8. B. Ḥul 54a.
9–10. B. Ḥul 53b.
10. "the slightest degree"—B. Ḥul 54a.
11. B. Ḥul 53a.
"Similarly, if a fox," etc.—B. Ḥul 53b.
12. B. Ḥul 53a–b.

Chapter VI

1. Ḥul 3:1.
2. B. Ḥul 43b.
"We have already explained"—above, i, 6.
3. B. Ḥul 45a; Alfasi, Ḥul Chap. 3.
"Where the brain begins to lead off"—B. Ḥul 45b.
"a different law applies"—below, ix, 3.
4. B. Ḥul 45b.
5. Ḥul 3:1; B. *ibid.* 45b.
6. Ḥul 3:1; B. *ibid.* 48a.
7. B. Ḥul 49a.
"a kernel"—Hebrew *nĕwiyyah* (so Oxford MS and editio princeps; the editions misprint *nĕziyyah*); Arabic *nawāt,* "date stone."
8. B. Ḥul 45b; MhM *ad loc.*
"the blood originates"—the liver was regarded as the source of the blood; cf. B. Beḵ 55a, and Rashi *ad loc.;* Preuss, p. 108.
"Consequently"—B. Ḥul 48b.
9. B. Ḥul 49a.
"If the flesh of the liver is infested with worms"—Tos Ḥul 3:10; B. Ḥul 48a.
10. Ḥul 3:1; B. *ibid.* 49b; Alfasi *ad loc.*
"Similarly, in every case"—B. Ḥul 48a, 49b.
"The exceptions," etc.—B. Ḥul 49b, 50a.
"the membrane which covers the whole heart"—i.e. the pericardium.
"The fat of a wild beast," etc.—B. Ḥul 49b; HP, p. 198.
11. Ḥul 3:1; B. *ibid.* 50b, 51a; HP, p. 201.
12. B. Ḥul 50b, 51a; HP, p. 201; MhM *ad loc.*
13. B. Ḥul 58b.
"If the animal remains alive for three days"—so Oxford MS; cf. MM, KM, and R. David ibn Abi Zimra *ad loc.*
"the entrails . . . must be inspected"—ṬYD 51, and BY *ad loc.*
"and if found perforated"—Ḥul 3:1.
"the coils of the ileum"—B. Ḥul 48b.
14. B. Ḥul 50a.
"If a wolf," etc.—B. Ḥul 9a.
15. Ḥul 3:4; B. *ibid.* 56b.
16. B. Ḥul 50a, 51a.
"about four fingers"—Alfasi *ad loc.*

17. B. Ḥul 56a.
"if the roof of a bird's crop"—Ḥul 3:4; B. *ibid.* 56b.
18. Ḥul 3:4; B. *ibid.* 43a; HG(H), p. 522.
19. Ḥul 3:2; B. *ibid.* 55a–b.
20. B. Ḥul 58b. See KM *ad loc.* Cf. Ibn Adret, Responsa, I, 3.
"Similarly, if it was born with two such organs"—B. Ḥul 58b.
"two gall bladders"—HG(H), p. 524.
21. B. Ḥul 58b; KM and LM *ad loc.*

Chapter VII

1. Ḥul 3:1; B. *ibid.* 46a.
"If the windpipe is perforated"—B. Ḥul 45a.
"not valid for šĕḥiṭah"—see above, i, 7.
2. B. Ḥul 32b.
3. B. Ḥul 48b; LhR 1581(217).
"and a membrane has formed over the perforation"—B. Ḥul 47b.
"If the main lobe of the lung is perforated"—B. Ḥul 48a.
4–5. B. Ḥul 48a; MhM *ad loc.*
5. Cf. Responsa of Jacob Berab, 1.
6–7. B. Ḥul 47b.
8. Cf. below, xi, 6.
9. B. Ḥul 47b.
"empties itself like a ladle"—i.e. is so full of fluid decomposed matter that it can be poured out as if out of a ladle.
10. B. Ḥul 48a.
"malodorous secretion"—B. Ḥul 55b, and Alfasi. Cf. Joseph ibn Migas, Responsa, 34.
11. B. Ḥul 47a; HP, p. 199.
"there is no possible way of examining them"—to find the perforation.
12. B. Ḥul 53b.
"If the lung is found to be perforated in a place where the hand," etc.—B. Ḥul 49a.
"in another place"—B. Ḥul 50a, and Alfasi.
13. B. Ḥul 50a.
"If a perforation is found in one of the swellings"—B. Ḥul 46b.
"a comparison is not decisive"—the shape and color of swellings are not constant, but change, hence comparison would be of no use (cf. MM). Literally, "the matter cannot be recognized."
14. B. Ḥul 48b.
15. "a worm"—B. Ḥul 49a.
[15A]. "Another factor is color"—B. Ḥul 46b, 47b; HG(H), p. 526.
16. B. Ḥul 46b.
17–19. B. Ḥul 47b.
18. "until the lung is inflated"—the source for this ruling is found in a responsum of R. Hai Gaon; cf. MM *ad loc.* and R. Nissim to Alfasi, Ḥul Chap. 3; cf. also KM *ad loc.*

20. Ḥul 3:3; B. *ibid.* 56b.

21. B. Ḥul 56b; MO and MhM *ad loc.*
"Similarly, if the outer skin of the gullet," etc.—B. Ḥul 43a.

Chapter VIII

1–4. B. Ḥul 47a, for the lung. For the legs see Sec. 11.
"Should it be found to be perforated," etc.—this is a Gaonic decision (MM).

4. "the animal is permitted"—when the lobes are in line, the rule that "every additional organ is considered equivalent to the absence of that organ" (above, vi, 20) does not apply; Rashi *ad loc.*

5. B. Ḥul 46b; MM *ad loc.;* Levi ibn Ḥabib, Responsa, 6.

6–7. B. Ḥul 47b.

7. "Similarly, if the body of the lung is defective"—Ḥul 3:1; B. *ibid.* 47b.
"that it can be scraped off with the fingernail"—B. Ḥul 46b.

8. B. Ḥul 47b.

9. Ḥul 3:2; B. *ibid.* 55b; HG(H), p. 536.

10. B. Ḥul 55b; PhM to Ḥul 3:2.

11. B. Ḥul 58b; Bek 40a; cf. HG(H), p. 538, and n. 55.
"On the other hand," etc. — the principle "addition = absence" applies only to a hind leg.
"if a foreleg is amputated"—Ḥul 4:6; B. *ibid.* 76a.

12. Ḥul 4:6; B. *ibid.* 76b.
"Should flesh," etc.—cf. Levi ibn Ḥabib, Responsa, 83.

13. Ḥul 4:6; B. *ibid.* 76a; and the decision of Alfasi.
"sixteen fingerbreadths"—Solomon ibn Adret, Responsa, I, 36.

14. B. Ḥul 76b; PhM to Ḥul 4:6, 3:4; ThR 90; Solomon ibn Adret, Responsa, I, 29, 160.

15. B. Ḥul 76a. The translation here follows the text of the Oxford MS.
"as we have explained"—above, Sec. 11.
"as will be explained"—below, Sec. 17.

16. Ḥul 3:1 (liver); 3:2 (jaw, but see note to Sec. 23); 4:6 (meeting of the sinews).

17. "We have already explained"—above, Sec. 15.

18–19. B. Ḥul 76b, and Alfasi.

19. "only one"—so Oxford MS, editio princeps, and MM; variant reading: "every one"; the Gemara quotes both views.

20. Ḥul 3:6.
"just as is an animal"—above, Sec. 11. Cf. B. Ḥul 57a.

21. Ḥul 3:1; B. *ibid.* 46a.
"If the liver is torn," etc.—B. Ḥul 46a.

22. B. Ḥul 46a.

23. ThR 89; KM.
"lower jaw"—Ḥul 3:2.
"if it is detached," etc.—B. Ḥul 44a.

24. Maimonides' own summation.

25. Ḥul 3:2; B. *ibid.* 55b.

"Consequently if it was born," etc.—Alfasi *ad loc.*
"if the kidney is perforated"—B. Ḥul 55b.
26. B. Ḥul 55b.
"Similarly, if the kidney is afflicted"—B. Ḥul 55a, and Alfasi.
"Likewise, if secretion . . . is found"—B. Ḥul 55b.

Chapter IX

1. Ḥul 3:1; B. *ibid.* 45b.
"Similarly," etc.—Ḥul 3:2.
"if the marrow inside," etc.—B. Ḥul 45b.
2–3. B. Ḥul 45b.
4. B. Ḥul 45b, 46a.
"These three branchings-off are three bones"—so Oxford MS.
5. Ḥul 3:1; B. *ibid.* 50b.
6. B. Ḥul 50b.
7. Ḥul 3:2; B. *ibid.* 55b. Cf. PhM *ad loc.*
"a *sela'* 's breadth of hide"—LhR 1575(211).
"it would appear . . . permitted"—PhM declares it forbidden.
8. Ḥul 3:1; B. *ibid.* 51a.
"from a height of ten handbreadths"—B. BḲ 50b.
9. B. Ḥul 51b.
"If one leaves the animal on high ground"—B. Ḥul 51a.
10–11. B. Ḥul 51a.
10. "rams"—so Rashi *ad loc.;* literally "male animals."
12. B. Ḥul 51b.
13. B. Ḥul 51a.
14–16. B. Ḥul 51b, 52a.
17. Cf. above, Sec. 8.
"The sole exception is the womb"—B. Ḥul 51a; MhM to Secs. 17–18; LhR 1401–02(28–29).
19. Ḥul 3:3; B. *ibid.* 56b. Cf. Tosafoṯ to B. Ḥul 51b.
"as we have explained"—above, Sec. 17.
20. Ḥul 3:3; B. *ibid.* 56b.
"which we have explained"—above, Sec. 17.
21. B. Ḥul 44a; KM and MhM *ad loc.*
"as we have explained"—above, i, 6.

Chapter X

1. Ḥul 3:1; B. *ibid.* 52a.
2. B. Ḥul 52a.
3. B. Ḥul 54b.
4. B. Ḥul 57b.
"If the wing is dislocated"—B. Ḥul 57a, and Alfasi.
"If the foreleg of an animal is dislocated"—B. Ḥul 57a.
5. B. Ḥul 54b.

"If the skull is perforated," etc.—B. Ḥul 45a.

6. B. Ḥul 52b.

"length"—literally "height."

7. B. Ḥul 56a.

"If a land bird"—Ḥul 3:3; B. *ibid.* 56a.

"one should place his hand," etc.—both these interpretations of B. Ḥul 56a are in Alfasi.

8. Ḥul 3:5; B. *ibid.* 58b. PhM *ad loc.* interprets the terms as: "strangled by its own blood, or overpowered by its own black bile, or rendered unconscious by its own white secretion."

9. An enumeration of all the cases detailed previously. Aaron ben Jacob, *'Orḥoṯ ḥayyim,* ed. Schlesinger (Berlin, 1899–1902), p. 428, enumerates 71 cases. Cf. also KM *ad loc.*

10. B. Ḥul 57a

"defects of the kidney"—since the Talmud gives the sizes only for large and small animals; cf. above, viii, 26.

"round like a grape"—and has therefore no thick and thin parts; cf. above, vi, 19.

11. Ḥul 3:3; B. *ibid.* 56a. Cf. ThR 90.

12. B. Ḥul 54a; cf. *ibid.* 57b.

13. *"which* THEY *shall teach thee"*—B. Sanh 87a.

14. "since the evidence of only one witness," etc.—B. Yeḇ 88a; Ḥul 10b. Cf. also above, II, viii, 7; and XIV, II, xi, 7 (YJS, *3,* 106).

"And we have already explained"—above, II, viii, 7–8; xi, 25.

"If ṭĕrefah meat," etc.—cf. above, II, viii, 9; and XIV, II, xii, 9 (YJS, *3,* 110).

Chapter XI

1. B. Ḥul 57b, 58a; and above, iii, 11.

2. B. Ḥul 53b.

3. B. Ḥul 9a, 51a.

4. All the cases cited have already been explained.

5. B. Ḥul 48a; Isaac ben Sheshet, Responsa, 188; MhM *ad loc.*

6. Cf. Responsa of Jacob Berab, 1.

"inflate it in warm water"—as above, vii, 7; LM *ad loc.*

7. Cf. Tanḥ Lev. 11:2(8).

"suspended adhesion"—the elaboration of these laws of suspended adhesion belongs to the post-Talmudic period. They are extensions of the rule in B. Ḥul 48a, that if the lung is perforated and the flank of the animal seals up the perforation, it is permitted, provided that it is securely attached to the flesh. Any adhesion therefore which has a strain placed upon it renders the animal invalid. Cf. Secs. 8–9.

"in consecutive order"—cf. above, viii, 5; MM and MhM *ad loc.*

8. MhM *ad loc.*

10. "My . . . father"—Maimon ben Joseph, who died some time after 1165.

"those who declared it forbidden"—ShE(A) III, p. 49; SMG, positive commandment 63.

"In a few places . . . permitted"—so also RABD *ad loc.*

11. ShE(A) III, p. 48; *'Iṭṭur* 38b, 41b; BY to ṬYD 39.

12. "we have never heard," etc.—since the lung of a bird is not statutorily subject to special examination (cf. above, x, 10).

13. B. Ḥul 9a; KM, LM *ad loc.*

14. "only out of regard for the general custom"—since the examination of the lung *in situ* (above, Sec. 7), whose omission is thus rectified, is in itself only a matter of custom.

15. "the animal is declared forbidden"—on the ground that an adhesion is definite evidence of a perforation. Cf. MM *ad loc.;* BY to ṬYD 39.

"waste of Israelite money"—cf. B. RH 27a: "The Torah feels concern for the property of Israel."

Chapter XII

1–2. Ḥul 5:1–2.

"upon the second animal"—HG(H), p. 560.

"Consequently," etc.—B. Ḥul 82b.

2. "animals which may not be eaten"—and were devoted to the upkeep of the Temple.

"Consequently," etc.—PhM to Ḥul 5:1.

3. Ḥul 5:3.

"becomes nĕbelah in his hand"—by having been slaughtered not in full accordance with the pertinent rules.

4–5. Ḥul 6:3.

4. "since their šĕḥiṭah," etc.—cf. above, iv, 5.

6. B. Ḥul 85a.

"Consequently"—Ḥul 5:2–3.

"which had been condemned to stoning"—Exod. 21:28 ff.

"a heifer whose neck was to be broken"—Deut. 21:4.

"a Red Heifer"—Num. 19:1 ff.

"for the purpose of idolatry," etc.—PhM to Ḥul 5:2.

7. B. Ḥul 81b.

"he is liable to no more than a flogging"—since the death penalty due for idolatry, or any other penalty, cannot be inflicted when there was no previous warning.

8. "only in respect to a clean domestic animal"—but not to a clean wild beast.

"It obtains also for crossbreeds"—of domestic animal and wild beast. The deer is a wild beast, the goat a domestic animal. The principle involved is whether a crossbred young is to be classified with its sire or its dam. There was much controversy in this matter; see B. Ḥul 79b, and LM and MhM *ad loc.*

9. B. Ḥul 79b.

"Similarly, in the case of a crossbreed"—Tos Ḥul 5:1.

"he is liable to a flogging"—since sire and dam are both domestic animals.

10. LṬ III, 123; B. Ḥul 58a.

"emerges alive"—Tos Ḥul 4:5.

"sets its feet"—B. Ḥul 75b; cf. above, II, v, 14.

11. B. Ḥul 78b, 79a; LM and MhM *ad loc.*

12. Ḥul 5:3.

"and then the dam, he is liable to be flogged only once"—since it is the slaughtering of the dam which constitutes the transgression. This principle of the act which constitutes the transgression applies to all the instances which follow.

13–16. Ḥul 5:3.

"and seek a legal decision"—Tos Ḥul 5:4–5; B. *ibid.* 82a.

14. Ḥul 5:3; LM *ad loc.*

"must inform the purchaser"—since on those occasions people usually purchase animals for immediate slaughter.

15. "If . . . the day is still young"—so that there is no certainty that the purchaser will slaughter his animal on the same day; he may hold it over for another day. Cf. Solomon ibn Adret to B. Ḥul 83a.

17. Ḥul 5:5; B. *ibid.* 83a–b; Tos *ibid.* 5:8.

"the day follows the night"—as in the account of Creation; this applies to all Jewish law.

"at twilight"—concerning which it is uncertain whether it is part of the preceding day or of the following night.

Chapter XIII

1. B. Ḥul 115a.

"if he lets it go"—Ḥul 12:4.

2. Ḥul 12:4.

"the pertinent positive commandment"—formulated in the following verse: *Thou shalt . . . let the dam go.*

3. B. Ḥul 141a.

"Thou shalt in any wise let . . . go"—literally "with a letting go shalt thou let go," interpreted to mean "by thy conscious action shalt thou let go."

4. B. Ḥul 141b.

5. B. Ḥul 141b, and decision of Alfasi.

"If he sends it off and it returns"—Ḥul 12:3; PhM *ad loc.*

"four or five times"—this is merely a round number; he must continue releasing the bird until it flies off for good. Cf. XIV, 1, xiii, 1 (YJS, *3*, 37), where Maimonides renders the Mishnaic "four or five times" (Sanh 6:1) with "many times."

6. Ḥul 12:3.

7. Ḥul 12:3; B. *ibid.* 141b, and Rashi *ad loc.*

"he is not obligated"—since Scripture does not require setting her free more than once.

"If he sets the dam free"—having first taken her young.

8. Ḥul 12:1 (not domesticated) and 2 (clean); PhM *ad loc.;* Sif Deut. 22:7.

"chance to be," etc.—B. Ḥul 139b.

9. Ḥul 12:3; B. *ibid.* 140a.

"If the young are ṭĕrefah"—B. Ḥul 140a. Cf. Sif Deut. 22:6. According to R. Nissim (to Alfasi on Ḥul 12), the captor stretched his hand into the nest and performed incomplete šĕḥiṭah upon the young, thus rendering them ṭĕrefah.

10. Ḥul 12:2; B. *ibid.* 138b, 140b, and Alfasi.

"an unclean bird"—Ḥul 12:2.

11. B. Ḥul 140b.

"ṭĕrefah"—i.e. the šĕḥiṭah performed upon her was left incomplete; cf. above, note to Sec. 9.

12. B. Ḥul 140b.

"the organs"— of the mother, according to ṬYD 292; of the young, according to MM and KM; of both mother and young, according to Joel Sirkes to ṬYD 292.

13. Ḥul 12:3; B. *ibid.* 140b; LM *ad loc.*

14–16. B. Ḥul 140b.

14. "he is not liable to a flogging"—since in all these cases no decision is given and the matter remains in doubt.

17. Ḥul 12:3.

"on the surface of the water"—B. Ḥul 139b.

18. B. Ḥul 141b.

"and the fact that the courtyard belongs to him," etc.—although generally a person may claim possession of goods that are found on his property (cf. B. BM 11a: "The ground belonging to a person takes possession for him [of what is found upon it] even without his knowledge").

19. Ḥul 12:5; B. *ibid.* 141a; MhM, I, *ad loc.*

"a Scriptural commandment"—Lev. 14:4.

"since a positive commandment"—to take the bird for purification rites, cannot override a positive commandment, to release the dam, and a negative commandment, not to take the dam, combined.

"while a positive commandment," etc.—once he has taken the bird, he has only a positive commandment to fulfill, namely, to release it.

20. Ḥul 12:1; B. *ibid.* 138b, 139a.

21. B. Ḥul 138b.

"to be brought to court"—and it cannot therefore be taken "unto thyself."

Chapter XIV

1. "positive commandment"—B. Beṣ 8b.

"or bird"—B. Ḥul 85a.

"before covering up the blood, one must recite the benediction"—Tos Ber 7:11 and Ḥul 6:9; P. Ber 9:3; B. Ḥul 86b. HG(H), p. 569 requires benediction after covering up the blood.

2. Ḥul 6:1; B. *ibid.* 84a.

3. Tos Ḥul 6:7: "since the commandment to cover it up precedes its consecration." B. *ibid.* 139a.

4. Ḥul 6:1; B. *ibid.* 80a; Beṣ 8b. This crossbreed or doubtful animal is the *koy* referred to there.

"on the Sabbath for the sake of an invalid"—Tos Ḥul 6:4; B. *ibid.* 84b.

"Similarly," etc.—Ḥul 6:1; B. *ibid.* 84b. Cf. Tos Ḥul 6:5.

5. Ḥul 6:4; B. *ibid.* 86b.

6. Ḥul 6:5; B. Zeḇ 78a.

7. Ḥul 6:4; B. *ibid.* 87a.

8. Ḥul 6:6; B. *ibid.* 88a.
9. B. Ḥul 87a.
10. Ḥul 6:2–3.
"privately"—cf. above, xii, 4, and note.
11–13. Ḥul 6:7; Tos *ibid.* 6:11; B. *ibid.* 88a–b; PhM *ad loc.*
11. "earth dust"—so Oxford MS (*bĕ-ʿafar*).
12. "Gold dust," etc.—PhM to Ḥul 6:7; LM *ad loc.*
13. "wood ashes"—Bes 1:2.
"apostate city"—cf. Deut. 13:13–18; B. Ḥul 89a.
14. B. Ḥul 83b.
15. B. Ḥul 87a.
"If he does not cover it up"—Ḥul 6:4.
16. B. Ḥul 87a; Shab 22a.
"For reverence is due," etc.—B. Yeḇ 6b; Gen. R. 44; Deut. R. 6; P. Neḏ 9:1; MN III, 26, 46.
"by making the commandments"—so Oxford MS (*'oṯam*).

GLOSSARY

Absent (*ḥăserah*)
One of the categories of ṭĕrefah

Amoraim
literally "expounders, expositors"; Talmudic authorities who flourished about 200-500, and whose discussions are embodied in the Gemara

Animal (*bĕhemah*)
domestic creature, as opposed to wild beast or beast of chase (*ḥayyah*)

'Ăšlaḡ
a kind of alkali or similar mineral used as soap

'Ăsufi
foundling, a child whose parentage is unknown

Bĕhemah
see Animal

Benefit (*hănayah, hăna'ah*)
indirect use of an article—such as for sale or for fuel—as distinguished from the direct eating of it

Bible
the Hebrew Bible consists of three main groups: (1) the Law (Torah), i.e. the five books of the Pentateuch; (2) the Prophets, subdivided into Prior Prophets (Joshua through Kings) and Latter Prophets (Isaiah through Malachi); and (3) the Writings (Psalms through Chronicles)

Clawed (*dĕrusah*)
one of the categories of ṭĕrefah

Coins
see Money

Consummation
see Initiation

Cubit
see Measures

Daily burnt offerings
two he-lambs offered daily in the Temple, one in the morning and one in the afternoon, at dusk; cf. Num. 28:1–8

Day and night

in the Jewish system of time-reckoning, the day begins with the preceding night; the night is counted from dusk to dawn, and the day from dawn to dusk, or sunrise to sunset. A daylight hour means 1/12 of the day as thus defined. Concerning twilight—i.e. the time between the beginning of the decline of the sun and sunset—there was doubt as to whether it belonged to the preceding day or to the following night.

Denar

see Money

Dĕrasah

see Pressing

Dĕrusah

see Clawed

Digging (*ḥălaḏah*)

one of the malpractices which render šĕḥiṭah invalid

Dough offering

the heave offering from the dough (1/24 of it) which was given to the priests; cf. Num. 15:18–21.

Egg

see Measures

Extinction (*ḳareṯ*)

divine punishment variously defined as (1) premature death, (2) death without leaving any issue, or (3) eradication of the soul in the world to come. Maimonides himself (I, v, viii, 1) favors the third explanation.

Fallen (*nĕfulah*)

one of the categories of ṭĕrefah

Fat

(1) *ḥeleḇ:* that part of the fat of a clean domestic animal which may not be eaten; in the case of sacrificial animals, this fat was burned upon the altar; cf. Lev. 3:17; (2) *šuman:* the part of the fat which may be eaten.

Fingerbreadth

see Measures

First fruits

cf. Deut. 26:1–11

Flux

discharge of matter from the sexual organs; particularly, flow of blood from the womb outside of the menstrual period

Fractured (*šĕḇurah*)
one of the categories of ṭĕrefah

Gaon (pl. *Geonim*)
the title borne by the presidents of the two Babylonian academies at Sura and Pumbeditha down to the 11th century

Gĕluḏah
a flayed animal

Gemara
that part of the Talmud which contains the comments of the Amoraim upon the Mishnah

Hağramah
see Misplacement

Ḥălaḏah
see Digging

Ḥăliṣah
the ceremony described in Deut. 25:7–10 to mark the refusal of a man to marry the childless wife of his deceased brother

Ḥallah
the portion of the dough which must be separated as the priest's share; Num. 15: 17–21

Hănayah, hăna'ah
see Benefit

Handbreadth
see Measures

Ḥăserah
see Absent

Ḥayyah
see Animal

Heave offering
a portion of the produce (about 2 per cent on the average) which was given to the priests who alone were permitted to eat it; cf. Num. 18:8; Lev. 22:10; Deut. 18:4

Heave offering of the tithe
out of the tithe which he received the Levite was obligated to give 1/10 to the priest; in other words, 1/100 of the original produce harvested by the Israelite; cf. Num. 18:25–32

Heifer, Red
cf. Num. Chap. 19

Heifer whose neck was to be broken
cf. Deut. 21:1–9

Ḥeleḇ
see Fat

Hours, Daylight
see Day and night

Ḥuṭ (pl. *ḥuṭin*)
literally "thread"; sinew or vein

'Iḳḳur
see Wrenching

Initiation and consummation
as applied to the sexual act, the insertion of the corona only, and of the entire male organ, respectively. Hence, the male participant is designated as "initiator" and "consummator"

'Issar
see Money

Jubilee year
the year concluding a series of seven Sabbatical cycles comprising 49 years; cf. Lev. 25:8–16. There was a difference of opinion as to whether the Jubilee year was the 49th year or an additional—i.e. 50th—year, but the majority inclined toward the latter view

Kareṯ
see Extinction

Kĕlisin
variously identified as a kind of fig, a kind of pea or bean, the fruit of the Judas tree, acorn, and licorice

Ḳĕru'ah
see Torn

Kohl
a preparation used in the East for painting the edges of the eyelids

Koy
(a kind of bearded antelope) a creature concerning which the Rabbis were in doubt as to whether it was to be classified as a domestic animal or as a wild beast.

Kutaḥ
porridge or preserve, consisting of sour milk, bread crusts, and salt

Law, The
see Bible

Levirate marriage (*yibbum*)

the marriage of a man to the childless widow of his brother; Deut. 25:5 ff.

Loḡ

see Measures

Ma'ăśer

see Tithes

Maiden (*na'ărah*)

a girl between the ages of 12 and 12 1/2; heretofore she is regarded as a minor, thereafter as an adult

Measures

cubit = the distance from the elbow to the tip of the middle finger

egg = the bulk of a medium-sized hen's egg

fingerbreadth = the breadth of the middle finger

handbreadth = 4 fingerbreadths

loḡ = the contents of 6 eggs

mile = 2,000 cubits (a journey of 18 minutes; hence a day's—i.e. 12 hours'—journey is 40 miles)

sĕ'ah = 24 loḡ (a container 3/5 cubit deep with a base 1/2 cubit square holds 2 sĕ'ah; III, 1, xv, 16 [YJS, *14*, 88])

siṭ = 2 handbreadths; cf. YJS, *14*, 548

Mĕrukkam

as applied to a human foetus, articulated, with recognizable joints

Min (pl. *Minim*)

literally "peculiar person"; a heretic or sectarian

Mina

see Money

Misplacement (*haḡramah*)

one of the malpractices which render šĕḥiṭah invalid

Mi'un

see Refusal

Mixed seeds of the vineyard

cf. Deut. 22:9–11

Money

denar = 6 *ma'ah* = 1/2 common shekel

'issar = 8 *pĕruṭah* (worth the value of 4 barleycorns of silver)

mina = 100 denar = 4 gold denar

pĕruṭah = the smallest copper coin, worth the value of half a barleycorn of silver

sela' = 2 common shekels = 1 Temple shekel

zuz = denar

Muḳṣeh

see Set apart

Mur'ah

a bird's crop; *cf. Zefeḳ*

Na'ărah

see Maiden

Nathin (pl. *Nethinim*)

a descendant of the Gibeonites who deceived Joshua (Josh. 9:3 ff.) and were condemned to be hewers of wood and drawers of water

Nazirite

a person who has uttered a vow to be a Nazirite was not permitted to drink wine or cut his hair until the expiration of his Nazirite term; cf. Num. Chap. 6

Nĕḇelah

an animal slaughtered in any manner deviating, be it ever so slightly, from that prescribed by Jewish law

Nĕfulah

see Fallen

Nĕḳuḇah

see Perforated

Nĕṭulah

see Removed

Nisan

the seventh month of the Jewish religious year, and the first of the civil year

Noachian commandments

seven universal precepts held to be incumbent not only upon Israelites but also upon all the "sons of Noah," i.e. the whole human race; cf. XIV, v, ix, 1 (YJS, *3*, 230–31)

Noṯar

see Remnant

'Omer

the sheaf of the first fruits of the harvest, also called the sheaf of waving, brought as an offering on the 16th day of Nisan; Lev. 23:9–14

'Orlah

literally "foreskin"; the fruit of newly planted trees in the first three years which was forbidden to be eaten; Lev. 19:23–25

Pausing (*šĕhiyyah*)

one of the malpractices which render šěḥiṭah invalid

Perforated (*nĕḵuḇah*)
one of the categories of ṭĕrefah

Pĕruṭah
see Money

Pĕsuḵah
see Split

Piggul
see Refuse

Pressing (*dĕrasah*)
one of the malpractices which render šĕḥiṭah invalid

Prophets
see Bible

Red Heifer
see Heifer, Red

Refusal (*mi'un*)
the right accorded to a minor orphan girl betrothed to someone by her mother or brother, to bring about the annulment of the betrothal by registering her refusal to marry her betrothed husband (Yeḇ 13:1–2); no divorce is then necessary.

Refuse (*piggul*)
a sacrifice rejectable in consequence of an improper intention in the mind of the officiating priest; VIII, vii, xiii, 1 (YJS, *12*, 350–51)

Remnant (*noṯar*)
an offering, or a portion of it, left over after the time prescribed for eating it, and due to be destroyed by burning; cf. Lev. 7:17; VIII, vii, xviii, 9–10 (YJS, *12*, 374–75)

Removed (*nĕṭulah*)
one of the categories of ṭĕrefah

Resident stranger
a semiproselyte who renounces idolatry in order to acquire limited citizenship in the Land of Israel

"Rose" (*warda*)
small ear of the lung lying within a pouch

Sabbatical year (*šĕmiṭṭah*)
the last year in a cycle of seven years, during which cultivation of land was forbidden and the fields must lie fallow; whatever grows in that year is regarded as ownerless property; cf. Exod. 23:10–11; Lev. 25:2–7

Sages

or Scribes; the post-Biblical scholars dating back to Ezra the Scribe (ca. 440 B.C.); the term, however, is loosely used for the Rabbis of the subsequent period who preserved and transmitted the Oral Law

Scripture
: *see* Bible, Torah

Sĕ'ah
: *see* Measures

Šĕḇurah
: *see* Fractured

Šĕḥiṭah
: the slaughtering of a clean domestic animal in strict accordance with Jewish law

Šĕhiyyah
: *see* Pausing

Selaʻ
: *see* Money

Šĕmiṭṭah
: *see* Sabbatical year

Set apart (*muḳṣeh*)
: an article of food or an object set aside and not intended to be consumed or handled during the Sabbath

Šĕṯuḳi (pl. *Šĕṯuḳim*)
: literally "silenced"; a child who does not know his father's identity

Sheaf of waving
: *see ʻOmer*

Shekel
: *see* Money

Shewbread
: cf. Exod. 25:30; Lev. 24:4–9

Ṣilṣul (*ṣirṣur*)
: a stone vessel containing a strainer and having an indented (comb-like) rim; a sort of cooler

Šilya
: caul, the membrane sometimes covering the head of a child at birth

Sin offering
: (1) regular ("fixed"): female sheep or goat; (2) "rising and falling," varied with the sinner's means; IX, iv, i, 4 (YJS, *4,* 96–97)

Siṭ
: *see* Measures

Split (*pĕsuḳah*)
one of the categories of ṭĕrefah

Šuman
see Fat

Tannaim
authorities cited in the Mishnah and the Baraita who flourished up to about the year 200

Ṭariṯ
salted minced fish

Ṭeḇel
produce from which the priests' and Levites' dues have not yet been separated

Ṭĕrefah
an animal torn by a wild beast or suffering from a serious organic disease, whose flesh is forbidden even if it has been slaughtered in accordance with Jewish law

Thank offering
cf. Lev. 7:12 ff.

Tithes (*maʿăśer*)
were of three kinds: the first tithe was given to the Levite in each of the first six years of the Sabbatical cycle; the second tithe was separated in the first, second, fourth and fifth years of the cycle and was consumed by the owner in Jerusalem; the poor man's tithe was given to the poor in the third and sixth years of the cycle

Torah
the Pentateuch and the law set forth therein; *see also* Bible

Torn (*ḳĕruʿah*)
one of the categories of ṭĕrefah

Ṭumṭum
a person whose sex cannot be determined with certainty

Twilight
see Day and night

Warda
see "Rose"

Wrenching (*ʿiḳḳur*)
one of the malpractices which render šĕḥiṭah invalid

Writings
see Bible

Yibbum

see Levirate marriage
Zefeḳ
a bird's crop; cf. *Mur'ah*
Zuz
see Money

SCRIPTURAL REFERENCES

GENESIS

EXODUS

LEVITICUS

NUMBERS

DEUTERONOMY

JOSHUA

9:23, 85 f.

2 SAMUEL

21:2, 125

1 KINGS

11:7, 91

ISAIAH

1:15, 137
33:4, 260
58:7, 20

HOSEA

11:4, 92

MALACHI

2:11–12, 82

PSALMS

119:105, 322

PROVERBS

3:29, 139
5:8, 138
5:19, 138, 146
22:6, 254

JOB

5:24, 139
28:6, 321
31:1, 133 f.

RUTH

1:18, 90

EZRA

8:20, 86

NEHEMIAH

10:31, 80

INDEX

AARON, the High Priest, 123 f., 140
Abaye, 353
Absent (*ḥăserah*), 280, 287, 293 ff., 391
  difference between "absent" and "removed," 297 f.
Administrator, male, over house inhabited by woman, forbidden, 144
Adultery. *See* Incest and adultery
Agricultural produce, *see* Produce
'Aḳiḇa, Rabbi, 330
Alkali, used in testing stains for blood, 66
Ammon and Ammonites, 84 ff., 113 f., 124
Amnon, 141
Amoraim, 391, 393
Amulets, 104
Animals and beasts, chewing cud, have no front teeth in upper jaw, 153; chilled, 304; clean species of, 154 f.; definition of, 354; doubtfully ṭĕrefah, may not be sold to heathen, 308; fallen from roof, may not be slaughtered for 24 hours, 302; inedible parts of, 175; monster births, 154; naturally enfeebled and moribund, permitted for food, but not recommended, 172 f.; offspring, abnormal, of, 153 f.; poisoned, 304; presumed to be in good health unless contrary evidence is present, 308 f., 311; seized with congestion of the blood, 304; suffocated with smoke, 304; tokens of, 153 f.; unclean, flesh of, combines with one another, but not with flesh of unclean bird or fish, 174 f.; unclean species of, 158 f.; unclean species of, penalty for eating of, 158 f.; *see also* Crossbreeds, Nĕḇelah, Šĕḥiṭah, Ṭĕrefah
Antigonus, of Socho, 381
Aorta, perforated, 283
Apostate Israelite, as slaughterer, 278 f.
"Articles of value," 240 ff.
Asafoetida, 285
'Ašlag, meaning of, 338, 391
Assyria, 86
'Ăsufi, *see* Foundling
Atheist, definition of, 279, 381
Atonement, Day of, 208, 230 f., 265

BACK OF ANIMAL, torn, 274
Badan pomegranates, 240, 242, 374
Barren woman, *see* Woman
Bastard and bastardy, 21, 82, 125, 127, 142, 331, 349; child of, *see* Child; classes of, 99; credibility of father and mother as to status of, 99 ff.; definition of, 97; doubtful, 99 ff., 125 ff.; forbidden forever to marry Israelite, 97, 106; may marry bastard, but not doubtful bastard, 102; may marry bondswoman, 98; may marry Nathin, 105; may marry proselyte, 98, 124; rules affecting, 97 ff.;

Kohl, 104, 394
Koy, 155, 320, 355, 389, 394; *see also* Crossbreeds
Kutaḥ, meaning of, 364, 394

LASCIVIOUS and suggestive behavior, 133 ff., 144 ff., 348, 352; exceptions from: father and daughter, 134, 141; husband and wife, 135 ff., 141; mother and son, 134, 141; *see also* Seclusion
Leah, the Matriarch, 352
Leaven, 208, 227 f., 233 f., 240, 242 f., 372, 374
Leg, absent parts of, 293; dislocated foreleg, 303; fractured bone of, 295; "meeting of the sinews" in, 295 f.; missing or supernumerary, 295; severed foreleg, 295, 297; severed hindleg, 295 f.; veins of foreleg, 189
Leprosy, 47, 140, 241, 318, 343
Lesbianism, *see* Homosexuality
Levi, tribe of, 87
Levirate marriage, 20, 100, 109 ff., 114, 122, 131, 143, 329, 394 f.
Levites, 105, 124 ff., 129 f., 351, 393, 399
Libation wine, 208 ff., 229, 238, 250 f., 367 f., 372, 376; as wages, 224 f.; effect upon, of admixture of other foods, 232 f., 246 ff.; proceeds of sale of, 223 f.; proceeds of sale of, as wages, 224; things prohibited as precaution against, 222 ff.; wages of Israelite hired by heathen to smash jars of, 223
Limb, dislocated or crushed, 178; fractured, 178; or flesh, dangling, 178; severed, 178 ff.
Live creature, forbidden for food, 170, 259, 262; limb cut from, forbidden for food, 170, 172, 176 ff.; live fish permitted, 260; not neutralized by admixture of foods, 241
Liver, blood of, 182 f.; infested with worms, 284; lobe above, 187; membrane of, 284, 297, 309 f.; must be singed or scalded before cooking, 182; removed, 296 f.; scorched by fire, 292; source of blood, 382; tubes of, 283 f.; white area in center of, 284
Locusts, clean species of, 157; cooked in milk, 196; do not require šĕḥiṭah, 260; have no fluid in their bodies, 169; penalty for eating unclean species of, 159; pickled by heathen, 253; tokens of, 157; *see also* Brine
Loḡ, meaning of, 366, 395
Lost property, rule governing return of, 343
Lung, absent lobes of, 293 f.; adhesions in, 289, 294, 309 ff., 386; air escaping from, 289 ff.; arteries of, 288, 290 f., 309; carried away or lost before examination, 311; color of, 291 f.; decayed, 290; decomposed inner part of, 289 f.; defective, 294; examination of, 289 ff., 295, 309 ff., 387; fluid in, 289; lobes of, 288 f., 293 f., 307, 310; main lobe of, 288 f., 309 f.; membranes of, 288 ff., 309; minimum size of lobe of, 294; needle in, 291; nonarticulated, 294; obstructed section of, 289; of bird, exempt from rules governing defects, 307, 311, 387; of bird, has no articulated lobes, or else their number is not constant, 307; perforated, 283, 288 ff., 303, 309, 311 f., 386; puffed up, 294; pulled out before examination in situ, 311; reversed order of lobes of, 293; "rose" of, 293, 310, 397; shrunken, 294 f.; structure of, 293; supernumerary lobes of, 293 f.; swellings or growths upon, 290, 309; tube of, 283; worm in, 291

ative commandment together, 318, 389; the prohibition of eating implies the prohibition of benefiting, unless the contrary is specified in Scripture or Oral Law, 194; punishment may not be inflicted without prior warning, 10, 387; the result of two factors, one permitted and the other forbidden, is forbidden, 374; a scholar may not plead ignorance of the law, 327; the Scriptural interdict of illicit intercourse is the most difficult prohibition for man to observe, 145; "Scripture speaks only in terms of the most common occurrence or example," 172, 196, 280, 318; there can be no custom about a thing which is not of common occurrence, 311; there is no guardian against unchastity, 144; "the Torah feels concern for the property of Israel," 387; trading in articles prohibited by Scripture is forbidden, in articles prohibited by the Sages is permitted, 195; two witnesses are as good as a hundred, 131; uncleanness cannot be removed by fire, but only by immersion, 249; whatever emerges is regarded as having emerged from the majority, 193, 362; when a positive commandment rectifies the transgression of a negative commandment, its performance is obligatory, and its nonperformance punishable, 316; when a transgressor is liable only to a penalty, the article involved is forbidden to him alone, and not to others, 237; whosoever blemishes others projects upon them his own blemish, 125

Rumor and gossip, effect on status of person, 101 f., 112, 119, 131

SABBATH, court does not sit on, 342; šěḥiṭah performed on, valid, 265

Sabbatical year, 205, 207, 225, 230, 233, 370, 372, 397

Sadducees, 79, 279, 340, 381

Saliva, tasteless, definition of, 67; used in testing stains for blood, 66

Salt, draws out wine absorbed by vessel, 211; standing next to curdled milk (milk sauce), absorbs moisture from it, 201

Salted food, so salty as to be inedible, regarded as equivalent to boiled food, 200

Salting and rinsing of meat, *see* Meat

Salting vessel, should not be used for tableware, 186

Samson, 89 f.

"Sandal" of foetus, *see* Foetus

Sanhedrin (Great Court), 127, 129, 339, 350

Saul, King, 86, 125

Scalding of vessels, *see* Vessels

Sě'ah, definition of, 367, 395

Seal within seal, definition of, 221

Seclusion, improper, chief contributory factor to unchastity, 145; of Israelite child with heathen teacher, 142; of Israelite woman with heathen man, forbidden, even in presence of his wife, 142; of Israelite's animal with heathen caretaker, 142; of man and woman in room with door open to public thoroughfare, 143; of married woman with another man, while her husband is in town, 143; of one woman with several men, and vice versa, 142; of several women with several men, 142 f.; precedents, *see* Precedents; with child, 143; with heathen woman, 141; with hermaphrodite, 143; with males or animals, 141; with married woman, 141 f.; with relatives, 141; with two related women who usually dislike one another, 143; with unmarried woman, 141; with woman in presence of one's wife, 142; *see also* Lascivious and suggestive behavior, Modest behavior

half-slave and half-free, 98; male, should not be owned by woman, 144; marriage and intercourse with, 83 f.; refusing to be circumcised and immersed, must be sold after twelve months, or else assume status of resident stranger, 94; wine touched by, 209; *see also* Bondsman, Bondswoman
Slave, Hebrew, 23, 83
Slave, manumitted, 22 f., 84; acquires full rights, provided he marries Israelite mate, 84; child of, *see* Child; may marry bastard, but not after slave descent has sunk into oblivion, 98 f.; may marry Israelite mate, 98, 124; may marry priest's daughter, 124; must be immersed a second time in order to become full proselyte, 89; relatives permitted or prohibited to, 94, 96
Sleeping, on one's back, likely to give rise to erection, 138
Smelling, of heathen wine, permitted, 223; *see also* Odor
Snake's eyeball, is round like a human eyeball, 70
Sodomy, *see* Bestiality, Homosexuality
Solomon, King, 89 ff.
Son cursing or striking his father, 15
Spain, 76, 311
Spinal cord, crushed, 298; extent of, 299; liquefied, 299; membrane of, 298 f.; split, 298, 300
Spine, fractured, 298, 311; smitten by club, 301
Spleen, does not consist of blood, but is merely flesh which resembles blood, 183; membrane of, 188 f.; missing or duplicated, 287; of bird, exempt from rules governing defects, 307; of bird, round like grape, 307; perforated, 287; sinews of, 188
Split (*pĕsuḳah*), 280, 298 ff., 399
Stabbing, as method of slaughtering, 181, 279, 312, 360, 378
Stain, blood, *see* Bloodstain
Stillborn child, 44, 68, 270
Stillborn young, *see* Unborn, stillborn, or newborn young
Stomach, cooked with milk within it, 199; membrane of, used to curdle cheese, 199; perforated, 283 ff.
Stomach, second, fat of, 187; none in bird, 286; perforated, 283, 285
Stomach, third, *see* Omasum
Stoned ox, 175 f., 241, 313, 321
Stoning, for incest or adultery, 10 f., 13 ff., 21 f.; *see also* Place of Stoning
Strangulation, for incest or adultery, 10 f., 15, 21 f.
Suckling, by adult male, forbidden, 165; child may suckle for a period up to five years, but once weaned at the age of two years may not resume, 165; *see also* Human milk, Woman
Šuman, meaning of, 392
Suspected wife, *see* Wife, suspected
Syria, 204 f., 357

TABERNACLES, feast of, 315
Tail, fat of, 187, 200, 232, 235 ff., 371; veins of, 189
Tamar, 141
Tannaim, definition of, 399
Tarfon, Rabbi, 354

296.1
M91
V.5

46088

Date Due

3 4711 00228 9579